Ylva Söderfeldt
From Pathology to Public Sphere

DISABILITY STUDIES • BODY – POWER – DIFFERENCE • VOLUME 9

Editorial

The scientific book series Disability Studies: Body – Power – Difference examines disability as an historical, social and cultural construction; it deals with the interrelation between power and symbolic meanings. The series intends to open up new perspectives to disability, thus correcting and extending traditional approaches in medicine, special education and rehabilitation sciences. It views disability as a phenomenon of embodied difference. Fundamental cultural concepts of »putting things into order«, for instance normality and deviance, health and illness, physical integrity and subjective identity are thereby discussed from a critical point of view. The book series Disability Studies aims to contribute to the study of the central themes of the Modern age: reason, human rights, equality, autonomy and solidarity in relation to social and cultural developments.

The scientific book series Disability Studies: Body – Power – Difference is published by Professor Anne Waldschmidt (iDiS – International research unit Disability Studies, Faculty of Human Sciences, University of Cologne), together with Professor Thomas Macho (Institute for Culture and Art Sciences, Humboldt University Berlin), Professor Werner Schneider (Faculty of Philosophy and Social Sciences, University of Augsburg), Anja Tervooren (Department of Education, University of Duisburg-Essen) and Heike Zirden (Berlin).

Ylva Söderfeldt (M.A.) teaches History of Medicine at the University Hospital in Aachen, Germany. Her research tackles the juncture between intellectual and social history, focusing on the history of medicine and disability history.

Ylva Söderfeldt
From Pathology to Public Sphere
The German Deaf Movement 1848-1914

[transcript] DISABILITY STUDIES

Gedruckt mit Unterstützung der Prof. Dr. Walter Artelt und Prof. Dr. Edith Heischkel-Artelt Stiftung, Frankfurt am Main, und des Instituts für Geschichte, Theorie und Ethik der Medizin, Universitätsklinikum der RWTH Aachen.

D 93

Bibliographic information published by the Deutsche Nationalbibliothek
The Deutsche Nationalbibliothek lists this publication in the Deutsche Nationalbibliografie; detailed bibliographic data are available in the Internet at http://dnb.d-nb.de

© **2013 transcript Verlag, Bielefeld**

All rights reserved. No part of this book may be reprinted or reproduced or utilized in any form or by any electronic, mechanical, or other means, now known or hereafter invented, including photocopying and recording, or in any information storage or retrieval system, without permission in writing from the publisher.

Cover concept: Kordula Röckenhaus, Bielefeld
Cover illustration: Viennese pictures: »In the Coffee-House
  of the Deaf-Mutes«. Illustrirte Zeitung No. 2122, March 1st 1884,
  p. 173
Proofread & Typeset by Ylva Söderfeldt
Printed by Majuskel Medienproduktion GmbH, Wetzlar
ISBN 978-3-8376-2119-8

Contents

Table of Figures | 7

Abbreviations | 9

Acknowledgements | 11

Introduction | 13

1. The 'Deaf-Mutes' in Numbers, Words, and Practice | 29
Counting 'Deaf-Mutes': Context, Motives, and Methods | 29
What They Found: Contents of the Surveys | 39
Managing the 'Deaf-Mutes' | 54
Conclusion of Chapter 1 | 90

2. Deaf Lives in Social Context | 93
Class and Culture in 19th Century Germany | 93
Deaf Networks | 100
Exclusion: The Example of the 'Unknown Deaf-Mutes' | 124
Conclusion of Chapter 2 | 143

3. Ways to be Deaf | 145
Practicing Deaf Community | 148
Imagined Deaf Communities | 171
The Individual in Imagined and Local Deaf Communities:
A New Way of Being Deaf | 193
Conclusion of Chapter 3 | 217

4. Conflicts: The Debate in the Deaf Movement | 219
The issues and the channels | 221
Reactions | 252
Strategies | 257
Conclusion of Chapter 4 | 265

5. Epilogue: The Deaf Movement during and after World War I | 267

6. Conclusion | 271

Appendix: List of Deaf Press Biographies | 279
Obituaries | 279
Other Celebrations | 281
Warrants, Criminals, and Warnings | 282

Bibliography | 285
Archives | 285
Printed Sources and Literature | 289

Abstract | 309

Zusammenfassung | 313

Table of Figures

Figure 1: Registry card for "blind, deaf-mute, feeble-minded and insane" persons used in the Saxon census from 1875 | 35
Figure 2: The most common occupations among 'deaf-mutes' in 1900 vs. the gainfully working in 1895 in size order | 42
Figure 3: Number of 'deaf-mutes' in 'deaf-mute asylums' in 1900, according to sex and age | 45
Figure 4: Chart of applications for bonuses in Bavaria and Berlin | 76
Figure 5: Deaf painters and their stays at the Royal Deaf-Mute Asylum and the Royal Academy of Arts | 113
Figure 6: Advertisements of cafés from the TsF | 119
Figure 7: "Viennese pictures: In the Coffee-House of the DeafMutes" | 121
Figure 8: Number of deaf clubs in Germany, their locations and representatives, as listed in 1873, 1891, and 1913 | 160
Figure 9: Number and type of deaf club activities as advertised in the TsF in 1873, 1892, and 1911 | 163
Figure 10: The first wave of international deaf congresses and the German deaf congresses until 1914 | 188

Abbreviations

AATD	Arbeitsausschuss für die Allgemeinheit der Taubstummen Deutschlands
AWdT	Arbeitsausschuss für das Wohl der deutschen Taubstummen (new name of the AATD after the Great War.)
ATV	Allgemeiner Taubstummenverein
ATZ	Allgemeiner Taubstummen-Zeitschrift
BezA	Bezirksamt
BGB	Bürgerliches Gesetzbuch (German national civil law from 1900)
CODA	Child of Deaf Adults
CVWITD	Central-Verband für die Wohlfahrt und die Interessen der Taubstummen Deutschlands
CVWT	Centralverein für das Wohl der Taubstummen (sometimes spelled Zentralverein)
DTZ	Deutsche Taubstummen-Zeitung
GstA PrK	Geheimes Staatsarchiv Preussischer Kulturbesitz
HLA	Hauptlandesarchiv
HStA	Hauptstaatsarchiv
LA	Landesarchiv
Mk	Mark
NSDAP	Nationalsozialistische Deutsche Arbeiterpartei
NZT	Neue Zeitschrift für Taubstumme
REGEDE	Reichsverband der Gehörlosen Deutschlands
RTD	Reichsverband der Taubstummen Deutschlands
SPD	Sozialdemokratische Partei Deutschlands
StA	Staatsarchiv
TC	Taubstummencourier
TPB	Taubstummen-Parteibund
TsF	Taubstummenfreund
TsV	Taubstummenverein
VGTHOB	Verein zur Gründung eines Taubstummen-Heims in Oberfranken zu Bamberg

WTFV	Württembergischer Taubstummen-Fürsorgeverein
WTV	Württembergischer Taubstummenverein
ZVWhT	Zentral-Verband für das Wohl hilfsbedürftiger Taubstummen e. V. (Bavaria)

Acknowledgements

The work with this study has been both a challenge and a pleasure. Overcoming the challenge, and making it an enjoyable experience, has only been possible with the help of others. My advisor, Professor Dr. Robert Jütte, and Professor Dr. Martin Dinges at the Insitute for the History of Medicine (IGM), Stuttgart, have been very generous with their time and effort. They saw the potential in this history of ideas for it to also become a social history, and prodded me in the right direction.

Professor Douglas Baynton at the University of Iowa offered me the opportunity to spend a few months there as a visiting scholar. Attending his courses in disability history, and thoroughly discussing my texts with him gave me perspectives that profoundly influenced the entire project. His knowledge of the subject area, genuine interest in the topic, patience, and scholarly integrity have greatly enhanced the analysis.

Professor Elisabeth Mansén at Stockholm University encouraged me to pursue a doctorate and offered me valuable help in the long and sometimes tiresome application process. Professor Dr. Klaus-B. Günther at the Humboldt University in Berlin created the possibility for me to begin my graduate studies, and introduced me to German Deaf History.

A scholarship from the Robert-Bosch-Stiftung enabled me to work full-time for three years on the project. Before that, a grant from the Swedish Deaf Association (SDRF) gave me the opportunity to perform the initial literature studies. Grants from the Professor Dr. Walter Artelt und Prof. Dr. Edith Heischkel-Artelt-Stiftung and the Institute for History, Theory and Ethics in Medicine in Aachen supported the publication of the study.

I have been very lucky to have Matilda Svensson as both a colleague in Disability History and as a friend. Our discussions on everything related, and unrelated, to the field were among the most enjoyable parts of this journey. Andreas Hellerstedt has also been a constant source of pep talks, advice, and welcomed distractions. Furthermore, I would like to thank the staff at the IGM for contributing to the stimulating and friendly environment there. During my frequent visits in Stuttgart, Birgit Buchholz offered me a home away from home.

In the course of the project, I visited several archives and libraries across Germany and in the United States. Apart from those listed in the bibliography, I would like to especially mention the Bibliothek für Sprach- und Hörgeschädigtenbildung in Leipzig, the Bibliothek für Bildungsgeschichtliche Forschung, and the Staatsbibliothek preußischer Kulturbesitz, both in Berlin. Without the knowledge and patience of librarians and archivists, this book would never have been written.

Finally, I have had the great privilege of having supportive parents. Björn Söderfeldt read and unsentimentally criticized the entire text at various stages. Birgitta Axelsson-Söderfeldt introduced me to the Deaf community and, most importantly, to the normality of difference. Thank you.

Introduction

How does a group of people take shape? This is the overarching question of this study. The group in question here is deaf people – or, with the contemporary term, 'deaf-mutes' – in 19th and early 20th century Germany. During this time, a movement emerged, consisting of numerous clubs, publications, and events organized by and for deaf people. Instead of being only the carriers of a pathological phenomenon, being made objects of social intervention, education, and medicine, deaf people started to appear in a new way – as sociable peer groups, as lobbyists, organizers, writers, thinkers. The emergence and expression of this new way of being deaf is the object of analysis.

In the following, I shall ask under what social circumstances the role shift occurred, how it came to be, and what the results were. The aim is to write a history of the German deaf movement, including its context, origins, and ideas, from the beginning around the middle of the 19th century, until the First World War.

Theoretical Standpoints

In the course of the text, the ideas of several theorists and schools will be used as tools in the analysis. Below, I comment briefly on the most important influences. Each of them will be discussed more thoroughly in the appropriate sections. The overall theoretical base of this work, however, is that of a social history of ideas. This is not mainly because the issues addressed happen to belong both to social and intellectual history, but it is rather an ambition to understand history in a certain way. The approach of a social history of ideas is to emphasise the function of ideas, that is, not only to analyze the plain expressions and finding their parallels in the past, contemporary era, or aftermath, but their relationship to the realities in which they existed.[1]

It is this perspective that makes it possible to bring together such disparate genres as club statutes, pedagogical manuals, and police records into one body of sources. The authors and actors in the sources came from a range of different social, geographical, and intellectual backgrounds. They did not form a society, nor a school of thought. However, the ideas and actions described in the documents were united by their function: managing people who were deaf.

The interdependence of conceptual, institutional, and personal levels in classifying, treating, and living as a kind of people is an idea deriving from Ian Hacking. His studies of how categorization creates practices that influence the categorized people, so that the group itself changes, what he calls a "looping effect",[2] also helps connecting the many actors and texts involved.

As for the social and communicative preconditions for deaf people in the German Empire, Jürgen Habermas' models of the 'bourgeois public sphere' and the 'life-world' versus the 'system' have been crucial to the analysis.[3] Habermas allows us to consider the impact of socio-economic and cultural factors as a backdrop to communication, and distinguishes between communicative and instrumental interactions between people and institutions. The implementation of the concept of the bourgeois public sphere in the specific setting of 19th century Germany relies on the work of Jürgen Kocka, who demonstrates that the *Bürger* at this point were a cultural factor, rather than a socio-economic class.[4] This made it possible to discern the *bürgerliche*, or bourgeois, elements of people who admittedly mostly belonged to lower social strata.

---

1 Peter Gay, "The Social History of Ideas: Ernst Cassirer and After," in *The Critical Spirit. Essays in Honor of Herbert Marcuse*, ed. Kurt H. Wolff and Barrington Moore (Boston: Beacon Press, 1967), pp. 106-120.

2 This concept is summarized in: Ian Hacking, "Kinds of People: Moving Targets," British Academy lecture, 2006, *Proceedings of the British Academy* Vol. 151 (2007): pp. 285-318.

3 The works I have used are Jürgen Habermas, Strukturwandel der Öffentlichkeit. Untersuchungen zu einer Kategorie der bürgerlichen Gesellschaft, 5th ed. (Neuwied: Luchterhand, 1971); idem, Theorie des kommunikativen Handelns. Vol. 1. Handlungsrationalität und gesellschaftliche Rationalisierung. Vol. 2. Zur Kritik der funktionalistischen Vernunft (Frankfurt am Main: Suhrkamp, 1981).

4 *Bürger* is a term that is notoriously difficult to translate. It denotes both bourgeoisie and citizens. *V.* below, pp. 96ff for a thorough discussion of the concept.

Furthermore, this study has benefited from recent scholarship on disability and deafness. Traditionally, disability has been regarded as something given by nature, concerning only the individual. According to this model, disabilities are caused by one or the other physical or mental impairment and render the individual depending on certain aids or assistance. Questioning this, activists and scholars have since the 1970s found that using a social model of disability offers insights that the individual, or medical, model does not. According to this new understanding of disability, the able body is not only a temporary condition, but also varies in its shape and traits, over time and in different contexts. Thus, disability is not located in certain bodily dispositions, but appears in the social setting, for instance inaccessible buildings or prejudiced attitudes.[5] When studying history, the impairments themselves are of less interest than what made people identify them as disabling, unsightly, or deviant, and what function and effects this judgment had. Whereas earlier 'histories of disability' focused on non-disabled professionals and benefactors and the 'solutions' they offered to the 'problem' of disability, Disability History lets disabled people appear as subjects, beyond the stereotypical roles as victims or objects of benevolence.[6]

Although the social model of disability has proven a useful tool in scholarship as well as activism, it has not escaped criticism. The bracketing of different kinds of bodily (or sensory, or mental) difference under the label "disability" often does not represent how people experience themselves, and it might also conceal internal conflicts and power structures.[7] There is an obvious risk that the dichotomy between the 'natural, bodily, real' impairment and the 'social, constructed, oppressive' disability over-simplifies the experience of disabled people. Structural oppression is presupposed, rather than critically examined, and the body itself remains outside the realm of cultural analysis.[8] Thus, the social

---

5   Catherine Kudlick, "Disability History: Why We Need Another 'Other'," *American Historical Review* Vol. 108, No. 3 (June 2003): pp. 763-793; Colin Barnes, Geof Mercer and Tom Shakespeare, *Exploring Disability: A Sociological Introduction* (Cambridge: Polity Press, 1999), pp. 20-31.
6   Elsbeth Bösl, "Was ist Disability History? Zur Geschichte und Historiografie von Behinderung," in *Disability History. Konstruktionen von Behinderung in der Geschichte. Eine Einführung,* eds. Elsbeth Bösl, Anne Klein, and Anne Waldschmidt (Bielefeld: transcript, 2010).
7   Markus Dederich, Körper, Kultur und Behinderung. Eine Einführung in die Disability Studies. (Bielefeld: transcript, 2007) pp. 54-55
8   Tom Shakespeare, "The Social Model of Disability" in *The Disability Studies Reader,* 3rd. Ed., ed. Lennard J. Davis (New York: Routledge, 2010), pp. 266-273.

model allows for a continued essentialist view of embodied difference – it merely moves the unquestioned, medical content away from one concept (disability) to another (impairment). As a remedy, Anne Waldschmidt has suggested that the humanities turn instead to a *cultural* model of disability. This means making disability a central category of analysis, on a par with gender, class, or ethnicity. According to the cultural model, disability is not something that certain people "have" and others "do not have." Instead, dis/ability is a further perspective that can be used to describe society. To Waldschmidt, disability history is not mainly a matter of recovering the lost history of people 'with' disabilities. Rather, she argues, it is a change of perspective relevant to all of the humanities: to view the mainstream from the 'deviant' position, instead of looking at the 'deviants' from the 'normal' point of view.[9] Philipp Sarasin goes even further, suggesting that deviant bodies are in fact not peripheral, but central phenomena to the construction of norms.[10]

Contemporary to the emergence of the social model of disability, in the 1970s and -80s, a new self-awareness grew among Deaf[11] activists and scholars concerned with signed languages, according to which deafness should not be seen as a disability, but rather that deaf people form a linguistic minority. One important function of this view is to support criticism of attempted medical and educational "cures", such as articulation training and cochlear implants. By claiming Deafness as a cultural category, not a medical diagnosis, the proponents of this view explained that there is, in fact, no need to "cure" it.[12] This approach

---

9   Anne Waldschmidt, "Warum und wozu brauchen die Disability Studies die Disability History?" in *Disability History,* eds. Bösl, Klein, and Waldschmidt, pp. 15-20; idem: "Brauchen die Disability Studies ein ‚kulturelles Modell' von Behinderung?" in *‚Nichts über uns – ohne uns!' Disability Studies als neuer Ansatz emanzipatorischer und interdisziplinärer Forschung über Behinderung,* eds. Gisela Hermes and Eckhard Rohrmann (Neu-Ulm, AG SPAK, 2006), pp. 90-92. *Cf.* also Rosemarie Garland-Thomson, *Extraordinary Bodies. Figuring Physical Disability in American Culture and Literature* (New York: Columbia University Press, 1997), pp. 8-9, 21-23, in which a similar approach is advocated; Garland-Thomson suggests calling this a "universalizing" view on disability, ibid, p. 22.

10 Philipp Sarasin, *Reizbare Maschinen. Eine Geschichte des Körpers 1765-1914* (Frankfurt a. M.: Suhrkamp, 2001), pp. 207-211, 251.

11 Deaf with capital D refers to cultural Deafness, instead of physical. See discussion of this concept below, p. 28.

12 Carol J. Erting, "Introduction," in *The Deaf Way. Perspectives from the International Conference on Deaf Culture,* ed. Carol J. Erting et al. (Washington, D.C.:

has accompanied the emergence of Deaf History as a field of study not of the institutions and (hearing) people concerned with cures and coping strategies, but of deaf people and their lives.[13] By viewing Deaf people as a linguistic minority, comparable to an ethnic group, it has also inspired scholars to use post-colonial theories in their research on contemporary and historical Deaf communities and the suppression of signed languages.[14] In this study, Benedict Anderson's concept of 'imagined communities' has aided the analysis.[15] Originally intended to describe the roots of nationalism, the idea of uniting the deaf, and the way in which this unification took place, can also, as will be discussed in Chapter 3, be understood as deriving from the idea of an imagined community.

However, the dissociation of deafness and disability is problematic in several ways. First, it could be interpreted as deprecatory towards people with disabilities, as the Deaf thereby try to distance themselves from that group. Second, it implies the false notion that the cultural affiliation with a Deaf community, or the self-identification as Deaf, contradicts also being disabled. Third, although its subscribers are aware of the social model of disability, the model from which

---

Gallaudet University Press, 1994), pp. xxiii-xxxi; Harlan Lane, *The Mask of Benevolence: Disabling the Deaf Community* (New York: Alfred A. Knopf, 1992), pp. 13-28, 203-238; idem, with Robert Hoffmeister and Ben Bahan, *A Journey into the DEAF-WORLD* (San Diego, CA; DawnSignPress, 1996), pp. ixf, 124-173, 335-407.

13 "Preface" in *Deaf History Unveiled. Interpretations from the new Scholarship*, ed. John Vickrey Van Cleve (Washington, D. C.: Gallaudet University Press, 1993), pp. ix-x; some important works in this genre are Carol Padden and Tom Humphries, *Deaf in America. Voices from a Culture* (Cambridge, Massachusetts: Harvard University Press, 1988); Carol Padden, "The Deaf Community and the Culture of Deaf People," in *Sign Language and the Deaf Community. Essays in Honor of William C. Stokoe*, eds. Charlotte Baker and Robbin Battison (n.pl.:National Association of the Deaf, 1980), pp. 89-103; Lane, Hoffmeister and Bahan, *DEAF-WORLD;* Harlan Lane: *When the Mind Hears. A History of the Deaf* (New York: Random House, 1984); idem, *The Mask of Benevolence*; idem (Ed.): *The Deaf Experience. Classics in Language and Education* (Cambridge, MA.: Harvard University Press, 1984).

14 V. Christopher Krentz, *Writing Deafness. The Hearing Line in Nineteenth-Century American Literature.* (Chapel Hill, NC: University of North Carolina Press, 2007); Owen Wrigley, *The Politics of Deafness* (Washington, D.C.: Gallaudet University Press, 1996).

15 Benedict Anderson, Imagined Communities. Reflections of the Origin and Spread of Nationalism. rev. ed., (London: Verso, 1991).

they seek to separate themselves is in fact the medical one.[16] Thus, the social model of disability and the work associated with it are left unconsidered, on false grounds. Fourth, the rigidity with which the cultural model of Deafness is sometimes advocated fails to acknowledge the sensory experience of deafness, and the significance that the physical condition in fact does have for d/Deaf people. Groups on the borderlines, such as oral deaf, or hearing signers, risk being forgotten, with the result being an incomplete picture of the complex social settings of Deaf communities and individuals.[17] Nevertheless, the cultural model of Deafness has been successful in emphasising the significance of signed languages as cultural transmitters and valuable collective resources shared by certain groups of people, who use them in varying ways. As for the critical position towards imposed cures and assimilation, it is in fact fully compatible with the perspectives from Disability Studies and the social and cultural models. By acknowledging this – that it is the medical model that needs to be abandoned – Deaf Studies can benefit from Disability Studies, while at the same time drawing from post-colonial ideas regarding linguistic and cultural minorities. What common traits and experiences caused the formation of the deaf movement is one of the issues addressed by the study, but an awareness of the significance of signed languages as a core property of deaf people will accompany the analysis.

For this study, the social model of disability has meant that it is not a history of the treatment of, or coping with, a physical condition. Neither is it a study of deafness as a sensory experience – people deafened as adults are not included. Institutions and professionals are parts of the story, but the focus is the ideas and

---

16 Douglas Baynton, "Disability and the Justification of Inequality in American History," in *The New Disability History*, eds. Paul Longmore and Lauri Umansky (New York, NY: New York University Press, 2001), p. 51; idem,"Beyond Culture: Deaf Studies and the Deaf Body," in *Open Your Eyes. Deaf Studies Talking*, ed. H-Dirksen L. Bauman (Minneapolis, MN: University of Minnesota Press, 2008) pp. 293-313; Mairian Corker, *Deaf and Disabled or Deafness Disabled? Toward a Human Rights Perspective.* (Buckingham: Open University Press, 1998), pp. 62-64.

17 Brenda Jo Brueggemann, *Lend Me Your Ear. Rhetorical Constructions of Deafness* (Washington D. C.: Gallaudet University Press, 1999), p. 182; idem, *Deaf Subjects. Between Identities and Places* (New York; London: New York University Press, 2009), p. 7; Lennard J. Davis, "Postdeafness," in *Open Your Eyes,* ed. Bauman, pp. 314-325; for a model based on the sensory experience of being deaf, *v.* Benjamin Bahan, "Upon the Formation of a Visual Variety of the Human Race," in *Open Your Eyes,* ed. Bauman, pp. 83-99.

deeds of people who were deaf. The cultural model of disability has influenced this study so that I consider the other side of the coin: Disability has to enter the analysis of structures of – for instance – class and gender. At the same time, there is a need for such categories to enter the Disability Studies. Thus this study does not stop at disability, in this case deafness, as a category of social or discursive exclusion. It asks how deafness worked together with other markers in the emergence of the German deaf movement.

Method

This is a study of statements, the emergence and dispersion of which form and transform a discourse. Although making use of statistics, it is not a quantitative study. In spite of containing the individual histories of certain people, events, and institutions, it is not a case study. Instead, the texts on these matters are read as different types of enouncements among many. Guided by the methodological suggestions made by Michel Foucault, the object of study is the system according to which the statements concerning deaf people were dispersed. The questions are which objects appeared in the statements, who was able to make the statements and be listened to, and what types of statements were possible to make. Thus, the views expressed by the authors, both the hearing professionals and the deaf activists, are not in themselves the main focus, but instead the rules according to which they took shape and appeared.[18]

In this study, the most crucial of Foucault's methodological principles is that of reversal.[19] When encountering deaf people, both as individuals and as faceless, stylized 'deaf people in general', the question is not only who they were and how they were described, but also who they were *not*. Determining which objects did not appear is as essential as recounting those that did appear. Through exclusion, borders were constantly drawn between different kinds of people. Where these processes of exclusion were at work – inside as well as outside of the group – demarcated the kind of people called 'the deaf-mutes'.

Discourse, however, does not exist in a void, neither is it the only thing that exists. The practices used when instances such as governments, police, and institutions handled 'the deaf mutes', the socio-economic conditions in Imperial Germany, the location of the deaf in the geographical space, and the social and

---

18 Michel Foucault, *The Archaeology of Knowledge,* trans. A.M. Sheridan Smith (New York: Pantheon Books, 1982), pp. 37-44; idem, *The Discourse on Language,* trans. Rupert Swyer, 1971, in Foucault, *Archaeology*, pp. 216-217, 223-233.
19 Foucault, *Discourse,* pp. 229-233.

sensory experience of belonging to a linguistic minority founded on a certain bodily difference, are comparative facts that, in different ways and to varying extent, co-determined what statements were made and what objects appeared in discourse.[20] Thus, these factors always accompany the analysis and are compared with the statements that were produced in association with them.

Sources

This study is based on a large and rather eclectic source material. For the deaf movement, I have relied above all on the periodicals issued by, or affiliated with, deaf organizations. These contain information about clubs and events, as well as biographies of deaf people, and debate articles. There were a number of different publications in this genre during the period in question. I have chosen not to use those that were not connected to the deaf movement. The editors and contributors were not necessarily all deaf, but the publication should serve the communication of deaf people, not the edifying of the deaf through hearing authorities. Such papers are sometimes called the "Silent press",[21] a concept I will also make use of. Of those publications that meet this standard, I have chosen to concentrate on those that were intended for all of Germany, and had the longest publication spans. They are the *Taubstummenfreund* (TsF), published between 1872 and 1911, and affiliated with the *Centralverein für das Wohl der Taubstummen* (CVWT), although with hearing editors for most of its history; *Taubstummencourier* (TC), issued from 1885 to 1903 by the deaf Bernhard Brill in Vienna; the *Allgemeine deutsche Taubstummenzeitschrift* (ATZ), published from 1913 as the successor of the *Taubstummenfreund* and official organ of several deaf clubs; the *Taubstummen-Korrespondenz* (TK), which was issued between 1902 and 1916 by "a union of Leipzig deaf-mutes";[22] and the *Deutsche Taubstummen-Zeitung* (DTZ), issued between 1898 and 1914 by a union of deaf organizations from the Rheinland, Silesia, and Mecklenburg.[23]

These publications are sources to the organizational structure of the movement, since they printed lists of clubs, and news and announcements from them. They are also sources to the ideas prevalent within the movement, expressed

---

20   Foucault, *Archaeology*, pp. 67-68, 157-165.
21   Jack R. Gannon, *Deaf Heritage. A Narrative history of Deaf America* (n.pl.:National Association of the Deaf, 1981), p. 238.
22   "einer Vereinigung Leipziger Taubstummer" TK (1903), title page.
23   However, only the volumes 1902-1912 survive to this day.

through debate articles, or reports and protocols from congresses.[24] Furthermore, they are sources to the social history of deaf people, at least of those affiliated with the movement. Advertisements and notices, foremost those on the individual lives of deaf people, combine into a body of biographical material about the people behind the ideas and organizations.

Other documents from deaf clubs are sparse. In the course of work, I contacted all regional sections of today's German Deaf Association[25] and asked if they kept an archive; none of them replied affirmatively. Requests for material relating to deaf organizations to all German state archives resulted in a few positive replies. For efficiency, I decided to concentrate on those regions where the most files on deaf clubs and deaf individuals – mostly recipients of support, or police investigations – existed. These regions were Berlin, Bavaria, and Württemberg. A further advantage of this selection is that it allowed me to follow the treatment of deaf people and the development of the deaf movement in three German regions with rather contrasting characters, from the urban Berlin and Munich, to the rural areas of catholic Bavaria and protestant Württemberg. A comprehensive study of the entire territory of the German Empire would have been too time-consuming, but with this selection, in-depth studies and identifying regional peculiarities and national commonalities were possible to combine.

As mentioned above, different kinds of files on deaf individuals kept in the archives were also part of the study. The purpose of this was to gain access to the lives of deaf people who did not appear in the deaf press. The selection of these files has been made based on accessibility and substance. Again, for efficiency, I was only able to use those files that were clearly designated by the word *taubstumm* [deaf-mute]. More extensive archive studies to find other records would have been too time-consuming. As for substance, I concentrated on those records that contained information about the biography and social circumstances of deaf adults. Medical records and documents about deaf children, typically concerning their enrolment in deaf school, were of less interest, since they relate to deafness as a physical trait rather than its social implications.

---

24   The protocols were in most cases either printed in one of the papers, or as an appendix. However, in a few cases, the protocols were independently published as booklets. *Cf.* for instance "Protocoll," TsF 21 (1878), p. 79; *Protokoll der Verhandlungen des dritten Deutschen Taubstummen-Kongresses zu Nürnberg,* [Appendix to the TsF 1896]; *Protokoll über die Verhandlungen des IX. Allgemeinen Deutschen Taubstummen-Kongresses zu Breslau, am 31. Mai und 1. Juni 1914,* (n.p.: AATD, 1915).

25   Deutscher Gehörlosen-Bund e.V., registered office Am Zirkus 4, Berlin.

The statistics on deaf people in Germany also emerged as a voluminous material, making some demarcations necessary. This selection was made based on two criteria: consistency with the previous selection, and type of information included in the surveys. Since I concentrated on Berlin, Bavaria, and Württemberg in other parts of the study, I used the statistics from these areas, as well as those that covered the entire nation. Coincidentally, all of these were reasonably detailed in their information about social circumstances of 'the deaf-mutes', and were produced quite regularly for a long time. In addition, I also used statistics from the Kingdom of Saxony, since they too fulfilled these criteria.

To grasp the context of the deaf movement, both in terms of the legal, educational, financial, and social possibilities and limitations applying to people who were deaf, and the views on deaf people held by the professionals employed to administer their lives, professional literature, foremost in pedagogy, has been used. Deafness was in 19th and early 20th century Germany above all an educational issue, which means that works on deaf education are the best sources to general information about the situation of deaf people. Regarding some institutions, however, the information in the literature is scarce. Therefore, archive material concerning a few asylums for deaf adults, and workplaces with deaf employees, has been added.

Chronologically, the study focuses on the time between 1848 and 1914. 1848 was the year in which the first German deaf club was formed and thus when the movement formally began. Of course, there was a pre-history of people, events, and publications leading up to this, which is why the study sometimes reaches back to the first half of the 19th century. The second demarcation has been more difficult to make, and stands more for necessity than a natural end. The German deaf movement, including several organizations founded in the 19th century, still exists today. It has gone through several structural transformations, but none of them seemed to be a suitable end point. Instead, the outbreak of the First World War has to serve as such. For Germany, this meant a profound crisis and resulted in far-reaching social, geographical, ideological, and governmental transformations, so that the German deaf movement during and after the Great War found itself in a radically altered context. In order not to end the study so abruptly, an epilogue has been added briefly discussing the further history of the movement until the takeover by the national socialists in 1933.

A final note: I have deliberately chosen not to anonymize any of the people that appear in the text. First, all of them are long ago deceased. Second, and more important, the anonymizing of these people from the past would give the impression that their condition was, in some way, shameful.[26]

Previous Research

A comprehensive work on the German deaf movement, covering the entire territory and/or longer periods of time, does not exist. In fact, the clubs and associations of deaf people are so unknown even within the scholarly community that the origins of the German disability rights movement – defined as groups of disabled people demanding self-determination and a subject, instead of object, position in the welfare system, and practicing mutual aid – have been dated to the Weimar Republic.[27] At that point, however, there had been organized deaf people for well over fifty years.

The available research about the German deaf movement focuses on individual clubs, cities, or deaf leaders. The Hamburg deaf movement is the most thoroughly investigated, being the topic of a 2006 monograph by Christian Hannen, which, however, focuses mainly on the 20th century.[28] The relationships between the 19th century Hamburg deaf clubs and leading personalities are also the subject of a few articles from 1995 by Renate Fischer, Karin Wempe, Silke Lamprecht, Ilka Seeberger, and Iris Groschek.[29] Fischer's work covers wide aspects of Deaf History. Especially important to this study have been her studies

---

26   This decision was influenced by Alice Dreger's discussion on anonymized images in medical case studies, *v.* "Jarring Bodies: Thoughts on the Display of Unusual Anatomies," *Perspectives in Biology and Medicine*, Vol. 43, No. 2 (Winter 2000): pp. 161-172.

27   Petra Fuchs, "Von der ‚Selbsthilfe' zur Selbstaufgabe. Zur Emanzipationsgeschichte behinderter Menschen (1919-1945)," in ed. Petra Lutz et al. *Der [im-]perfekte Mensch. Metamorphosen von Normalität und Abweichung* (Cologne: Böhlau Verlag, 2003), pp. 435-447.

28   Christian Hannen, Von der Fürsorge zur Barrierefreiheit. Die Hamburger Gehörlosenbewegung 1875-2005 (Seedorf: Signum Verlag, 2006).

29   Renate Fischer et al., "John E. Pacher (1842-1898) – ein ‚Taubstummer' aus Hamburg. Zusammenstellung von Quellen als Versuch einer biographischen Skizze," *Das Zeichen* 32 (1995), pp. 122-133[Part 1], *Das Zeichen* 33 (1995), pp. 254-266 [Part 2]; Iris Groschek, "John Pacher und die Hamburger Taubstummenvereine," *Das Zeichen* 34 (1995): pp. 409-411

of the treatment of deaf people in the institutional setting.[30] Jochen Muhs has done research on the biographies, work, and ideas of certain deaf and hearing people who were significant to the 19th century deaf movement. In his articles, the biography is always accompanied by a history of the organizations and debates they helped shape.[31] A similar achievement belongs to Helmut Vogel for his biography on deaf teacher Otto Friedrich Kruse.[32]

Hans-Uwe Feige has explored the social history of deaf people, with focus on the late 18th and early 19th centuries. He uses letters, diaries, and other archive material to reconstruct the biographies of what could be designated more ‚ordinary' deaf people, rather than famous deaf leaders.[33]

Most research in German Deaf History is however about deaf education. Paul Schumann's monumental *Geschichte des Taubstummenwesens* from 1940 is, although from an oralist standpoint tainted with national socialist rhetoric, a detailed history of the school system and its methods from antiquity onward, focusing on Germany in the 18th, 19th, and 20th centuries. A brief history of the deaf

---

30   Renate Fischer, "'Schläge auf die Hand rauben den Verstand'. Ein historisches Beispiel für den Zusammenhang von Strafe und Gebärdensprachverbot an Gehörlosenschulen," *Das Zeichen* 61 (2002): pp. 336-342; idem et al., "'mir mußten dann die Flügel abgeschnitten werden' Hörgeschädigte in einer Hamburger 'Heil- und Pflegeanstalt' in der ersten Hälfte des 20. Jahrhunderts," *Das Zeichen* 39 (1997): pp. 20-33.

31   Jochen Muhs, "Eduard Fürstenberg," *Das Zeichen* 30 (1994): pp. 422-423; idem, "Johann Heidsiek (1855-1942) – Wegbereiter des Bilingualismus," *Das Zeichen* 47 (1999): pp. 11-17; idem, *Johann Heidsiek. Einer der letzten großen Vorkämpfer für gebärdensprachliche Erziehung Gehörloser an Taubstummenanstalten (1855-1942)*, Deaf History 1 (Berlin: Deaf-History Deutschland, 1998).

32   Helmut Vogel, "Otto Friedrich Kruse (1801-1880). Gehörloser Lehrer und Publizist," *Das Zeichen* 56 (2001): pp. 198-207; idem, "Otto Friedrich Kruse (1801-1880). Mahner gegen die Unterdrückung der Gebärdensprache," *Das Zeichen* 57 (2001): pp. 370-376.

33   Hans-Uwe Feige, "Denn taube Personen folgen ihren thierischen Trieben..." (Samuel Henicke). Gehörlosen-Biografien aus dem 18. und 19. Jahrhundert (Leipzig: Gutenberg Verlag, 1999); idem, "Die Geburt der 'Taubstummenprämie' im Königreich Sachsen", Das Zeichen 54 (2000): pp. 548-557; idem, "Lebenswirklichkeit gehörloser Kinder gegen Ende der frühen Neuzeit", Das Zeichen 55 (2001): pp. 18-33; idem, "Gehörlose Handwerker vor 200 Jahren," Das Zeichen 58 (2001): pp. 526-535.

movement is also included.[34] The most comprehensive work since then is Iris Groschek's 2008 history of the deaf education in Hamburg, which also discusses the deaf movement.[35] Sylvia Wolff and Günther List have investigated the ideology and practice of German deaf education in the 19th century, both concentrating on the use of signing versus articulation and lip reading.[36] List has also surveyed the periodicals of the deaf movement, and Heidi Grötz has summarized and analyzed the debate in the *Taubstummencourier*.[37] Joachim Gessinger has explored the philosophical roots of the education of deaf people.[38]

In some other countries, there has been more research about the history of their deaf movements. One that has been most informative to this study is Joseph

---

34 Paul Schumann, Geschichte des Taubstummenwesens vom deutschen Standpunkt aus dargestellt (Frankfurt a. M.: Moritz Diesterweg, 1940).

35 Iris Groschek, Unterwegs in einer Welt des Verstehens. Gehörlosenbildung in Hamburg vom 18. Jahrhundert bis in die Gegenwart, Hamburger historische Forschungen 1 (Hamburg: Hamburg University Press, 2008).

36 Sylvia Wolff, "Von der 'Taubstummen-Unterrichtskunst' zur Didaktik des Gehörlosenunterrichts," *Das Zeichen* 42 (1997): pp. 502-507 [Part 1], *Das Zeichen* 43 (1998): pp. 10-18 [Part 2]; idem, "'Taubstumme zu glücklichen Erdnern bilden' – Lehren, Lernen und Gebärdensprache am Berliner Taubstummen-Institut. Teil I: Selbstverständlich Gebärdensprache! Ernst Adolf Eschke in der Zeit von 1788 bis 1811," *Das Zeichen* 51 (2000): pp. 20-29; idem: "Lehren, lernen und Gebärdensprache am Berliner Taubstummen-Institut. Teil II: Die Willkür der Zeichen," *Das Zeichen* 52 (2000): 198-207; idem, "Gehörlose im Land Brandenburg zwischen 1750 und 1900. Teil I: Von Zöglingen, Künstlern und Handwerksgesellen – Schulleben und berufliche Bildung," *Das Zeichen* 68 (2004): pp. 348-357; Günther List, "Pädagogische Inklusion und die 'Bildbarkeit' der Taubstummen," *Das Zeichen* 51 (2000): pp. 8-18 [Part 1]; *Das Zeichen* 52 (2000): pp. 186-196 [Part 2]; idem, "Assimilation durch Zweisprachigkeit. Die preußisch-deutschen Projekte Taubstummen-Bildung und Polenpolitik im 19. Jahrhundert," *Das Zeichen* 68 (2004): pp. 338-347; idem, "Deaf History: A Suppressed Part of General History," in *Deaf History Unveiled*, ed. Van Cleve, pp. 113-126.

37 Günther List, "Zeit-Schriften. Periodica als Quellengattung für die Geschichte der Gehörlosen bis zum Beginn des 20. Jahrhunderts," *Das Zeichen* 29 (1994): pp. 278-287; Heidi Grötz, "Der 'Taubstummen-Courier' – Eine Zeitschrift von Gehörlosen für Gehörlose," *Das Zeichen* 30 (1994): pp. 412-421 [Part 1]; *Das Zeichen* 31 (1995): pp. 8-13 [Part 2].

38 Joachim Gessinger, Auge und Ohr. Studien zur Erforschung der Sprache am Menschen 1700-1850 (Berlin: de Gruyter, 1994).

Murray's dissertation on the transnational level of 19th and early 20th century American and European deaf movements. Murray includes in his study several German deaf leaders, organizations, and events.[39] Anne Quartararo has written the history of the French deaf movement in the 19th century, offering many parallels to the developments in Germany.[40] John Vickrey Van Cleve's and Barry A. Crouch's 1989 history of the American deaf movement is one of the earliest scholarly works on the subject, and has also been helpful in understanding the German situation.[41] Especially in the United States, there is a growing body of work on different aspects, apart from the organizations, of Deaf History, which has been useful both as inspiration, reference, and examples of theoretical approaches. These works are too numerous to mention in the introduction, but will be cited in the appropriate sections below.

Disposition

The study is divided into four main chapters, followed by an epilogue and a conclusion. Chapter one concerns the view on the deaf from outside. Statisticians identified, counted, and described a group of people they called 'the deaf mutes'. Legislators determined their rights. Governments and charities assisted them. Employers hired them, and institutions confined them. Teachers educated them. I will ask what image these instances created of the deaf, and what space they allowed for them.

Chapter two is about the social conditions in 19th and early 20th century Germany. The question is how the structure and transformation of society affected people who were deaf.

Chapter three examines the history of German deaf organizations, their structure, activities, and ideological roots, from their origins and until 1914. The question is on what social and ideological basis deaf people organized, and what these conditions tell us about the self-images and spaces deaf people created for themselves.

---

39   Joseph Murray, "One Touch Of Nature Makes The Whole World Kin:" The Transnational Lives Of Deaf Americans, 1870-1924 (Ph.D. Diss., University of Iowa, 2007).

40   Anne T. Quartararo, *Deaf Identity and Social Images in Nineteenth-Century France* (Washington D.C.: Gallaudet University Press, 2008).

41   John Vickrey Van Cleve and Barry A. Crouch, *A Place of Their Own. Creating the Deaf Community in America* (Washington, D.C.; Gallaudet University Press, 1989).

Chapter four concerns the debate within the movement, and between the deaf and hearing authorities; how it was conducted, and what effects it had. The epilogue is an outlook at the further development of the German deaf movement during and immediately following the First World War.

A Word on Words

From one point of view, this study is about deaf people, more precisely: people with congenital or early hearing loss, to a degree that rendered them unable to learn, or maintain their knowledge of, spoken language by use of their ears. It is not a study about deafened adults or hard of hearing people. These groups were already in the 19th century demarcated from the 'deaf-mutes'.[42]

Due to the numerous variations in the physical and social characteristics of deafness, it is nevertheless no easy task to decide who counts as deaf, and who does not. Today, many have settled on a cultural definition, including those who use Sign Language and are affiliated in one way or another with what is called Deaf culture. Considering oneself deaf, or Deaf, capitalized to mark the cultural (or national/ethnical) content of the term, is a crucial part of being Deaf. Nevertheless, the sensory side of deafness remains important. Children of Deaf adults, (CODAs), are often fluent signers and firmly integrated in the Deaf culture, but as long as they hear, they are not Deaf.[43]

Throughout history, we find people whose deafness, both physically and culturally, is ambiguous. Brenda Jo Brueggeman's suggestion that the characteristic trait of the deaf subject is in fact betweenity,[44] implies that a study like this one is not the place to install thresholds and to disregard those who were not 'proper' deaf people.

The terminology to use relating to people who cannot hear continues to be a controversial topic. The antiquated term 'deaf-mute', and its equivalents in other languages, has gone from general acceptance, to criticism of inaccuracy, to today being considered derogatory. On the other hand, it was the most commonly used word for deaf people at the time in question here.[45] In that sense, this study is in

---

42   Eduard Walther (Ed.) *Handbuch der Taubstummenbildung* (Berlin: Elwin Staude, 1895), pp. 33, 47, 56, 68.
43   Baynton, "Beyond Culture", pp. 293-295.
44   Brueggemann, *Deaf Subjects,* p. 7.
45   In German: "Taubstumm". Sometimes the word "Gehörlos", "hearingless", today the generally accepted German term for deaf people, was also used. See for instance

fact about 'deaf-mutes'. Nevertheless, I have chosen to avoid the word in most cases and to use it only when discussing terminology and the closely related construction of 'the deaf-mutes' as a demographic group. This is because it would be misleading to label this process the construction of 'the deaf' as a group, when that term was in fact not used. To signify my critical position towards this and related terms, I write them in single quotation marks ('').

Instead, I have chosen to use the word 'deaf' in most of the text. Some scholars choose instead to write 'Deaf' when referring to deaf signers who form a community, and deaf when referring to the condition of not hearing.[46] However, knowing when to use this distinction is, to the historian, troublesome and may be misleading. The capitalized Deaf was not only invented much later than the period studied here, but also implies a certain self-image and cultural identification, which often cannot be imposed on the people in the 19th century.[47] It is my intention to investigate, not to presuppose, the self-image of 19th century deaf people. Using 'Deaf' would suggest that I already decided that they saw themselves in a similar way as today's Deaf. Furthermore, their physical ability to hear is impossible to determine today, and of little importance to the study. Therefore, there is in this case no real need to distinguish between the two sides of d/Deafness. Only when referring to the contemporary concept of Deaf(ness), and modern Deaf communities and -people, I will use the capital D.

In the 19th century, no distinction was made between different national sign languages.[48] In German, Sign Language was called simply *Gebärdensprache* ("gesture-language", sometimes spelled *Geberdensprache*) or *Zeichensprache* ("sign-language"). How much this language had in common with that used in contemporary Germany is unknown. Whether there was a German Sign Language at the time, or rather different regional languages, is still an open question. Therefore, I do not use today's denomination DGS, *Deutsche Gebärdensprache*, but Sign Language or Sign, capitalized to signify awareness of this as a genuine, idiomatic language.

H. Lingelmann, *Aus der Taubstummen-Welt. Biographien, Charakterzüge und Erzählungen aus dem Leben der Gehörlosen für Leser jeden Standes* (Berlin, 1876).

46 For instance: Murray, *Touch of Nature*; Lane, Hoffmeister and Bahan, *DEAF-WORLD*; Susan Burch, *Signs of Resistance: American Deaf Culture History, 1900-1942* (New York: New York University Press, 2002).

47 v. Douglas Baynton, *Forbidden Signs. American Culture and the Campaign Against Sign Language* (Chicago, IL: University of Chicago Press, 1996), pp. 11-12.

48 Murray, *Touch of Nature*, p. 2; Baynton, *Forbidden Signs*, pp. 12-13.

1. The 'Deaf-Mutes' in Numbers, Words, and Practice

Regardless of our current understanding of deafness, cultural or medical, we cannot test the hearing of people long gone. Neither can we impose a 21st century understanding of the Deaf retrospectively. This leaves us with the 19th century concept, the 'deaf-mutes', '*Taubstummen*', a word that in 19th century Germany was used to describe certain people. The obvious question becomes: what kind of people did officials and professionals mean when they used this term? Who were the 'deaf-mutes'?

COUNTING 'DEAF-MUTES': CONTEXT, MOTIVES, AND METHODS

The practice of counting 'deaf-mutes' in the German states began in the early 19th century.[1] Over the years, the accounts became more frequent and elaborate. A literature emerged, consisting of charts and lists of numbers of 'deaf-mutes', ordered according to different categories. In the earliest surveys, the number of

---

[1] An "account of deaf-mutes" ("Taubstummenzählung") was performed in Bavaria as early as 1801. V. Georg Pongratz, Allgemeine Statistik über die Taubstummen Bayerns. Zugleich eine Studie über das Auftreten der Taubstummheit in Bayern im 19. Jahrhundert (Munich: Max Kellerer's Hof-Buchhandlung, 1906), p. 1. However, in Gertrud Hesse's comprehensive overview from 1935, a Prussian account from 1823 is the earliest entry. Gertrud Hesse, Beiträge zur Geschichte und Methodik der deutschen Taubstummenstatistik Inaugural-Dissertation, Johann Wolfgang Goethe-Universität, Frankfurt a. M. (Saarlouis: Haufen Verlagsgesellschaft, 1935), p. 15. I have been unable to confirm Pongratz's claim about an 1801 survey.

deaf people in a certain area, their age and sex were listed.² Later, information about their social situation, their occupation, and their medical history appeared. The earliest more elaborate surveys, according to an overview by Gertrud Hesse, were the Bavarian official statistics from 1840 and a private survey performed in Saxony by Eduard Schmalz in 1836. However, these were rare exceptions. It was not until the German unification in 1871 that more extensive accounts became common.³ In 1901, legislation was passed prescribing the registration of all 'deaf-mute' children in the nation.⁴

The emergence and growth of German 'deaf-mute statistics' was part of an international development which has been described by philosopher Ian Hacking as an "avalanche of printed numbers".⁵ Above all, 19th century statisticians were interested in the population, especially minorities, deviant people, and -behaviours. Hacking's argument is that categorization and collection of data can, in a sense, help create certain categories of people.⁶ In the following, we shall see if and how this was the case with the 'deaf-mute statistics.'

The first section is concerned with the motives and methods for developing these statistics. After describing the different types of surveys, I will analyze the contents of a selection of statistical publications, in order to determine what characterized the new representative of the deaf, the 'average deaf-mute'.⁷

Motives

Counting and calculating 'deaf-mutes' could be done in several different ways, depending not only on resources, but also on the type of information the surveyors wished to extract, and how the results were to be used. Most surveys were

---

2 Cf. for instance Hesse, *Taubstummenstatistik*, pp. 15, 43.
3 Hesse, *Taubstummenstatistik*, pp. 4, 27, 68.
4 Engelmann, "Die Ergebnisse der fortlaufenden Statistik der Taubstummen während der Jahre 1902 bis 1905," Medizinal-statistische Mitteilungen aus dem Kaiserlichen Gesundheitsamte. (Beihefte zu den Veröffentlichungen des Kaiserlichen Gesundheitsamtes) Vol. 12. Part 1 (Berlin: Julius Springer, 1909), pp. 1-5
5 Ian Hacking, *The Taming of Chance* (Cambridge: Cambridge University Press, 1990), pp. 2, 33.
6 Hacking, *The Taming of Chance,* p. 3; idem, "Kinds of People: Moving Targets."
7 The words 'average', or 'average deaf-mute', were not used in any of the sources of this chapter. In the following, I will sometimes use the expression to designate the combined image conveyed in statistic surveys. They do give the impression of an average 'deaf-mute', although they never explicitly make use of this concept.

commissioned by the local or central governments as a part of a scheme to, in one way or another, manage the 'deaf-mutes'. Planning educational measures entailed finding out how many 'deaf-mutes' of suitable age lived on the territory. These were the first surveys.[8] When later on inquiries about the social, occupational and medical circumstances of the 'deaf-mutes' were added, this suggests an extended ambition of managing their lives. Furthermore, it indicates that the 'deaf-mutes' were understood not only as an educational, but increasingly also as a medical and social matter.

In 1880, otologist Arthur Hartmann discussed the advantages of statistics on 'deaf-mutes' in a treatise on "deaf-mutism and the education of deaf-mutes".[9] Hartmann considered the 'deaf-mutes' a threat to the state by being unproductive and in the need of relief. Statistics were a tool to remedy this, but not by integrating or educating the 'deaf-mutes'. Instead, Hartmann writes: "It must be the aim of the statistics on one hand to determine the prevalence of the defects, on the other to discover their nature and causes, so that measures can be taken through which their incidence can be prevented as far as possible."[10] Thus, approaching the end of the century, statistics had become a tool for prevention and elimination of 'deaf-mutism'. This is the background to the registration of all deaf children, focusing on their medical histories, commenced in 1902.[11]

Methods

Statisticians battled with the question over the most effective and accurate way to count 'deaf-mutes'. A number of different strategies were tried over the years.

---

8   Hesse, Taubstummenstatistik, 4; Pongratz, Allgemeine Statistik, p. 1; cf. Hacking, The Taming of Chance, pp. 118-121.

9   Arthur Hartmann, Taubstummheit und Taubstummenbildung nach den vorhandenen Quellen, sowie nach eigenen Beobachtungen bearbeitet (Stuttgart: Ferdinand Enke, 1880).

10 "Sache der Statistik muss es sein, einerseits die Verbreitung der Gebrechen festzustellen, andererseits das Wesen und die Ursachen derselben zu ermitteln, damit Massregeln getroffen werden können, durch welche dem Auftreten derselben, soweit als dies überhaupt möglich ist, entgegengewirkt werden kann." Hartmann, *Taubstummheit*, p. 30; *cf.* Friedrich Prinzing, "Die Methoden der medizinischen Statistik," in *Handbuch der biologischen Arbeitsmethoden*, Vol. 5, part 2, ed. Emil Aberhelden (Berlin: Urban & Schwarzenberg, [1928]), p. 663, on the importance of medical statistic for research on hereditariness of illnesses.

11 *V.* below pp. 37f.

Gertrud Hesse identified six main methods that were used to gain statistical data on deaf people during the 19th and early 20th centuries: Statistics made in connection with general censuses, independent surveys, combinations of these, counting of 'deaf-mute' institutional wards, continuous registration of 'deaf-mute' school children, and registration of 'deaf-mute' patients in special clinics.[12] Hartmann made another distinction between two kinds of statistics: the general and the particular. The general were those surveys that merely listed the same information any census would: age, sex, religion, etcetera. The particular surveys had specialized questions, designed especially for gaining information about "the essence and causes of the infirmity".[13] Different models within each category were also possible. The information could be gathered by lay people or by local medicals or clergy, with or without direct contact with the surveyed households.

The general agreement was that there was a fundamental conflict between comprehensiveness and accuracy. How many, and which, people were counted as 'deaf-mutes' depended on the method. Asking every household for any 'deaf-mute' members led to more cases being identified, but, on the other hand, the professional surveyors doubted that the average citizen was competent enough to make a correct judgement. The 'combined' method mentioned above included a general census performed face-to-face in each household, which provided the names of all 'deaf-mutes' in each area. Then a physician could visit them to confirm that they were indeed 'deaf-mutes' and ask further questions about their medical and social circumstances. This procedure combined the comprehensiveness of the information collected in each household with the professional gaze of the medicals. Although advocated by some professionals, this labour-intensive method was only seldom used in practice.[14]

---

12   Hesse, Taubstummenstatistik, p. 7.
13   "das Wesen und die Ursachen des Gebrechens [...]." Hartmann, Taubstummheit, p. 31.
14   Kurt Weißback, "Die Gebrechlichen und ihre Versorgung," Zeitschrift des Sächsischen Statistischen Landesamtes 64/65 (1918/19): p. 117; "Hauptergebnisse der Ermittelung der Blinden, Taubstummen, Blödsinnigen und Irrsinnigen nach Regierungsbezirken, auf Grund der Volkszählung vom 1. Dezember 1871," Zeitschrift des kgl. bayerischen statistischen Bureaus 8, no. 2. (1876): p. 107; Hartmann, Taubstummheit, pp. 31-35; Pongratz, Allgemeine Statistik, pp. 1-5; Heinrich Schmaltz, Die Taubstummen im Königreich Sachsen. Ein Beitrag zur Kenntniss der Ätiologie und Verbreitung der Taubstummheit (Leipzig: Breitkopf & Härtel, 1884): p. 8

Thus, the particular ways of counting 'deaf-mutes' varied over place and time. In the following, a few surveys shall be presented in detail. First, the developments in two German states with especially long traditions of elaborate 'deaf-mute statistics.' Second, two nation-wide initiatives to count and describe the totality of the German 'deaf-mutes'.

The Early 'Deaf-Mute Statistics' in Bavaria

Georg Pongratz, teacher at the Royal Central Deaf-Mute Institute in Munich, was appointed by the Bavarian government to revise the 'deaf-mute statistics' contained in the 1900 census. In his report, he included a brief history of the 'deaf-mute statistics' in Bavaria. According to him, Bavaria counted its 'deaf-mutes' for the first time in 1801, as a part of the preparations for the first deaf asylum. In 1840 and 1858, Bavaria became the first German state to commission medical statistics on the 'deaf-mutes'. These were performed by forensic physicians in cooperation with the police, and included an examination of the 'deaf-mute' and the gathering of information from his or her family.[15] They included questions about the reason for the 'deaf-mutism' and the medical state and history of the 'deaf-mute' and his or her family. The answers included cases of 'deaf-mutism' as a result of fright, a lightning striking nearby, a cold bath, and in one case, quoted in a footnote, a woman gave birth to five 'deaf-mute' children after seeing a 'deaf-mute' child during her first pregnancy.[16] Worth noticing is also the inquiry into the 'deaf-mute's' ability to speak, since it implies a view on 'deaf-mutism' as a condition not necessarily consisting of lack of both hearing and speech. Apparently, one could be 'deaf-mute' but still be able to speak. In 1840, it was found that six percent of the 'deaf-mutes' had this ability.[17]

---

15   Pongratz, *Taubstummheit,* p. 1; the results of the 1840 and 1858 surveys were published in *Beiträge zur Statistik des Königreichs Bayern,* ed. F.B.W. von Hermann (Munich: J. G. Cotta'schen Buchhandlung), Vol. 1 (1850): pp. 225-232; Vol. 8 (1859): pp. 259-263; I have been unable to find any published results of the 1801 survey.

16   Hermann, *Beiträge,* Vol. 1. (1850): pp. 226-227, Hermann, *Beiträge,*Vol. 8. (1859): p. 259.

17   However, only one percent had gained this skill through education. The others were likely post-lingually deaf who had maintained their speech. In 1858, still about six percent of the deaf could speak, but they had all learned it at school. It was no longer asked whether the deaf person could speak, but only if he or she had learned to

According to Pongratz, these early surveys were widely believed to be incomplete. The doctors had, so he argued, not been able to find all 'deaf-mutes'. To remedy this, a section on 'deaf-mutes' was listed in a separate section of the general census in 1871. However, this led to the opposite problem and the surveyors ended up with many "non-deaf-mutes" listed as 'deaf-mutes'.[18] In the face of this, Pongratz' revision of the 1900 survey results was supposed to make sure that all those who, according to present medical definitions, were 'deaf-mute' were included – and no one else. The information he was able to gather was slightly more detailed than in the general survey, and focused on the epidemiological and social aspects of 'deaf-mutism'.[19]

Systematizing the Efforts in Saxony

In the Kingdom of Saxony, the counting of 'deaf-mutes' began as a part of the general censuses in the 1830s. These surveys were performed about every three to five years, more frequently than in most other German states. Until 1875, they merely listed the number and sex of the 'deaf-mutes' in each locality. In that year, a registry card for every "blind, deaf-mute, feebleminded, [or] insane"[20] inhabitant was introduced (fig. 1).

In each household, the master was asked if any of the members had one of these afflictions. If so, the surveyor filled out the special card, which facilitated the evaluation of results but contained no medical or extended social

---

    speak through education. Hermann, *Beiträge,* Vol. 1. (1850): p. 27; Hermann, *Beiträge,* Vol. 8. (1859): p. 260.

18 "Nichttaubstummen", Pongratz, Allgemeine Statistik, p. 1. The results of the 1871 survey appeared in Georg Mayr, Die Verbreitung der Blindheit, der Taubstummheit, des Blödsinns und des Irrsinns in Bayern nebst einer allgemeinen internationalen Statistik dieser vier Gebrechen, Beiträge zur Statistik des Königreichs Bayern, Vol. 35 (Munich: Adolf Ackermann, 1877).

19 Pongratz, *Allgemeine Statistik,* pp. 2-5.

20 "blind, taubstumm, blödsinnig, irrsinnig" Victor Böhmert, "Die Statistik der Gebrechlichen im Königreich Sachsen in den Jahren 1834-1875," *Zeitschrift des Sächsischen Statistischen Bureau's* 23 (1877): p. 21; *cf.* Prinzing, *Die Methoden der medizinischen Statistik,* pp. 531-532.

information. As a result, the 1875-1910 surveys offered somewhat more detailed information, including family structure and, sometimes, occupation.[21]

Figure 1: Registry card for "blind, deaf-mute, feeble-minded and insane" persons used in the Saxon census from 1875.

Blind:	Taubstumm: ....
Ort:	Amtshptmsch.: ....
Cat.-(Haus-)Nr.	Anstalt: ....
Name:	
Beruf:	Familienstand: ....
Männlich: .... Geburtstag u. Jahr: .... Weiblich:	
Geburtsort u. Land: .... vorh. Wohnort:	
Staatsangehörigkeit: .... Muttersprache:	
(wenn nicht sächsisch) (wenn nicht deutsch)	
Irrsinnig: .... **1. December 1875.** Blödsinnig:	

The card asks for name, age, sex, occupation, marital status, present and previous address, place of birth, citizenship, and native language. Source: Böhmert, "Statistik", p. 21.

In 1881, the Dresden physician Heinrich Schmaltz initiated a private investigation into the lives of Saxony's 'deaf-mutes'. With the aim of finding the medical reasons for 'deaf-mutism', he designed a form to be filled out with a detailed medical history and description, including a genealogy. Schmaltz thought of his survey as a medical research project, but mentioned that some of the information he gathered could also give an idea of the social circumstances of the 'deaf-mutes'. For assistance in gathering the data he turned to the clergy.[22] He expected local pastors to be sympathetic to the "humanitarian concept"[23] of such research, and educated enough to be able to accurately answer the questions. Of

---

21 Böhmert, "Statistik," p. 24; Kurt Weißback, "Die Gebrechlichen und ihre Versorgung," *Zeitschrift des Sächsischen Statistischen Landesamtes* 64/65 (1918/19): pp. 123-124.
22 Schmaltz, *Taubstummen*, pp. iii-9.
23 "humane Grundgedanke" Schmaltz, *Taubstummen*, p. 8.

the nearly 1800 copies he sent out, he received data on about 1500 deaf people in return. However, he did not always receive the type of information he wanted: "Out of obvious misunderstanding, even the well-educated answered the seemingly very simple queries inaccurately, incompletely, and sometimes even in a contradictory manner."[24] Nevertheless, Schmaltz used his material for a sociomedical discussion of the causes of 'deaf-mutism'.[25]

A Comprehensive Survey: The German 'Deaf-Mutes' in 1900

In the Chancellor's order to perform a general German census in the year 1900, he stipulated that it should include counting all 'deaf-mutes' and all those who were blind on both eyes. Any 'deaf-mute' member of a household was registered separately on a special card, giving the opportunity of answering questions explicitly concerning deafness. The information was not gathered by professionals. Whether a person was 'deaf-mute', and since when, was answered based on the information given by the deaf person's family members or by themselves.

Identical, rather brief, forms were used for registering blind and 'deaf-mute' people. Only three questions particularly concerned the 'deaf-mutes': "Deafmute: Since earliest childhood? or later arisen? [...] If inmate of an institution: Address of the institution: If one or more further cripples belong to the same *ordinary* household (not institutions): Record of the number(s) of the card(s) in question for the administrative district".[26] All in all, there were 15 questions on the form, the others being identical with the ones used in the general survey. Thus, the 1900 census primarily offered the opportunity of conveniently

---

24 "Selbst Hochgebildete beantworteten die anscheinend so überaus einfachen Anfragen aus offenbarem Missverständniss falsch, unvollständig, ja bisweilen so, dass sich Einzelheiten gegenseitig widersprachen." Schmaltz, *Taubstummen*, p. 7.

25 In his conclusion, he emphasized poor social conditions in childhood as the main reason for deafness. Schmaltz *Taubstummen*, pp. 178-179

26 "Taubstumm: Seit frühester Jugend? oder später entstanden? [...] Wenn Anstaltspflegling: Adresse der Anstalt: Wenn noch ein oder mehr Gebrechliche derselben *gewöhnlichen* Haushaltung (nicht Anstalt) angehören: Angabe der betreffenden laufenden Nummer(n) der Karte(n) für den Verwaltungsbezirk" Engelmann, "Die Taubstummen im Deutschen Reiche nach den Ergebnissen der Volkszählung von 1900," *Medizinal-statistische Mitteilungen aus dem Kaiserlichen Gesundheitsamte. (Beihefte zu den Veröffentlichungen des Kaiserlichen Gesundheitsamtes.)* Vol. 9. Part 1 (Berlin: Julius Springer, 1905), p. 8.

comparing the 'deaf-mutes' to the general population. It was not suited as a base for in-depth analysis of 'deaf-mutism' in the medical sense, nor did it offer insights in the success, failure, or present stand of deaf education. When the cards had been filled out, they were sent to the Imperial Office of Public Health. This agency evaluated the material and issued a 200-page report in 1905.[27]

The Continuous Registry of Deaf Children

The Office of Public Health considered the 1900 survey to be flawed in terms of medical detail and accuracy, but as it was being performed, a new initiative was already underway. At a congress for German teachers of the deaf in 1897, the idea of a continuous registration of 'deaf-mute' children had been presented. The suggestion met great approval among teachers and in the government, and in 1901, an order was issued to register all 'deaf-mute' children in Germany.[28]

This type of survey was completely new. It encompassed the entire nation and was designed to include all 'deaf-mute' children, not on one single occasion, but through continuous registration. All deaf children were to be registered when they entered deaf school, or at reaching the age at which hearing children started school.[29] A committee of state bureaucrats, medical doctors, teachers of the deaf, and representatives of local governments designed the forms. They were remarkably extensive, including twenty main questions, many with several follow-up questions, divided into three sections. The first was to be filled out by the local police authority (concerning the name, age, place of birth, residence, and religion of the child, and the occupations of its parents), the second by a physician in cooperation with the family, local clergy, and schoolteachers (concerning the medical history of the child and its relatives), the third by a specialist physician and a teacher at the deaf school to which the child was enrolled. This last section related to the child's current medical and educational status. The order was implemented on the 1st of January 1902. In 1908, the Office of Public Health published a report based on the data collected until the 1st of June 1905.[30]

---

27 Engelmann, "Die Taubstummen," pp. 8-9.
28 Engelmann: "Die Taubstummen", p. 9; idem, "Ergebnisse", pp. 1-2; Ernst Schorsch, "IV. Deutsche Taubstummenlehrer-Versammlung in Dresden vom 29. September bis 2. Oktober 1897," *Blätter für Taubstummenbildung* 20 (1897): pp. 315-316.
29 Including those who were "suspected of deaf-mutism" ["der Taubstummheit verdächtige"] Engelmann, "Ergebnisse", p. 1.
30 *Ibid.* pp. 1-6.

Although the idea originated with teachers of the deaf, and the survey was designed and performed in close cooperation with the educational system, it seems that there was never an intention to apply the findings to improve educational practices. The report mentions acquiring knowledge of the causes of 'deaf-mutism' as the main motive of the survey. These causes, as assumed in the report, may be "inheritance, blood relations, economic circumstances, or earlier illnesses".[31] Judging by the questions, the physical and mental health and medical family history of the children was considered most important. Special attention was paid to congenital deafness.[32]

Compared to the magnitude of the project, the results appear to have been meagre. The 1900 report begins by stating that it will ask what part social circumstances, inheritance, and illness play in causing 'deaf-mutism'. After discussing the results, the conclusion was that all three factors apparently contributed, and that improving social and medical conditions may reduce the occurrence of 'deaf-mutism'.[33]

The Development of 'Deaf-Mute'-Statistics: Conclusion

The German 'deaf-mute statistics' started as a mere counting of 'deaf-mutes' in individual states. During the course of the 19th century, these surveys became more common, more frequent, and more elaborate. The idea started to emerge that counting 'deaf-mutes' not only could help planning education and welfare, but also find the causes of the condition. Prevention replaced remedy as a motive. At the turn of the century, within only three years, two major surveys of 'deaf-mutes' were performed, covering the entire German territory. Apart from the area they covered, however, they had little in common. The survey of 'deaf-mutes' in connection with the 1900 census offered information almost exclusively on socio-economic circumstances, whereas the registry of 'deaf-mute' children was concerned with intricate medical histories. Nevertheless, both surveys were published in the same series, the *Medizinal-statistische Mitteilungen,* which was issued by the Office of Public Health. The counting of 'deaf-mutes' had, regardless of the type of information recorded and the circumstances of the surveys, definitely arrived in the medical realm.

---

31 "Vererbung, Blutsverwandschaft, wirtschaftliche Verhältnisse oder vorausgegangene Erkrankungen" ibid, p. 1; "blood relations" alludes to inbreeding.
32 Engelmann, "Ergebnisse", pp. 1-6.
33 Ibid., p. 25.

WHAT THEY FOUND: CONTENTS OF THE SURVEYS

The classification process through which the 'deaf-mutes' emerged as a medically deviant subgroup in the German population took a century to be completed. In the early 20th century, it was finally possible to define with some certainty what type of person an 'average (German) deaf-mute' was. The following sections will describe the characteristics of this demographic category. Because of its comprehensiveness, the 1900 nation-wide survey has been selected as the main source. Two parts of the survey are of particular interest, since they contain socio-economic data: the one on the vocations, and the one on the family structure of the surveyed. In the following, these data will be used to find the settings where the 'deaf-mutes in general' could be found. Of course, the survey also presented variations within the group. The final part is therefore devoted to these contrasts, since they suggest what factors, besides the 'deaf-mutism' itself, helped determine the situation of the average 'deaf-mutes'.

The 1900 survey followed the disposition of the general census of which it was a part. This meant that the information about the 48 750 'deaf-mutes' that the surveyors identified was rather limited. The forms asked for age, sex, citizenship, religion, origin, occupation, marital status, mother tongue, and the type of relationship to the head of the household. With these facts, a basic sense of their social situation could be gained, and they could be sorted according to membership in other demographic subgroups.[34]

Occupation

In the presentation of the 1900 survey, all 'deaf-mutes' born in 1884 or earlier, and not living in asylums, were divided into twenty-five groups according to occupation. Housewives and other family members who did not work were probably included in the last group, "Without vocation and none stated".[35] Eighteen percent of the male and half of the female 'deaf-mutes' belonged to this group.[36]

---

34   Religious, ethnic, linguistic, and geographical.
35   "Ohne Beruf und Berufsangabe." Engelmann, "Die Taubstummen," p. 28.
36   This conclusion is made based on the fact that 36 929 people were included in the list of vocations. Counting out all deaf between 0 and 15 years of age and all adult inmates of deaf asylums, as stated in the survey, there were 849 people left not included in the survey of vocations, not living in asylums and not above 15 years old. That only 849 deaf people, or hardly 2%, were either dependants, live-in

Type of industry, not type of work, was decisive for the disposition of the statistics. It must therefore be kept in mind that the figures do not necessarily tell us anything about the position of the workers within their particular branch. In the "Commerce" group, for instance, stockbrokers, travelling salesmen and packers were all included. "Clothing and cleaning" included, among others, tailors, shoemakers, hairdressers, laundresses and pressers.[37] Consequently, the vocational statistics did not principally serve the purpose of positioning the 'deaf-mutes' in a socio-economic class. Rather, it assigned them to a functional subgroup in society. Categories were defined by the type of material they were involved in handling, for instance wood or leather, or by the basic societal function they had, like agriculture, trade, or civil service. The people in each category belonged to a class, not in any Marxist sense, but by filling a certain function in the body of society.

Not only was a wide range of different vocations combined in the same category; neither was it discriminated between people currently working, and people who were not. There was no category for unemployed people, only for people without vocation, which of course is something completely different. Whether they actually performed their stated occupation, and if they were able to make a living out of it, is obscure. The report states: "24 262 or 66,8 % were able to perform gainful work, although probably not as skilfully and successfully as the hearing".[38]

This statement likely alludes to what in the survey is called "occupational position".[39] Those who owned their business were differentiated from those who were employed. The numbers of self-employed (*selbständig*) 'deaf-mutes' varied

---

    servants or self-sufficients seems unlikely, since these groups together accounted for about 40% of the adult population in 1895. It seems more probable that the divergence is caused by different age limits in the different parts of the survey. The 'vocations' part mentions those born before 1885, while the general age categorization in the deaf population draws the line between those aged 15, and those older than 15. Thus a divergence due to the exact date of birth is possible. Engelmann, "Die Taubstummen," pp. 72, 198, 242-243; *Statistik des Deutschen Reichs herausgegeben vom Kaiserlichen Statistischen Amt,* Vol. 111 (Berlin: Puttkammer & Mühlbrecht 1899): p. 15.

37   Statistik des Deutschen Reichs, Vol. 111. (1899): pp. 23-24.

38   "24 672 oder 66,8 % einem Erwerbe, wenn auch vermutlich nicht mit den gleichen Geschick und Erfolg wie die Hörfähigen, nachzugehn [sic] im Stande waren." Engelmann, "Die Taubstummen," p. 27.

39   "Stellung im Beruf", ibid.

greatly according to business branch, between 73 and 0,5%, with an average of 14%. This, according to the report, showed that "the deaf-mutes are apparently, due to their infirmity, mainly reliant on the position as *sub*workers."[40]

Evaluating these figures is complicated by the fact that the presentation did not compare the vocational structure of the 'deaf-mutes' with that in the general population. Instead, it was the relative size of the groups themselves that was compared, without making any reference to which vocations were generally most common at the time. The conclusion was that 'deaf-mutes' rarely performed advanced tasks and preferred work that did not demand verbal communication.[41]

Contrasting the class structure of the 'deaf-mutes' with that of the population as a whole aids the understanding of the section. However, a number of factors complicate such a comparison. First, no general survey of vocations from the same year is available. Although this information was required in the general census, the results of this particular question were not published.[42] The closest alternative for comparison with the entire population is instead the general survey of vocations from 1895. Second, the survey of the 'deaf-mutes' was diffuse on what methods it had used in developing this rather complex type of statistics. It simply listed the number of 'deaf-mutes' in each trade, but did not say according to what definitions the disposition was made. Hence, one cannot be certain what differences exist between the two surveys. In the 1895 survey, the definitions were differentiated and clearly stated to a much higher degree. A distinction was made between four groups: the gainfully working, the live-in servants, the dependents (people primarily living off the income from another household member's gainful work), and the self-sufficient, that is, people living on pensions or own capital, including inmates of asylums. Children were also included in the respective groups, and everyone was counted as belonging to the vocational group of their main provider.[43]

---

40 "[…] sind offenbar die Taubstummen durch ihr Gebrechen hauptsächlich auf die Stellung als Arbeits*gehilfen* angewiesen […]." [emphasis in original] Engelmann, "Die Taubstummen," p. 28.

41 Ibid., p. 28.

42 *V. Statistik des Deutschen Reichs herausgegeben vom Kaiserlichen Statistischen Amt*, Vol. 150 (Berlin: Puttkammer & Mühlbrecht, 1903), in which the results of the census were published. The census form, asking for vocation, is depicted in ibid., p. 12.

43 Statistik des Deutschen Reichs, Vol. 111 (1899), pp. 15-18.

Instead of comparing the percentage of deaf within each vocational group with that in the entire population, which would be very unreliable, a list of the most common occupations in each group can give an idea of how they compared (fig. 2).

Figure 2: The most common occupations among 'deaf-mutes' in 1900 vs. the gainfully working in 1895 in size order.[44]

	Vocational groups according to number of occupied 'deaf-mutes' in 1900	Vocational groups according to share of the gainfully working in 1895
1.	Agriculture	Agriculture
2.	Clothing and Cleaning	Clothing and Cleaning
3.	Woodworks	Military- court- and civil service, free professions
4.	Domestic service and miscellaneous paid work	Building
5.	Building	Commerce
6.	Textile industry	Textile industry
7.	Food industry	Food industry
8.	Mineral industry	Metal manufacturing
9.	Printing	Woodworks
10.	Metal manufacturing	Communications
11.	Art	Mining
12.	Miscellaneous factory work	Mineral industry
13.	Paper	Hosting
14.	Leather	Domestic service and miscellaneous paid work
15.	Commerce	Machine and tool production
16.	Machine and tool production	Leather
17.	Military- court- and civil service, free professions	Forestry and fishing
18.	Forestry and fishing	Paper
19.	Mining	Printing
20.	Communications	Chemical industry
21.	Hosting	Firewood, lighting, oils
22.	Chemical industry	Miscellaneous factory work
23.	Firewood, lighting, oils	Art
24.	Insurance	Insurance

Sources: Medizinal-statistische Mitteilungen Vol. 9 p. 29, Statistisches Jahrbuch für das Deutsche Reich 1898, Berlin: Puttkammer & Mühlbrecht, 1898, p. 7

Nearly half of all 'deaf-mute' adults belonged either to the categories agriculture (one in four) or "Clothing and cleaning" (one in five). Agriculture had the largest single workforce in Germany at this time, so that its heading the list is not surprising. "Clothing and cleaning" was the second largest category also in the

---

44 No 'deaf-mutes' worked in insurance.

general survey, but relatively smaller than in the survey of 'deaf-mutes'.[45] The rest of the lists show some obvious differences. Some appear to reflect social- and communication barriers: Military-, court- and civil service, commerce, communications and mining belonged to the upper half of the general ranking, but did not make it to this position among the 'deaf-mutes'. The professions of the first category were virtually closed to deaf people due to the inaccessibility of higher education.[46] In mining, hearing played an important part in determining and avoiding hazards.[47] Most positions within commerce and communications entailed frequent communication with strangers, making them difficult or in some cases even impossible to manage without speech and hearing. Domestic service, which was a relatively larger category in the survey of 'deaf-mutes' than in the general one, also poses demands of communication skills. In this case, however, communication typically occurs with only a few known people, rather than with many complete strangers. Within a household, satisfactory modes of communication can be agreed upon and accustomed to. Neither did deaf servants necessarily work for hearing people, whereas a deaf shop assistant having only deaf customers is hard to imagine. The high ranking of printing and art among 'deaf-mutes' compared to the 1895 survey complies with practices in deaf education and traditions in the deaf community. These were typical 'deaf vocations', traditionally favoured and encouraged in the deaf schools and by the deaf community elite.[48]

Altogether, the overview of vocations in the 1900 survey of 'deaf-mutes' placed them foremost in categories associated with physical labour, serving the small world of private households rather than the state. In society, they attended to the basic needs – agriculture, clothing, and cleaning – but were rarely found in those sectors that connected, administered and supervised the system.

---

45   Hardly seven percent of the total workforce belonged to "Clothing and cleaning", compared to nearly one in five deaf people. Engelmann, "Die Taubstummen," p. 29; *Statistisches Jahrbuch für das Deutsche Reich,* 1898 (Berlin: Puttkammer & Mühl- brecht, 1898), p. 7.

46   Armin Löwe, "Gehörlosenpädagogik," in *Geschichte der Sonderpädagogik,* ed. Světluše Solarová (Stuttgart: Verlag W. Kohlhammer, 1983), p. 40.

47   Karin Hartewig, Das unberechenbare Jahrzehnt. Bergarbeiter und ihre Familien im Ruhrgebiet 1914-1924 (Munich: C. H. Beck, 1993), p. 105.

48   Yves Bernard, "Silent Artists," in *Looking Back. A Reader on the History of Deaf Communities and their Sign Languages,* eds. Renate Fischer and Harlan Lane (Hamburg: SignumVerlag, 1993), pp. 75-87; Feige, *Gehörlosen-Biographien,* p. 45; below p. 239.

Social and Family Life

The 1900 survey also revealed the position of the 'deaf-mutes' within their households. Excepting those who were living in institutions, it categorized them according to their relationship with the head of their household. Only a minority, about one in six, of the 'deaf-mute' men themselves headed a household, and an even smaller fraction of the women were married to the master of their house.[49] Instead, the 'deaf-mutes' were mostly found in dependent situations, mainly as children or grandchildren of the master or mistress of the house. Especially the 'deaf-mute' women were often found to be living with their parents, grandparents, or other relatives.

The survey also recorded the marriage rate among the 'deaf-mutes', and noticed that it was considerably lower than average. One in five adult deaf men were, or had been, married in the year of 1900. Deaf women married even less frequently: barely 13 percent of them were married, widowed, or divorced. In the population as a whole, about 40% were or had been married, noticeably with a higher marriage rate among women than men.[50] From this, the 'deaf-mutes' appeared as people of low status in their immediate social settings. Furthermore, their dependent situation indicated low status also in the wider sense. Not being able to start a family of their own could indicate meagre earnings and social stigma.

Institutional confinement was, as far as the 1900 survey reveals, a relatively uncommon place for 'deaf-mutes', apart from those children who went to residential school. However, only those who lived in 'deaf-mute asylums' were counted. Most states did not accommodate any adults at all in such institutions.[51]

Gender

The combination of gender- and disability related discrimination put the 'deaf-mute' women in a difficult situation. Due to their disability, the stereotypical female role as wife and mother was beyond reach for most of them. All skilled occupations except sewing and associated crafts were closed to them because of

---

49   The opposite, deaf women heading the household and deaf men being listed as spouses, was even rarer. Engelmann, "Die Taubstummen," pp. 25-27.
50   Engelmann, "Die Taubstummen," p. 23.
51   683 individuals over age 15 were in "deaf-mute-asylums" ["Taubstummen-Anstalten"] Engelmann, "Die Taubstummen," pp. 242-241.

their gender.⁵² From the professions they were excluded both as women and as 'deaf-mutes', although, before oralism closed the teaching profession to deaf people, there had been a few deaf women teachers.⁵³

Compared to their male counterparts, 'deaf-mute' women appeared to be in a weaker position in almost every aspect. They were even less likely than the men to marry and form their own household. Instead, they often remained at home in their family of origin. They were also more likely than men to remain in 'deaf-mute asylums' as adults (fig. 3).⁵⁴

Figure 3: Number of 'deaf-mutes' in 'deaf-mute asylums' in 1900, according to sex and age.

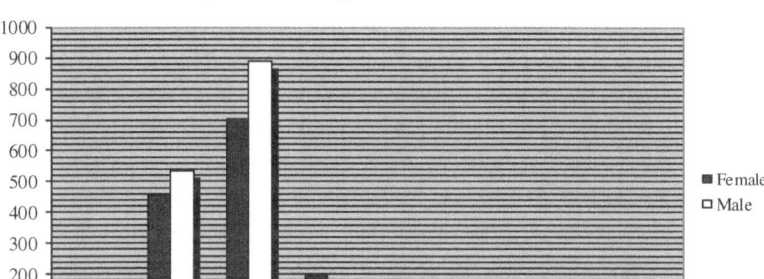

In the ages when schooling took place, boys were more likely than girls to live in institutions. Before and after that age, the relation was the opposite. Medizinalstatistische Mitteilungen, Vol. 9, pp. 242-243.

The combined picture is that 'deaf-mute' women were infantilized. They appear as a group lacking autonomy both in the social and economic realms. Perhaps as

---

52   The vocational education for girls was less regulated than that for boys, but a number of skilled and semi-skilled vocations, all in textile crafts, were available to them. v. Anne Schlüter, *Neue Hüte – alte Hüte? Gewerbliche Berufsbildung für Mädchen zu Beginn des 20. Jahrhunderts – Zur Geschichte ihrer Institut–ionalisierung* (Düsseldorf: Pädagogischer Verlag Schwann-Bagel, 1987), pp. 75-79.

53   Jochen Muhs, "Margaretha Hüttmann," *Das Zeichen* 28 (1994): pp. 156-157; Albin Maria Watzulik, "Das Neujahr 1901 in Leipzig," TC 2 (1901): pp. 17-18.

54   Engelmann, "Die Taubstummen", pp. 23-27, 30.

a symptom of this, some institutions called their female inmates "girls"[55] regardless of their age.

Types of Deafness

In addition to gender, age, and region, the 1900 survey differentiated among the 'deaf-mutes' according to the age when deafness had occurred. The vocational status and position in the household of those who had become 'deaf-mute' at age two or older was compared with that of those whose deafness had occurred earlier – including those who were born deaf.[56] Accordingly, some differences between the two groups appeared in the charts. Those who had become 'deaf-mute' at two years of age or later were more likely to be in charge of their own household or, in the women's case, be married to the person in charge. They were less likely to live with their parents, other relatives, or employers, but more likely to live with their grown children or grandchildren.[57] In short, 'deaf-mutes' in this group tended to have a higher status in the family.

They also appeared in trades with a higher status more often than those in the earlier deafened category. Noticeably higher relative numbers of later deafened people were employed in printing, trade, arts, building, stone industry and in the category "Military-, court-, civil-, and clerical service, as well as so-called free professions". As mentioned above, no definite statements on social status can be made based on these statistics. Several groups include both blue- and white-collar occupations. However, there was a certain covariaton between high levels of skilled labour, low numbers of 'deaf-mute' women, and higher numbers of later-deafened men in these vocational groups. Also, the later-deafened men were less likely to be without vocation than their earlier-deafened counterparts. For the women, the covariation was the opposite.[58]

---

55   "Mädchen", Bericht über die Ursberger Anstalten 1909, p. 5, BayHstA Rep. MInn Nr. 79999; *Jahres-Bericht über die Erziehungs- & Versorgungsanstalt taubstummer Mädchen in Hohenwart,* 1900-1911, StA Munich [no signature].

56   The latter group accounted for the vast majority, 37 693 of the total 48 750 'deaf-mutes'. Engelmann, "Die Taubstummen", pp. 19-20, 27-29

57   Engelmann, "Die Taubstummen", pp. 26-27

58   *Statistik des Deutschen Reichs,* Vol. 111, pp. 22-25; Engelmann, "Die Taubstummen," pp. 28-29; *cf.* Hans-Heinrich Müller (ed.), *Produktivkräfte in Deutschland 1870 bis 1917/18* (Berlin: Akademie-Verlag 1985), p. 416. In spite of their relatively higher proportions, there were still fewer late-deafened than early-deafened persons in the mentioned trades in absolute numbers.

Thus, the division of the 'deaf-mutes' into two groups differentiated the rather bleak image given by the survey. Being 'deaf-mute' was not an absolute state, but could manifest itself in varying ways – with correspondingly diversified consequences. The general rule, implied in the charts, was that the more one had in common with the norm, the better the prospects. In this case, the correspondence with the norm was having been hearing for some length of time. Degree of deafness, or coping skills such as lip reading, were not taken into account in this survey.

A distinction between profoundly and partially deaf was added by Pongratz in his revision of the census. His results enhanced the impression that similarity to the hearing meant higher status. He claimed to have found that every deaf person working in high-status professions within administration, teaching, medicine and the church, as well as to a great extent in commerce, was in fact not 'deaf-mute', but either deafened as an adult or hard of hearing. He argued that this had been the case in earlier studies as well.[59] The implications of this claim reversed the differentiation in the original survey. By eliminating the exception to the rule, Pongratz confirmed the image of 'deaf-mutism' as a severe handicap to the mental and intellectual functions.[60]

Differentiation between different kinds of 'deaf-mutism' according to degree or time of occurrence offered a way of handling individuals who did not fit the stereotype. In the 'deaf-mute' demographic subgroup, there were not exclusively people in modest positions. By introducing a further category of not-quite-so-'deaf-mute' people, the statisticians de-emphasised the disturbing inconsistencies.

Regional Differences

The division of the 'deaf-mutes' according to state and parish allowed contrasts to appear between areas of different character. The following section consists of a comparison between four areas: Berlin, as the capital and largest city of the Empire; the Kingdom of Saxony, which was also a predominantly urban-industrial area; catholic Bavaria, and protestant Württemberg, both mostly rural-agricultural states. For each of these regions, the 'deaf-mute' population can be followed over a number of decades, offering a further perspective on the results of the 1900 survey.

---

59   Pongratz, *Allgemeine Statistik*, pp. 94-95.
60   *Cf.* Walther, *Handbuch*, pp. 87-90.

City Life: Berlin

In the surveys made in the thirty years between 1880 and 1910, Berlin's 'deaf-mutes' were presented as increasingly independent citizens. Joining the urban working class appeared to better their standing. In 1900, their marriage rate was roughly the same as that of the population as a whole, and they were much more likely to have their own household than the average 'deaf-mute'. The general picture suggests that they increasingly, as workers and craftsmen, could support a family and maintain a household organized along traditional gender-patterns, instead of being secluded in asylums or dependent on their parents or relatives. According to the 1900 survey, there were no inmates over age 20 in Berlin's 'deaf-mute asylums'.[61] During the period in question, however, no advancement beyond the working class existence took place. The number of independents with their own business hardly increased, and neither did the number of deaf white-collar workers. The second most common way of living for a 'deaf-mute' man remained being a lodger.[62]

An Industrialized Kingdom: Saxony

The Kingdom of Saxony was highly industrialized. Compared to the German average, agriculture was a relatively small sector in terms of labour force. Manu-

---

61 Engelmann, "Die Taubstummen," pp. 242-243.
62 Preussische Statistik. (Amtliches Quellenwerk.) Herausgegeben in zwanglosen Heften vom Königlichen statistischen Bureau in Berlin. Vol. 69: Die Gebrechlichen in der Bevölkerung des preussischen Staates nach den Ergebnissen der Volkszählung vom 1. December 1880 (Berlin: Verlag des Königlichen Statistischen Bureaus, 1883): pp. 56-57; Preussische Statistik, Vol. 148: Die endgültigen Ergebnisse der Volkszählung vom 2. December 1895 im preussischen Staate, Part 2 (Berlin: Verlag des Königlichen statistischen Bureaus, 1898): pp. 190-191; Engelmann, "Die Taubstummen," pp. 72-73, 156, 182-183, 201; Albert Guttstadt, "Die Taubstummen und Blinden in Preussen," Zeitschrift des Königlich preussischen statistischen Landesamts Vol. 48 (1908): pp. 141, 144-146; Robert Behla, "Die Taubstummen in Preussen," Zeitschrift des Königlich preussischen statistischen Landesamtes Vol. 52 (1912): pp. 285, 288-290.

facturing industries, concentrated to the urban areas, placed Saxony among the leading areas in the German economy.[63]

In the 1900 survey, the social situation of Saxony's 'deaf-mutes' appeared to be rather similar to that in Berlin: they had a stronger, more independent position, than the 'deaf-mutes' in general.[64] In a digest of nearly a decade of 'deaf-mute statistics', Kurt Weißback made a rather positive evaluation of the numbers. The 'deaf-mutes' were integrated on the labour market, mainly in crafts and industry. Their tendency to marry had risen considerably. From this, Weißback concluded that the aid to the 'deaf-mutes' had proven to be effective.[65]

For the year 1900, the Saxon part of the general census offered a somewhat more detailed picture of the labour and earnings of the 'deaf-mutes'. The overview showed that the most common occupation among the men was to be a skilled worker. The women also worked in industry in considerable numbers, but their most common position was that of a "household member without primary occupation".[66] After Prussia, Saxony also stood out as having above-average numbers of 'deaf-mutes' heading their own households.[67] Less than 50 'deaf-mutes' were living off welfare, in poorhouses or in charitable institutions – only slightly more than those who lived from pensions and property.[68] The 'deaf-mute asylums' had relatively few adult wards.[69] Although Weißback made no comparison to the population in general, the impression gained was that Saxony's 'deaf-mutes' were reasonably comfortable.

Rural Bavaria and Württemberg

As mentioned above, detailed statistics on the Bavarian 'deaf-mutes' were made already in the 1840s and -50s. According to these early surveys, the 'deaf-mutes' were evenly distributed in different occupations. Agriculture, crafts, service and trade each stood for between 10 and 20 percent of the deaf labour force.

63　Roland Zeise and Bernd Rüdiger, "Bundesstaat im Deutschen Reich (1871-1917/18)," in *Geschichte Sachsens,* ed. Karl Czok (Weimar: Hemann Böhlaus Nachfolger, 1989), pp. 382-387.
64　Engelmann, "Die Taubstummen," pp. 72-73, 156, 185, 210.
65　Weißback, "Gebrechlichen," pp. 124-126, 139.
66　"Haushaltungsangehörige ohne Hauptberuf", Weißback, "Gebrechlichen", p. 124.
67　Engelmann, "Die Taubstummen," p. 26.
68　Weißback, "Gebrechlichen," p. 124.
69　Engelmann, "Die Taubstummen," pp. 242-241.

"Professional trade, art and science"[70] also employed a comparatively large share of the 'deaf-mutes', as many as ten percent in 1859.

Bavaria was not industrialised to the same extent as Berlin and Saxony, and the population density was below the German average. Agriculture was by far the largest sector in terms of labour force.[71] This sector also occupied the largest share of 'deaf-mutes' according to all surveys; still, it was surprisingly small among the 'deaf-mutes' compared to the population in general. More than half of the population worked in agriculture in the early 20th century, but only one in four 'deaf-mutes'. Earlier studies compared the occupation of the 'deaf-mutes' with that of their parents, and found a similar pattern: The 'deaf-mutes' were less prone than their parents to work in agriculture.[72]

In his revision of the 1900 survey, Pongratz explained this by arguing that a distinction between agricultural work, forestry, and domestic service cannot be made with any certainty, since most of the 'deaf-mutes' working in these sectors were sons and daughters of farmers, helping out with various chores at the family farmstead. Only thirteen individuals were landowning farmers.[73] Instead, Pongratz divided the 'deaf-mute' male workers into three main groups: "Agriculture, forestry and domestic service", "Crafts and industry (including commerce)" and "Art and artistic handicraft".[74]

Pongratz found 'deaf-mute' women only in the first two categories. The majority belonged to the "Agriculture, forestry and domestic service" sector, where the possibility of financial independence was considerably smaller than in "Crafts and industry". For the men, the distribution was the opposite. Typical crafts among the men were shoemaking, tailoring and carpentry, whereas the 'deaf-mute' craftswomen were mostly seamstresses and dressmakers. Both men and women remained largely dependent on others for their sustenance, but

---

70 "Berufsgeschäften, Künsten und Wissenschaften", Hermann, *Beiträge,* Vol. 1 (1850): p. 230; Hermann, *Beiträge,* Vol. 8 (1859): p. 260.

71 Rainer Gömmel, "Gewerbe, Handel und Verkehr," in *Handbuch der Bayerischen Geschichte,* Vol. 4: *Das neue Bayern. Von 1800 bis Gegenwart,* Part 2: *Die innere und kulturelle Entwicklung,* ed. Alois Schmid (Munich: C.H. Beck, 2007), pp. 241-247; Norman Stoe and Geoffrey Barraclough (Eds.), *The Times Atlas of World History,* 3rd ed. (London: Times Books, 1990), pp. 208-210.

72 Hermann, *Beiträge* Vol. 1 (1850): pp. 227, 230; Hermann *Beiträge* Vol. 8. (1859): p. 260; Engelmann, "Die Taubstummen," p. 209.

73 Pongratz, *Allgemeine Statistik,* pp. 96, 108.

74 "Land- Forst- und Hauswirtschaft"; "Gewerbe und Industrie (auch Handel)"; "Kunst und Kunsthandwerk", Pongratz, *Allgemeine Statistik,* p. 96.

women to a greater extent than men. A slight majority, 60%, of the 'deaf-mute' men deemed able to work actually managed to support themselves. Of the women, it was only 35%.[75] The marriage rate was also low. A mere seven percent of the 'deaf-mute' adults were married, according to the 1900 survey. A 'deaf-mute' woman or girl was substantially more likely to live in an institution than to be married.[76]

Württemberg and Bavaria stand out in the 1900 survey as the only states that accommodated adults in 'deaf-mute asylums' to any significant extent. Together, they were home to 60% of the total deaf adult institutional wards.[77] According to Pongratz, one in ten 'deaf-mutes' in Bavaria lived in institutions, excluding those who went to deaf schools. Two-thirds of them were women. Most were adults between 21 and 40 years of age, and they had typically been transferred to their respective asylums before they turned 20. In other words, the stay at an asylum was mostly long-term, and decided in youth. Most of the inmates were deemed capable of receiving education, in fact, most of them had attended school. Even in so-called 'Idiot-' or 'Cretin-Asylums' there were 'deaf-mute' wards without any intellectual disability.[78] Pongratz viewed the institutionalisation of 'deaf-mutes' as problematic in two ways: Those 'deaf-mutes' he regarded as most in need of institutional care – the elderly and the "uneducable feeble-minded"[79] did not receive it. On the other hand, young and able 'deaf-mutes' were often admitted, since they were able to work and thus contribute to the maintenance of the institution.[80]

Pongratz noticed a difference in labour structure over the generations. Younger 'deaf-mutes' of both sexes tended to work in crafts and industry more frequently than the older, a fact that Pongratz explained by referring to industrialization and the growth of deaf education.[81] A comparison of all four Bavarian studies shows that manufacture and industry appeared to have grown as

---

75 Pongratz *Allgemeine Statistik*, pp. 96-98, 101-106, 108-113.
76 Pongratz identified 113 married, widowed or divorced 'deaf-mute' women, and 369 'deaf-mute' women and girls living in different asylums. Pongratz , *Allgemeine Statistik,* pp. 25, 86; In the 1871 survey, the numbers were 69 married, widowed and divorced, and 258 living in asylums. Mayr, *Verbreitung* (Appendix), pp. 184-185, *cf.* Engelmann, "Die Taubstummen," p. 26.
77 Engelmann, "Die Taubstummen," pp. 30, 242-243.
78 Pongratz, *Allgemeine Statistik*, pp. 86-87.
79 "bildungsunfähigen schwachsinnigen", *ibid.,* p. 90.
80 Ibid., pp. 90-91.
81 Ibid., p. 101.

an employer of 'deaf-mutes', but only slowly. The difference between the 1840 and 1900 surveys was five percent.[82]

Considered together, the Bavarian surveys displayed a rise in education rates during the 19th century, although at a moderate pace. In 1858, half the 'deaf-mutes' had allegedly received education. At the turn of the century, three out of four deaf born between 1874 and 1893 had been educated. The state relied on private charities to provide deaf children with education, an apparently ineffective system, as a large share of Bavaria's 'deaf-mutes' remained uneducated.[83]

According to Pongratz's survey, educational level had great influence on the vocational life of the 'deaf-mutes'. Most of the men who had attended deaf school worked in art, crafts and industry, whereas their uneducated counterparts mostly worked in agriculture. The women showed a similar but weaker tendency. Consequently, the educated 'deaf-mutes' were more likely to be able to make their own living.[84] Here, Pongratz offered results that supported the educational theory and practice. His charts confirmed the value of deaf education and training in manual trades as the most advantageous career choice for 'deaf-mutes'.[85]

In Württemberg, industrialization was also comparatively slow, making agriculture a larger sector there than in most of the German Empire.[86] Earlier surveys had established a reasonable outreach of the education system to deaf children.[87]

---

82 Hermann, *Beiträge,* Vol. 1 (1850): p. 230; Pongratz, *Allgemeine Statistik,* p. 44.

83 Numbers concern the "educable" ("bildungsfähige") 'deaf-mutes'. Hermann, *Beiträge,* Vol. 1 (1850): p. 227; Hermann, *Beiträge,* Vol. 8. (1859): pp. 260; Pongratz, *Allgemeine Statistik,* p. 75; Hartmann, *Taubstummheit,* p. 185.

84 Pongratz, *Allgemeine Statistik,* pp. 117-118.

85 *Cf.* below p. 70.

86 Wolfgang von Hippel, "Wirtschafts- und Sozialgeschichte 1800 bis 1918," in *Handbuch der baden-württembergischen Geschichte* Vol. 3, ed. Hansmartin Schwarzmaier (Stuttgart: Klett-Cotta, 1992), p. 625.

87 The majority of Württemberg's 'deaf-mute' children were enrolled in one of the seven deaf schools in the 1870s. A. Hedinger, *Die Taubstummen und die Taubstummen-Anstalten nach seinen Untersuchungen in den Instituten des Königreichs Württembergs und des Grossherzogtums Baden* (Stuttgart: Ferdinand Enke, 1882), pp. 2, 4. Worth noticing is also that a government agency, the Commission for Reformatories, performed a survey of deaf children between ages 6 and 15 already in 1831. The results were used to gain an idea of the proportions of 'deaf-mute' vs. hearing people in different areas, which raised interest due to the surmised connection between geological conditions and 'deaf-mutism'. *Württembergische*

Nevertheless, the 1900 survey showed low levels of 'deaf-mutes' performing or at least being trained in a vocation. "Without (known) vocation" was the largest group in the 1900 overview of Württemberg's 'deaf-mute' workers. The deviation was especially strong in men; the 'deaf-mute' women were frequently without profession throughout Germany. In Württemberg, one-third of the 'deaf-mute' men had no vocation, as opposed to one in five in the entire nation. Especially agriculture displayed low numbers of 'deaf-mutes'. A mere 8% of the women belonged to this group, as opposed to the 20% average. Also, the marriage rates and the number of 'deaf-mutes' having a strong position in the household were below average. As in Bavaria, this corresponded with unusually high numbers of adult asylum wards.[88]

Conclusion: The 'Average German Deaf-Mute'

Of course, the concept 'deaf-mute' existed long before statistics. There was legislation, science, and institutions concerned with 'deaf-mutes' before anyone counted them.[89] However, the 'deaf-mutes' of the Bible, of the French Enlightenment, and of Prussian statistics are not necessarily the same kind of people. The invention of the 'deaf-mutes' as a subgroup in the population was a new way of understanding and creating knowledge about them, that is, by numerical means. The 'deaf-mutes' of scientific treatises, or the pupils in early deaf schools, were real individuals who walked the earth. The statistics, on the other hand, created an image of an 'average deaf-mute', who was not a person, but the sum of many people. In 19th century statistics, this type of average person was often used as a representation of the group.[90] Public displays of the most talented deaf pupils were used to represent 'the deaf-mutes' from the early days of deaf education.[91]

Jahrbücher für Geschichte, Geographie, Statistik und Topographie, Vol. 1833, No. 1 (Stuttgart: J. G. Cotta'sche Buchhandlung, 1834): pp. 382-383, 393.

88 Engelmann, "Die Taubstummen," pp. 26, 30, 211, 242-243.
89 Jonathan Rée, *I See a Voice. Deafness, Language and the Senses – A Philosophical History* (New York, NY: Metropolitan Books, Henry Holt and Company, 1999), pp. 92-95, 97-109, 133-137; Harlan Lane, *When the Mind Hears. A History of the Deaf* (New York, NY: Vintage Books, 1989) [reprint; first ed. Random House, 1984], pp. 67-111
90 Hacking, *The Taming of Chance*, pp. 107-110.
91 Cf. Lane, When the Mind Hears, pp. 34-38; Jan Branson and Don Miller, Damned for Their Difference: The Cultural Construction of Deaf People as Disabled. A Sociological History (Washington, D.C.: Gallaudet University Press, 2002), p. 125;

Such remarkable individuals became, at best, insignificant exceptions to the rule in statistical investigations.

It was a bleak image that emerged when the German authorities counted 'deaf-mutes'. Contrary to their intentions, they were unable to identify any clear patterns in the occurrence of 'deaf-mutism'. In terms of social standing, however, the tendency was beyond question: The surveys varied in methods, comprehensiveness, and thoroughness, but the 'average deaf-mutes' they found always seemed to be the same kind of people, characterized above all by their subordinate position at home and in society.

Managing the 'Deaf-Mutes'

'Deaf-mutes' were not only a concern of the statistician. Legislators, officials, organizations, and professionals of different fields were also involved in producing knowledge about, and interacting with, deaf[92] people. Practices such as distributing welfare, educating, or policing comprise ways of understanding their objects. They reveal the perceptions that these instances had of deaf people. By means of their real influence on individual lives, practices also determined spaces of action for deaf persons. The following section will ask in what ways the agencies of power treated the deaf.

The section begins with an overview of power in its most trivial form: legislation. This is to establish the formal prerequisites for deaf participation in civil society. The subsequent sections explore education and labour, and the options when these systems were insufficient: welfare, charity, and institutional confinement.

Legislation

Whether a deaf person was legally capable or not under German law depended on his or her ability to communicate and to what extent their language mode was accepted and understood by the authorities. Prussian law declared that anyone

---

cf. also Groschek, Unterwegs in eine Welt des Verstehens, pp. 75-76, 84-85, on another type of public display of successful pupils (through publishing their letters in the annual reports) and on late-19th century public displays of lip-reading pupils.

92 Leaving the statistics behind, I will from now on use the term 'deaf' instead of 'deaf-mute' in most cases. 'Deaf-mute', 'taubstumm', was, however, the term used in the sources.

who as a result of deafness or muteness could not care for their own personal responsibilities and concerns was to be placed under the authority of a guardian. The implementation of this paragraph was decided in court.[93]

With the *Bürgerliches Gesetzbuch* (BGB) of 1900, the regulations were somewhat moderated. Another type of guardianship was introduced, according to which it was possible to exclude certain fields of action from the guardian's power. It was conceived as a service to the deaf person, who in this type of arrangement remained legally capable in the case that he or she attempted to take any legal action. The legislator assumed that he or she would neither be able to, nor want to make, own legal decisions. After all, the guardianship was voluntary on behalf of its object. A guardian could not be appointed against the will of the deaf person, given that it was possible to communicate with him or her. What sort of communication this refers to was open to interpretation.[94] Other legal paragraphs were inconsistent in their acceptance of different language modes. Sign language was accepted in courtroom negotiations, but a will could only be made in writing or spoken language.[95] Thus, an illiterate deaf person could testify in court using an interpreter, but not make up a will. Statistics of the number of people standing under guardianship in the German Empire exist neither in the entire population, nor concerning the deaf. References to the practice appear relatively seldom in the sources.[96] Guardians of deaf people were, furthermore, not necessarily hearing. Eduard Fürstenberg, founder of the

---

93   *Vormundschaftsordnung* of July 5, 1875, § 81; Hartmann, *Taubstummheit*, p. 191.

94   BGB § 1910; Unser neues Recht in gemeinfasslichen Einzeldarstellungen, Vol. 12/13: Die Vormundschaft (Berlin: Pass & Garleb, 1900), p. 40.

95   P. Schlotter, Die Rechtsstellung und der Rechtsschutz der Taubstummen. Eine juristische Plauderei (Leipzig: Hugo Dude, 1907), pp. 26, 32-42; Paul Kockelmann, Taubstummenbildung und Taubstummenfürsorge. Ein Wort der Aufklärung für alle gebildeten, besonders für Seelsorger, Lehrer und Lehrerinnen und für die Eltern Taubstummer Kinder 2nd Ed. (Düsseldorf: L. Schwann, 1914), pp. 54-57.

96   One of the few examples was a case of abuse of guardianships reported in the TC. Franz Schmitt, a deaf man who had inherited 50 000 Mk from his father, was deceived by his nephew into consenting to him as a legal guardian. The nephew embezzled Schmitt's inheritance, abused him physically, and refused him to marry. Only with the help of a group of deaf friends could he escape the abuse, concluded the article. Adolph Itzstein et al., "Die Leidensgeschichte eines Taubstummen," TC 12 (1885): pp. 134-135, TC 5 (1886): pp. 50-51

first German deaf club, had some 50 deaf charges.[97] Thus, the guardianship system was not always a transfer of power and integrity from deaf to hearing individuals.

A deaf person who could read and write, or indeed speak, was legally capable with a few exceptions: he or she could not be elected to local or national parliaments, neither could he or she take a legal office, nor countersign legal documents. Finally, the license to be a travelling salesman was available only as an exception to deaf people, since the authorities feared that it might be used for begging.[98] Voting was granted with difficulty, since the law required voters to vocally articulate their votes. Following discrimination of deaf voters, the legislative court in 1913 decided to allow votes in writing or through an interpreter.[99]

If a deaf person was accused of a crime, the prosecution had to prove that he or she had the mental ability of at least a 13-year-old. Otherwise he or she could not be punished. Under civil law, on the other hand, the deaf person him/herself was obliged to prove that he or she had not reached the mental state of a child of at least eight. Otherwise it was presumed that he or she was responsible for his/her actions.[100]

Earlier legislations in different German states had not allowed uneducated (and in some cases even educated) deaf people to marry. In united Germany, no law explicitly prohibited deaf marriages. It was even possible to have a Sign Language interpreter translate the ceremony.[101] However, the guardian system could be used to bar deaf people from marriage, since the guardian had to give his or her permission.[102]

---

97   Lingelmann, *Aus der Taubstummen-Welt* (1876), pp. 34-35; August Schenck, "Eduard Fürstenberg," TsF 8 (1888): p. 32.
98   Schlotter, *Rechtsstellung*, 43-47, Hartmann, *Taubstummheit*, pp. 191-194
99   "Berlin (Taubstumme Wähler.)," ATZ 1 (1913): p. 3; "Wie hat der Taubstumme zu wählen?" ATZ 16 (1913): p. 131.
100 Schlotter, *Rechtsstellung*, pp. 18-22.
101 August Richter, "Die Eingliederung des Taubstummen in die deutsche Kulturgemeinschaft," in *Handbuch des Taubstummenwesens*, ed. Paul Schumann (Osterwieck am Harz: Erwin Staude Verlagsbuchhandlung, 1929), p. 696.
102 *V.* p. 55 and *Unser neues Recht*, pp. 19, 39.

Education: Origins

Of all aspects of deaf people's lives, education has been the area attracting most interest among professionals and decision-makers. Accordingly, education has been the main area of interaction between deaf people and powerful institutions such as the state, the church, and science. This study is not about deaf education; nevertheless, education was such an important part of the individual and collective deaf lives, and had such impact on the understanding of deafness that a section on education is necessary.

Institutional deaf education originated in France and Germany almost simultaneously, but in different contextual settings. Whereas the early French institutions were led by members of the clergy, their German counterparts were mostly secular. Samuel Heinicke (1727-1790) came from a military background, later entered university and made his living as a private teacher in Hamburg. Some time during the 1760s he started to teach deaf children with the aid of fingerspelling and writing. Soon, however, he developed his own method for the education of the deaf, based on speech. His reputation as a teacher led to the Elector of Saxony appointing Heinicke in 1778 to offer education to poor deaf children free of charge. This was the origin of the Royal Deaf-Mute-School in Leipzig, the very first state-funded deaf school in the world.[103]

Heinicke was not the inventor of oral education, but his embrace of the method led to oralism being associated with Germany, in opposition to the 'French' manualism. It has been much disputed whether Heinicke himself was a true oralist or not. Clearly, his methods and ideas differed radically from late-19th-century oralism.[104] Deaf education spread from Leipzig to other parts of Germany through personal bonds between Heinicke and the next generation of teachers of the deaf. However, German deaf teachers in the generations following Heinicke were undeniably using the combined rather than oral

---

103 Schumann, *Geschichte*, pp. 145-147; Andreas Möckel, *Geschichte der Heilpädagogik* (Stuttgart: Klett-Cotta, 1988), pp. 40-43.

104 Later oralists used vision and touch as the main channels for speech production and understanding. Heinicke was convinced that the sense of taste was the proper foundation for a real understanding of speech among the deaf. He kept this rather unconventional idea in part secret, and its use was discontinued with his death. Furthermore, Heinicke used pantomime in his classrooms and offered manual education as a low-budget alternative to speech. Schumann, *Geschichte,* pp. 149-151; Joakim Winkler, "Samuel Heinicke – Einige Betrachtungen zu seinem Leben und Wirken," *Das Zeichen* 15 (1991): pp. 7-18; Rée, *I See a Voice*, pp. 162-165.

method.[105] Several schools, foremost in southern Germany, were influenced by the French manual tradition during the first decades of the 19th century.[106]

The first half of the 19th century was characterized by mainstreaming attempts. Schoolteachers were given classes in deaf education methods in the many deaf schools founded in connection with teacher seminars. Teaching deaf children was considered an especially effective pedagogical training for the seminarists, and was expected to make possible the integration of deaf children in mainstream schools. This would be cheaper, thus making education available to more deaf children, and favourable to the integration of the deaf. In reality, the deaf children ended up in over-populated classes without any special provisions. The mainstreaming was gradually abandoned during the latter half of the 19th century.[107]

Instead, the education of deaf children in special schools continued to expand. Deaf education had not been absorbed by general pedagogics, but established itself as a specialized discipline.[108] Around 1850, this discipline experienced what has been described as a radical breaking point, associated with the teacher Friedrich Moritz Hill (1805-74) in Weißenfels. Hill applied state-of-the-art German pedagogics as a foundation for oral education, and developed clear didactic guidelines.[109] Through his publications, he acquired a large following among younger teachers, who further developed the method. Foremost of these was Johannes Vatter (1842-1916) in Frankfurt a. M., according to Paul Schumann's history of German deaf education the "embodiment of the pure German method".[110] This method was based on the tenet that deaf children should learn to speak by the same means as hearing children do, that is, without the use of explanatory signs.[111] Oralism had long been a theory rather than a practice, but state schools with specialized teachers of small classes, following a

---

105 Schumann, *Geschichte*, pp. 148, 181-186; Wolff, "Selbstverständlich Gebärdensprache!" pp. 20-29; Heinz Weithaas, "Die Leipziger Taubstummenanstalt und die Gebärde – Ein geschichtlicher Rückblick," *Das Zeichen* 24 (1993): pp. 163-166.

106 Löwe, "Gehörlosenpädagogik," pp. 20-21; on the Austrian deaf education system, v. Walter Schott, *Das k. k. Taubstummen-Institut in Wien 1779-1918* (Vienna: Böhlau Verlag, 1995), and idem, *Das Allgemeine österreichische israelitische Taubstummen-Institut in Wien 1844-1926* (Vienna: self-published by the author, 1999).

107 Löwe "Gehörlosenpädagogik", pp. 22-25.

108 Schumann, *Geschichte*, pp. 399-401.

109 Ibid., pp. 304-323.

110 "Verkörperung der rein deutschen Methode," ibid., p. 387.

111 Ibid., pp. 387-396.

standardised curriculum, made it possible to enforce oralist practices. Oral education thus became the dominant method in the deaf schools in the latter half of the century.[112]

The School System

Eduard Walther (1840-1908) headed the Royal Deaf-Mute Asylum in Berlin, including the teacher's seminar, from 1885. This position was a most influential one, since the Berlin institution was the only training school for German teachers of the deaf. Walther was a follower of Hill's, and author of a textbook in deaf education from 1895, the voluminous *Handbuch der Taubstummenbildung*.[113] This book described the present organization and method of deaf education at the time. It is the main source of the following overview. Further sources include treatises by other teachers of the deaf at the time, and previous research on the history of German deaf education.

The German deaf education system was a diversity of state, municipal, and private schools of different kinds. There was no central administration.[114] Nor was obligatory schooling a matter of central legislation, but was regulated by each German state. Different regions introduced compulsory education for deaf children at different points in time. Compared to manual education, and certainly to mainstreaming, oral education is expensive. Due to high costs, an education available to all deaf children was delayed in many states. Theoretically, deaf children were obliged to attend school just like the hearing. In practice this obligation was often impossible to enforce, since most deaf children had no opportunity to go to school where they lived. Laws requiring deaf children to visit institutions away from home were introduced from the last decades of the 19th century in individual states.[115] In Prussia, one of the last states to make education mandatory for deaf children, little over half of the children between eight and sixteen years were currently receiving education in public schools or

---

112 Günther List, "Deaf History," pp. 118-124; Löwe, "Gehörlosenpädagogik," pp. 25-31.
113 Schumann described him as a moderate man, who avoided the extreme. However, both Schumann's characterization of him and his own work reflect a strong opposition to Sign Language. Schumann, *Geschichte*, pp. 375, 379; Walther, *Handbuch*, p. 109; below pp. 62, 234.
114 Hartmann, *Taubstummheit*, pp. 183-186.
115 Hartmann, *Taubstummheit*, pp. 189-190.

schools for the deaf in 1873.[116] An overview from 1880 shows that almost 5000 children were taught in Germany's eighty-two deaf schools in the late 1870s. Compared to the estimates of the total number of 'deaf-mute' children of school age, this would leave nearly two out of five children outside the deaf education system, but the variations in different areas were significant. In Saxony, all deaf children went to school. In East Prussia on the other hand, only one-third were receiving education.[117]

The last decades of the 19th century was a period of expansion for the deaf education system. An overview from 1906 listed ninety-three deaf schools in Germany, teaching a total of 7000 children. Thus, not only had the number of institutions increased, but also the number of pupils in each school.[118] Still, an education at a special school for the deaf was not an experience common to all people who were deaf. Not having any education at all was probably at least as common among deaf people as the experience of deaf school was.[119] Where no specialized deaf education was available, parents could place their child in the mainstream school, and were sometimes obliged to do so. The education the children received there was limited to behaving properly, taking part in physical games, drawing and writing.[120]

Equally great was the variation in type of school, the age at enrolment, and in duration of the education. In entire Germany, day schools and boarding schools each accommodated about half of the pupils. However, Prussia had mainly day schools, whereas the boarding school system dominated in most other states, and Saxony, Baden, and some city-states had only boarding schools.[121] Most deaf schools admitted children in their seventh year, although some institutions were

---

116   Preussische Statistik (1883): p. XXVIII.
117   Hartmann, *Taubstummheit*, pp. 209-210.
118   Josef Radomski, Statistische Nachrichten über die Taubstummenanstalten Deutschlands und der russischen Ostseeprovinzen, sowie über deren Lehrkräfte für das Jahr 1906 (Posen: Friedrich Ebbecke, 1908), pp. 12-19.
119   There exists no statistics on how many of the total number of deaf people had received education. Given, however, the limited outreach of the system to deaf children at certain moments in time, and the backlog of earlier generations, it seems likely that a large minority, or even the majority, of the deaf had not gone to deaf school.
120   Walther, *Handbuch*, pp. 6-7.
121   For 20% of the children there are unfortunately no certain data as to their housing. Hartmann, *Taubstummheit*, pp. 209-210.

forced to accept pupils as old as thirteen or fourteen due to long waiting lists. Six to eight years was considered the preferable duration of schooling.[122]

Teaching Methods

According to Walther, the first year of school was to be almost entirely devoted to the pronouncing of basic sounds. During the following years, the children practiced articulation and learned German vocabulary and grammar. Other subjects than speech training were not introduced until the fifth or sixth school year.[123]

The much-cited ban on signs in deaf schools has been interpreted in diverse ways. Contradicting sources, the vagueness and uncertainty on what signs really are, and what banning them really means, has led to disagreement on the matter. According to the oralist biased account by Armin Löwe, a ban of signs was never *typical* of the German method.[124] This is true in the sense that to the purifiers and ideologists of the method, it was not the main issue. Most crucial and characteristic to the German method was considered its philosophical dogma: the immediate learning of spoken language. It was in the difference between translation from signs to speech or writing on the one hand, and bringing deaf children to *think* in spoken language on the other that the essential difference between French and German methods lay, they claimed.[125] How the theoretical foundations of the method were put into practice varied, likely depending on individual teachers and schools. In Berlin in 1888, deaf adults were banned from the Berlin Royal Deaf-Mute Asylum in an effort to exclude Sign Language. In the Leipzig school on the other hand, signing was never completely abandoned.[126]

Regardless of the theoretical roots of oralism and the teacher's proficiency in Sign Language, the latter half of the 19th century saw a hardening attitude toward signs. In a footnote to his 1895 textbook, Eduard Walther recommended every teacher of the deaf to learn to sign, since society needs hearing signers. Sign Language was necessary for communicating with many deaf people at once, to translate court procedures, and to assist uneducated deaf. However, on the same

---

122 Hartmann, *Taubstummheit*, pp. 118, 171.
123 Walther, *Handbuch*, p. 11.
124 Löwe, "Gehörlosenpädagogik," p. 28.
125 Schumann, *Geschichte*, p. 348.
126 Wolff, "Zöglingen, Künstlern und Handwerksgesellen," p. 354; Weithaas "Die Leipziger Taubstummenanstalt," pp. 163-166 .

page he stated: "*Sign Language is to be pushed back out of the deaf education and the communication with deaf-mutes.* [...] The deaf-mutes must be *forced* to express themselves in spoken language as far as their capabilities allow."[127] Only with very small children, signs should be used.[128]

Oralism: Context and Results

Imperial Germany encompassed regions and peoples of great diversity, geographically, economically and historically, with religious and cultural plurality. To manage the vast country with all its differences, the young empire chose to strive for unity. In this context, the idea of linguistic assimilation became fundamental. Linguistic minorities were no longer tolerated, but were put under pressure to become German-speaking. These policies affected above all the Polish-speaking minority, and the main tool to introduce them to German was the school system. To find theoretical inspiration for this, nationalists needed to look no further than to deaf education. Renowned pedagogue Wilhelm Harnisch referred to how German replaced Sign Language in oral education when he envisioned the assimilation of Polish-speakers.[129] This was at the time not unique for Germany; both in Third Republic France and post-civil war USA, the attitudes towards linguistic diversity hardened and fuelled oralism.[130]

The enforcement of oralism in the classroom affected social patterns within and outside the schools. The way the teacher interacted with the pupils changed, as oral education demanded the teacher to pay close personal attention to each pupil, including physical contact. Typically, the teacher practiced articulation with one child at a time, while the rest of the class was "occupied with other things".[131] Renate Fischer writes: "The solidity of Sign Language use is replaced

---

127 "*Die Gebärdensprache ist von dem Taubstummenunterrichte und dem Verkehre mit Taubstummen zurückzudrängen.*[...] Die Taubstummen müssen *gezwungen* werden, soweit es ihre Fähigkeiten gestatten, bei ihren Äußerungen die Lautsprache anzuwenden." [emphasis in original] Walther, *Handbuch*, p. 109

128 Walther, *Handbuch*, pp. 109-110

129 List, "Nationale Inklusion" (Part 2), pp. 186-192; idem, "Assimilation," pp. 338-347, Siegmund Prillwitz, "Der Lange Weg zur Zweisprachigkeit im deutschen Sprachraum," *Das Zeichen* 12 (1990): p. 133.

130 Anne T. Quartararo, "Republicanism, Deaf Identity and the Career of Henri Gaillard in Late-Nineteenth-Century France" in: *Deaf History Unveiled*, pp. 44-45; Baynton, *Forbidden Signs*, pp. 26-34.

131 "auf andere Weise beschäftigt", Walther, *Handbuch*, p. 12.

by forced physical closeness in speech training; the bad breath of the skin-close speaker, causing nausea, replaces the airy pictures of communicating hands."[132]

The school as a place for encounters between deaf people lost some of its significance. Deaf teachers were no longer employed, and some educators attempted to cut off contact between deaf children and deaf adults, creating a generational gap between manually and orally educated deaf.[133] Within the schools themselves, the deaf children were also divided as a part of oral education. Walther favoured a division in two, or even three, groups according to a perceived higher or lower capability of the pupils. He suggested they be kept physically apart at different schools. Decisive for which group a child belonged to was his or her ability to learn spoken language.[134]

Counter to its intention, oral education, judging by the professional literature, did not seem to aid deaf people to integrate in hearing society. Albert Gutzmann, principal of the City Deaf-Mute School in Berlin, noticed that deaf children were reluctant to communicate in spoken German at home with their families. They did not speak in complete sentences, but only pronounced single words, and 'pointed out' or 'showed' (*Zeigen*) their wishes instead of articulating. Rather than reading on the lips, they tried to guess the ideas of their opposites.[135]

Other educators expressed similar opinions: Teaching deaf children to articulate and read lips in the classroom did not mean that they spoke, or understood speech, outside the school. Jakob Huschens, teacher at the deaf school in Trier and also a writer of several books on deaf education, gave some advice to hearing people: in order to be understood, they needed to allow for sufficient lighting, speak slowly, first make sure that their deaf conversation partner understood what topic they spoke about, and not use difficult words. When Huschens claimed that ninety percent of the deaf children could communicate in spoken language upon leaving school, it was under these very particular circum-

---

132 "Die Körperlichkeit der Gebärdensprachverwendung wird ersetzt durch erzwungene körperliche Nähe beim Sprechtraining; der Übelkeit erregende schlechte Atem des hautnah Vorsprechenden ersetzt die luftigen Bilder kommunizierender Hände." Renate Fischer, "'Schläge auf die Hand," p. 342.

133 Wolff, "Zöglingen, Künstlern und Handwerksgesellen," p. 354; Fischer, "Schläge auf die Hand," pp. 337-338.

134 Walther, *Handbuch*, pp. 16-23.

135 Albert Gutzmann, *Vor- und Fortbildung der Taubstummen*, Vol. 2 (Berlin: Elwin Staude, 1899), p. 26.

stances.[136] Gutzmann was also aware of that hearing people might avoid communication with deaf people, since they found the sound of their voices annoying.[137] Furthermore, articulation skills required the constant control and correction by hearing people if not to degenerate, which meant that they were often lost after graduation.[138]

Based on this, it can be assumed that there was a communication barrier between non-signing hearing people and educated as well as uneducated deaf, especially regarding casual conversation. Writing, articulating, and reading lips is more suitable for the exchange of information necessary to work and attend to ones basic needs and duties in society. Many deaf people probably could not communicate with the hearing even on this basic level. Those who remained in institutions, with their parents, or other relatives, depended on others for their financial support and all other affairs, and had little use for oral skills.

Sources are scarce on to what extent 'home sign' was used, and how well deaf children could communicate with their immediate family. Paul Kockelmann, principal of the deaf asylum in Aachen, described how uneducated deaf children in their home environment communicate on relatively complex matters using pantomime.[139] Historian Hans-Uwe Feige has found that deaf children in

---

136 Jakob Huschens, Die soziale Bedeutung der Taubstummenbildung. Ein Beitrag zur richtigen Bewertung des der menschlichen Gesellschaft wiedergegebenen sprechenden Tauben (Trier: Paulinus-Druckerei, 1911), pp. 78, 82-85; Modern-day research confirms that true comprehension in oral communication between hearing and deaf people is seldom found, especially not between strangers. If both parties know each other well, they can get accustomed to the voices and expressions of the other. This means that oral communication does not necessarily have the advantage over signs often assumed – enabling deaf people to communicate with a greater variety of people. Just like Sign Language, oral communication must be learned by the hearing person in order to be useful. V. Horst Ebbinghaus and Jens Heßmann, "Wie gefällt dir meine Stimme? Zur sozialen Wirklichkeit des Sprechens Gehörloser," Das Zeichen 2 (1987): pp. 24-29.

137 Albert Gutzmann, Kleine Streiflichter auf die kirchliche, soziale und gesetzliche Stellung der Taubstummen (Berlin: Elwin Staude, 1899), p. 19.

138 Hartmann, *Taubstummheit*, p. 178.

139 Kockelmann, *Taubstummenbildung und Taubstummenfürsorge*, pp. 12-14. Home sign denotes the gestural communication that develops in families with deaf children, *cf.* Nancy Frishberg, "Home sign" in *Gallaudet Encyclopedia of deaf people and deafness,* Vol. 3, ed. John Vickrey Van Cleve (New York: Mc Graw Hill, 1987), pp. 128-131.

the late 18th and early 19th centuries were largely isolated in their families, and often victims of violence as a result of communication problems. The deaf asylums were, according to Feige, where a socialization of deaf children began, and they formed more intimate bonds with their schools than with their parental homes.[140]

Medicine and Deaf Education

In the second half of the 19th century, medical treatment of deafness was relatively uncommon. Earlier treatments with surgery, electricity, and letting of blood had all proven unsuccessful, as well as painful and risky. Thus, the medical professionals resigned and drew back from treating deafness in the 1830s and -40s. Interest in deaf people's ears declined quickly, and the services of otologists were less frequently demanded. Deafness became generally accepted as incurable and a matter of education, not of medical treatment. Instead of focusing on deafness, otology evolved as the area of expertise on ears in general. Efforts were put into the anatomical examination of the ear, which towards the turn of the century led to safer and more successful operations. At the turn of the 19th century, nearly one-third of the 'deaf-mute' children had received some kind of medical treatment.[141]

Another development within medicine had more impact on the lives of deaf people: the so-called "hearing movement." Based on the discovery that most "deaf" children have residual hearing, Austrian otologist Viktor Urbantschitsch attempted to train the ears of deaf children by exposing them to sound. He believed that the ability to hear could be improved through special exercises. German otologist Friedrich Bezold rejected Urbantschitsch's method, but confirmed the importance of residual hearing. Bezold's suggestion was to differentiate the school system according to level of hearing. Although no hearing aids were yet available, and the ear cannot be trained like a muscle, the hearing movement had discovered residual hearing as an important factor in oral education.[142]

---

140 Hans-Uwe Feige, "Lebenswirklichkeit," pp. 23-32.
141 Engelmann, "Ergebnisse," p. 20; Tomas Stichnoth, *Taubstummheit. Die medizinische Behandlung der Gehörlosigkeit vom 17. Jahrhundert bis zur Gegenwart*, Kölner medizinhistorische Beiträge: Arbeiten der Forschungsstelle des Instituts für Geschichte der Medizin der Universität zu Köln. Vol. 37 (1985), pp. 40-63.
142 Löwe, "Gehörlosenpädagogik," pp. 34-36; Stichnoth, *Taubstummheit*, pp. 66-67.

As we saw in the section on statistics, the medical understanding of deafness in the late 19th century was focused on the causes of the condition. In the United States, Alexander Graham Bell gained attention by claiming that deafness was a question of heredity, which was to be curbed by eugenic measures. His treatises on a 'deaf variety of the human race' was translated and appeared in different German publications for the deaf and teachers of the deaf during 1892. There was, however, not much enthusiasm on either side for the idea of hindering deaf people from marrying and conceiving.[143]

Graduation: The Transition of Deaf School Alumni into Hearing Society

Special schools distinguished deaf children from the rest of society and kept them in a segregated environment, designed for their perceived needs. At some point segregation and special attention must cease, lest the deaf indefinitely remain in institutions. As we have seen, only a small minority of Germany's 'deaf-mutes' lived in institutions. For the majority of those who received special education, the existence in a predominantly deaf subdivision of society was limited to a few years in childhood. This meant that deaf children were expected to go through two significant social transfers, first when they entered deaf school, then when graduating. As children of hearing parents, they had been linguistically and sensory deviant. On being enrolled in deaf school they were singled out of mainstream, hearing society and were integrated in a deaf majority. After graduation, this social transfer was reversed when they were required to leave their deaf peers and re-enter hearing society. Their hearing acquaintances during the school years – teachers, other personnel, boarding families, parents and other relatives – had been in possession of a certain competence concerning, and familiarity with, deaf people. Hearing people in general did not have this knowledge.

Oral education aimed at preparing pupils for this moment by teaching them to communicate with hearing people in the spoken mode. Theoretically, a suc-

---

143 Alexander Graham Bell, "Die Ehe," TsF 42 (1892): pp. 180-182, continued in subsequent issues; ibid., TC 9 (1892): pp. 105-107, continued in subsequent issues; F. Werner, Review of Bell, *Marriage. An Address to the Deaf, Blätter* Vol. 5, No. 4 (1892): pp. 62-64; Alexander Graham Bell, "Die Ehe," transl. Renz, *Organ* Vol. 38, No. 7 (1892): pp. 194-207; cf. idem, *Memoir upon the Formation of a Deaf Variety of the Human Race*, National Academy of Sciences lecture, Memoirs of the National Academy of Sciences [1883]; Baynton, *Forbidden Signs.* pp. 30-31.

cessful oral education would produce graduates so fluent in articulation and lip reading that their integration posed no problem. Graduates of an oral school would, in the ideal case, be left with no further action, and find their way under the same conditions as the hearing. In reality, oral schools did not follow this practice. Graduating students were not expected to simply leave school and integrate into mainstream society. Professionals of the education system kept in touch with former pupils through informal relationships and formal extensions of education.

An overview from 1886 of thirty-nine Prussian deaf schools shows that half of them helped their former pupils in finding an apprenticeship or employment. The type of assistance in the transition to working life varied:

- Continued contact was offered at eight schools;
- preparation[144] at six schools;
- help in finding a master or work at twenty-two schools;
- vocational education at one school;
- financial support at sixteen schools, and
- secondary courses at eight schools.[145]

Financial support was in most cases provided through private foundations associated with the schools, offering grants to especially needy and worthy alumnae. Both financial and other support was given on a voluntary basis on part of the schools. A duty to assist graduates did not exist. Only their parents were formally obliged to care for them.[146]

Secondary schools attended by apprentices a few hours per week as a complement to their manual training emerged in Germany in the first half of the

---

144 Six schools stated that they "already in the course of education prepare and begin the transfer of the pupils into practical life", "schon während des Unterrichtkursus den Uebergang der Zöglinge in das praktische Leben vorzubereiten und einzuleiten", Guttstadt, *Krankenhaus-Lexikon,* p. 259. What this meant in practice was not specified.

145 Guttstadt, Krankenhaus-Lexikon pp. 259-263.

146 The asylums in Angerburg, Königsberg and Rössel considered it a duty to prepare their students for life after graduation, but none of the institutions had the obligation to assist them after graduation. Albert Guttstadt, *Krankenhaus-Lexikon für das Königreich Preussen: die Anstalten für Kranke und Gebrechliche und das Krankenhaus-, Irren-, Blinden- und Taubstummenwesen,* Vol. 2 (Berlin: Verlag des Königlichen Statistischen Bureaus,1886), pp. 259-263.

19th century. Over the years, they developed into differentiated institutions suiting the needs of individual occupations, and gradually became obligatory.[147] Special secondary schools for deaf apprentices followed in many places.[148] Whereas mainstream secondary courses were designed to enhance the skills of apprentices in a certain trade by deepening their theoretical competence, secondary deaf schools focused on integration. They offered continued oral education and extension of general knowledge.[149]

These schools maintained the contact between the education system and the deaf. Simultaneously, they brought deaf youth together. Graduation scattered the peer groups formed at school. Together they had experienced the transfer from being deviants in the mainstream, to forming a majority at school. Often they had lived together in boarding schools far away from their original homes and families. Graduation separated them and sent them to workplaces where the majority was hearing. Through the special secondary school, they remained in contact at least for a couple of hours every week.

Not all deaf graduates attended secondary school even when it was available. Its existence was still unknown to some, and certain mainstream secondary schools refused to enrol deaf pupils.[150] Furthermore, re-entering hearing society was associated with a division into two groups of young deaf people. Teachers and parents organized work or training for some of them, while others returned to their families to help in the household or on the fields. We do not know how common this was. According to the 1900 census, around half of all 'deaf-mutes' lived with their parents, grandparents, or other relatives, which can give some idea of the extent of the practice.[151]

According to Walther, some teachers visited their former students regularly to impose good moral behaviour, supervise their material situation and their

---

147 Rainer Fischbach, Von der Sonntags- und Fortbildungsschule zur Berufsschule. Ein Beitrag zur Wirtschafts und Sozialgeschichte des Preußischen Siegerlandes 1815-1918 (St. Katharinen: Scripta Mercaturae Verlag, 2004), pp. 1, 128-138.
148 In Prussia, one in five surveyed deaf schools offered secondary courses in 1886. Guttstadt, *Krankenhaus-Lexikon,* pp. 259-263. A secondary school for the deaf in Munich was not founded until 1912. Kgl. Staatsministerium des Innern für Kirchen- und Schulangelegenheiten to Inspektion des Kgl. Zentraltaubstummeninstitutes Munich 26 March 1912, BayHStA, Rep. MK, Nr. 62358.
149 Walther, *Handbuch,* pp. 723-728; Hartmann, *Taubstummheit,* pp. 178-179.
150 Application concerning Karl Bernau, 1910, LA Berlin A Pr. Br. Rep. 030 Nr. 1886; *cf.* Guttstadt, *Krankenhaus-Lexikon,* p. 259.
151 Engelmann, "Die Taubstummen," p. 182.

language skills. Others kept in touch by correspondence, and most schools invited adult deaf to annual social gatherings.[152] Many children had grown up with their teachers rather than with their families. Sometimes, the staff, their families, and the pupils even lived under the same roof. This long-enduring and close contact was not only emotional, but also of great importance for communication. Jakob Huschens claimed that only professionals were able to truly understand the deaf.[153]

Preserving the bond between former students and their school was a way of supporting the deaf, but also gave the opportunity of maintaining control over them. If left on their own without some supervising authority, Huschens feared that the former students would easily descend into begging and crime.[154] Keeping in touch also had the potential of enlightening the teachers as to the success of the education. Yet, as we have seen, there was a reluctance in letting adult deaf mingle with current students.[155] The contact with the alumni was to be between them and the teacher, excluding younger generations.

Another way of maintaining the bond were the religious services for the deaf arranged in several places. In 1866, Reinhold Schönberner, a teacher of the deaf with a degree in theology, was appointed to the spiritual care of the deaf in Berlin. He held regular services in Sign.[156] In Brandenburg, a travelling priest fluent in Sign Language held services in the entire province for a period.[157]

Oralist visions of diminishing the linguistic barrier between deaf and hearing people were not fulfilled. By making special provisions for former deaf school pupils, professionals and authorities continued to acknowledge that there was a need for special measures to facilitate their entrance on the labour market. Vocational training within the apprentice system was sanctioned with financial incentives for masters and by negotiation of apprenticeships through the school. Ironically, the integration the oralists strived for undid their efforts in speech

---

152 Walther, *Handbuch*, p. 711.
153 Huschens, *Bedeutung der Taubstummenbildung*, p. 91; *cf.* Groschek, *Unterwegs in einer Welt des Verstehens,* pp. 38, 64-65, 87-88, and Weithaas, "Die Leipziger Taubstummenanstalt und die Gebärde," p. 164, on the rooming conditions in Hamburg and Leipzig deaf schools.
154 Huschens, Bedeutung der Taubstummenbildung, p. 80.
155 *V.* above p. 61.
156 Ernst Schorsch, Das Taubstummenwesen der Stadt Berlin. Anläßlich des fünfzigjährigen Bestehens der Städtischen Taubstummenschule (Berlin: Verlag der Städtischen Taubstummenschule, 1925), p. 61.
157 Gutzmann, *Streiflichter,* p.16.

training. Speech was supposed to make the deaf close-to-normal, and facilitate their mingling with the hearing, but, away from school, the former students often stopped using their voices. The artificial movements of their tongues could only be maintained through constant, professional supervision. Therefore, oralism created continued segregation in the secondary courses, where deaf apprentices were supposed to remain with one foot in the special education system.[158]

Vocational Education

Early German deaf schools were sometimes combined with workshops where the pupils produced commodities contributing to the maintenance of the school. In some cases, they offered the opportunity of learning a specialized trade, which would otherwise not be available to deaf youth.[159] Oral education, as practiced both in Germany and elsewhere, was not suited to combine with learning a trade. First, training children in articulation and lip reading is time-consuming and thus leaves little room in the curriculum for vocational instruction. Not only do the actual speech classes demand much time and attention, but teaching deaf children any other subject using spoken language is also much slower than using Sign. The ideology of German schools prescribed that 'in everything is language (i.e. speech) education', meaning that craft teachers were supposed to communicate with the students through spoken language only.[160] One might doubt that this was always implemented, but on an ideological level there was no support for an exception to the oral rule. Instead, oralist educators opposed vocational education in the deaf schools since it did not comply with their aim: to make the deaf children as similar to the hearing as possible. Oral education was supposed to enable deaf people to integrate in hearing society, so that the need for special provisions diminished.[161]

---

158 Walther, *Handbuch*, pp. 723-728; *v.* also Günter List, "Deaf History," p. 122: "In short, by relieving hearing people of the necessity to think things through, oral teachers made themselves nearly indispensable."
159 Schumann, *Geschichte*, pp. 654-657; Sylvia Wolff, "Didaktik des Gehörlosenunterrichts," pp. 13-14.
160 Wilhelm Weise, "Der Knaben-Handarbeitsunterricht," pp. 686-687, Bertha Kätzke, "Der Unterricht in weiblichen Handarbeiten," pp. 706-707, both in Walther, *Handbuch*; *v.* also Groschek, *Unterwegs in eine Welt des Verstehens*, pp. 92-94, on the role of handicraft in the Hamburg deaf school.
161 Walther, *Handbuch*, p. 710; Löwe, "Gehörlosenpädagogik," pp. 40-41.

Complying with this ideology, very few of the German deaf schools offered vocational education. To learn a trade, deaf people just like the hearing were required to find an apprenticeship. Walther pointed out that the school and its teachers had no obligation to help former students with this. Still, he and others asserted that many teachers did so: they kept in touch with their students and tried to find masters willing to take them on.[162] Where crafts were included in the curriculum, they instead served a moral and general pedagogic purpose. Performing simple manual tasks was supposed to shape the character and educate the boys in work morale and handiness. The girls were taught the practical skills needed in a household. The purpose was to offer them the same education that hearing girls obtained at home, not vocational training.[163] However, vocational training at deaf schools was not completely abandoned.[164] The scarcity of sources in this context is symptomatic for the ideologically motivated aversion of educators towards the practice.

Concerning higher learning, the same argument was used. Rather than teaching more advanced subjects, the school should equip their pupils with basic skills. Any further intellectual development should take place on their own initiative and in association with the hearing.[165] However, the system of higher education was practically inaccessible to deaf people until the 1950s.[166] Thus,

---

162   Walther, Handbuch, pp. 711-712; Huschens, Bedeutung der Taubstummenbildung, p. 78; H. Stolte, Über die Erziehung des Taubstummen zur Religiosität und Sittlichkeit. Ein Beitrag zur Methodik des Religionsunterricht in der Taubstummenschule (Soest: P. G. Capell, 1891), p. 83.

163   Weise, "Der Knaben-Handarbeitsunterricht," pp. 684-701; Kätzke, "Unterricht," p. 702; Walther, *Handbuch*, pp. 709-710.

164   Paulinenpflege in Winnenden, Württemberg, was both a school and an asylum. In the asylum, they occasionally trained young deaf in tailoring and shoemaking. Annual Reports from the Paulinenpflege in Winnenden, 1886/1887, 1887/1888, StA Ludwigsburg, Bestand E 191, Bü 5056. The Asylum in Stralsund offered girls a one-year sewing course after graduation. Guttstadt, *Krankenhaus-Lexikon*, p. 260. Paul Schumann confirmed as late as 1929 that some schools continued to sell articles produced by the children. Schumann, *Handbuch*, p. 94.

165   Friedrich Moritz Hill, Der gegenwärtige Zustand des Taubstummen-Bildungs-Wesens in Deutschland : eine Mahnung an die Taubstummen-Lehrer und ihre Vorgesetzten, die Communal- u. Kreis-Schulbehörden, die Geistlichen und Aerzte, die Staatsregierungen und Landesvertreter (Weimar: Böhlau,1866), pp. 86-87, 150-152; cf. also Baynton, Forbidden Signs, p. 98.

166   With very few exceptions. Löwe, "Gehörlosenpädagogik," p. 40.

deaf people were integrated in the mainstream system of vocational education, but as opposed to the hearing, they had no other option and were thereby kept back in the manually working classes.

The Bonus System

The placement of deaf apprentices with masters was facilitated by the 'deaf-mute bonus' (*'Taubstummenprämie'*) first introduced in Saxony in 1811 and then in several other German states, including Prussia. It meant that the state offered a grant of up to 200 Mk to any master who trained a deaf apprentice.[167] Around the deaf schools, craftspeople became accustomed to this practice, and some masters took on several deaf apprentices over the years. In other cases, deaf boarders remained in their foster families and were trained in the family trade.[168]

Hans-Uwe Feige concludes in his study of the 'deaf-mute bonus' that the system had a positive effect on the individual apprentices as well as on the deaf in general. Deaf craftspeople helped to alter the stereotypical image of 'the deaf-mute'. Deaf people became recognized in society as respectable workers, instead of indigents. On the individual level, Feige argues that the apprenticeship was mostly beneficial. Since a clergyman or other prominent person often initiated the contact, masters felt obliged to treat deaf apprentices well.[169] Apprenticeships could otherwise be hazardous: Exploitation of apprentices as cheap labour increased in the 19th century. Violence and other maltreatment were regular phenomena.[170]

Feige focuses on the early 19th century in his positive evaluation of the bonus system. In the course of the century, both the system of production and the deaf education changed significantly, placing the bonuses in another context. Educators were concerned that masters exploited deaf apprentices, making them perform household chores rather than giving them adequate training.[171] Below, a

---

167 Schumann, *Geschichte*, pp. 655-657; Feige, "Taubstummenprämie," pp. 553-555; Richter, "Eingliederung;" p. 670.
168 Walther, *Handbuch*, p. 712.
169 Feige, "Gehörlose Handwerker vor 200 Jahren," pp. 531-532.
170 Reinhold Reith, "Zur beruflichen Sozialisation im Handwerk vom 18. bis ins frühe 20. Jahrhundert. Umrisse einer Sozialgeschichte der deutschen Lehrlinge," *Vierteljahrschrift für Sozial- und Wirtschaftsgeschichte* 76 (1989): pp. 15-24.
171 Wende, speech at the "Fürsorgetag" in Berlin 1913, quoted in Richter, "Eingliederung," p. 670.

sample of applications for bonus payments from Berlin and Bavaria illustrate how the system worked in the early 20th century (fig. 4).

Prussia had introduced the 'deaf-mute bonus' in 1817. In the course of the 19th century the regulations were complemented through ministerial decisions. Conditions of receiving the bonus of 150, from 1907 200 Mk, were that the master, or the seamstress, educated a 'deaf and mute' apprentice completely, lodged and fed him or her in the household in those regions where this was common practice, covered all expenses and demanded no compensation for the education.[172] An upper limit was fixed for the total sum of bonuses, meaning that applicants could be denied payment if they applied late in the year.[173] Most apprenticeships were, according to Eduard Walther, negotiated by the school. Nevertheless, Walther estimated that the bonus system was unknown in many institutions and to the parents of deaf children.[174]

Some confusion about the conditions appears in the twenty-six sample applications further discussed below. A total thirteen, or nearly four out of ten, applications were declined, and often an initial decline due to misunderstood or incomplete applications preceded acceptance.[175]

Bavaria paid rewards to masters who had trained deaf apprentices in individual cases.[176] Bonuses according to the Saxon-Prussian model were introduced in 1906, following a request by the Bavarian Association of Teachers of the Deaf-Mutes. Training deaf youth in manual professions was time-

---

172   Bayerische Taubstummenlehrerverein to Landtag des Königreichs Bayern, 17 November 1905, Appendix 1., BayHstA MWi 1055.
173   Vertretung des Ministers für Handel und Gewerbe, Berlin 26. November 1889, Vertretung des Ministers für Handel und Gewerbe, Berlin 4. November 1890, LA Berlin A Pr. Br. Rep. 030 Nr. 1886, pp. 59, 55.
174   Walther to the Kgl. Polizei-Präsidium, Berlin 31 Januar 1893, LA Berlin A Pr. Br. Rep. 030 Nr. 1886, p. 60.
175   In part this was caused by the refusal by the teacher Dost at the Royal Asylum to confirm the 'deaf-mutism' of his pupils. Dost considered orally educated deaf to be deaf, not mute. Only masters who trained 'deaf-mutes' were, however, eligible to bonuses, and Dost was required to use this term in his certificates. *V.* for instance applications concerning Paul Ganzer and Wilhelm Hampicke (1910), Gustav Adermann (1911), and Karl Werner (1912), and Dost to Kgl. Polizei-Präsidium 28 November 1910; Kgl. Polizei-Präsident to Dost 3 December 1910, LA Berlin A Pr. Br. Rep. 030 Nr. 1886.
176   Staatsministerium des Kgl. Hauses u. des Aeussern to the Handwerkskammern, 22 November 1907, BayHstA MWi 1055.

consuming, the teachers argued. Regardless of the quality of education, their (spoken) language skills remained defective, and their understanding of the "conditions of life"[177] limited. Were they provided with training, however, their "manual accomplishment, the condition and sharpness of their eye, and the few distractions to their attention [make them] often very appreciated as useful workers [...]."[178]

The teacher's request prompted the government to ask the Chambers of Crafts for remit in the issue. They agreed that difficulties in the dialogue between deaf apprentices and hearing masters impaired the training as well as the relations in the family. In their opinion, deaf people were often suspicious and stubborn, making their training more demanding. Without a state grant, they argued, no masters were inclined to accept deaf apprentices in their homes and workshops.[179]

In 1907, the bonuses were introduced with conditions largely modelled on the Prussian ones. At their own request, the Chambers of Crafts were made responsible for selecting suitable masters. In cooperation with the deaf schools, they were also to identify possible candidates among the graduates.[180]

When advocating the bonuses, the teachers' association had estimated that the masters training almost fifty deaf apprentices, a third of whom were girls, would be eligible for a bonus every year. In reality, the bonus appears to have been granted considerably less frequently. An overview of the years 1906-1915 indicates that the average number of bonuses paid each year was only four.[181] Declinations were infrequent. The relatively small number of bonuses seems to be due to low demand. In their request, the teachers had argued that deaf children

---

177 "Lebensverhältnisse," Bayerischer Taubstummenlehrerverein to the Landtag des Königreichs Bayern, 17 November 1905, BayHstA MWi 1055.

178 "ihrer manuellen Fertigkeit, der Geübtheit und Schärfe ihres Auges und der geringen Ablenkung ihrer Aufmerksamkeit als brauchbare Arbeiter häufig sehr geschätzt [...]." Bayerische Taubstummenlehrerverein to the Landtag des Königreichs Bayern, 17 November 1905, BayHstA MWi 1055.

179 Die Handwerkskammer für die Oberpfalz und Regensburg to Staatsministerium des Kgl. Hauses und des Aeussern, 31 August 1905, BayHstA MWi 1055.

180 Staatsministerium des Kgl. Hauses u. des Aeussern to the Handwerkskammern, 22 November 1907, BayHstA MWi 1055.

181 Prämien an Handwerksmeister für Ausbildung taubstummer Lehrlinge, BayHstA MWi 1055.

usually came from poor households, unable to finance their apprenticeships.[182] Apprentice fees payable to the master was a practice from the guild system still practiced in parts of Bavaria.[183] Where fees still were common, bonuses relieved parents of the burden of paying for the apprenticeship, which appears to have been part of the motivation behind the suggestion. Otherwise, the bonus was an incentive to accept deaf apprentices. In Berlin, apprentice fees had been abandoned. Instead masters paid their apprentices a small salary.[184]

Perhaps, the teachers had underestimated the ability of the parents of deaf children to pay the fees, or over-estimated their desire to let their youth learn a craft. Walther's concerns about the bonus system being unknown appears less plausible as an explanation, due to the active part played by the Chambers of Crafts and deaf schools. Apprenticeships were negotiated and bonuses paid on their initiative, allowing all deaf graduates to be considered with the bonus explicitly in mind.

Based on samples of applications and decisions, declination seem to have been more frequent in Berlin than in Bavaria. In theory, bonuses could be paid for educating deaf girls in dressmaking, but in reality this was highly unusual. No seamstress or dressmaker applied for a bonus in Berlin, and only five, out of which two were declined, applied in Bavaria.[185] Nevertheless, tailoring, including dressmaking, was the most common trade among the masters receiving bonuses in both areas, followed by woodworks. Thus the structure corresponded with that of the most common vocations among the 'deaf mutes' as presented in the 1900 statistics (fig. 4).[186]

---

182 Bayerischer Taubstummenlehrerverein to the Landtag des Königreichs Bayern, 17 November 1905, BayHstA MWi 1055.

183 Karl-Jürgen Rinneberg, *Das betriebliche Ausbildungswesen in der Zeit der industriellen Umgestaltung Deutschlands,* Deutsches Institut für Internationale Pädagogische Forschung: Studien und Dokumentationen zur deutschen Bildungsgeschichte, Vol. 29 (Cologne: Böhlau Verlag, 1985), pp. 138-139.

184 Rinneberg, *Ausbildungswesen,* p. 139.

185 Apprentices Elise Auer (1911), Martina Winterer and Therese Glonner (1912), Maria Altmansperger and Fanny Altendorfer (1914), BayHstA MWi 1055.

186 V. above, p. 42.

Figure 4: Chart of applications for bonuses in Bavaria and Berlin.

	Bavaria	Berlin
Time span studied	1906-1914	1910-1912
Number of applications	40	26
Declinations	3	10
Blacksmith and wagoner	1	0
Bookbinder	1	3
Cabinet maker	9	0
Carpenter	0	4
Chiseller	1	0
Cooper	1	0
Leather worker	0	1
Painter	3	1
Plaster modeller	1	0
Saddler and upholsterer	2	0
Sculptor	1	0
Shoemaker	6	1
Tailor, seamstress, dressmaker	11	6

Source: BayHstA MWi 1055, LA Berlin A Pr. Br. Rep. 030 Nr. 1886

The bonus system had been invented long before the German method was 'purified'. Nevertheless, it fit well into the theoretical framework. It offered an incentive to integrate in the mainstream apprentice system, leading deaf youth to manual occupations. As we have seen, the 'pure' German school regarded this, not higher learning or segregated vocational training, as the proper place for deaf people. The bonus system helped to make this ambition come true.

Employment

As industrial development turned workshops into factories, some capitalists became aware of the potential advantages of hiring deaf people. In the United States, certain industries, notably Ford and Goodyear, began recruiting deaf workers in the early 20th century. Motivations were the assumed loyalty of deaf workers, labour shortage, and to some extent a genuine interest in diversity.[187] The quest for groups of people formerly unavailable as paid workers is typical of industrial capitalism. Capitalists turn to women, children, and inmates of institutions to extract surplus labour. These have the role of an auxiliary supply of a cheap, docile workforce.[188] Deaf people were under-employed and thus, to an extent, constituted such an unexploited source of surplus labour.

In general, the employment of deaf workers has left few traces. Employers did not record their strategies and motives for hiring deaf persons. In the following, two German examples of businesses specifically looking for deaf people to employ, and making use of the state authorities to reach this aim, will be presented. Although they were probably atypical, they are relevant as two of very few examples where the conditions at private employers of deaf people have been recorded and kept for the afterworld.

Benevolent Capitalists: Fischer & Walther

In 1873, factory owners Ernst Fischer and Franz Walther employed 50 young women in their silk spinnery in Wiesenthal, Württemberg. This factory was not only a workplace, but also had the ambition to be a social institution. The employees mostly came from poor households, lived on the premises, were obliged to follow house rules around the clock, and stood under the personal supervision of Mrs. Fischer. Bible studies and religious services were held regularly. According to Fischer and Walther, it had occurred to them after a state inspection in 1873 that their factory was in such a top condition that they could offer employment to deaf girls. Since the latter had difficulties finding employ-

---

187 Robert M. Buchanan, *Illusions of Equality. Deaf Americans in School and Factory 1850-1950* (Washington, D.C.: Gallaudet University Press, 1999), pp. 73-83.

188 Karl Marx, *Das Kapital. Kritik der politischen Ökonomie,* Vol. 1 [1890] (Berlin: Dietz Verlag, 1982), pp. 425, 430, 657-677.

ment, Fischer and Walther would do their best to "ease their sad condition."[189] In order to realize this ambition, they contacted the Board of Charity, which sent their request to the Württembergian deaf schools.

At first, Fischer and Walther had difficulties finding the six deaf girls they wanted to employ. Württembergian deaf schools had few female graduates. Of seven girls who were confirmed in 1873, three were to be sent back to their parents: one was "already since a long while awaited with yearning by her parents."[190] Two further girls had found employment elsewhere.[191] Only the Esslingen School took up Fischer and Walther's offer. Maria Wößner, born 1858, came from a dysfunctional family and was considered being of lesser intelligence, but good-natured and cleanly.[192] Fischer and Walther were highly satisfied with their first deaf employee, and requested further placements. In 1876, they had six deaf girls living and working at the factory.[193]

Work in the Wiesenthal factory went on for ten hours a day, six days a week. Except for shelter, food and medical care, workers received a minimum wage of 25 Gulden per year.[194] In their leisure time, the girls practiced sewing and

---

189 "ihre traurige Lage nach Kräften zu erleichtern", Fischer and Walther to the Centralleitung des Wohlthätigkeitsvereins, 20 March 1873, StA Ludwigsburg, E 191 Bü 3533.

190 "schon längst sehnlichst von seinem Eltern erwartet", Kgl. Taubstummenanstalt Gmünd to the Centralleitung des Wohlthätigkeitsvereins 10 April 1873; Inspektor Rizzmann, Paulinenpflege Winnenden, to the Centralleitung des Wohlthätigkeitsvereins, 15 April 1873, StA Ludwigsburg, E 191 Bü 3533.

191 A. F. Oßwald and J. Ziegler, Taubstummenanstalt Wilhelmsdorf, to the Centralleitung des Wohlthätigkeitsvereins 14 April 1873; Bericht des Seminar-Rektorates betr. die Vermittlung taubstummen Mädchen für die Seidezwirnerei in Wiesenthal Nürtingen, 12 April 1873, StA Ludwigsburg, E 191 Bü 3533.

192 The seventh girl was considered suitable by the school, but the consent of her parents had to be acquired; whether she was finally employed or not is unclear. Bericht des Sem. Rektorats betr. die Unterbringung eines taubstummen Mädchens, Eßlingen 21 April 1873, with appendix, StA Ludwigsburg, E 191 Bü 3533.

193 Pfarramt Schwarz to the Centralleitung des Wohlthätigkeitsvereins 14 February 1876, StA Ludwigsburg, E 191 Bü 3533.

194 25 Gulden was equivalent to about 40 Mk. As a comparison, the average income of a worker in the cotton textile industry was a yearly 524 Mk and 76 Pfennigs in 1873. However, the girls in Wiesenthal needed not pay for food and shelter. Hermann Kellenbenz, "Zahlungsmittel, Maße und Gewichte seit 1800." in *Handbuch der deutschen Wirtschafts- und Sozialgeschichte*, Vol. 2, eds. Hermann Aubin and

knitting.[195] To fill their factory, Fischer and Walther specialized in cheap and easily recruited labour: young women from difficult backgrounds or with disabilities. Officials and schools supplied them with the workers they needed. In exchange, Fischer and Walther provided the community with a safeguard against future costs. Relations with the clergy were well cultivated, and they intended to employ a woman supervisor with experience of deaf education.[196]

Deaf girls who could not be cared for by their families and found no other employment might need to be placed in institutions. Otherwise the fear was that they would become burdens to the poor relief system. Walther and Fischer profited on their employment policy, but so did the community. As for the deaf girls they employed, they lived strictly controlled lives, with practically no leisure time. On the other hand, they likely formed a small signing community, and were thereby saved from the isolation threatening deaf people on the countryside. Between 1873 and 1876, Fischer and Walther's business flourished. They repeatedly asked for more disadvantaged girls to employ, even from outside Württemberg. On their request to investigate if any deaf girls might be procured from East Prussia, the charity board replied that their trouble in finding labour was probably due to low wages. Nevertheless, the gentlemen's request was met.[197]

Benevolent Master: F. Pfluger

Another model of private initiative relating to the occupation of deaf school graduates appeared as a by-product to the Bavarian bonus system. After the intended bonuses became known to the Chambers of Craft in 1905, a board member of the Oberpfalz and Regensburg Chamber declared that he intended to

---

Wolfgang Zorn (Stuttgart: Ernst Klett Verlag, 1976), pp. 942-943; Ashok V. Desai, *Real Wages in Germany 1871-1913* (Oxford: Clarendon Press, 1968), p. 108.

195   Fischer and Walther to the Centralleitung des Wohlthätigkeitsvereins, 20 March 1873; Fischer and Walter to the Centralleitung des Wohlthätigkeitsvereins, 10 May 1873, StA Ludwigsburg, E 191 Bü 3533.

196   Whether this promise was kept is unclear. Centralleitung des Wohlthätigkeitsvereins to the Taubstummenanstalt zu Gmünd, Taubstummenschule zu Eßlingen, Taubstummenschule zu Nürtingen, Taubstummen Anstalt "Paulinenpflege" zu Winnenden, and Taubstummen-Anstalt Wilhelmsdorf, 3 April 1873, StA Ludwigsburg, E 191 Bü 3533.

197   Pfarramt Schwarz to the Centralleitung des Wohlthätigkeitsvereins, 14 Februar 1876, StA Ludwigsburg, E 191 Bü 3533.

set up a vocational school. Fritz Pfluger, a cabinet maker from Regensburg, proposed himself as leader of a workshop for six apprentices. Reactions were positive: Pfluger was a respected person and his project was perceived as answering to a societal need. Bonuses would be paid for each apprentice. Also, there was a possibility of further financial aid for fitting the shop.[198] Pfluger's original plan included employment of a teacher of the deaf to offer education in theoretical subjects, but this intention had to be abandoned. Instead Pfluger alone would be in charge of the teaching, and send the apprentices to the secondary deaf school for two hours per week.[199]

In spite of the favourable reactions from the state, Pfluger had limited success. Funding was not a problem, but the lack of prospective apprentices. At an early stage he had contacted all Bavarian deaf schools, but found not a single graduate who would enter his educational program.[200] In 1908 he was granted a bonus for educating one deaf boy, who seems to have been his only apprentice.[201]

Pfluger's and Fischer and Walther's efforts to find deaf workers and apprentices were most certainly not acts of mere charity. These entrepreneurs had realized that deaf youth were not only cheap and easily manageable labour, but sometimes even came with a cash bonus. Simultaneously, business owners hiring deaf people relieved society of the potential burden of providing for them, which gave their efforts a charitable quality. The examples of Fischer and Walther and Pfluger suggest that the administrative authorities were willing to support projects of this kind, but that the deaf schools and parents of deaf youth were more reluctant.

---

198 Reg. d. Obf. u. v. Regensburg, Kammer des Innern, to the Staatsministerium des Innern für Kirchen und Schulangelengheiten, 26 March 1906, BayHStA MK 62324; Staatsministerium des Innern für Kirchen und Schulangelengheiten to the Staatsministerium des Kgl. Hauses und des Aeussern, 18 April 1906, Staatsministerium des Innern für Kirchen und Schulangelengheiten to the Reg. d. Obf. u. v. Regensburg, Kammer des Innern, 15 May 1906, BayHStA MWi 1055.

199 Reg. d. Obf. u. v. Regensburg, Kammer des Innern to the Staatsministerium des Innern für Kirchen und Schulangelegenheiten, 30 April 1907, BayHStA MK 62324.

200 Brettreich: Regierungsbericht, BayHStA MWi 1055.

201 Application concerning Willy Hagn (1908), BayHStA MWi 1055.

Institutions

Boarding schools made life in institutions an integral part of the shared "Deaf experience"[202] from the 18th century onward. However, there were also deaf people to whom institutionalisation was not a temporary phase during the school years, but a long-term way of life. [203]

Due to the scarcity of specialist literature on the subject, I will in the following sections discuss four institutions with adult deaf inhabitants, using their statutes and annual reports. The purpose is to exemplify how such asylums could be organized and how their inmates lived. In some areas, staying at an institution was not uncommon as a way of life for people who were deaf, as pointed out above. Furthermore, institutional confinement was an important practice used to manage the deaf in Germany in terms of cost and effort. A relatively large number of people could be involved in founding, funding, and maintaining also a small institution.[204] In the individual case, they offered families and authorities an option to handle deaf persons.

Wagner'sche Anstalten

Johann Evangelist Wagner (1807-1886), a catholic priest, was the founder of a complex of eleven charitable institutions in Bavaria, with altogether 1771 deaf or intellectually disabled inmates (1914). In 1847, he had opened an asylum for deaf girls in connection with the convent school for the deaf in Dillingen.[205] Over the years, it was followed by similar institutions in Zell (1872), Hohenwart

---

202 To use a term coined by Harlan Lane. *v.* Lane (Ed.) *The Deaf Experience*.

203 *V.* above p. 51.

204 In addition to the actual staff, the institutions received contributions from numerous private people. See for instance the annual reports of the Paulinenpflege, StA Ludwigsburg, E 191, Bü 5053-5058.

205 Hermann Oblinger, "Johann Evangelist Wagner und Dominikus Ringeisen als Wegbereiter der Behinderten- und Sonderschulpädagogik im 19. Jahrhundert." in *Handbuch der Geschichte des Bayerischen Bildungswesens*, Vol. 2: *Geschichte der Schule in Bayern. Von 1800 bis 1918*, ed. Max Liedtke (Bad Heilbronn: Verlag Julius Klinkhardt, 1993), pp. 551-556; *J.E.Wagnersche Wohltätigkeitsanstalten. Taubstummenanstalt Dillingen. Erziehungs-, Unterrichts- und Versorgungs-Anstalt für taubstumme Mädchen. Jahresbericht 1913/14.* (Dillingen: J. Keller & Co, 1914), pp. 5-6; StA Amberg, Reg. d. Obpf, Kammer des Innern Nr. 14597.

(1878), and Michelfeld (1884). All obeyed the same administration and shared the same statutes.[206]

Catholic deaf girls were provided with a seven-year education, and thereafter had the option to remain in the asylum. According to the annual reports of the Hohenwart asylum from the first decades of the 20th century, most girls remained after completing their education. In 1901, Hohenwart had 75 adult inmates, several of whom had lived there since the opening in 1878. They were occupied with household work and delicate crafts such as embroidery. Items of their production were sold, often to churches, and contributed to the maintenance of the institution. Other funds came from offertories, secular authorities, and private assets of residents. The Wagnersche asylums aspired to accept all applicants, regardless of their financial status.[207]

Wagner's motivation for combining deaf schools with asylums was the observation that deaf girls educated in Dillingen often had no opportunity to find work or to be provided for at home. In the asylum, they could work for their living under secured circumstances.[208] Most teachers were nuns, and all personnel,

---

206 J.E. Wagnersche Wohltätigkeitsanstalten. Jahresbericht 1913/14, StA Amberg, Reg. d. Obpf, Kammer des Innern Nr. 14597; Statuten der Erziehungs- und Versorgungs-Anstalten für weibliche Taubstumme in Dillingen, Hohenwart bei Schreobenhausen und Zell bei Hilpolstein. (Donauwörth, 1879), StA Amberg, Bez.A. Eschenbach Nr. 4022; Franz Weigl, Johann Evangelist Wagner. Gründer der J.E. Wagnerschen Wohltätigkeitsanstalten in Bayern. Regens am Priesterseminar Dillingen a. D. Eine Lebensgeschichte (Munich: Seyfried & Comp., Schnell & Söhne, 1931), pp. 104-114, 126.

207 Statuten der Erziehungs- und Versorgungs-Anstalten für weibliche Taubstumme in Dillingen, Hohenwart bei Schreobenhausen und Zell bei Hilpolstein (Donauwörth 1879), StA Amberg, Bez.A. Eschenbach Nr. 4022; J.E.Wagnersche Wohltätigkeitsanstalten. Jahresbericht 1913/14, Jahres-Bericht über die Erziehungs- und Versorgungs-Anstalt für taubstumme Mädchen in Zell bei Hilpolstein (Mittelfranken) pro 1890/91, StA Amberg, Reg. d. Obpf. Kammer des Innern Nr. 14597; Jahres-Bericht über die Erziehungs- & Versorgungsanstalt taubstummer Mädchen in Hohenwart für das Jahr 1900/1901; 1901/1902; 1903/1904; 1907/1908; 1909/1910; 1912/1913, StA Munich, no signature.

208 Statuten der Erziehungs- und Versorgungs-Anstalten für weibliche Taubstumme in Dillingen, Hohenwart bei Schreobenhausen und Zell bei Hilpolstein (Donauwörth, 1879), p. 1, StA Amberg, Bez.A. Eschenbach Nr. 4022.

except for the dean, were women.²⁰⁹ As exceptions, girls of other confessions, and even boys, could be accepted as pupils or inmates.²¹⁰ Thus poverty, religion and even gender were no absolute borders limiting the possibility of enrolment. Intelligence, however, was. In the early 20th century, girls were repeatedly sent home from Hohenwart because they were considered uneducable.²¹¹

St. Joseph

Ursberg, Bavaria, was the home of a gigantic complex of charitable asylums called the St. Joseph. In 1913, the institutions for epileptics, 'deaf-mutes' with additional disabilities, indisposed workers and intellectually disabled had 1780 inmates. Out of these, probably about one hundred were deaf. This was a considerable increase since 1892, when the asylum had 38 deaf inmates.²¹²

Dominikus Ringeisen, also a catholic priest and a disciple of J. E. Wagner's, had founded the Ursberg institutions in 1884.²¹³ The asylum was open to both sexes, and without regard of religion – although the asylum considered itself to have a catholic character. Only 'educable' deaf and physically disabled children were excluded from the asylum. Three classes of care were offered, with fees between 250 and 550 Mark per year. Class, type of disability, age and sex determined in which ward the inmates were placed. Especially 'cretins' and epileptics were kept strictly apart from physically disabled and deaf inmates.

---

209 Jahres-Bericht über die Erziehungs- & Versorgungsanstalt taubstummer Mädchen in Hohenwart für das Jahr 1900/1901; 1909/1910, StA Munich, no signature.

210 Statuten der Erziehungs- und Versorgungs-Anstalten für weibliche Taubstumme, StA Amberg, Bez.A. Eschenbach Nr. 4022; Jahres-Bericht über die Erziehungs- & Versorgungsanstalt taubstummer Mädchen in Hohenwart für das Jahr 1904/1905, StA Munich, no signature.

211 Jahres-Bericht über die Erziehungs- & Versorgungsanstalt taubstummer Mädchen in Hohenwart für das Jahr 1907/1908; 1910/1911; 1912/1913, StA Munich, no signature.

212 An overview from 1908 listed 105 deaf inmates. From 1913, there are no exact figures. Franz X. Kerer, *Dominikus Ringeisen von Ursberg. Ein Lebens- und Charakterbild* (Regensburg: G. J. Manz, 1927), p. 40; *Uebersicht der zurzeit in den Ursberger Anstalten versorgten Pfleglinge, nach den Regierungskreisen geordnet* [1908]; Annual report of the Ursberg asylums, 1913, p. 10, BayHStA Rep. MInn Nr. 79999.

213 Oblinger, "Johann Evangelist Wagner," pp. 551-556.

Professional teachers taught all deaf, except the 'uneducable', without regards to age or gender.

Although the stay at the institution was paid for in cash, all inmates that were able to work were expected to do so. Opportunities were at hand in the household and associated facilities such as bakery, brewery, mill, or in the fields. St. Joseph also had workshops where manufacture of baskets, saddles, shoes, books, clothing and other products was taught and performed, as were feminine chores and crafts such as ironing and knitting. According to the statutes, the purpose of the work was therapeutical: to make the inmates useful members of society, "inside or outside of the asylum".[214] There was no mentioning of compensation for this labour. The statutes also regulated the use of punishments. Adult inmates were not to be physically punished, but could be deprived of food, isolated from the group, or locked up.[215]

Paulinenpflege

This Württembergian institution, like the 'Wagnersche' asylums, was essentially a school, but kept some pupils after graduation. Some were taught a trade, others remained their entire life. Deaf adults who had not attended school were also admitted.

Founded in 1823 by vicar Friedrich Jakob Philipp Heim, it educated nearly 300 pupils during its first 50 years.[216] They were, at first, mostly sent home or found work outside of the institution. During the late 19th century, the care of deaf adults came more into focus, as did teaching of deaf children with intellectual disorders. This in turn resulted in difficulties in finding suitable occupations for the latter group after graduation, so that the Paulinenpflege developed into an

---

214 "innerhalb und außerhalb der Anstalt," *Satzungen der St. Joseph-Versorgungsanstalt Ursberg*, 1898, p. 15, StA Amberg, Reg. d. Obpf. Kammer des Innern, 12823.

215 *Satzungen der St. Joseph-Versorgungsanstalt Ursberg*, 1898, pp. 16-17, StA Amberg, Reg. d. Obpf. Kammer des Innern, 12823.

216 Margarete Henninger, Friedrich Jakob Philipp Heim. 1789-1850. Gründer der Paulinenpflege Winnenden. Ein Beitrag zur Frühgeschichte der Diakonie in Württemberg (Winnenden: Paulinenpflege, 1990), p. 135; Jubiläumsbericht der Rettungs- und Taubstummenanstalt Paulinenpflege zu Winnenden, 1873, StA Ludwigsburg, E 191 Bü 5054.

institution for vocational education and became for some a life-long home and workplace.[217]

Male inmates worked in different crafts or tended the premises. The women were occupied with textile crafts.[218] Maintaining the asylum for deaf adults was associated with disciplinary challenges. Inmates often escaped, or behaved in ways that were considered unacceptable. Escapes and transfers to insane asylums occurred frequently. In the annual reports, the administration noted that the men were difficult to handle since they were discontent with their situation and longed for freedom. The women had what was regarded as impossible dreams, such as getting married. Their caregiver concluded that the continued care and control was in their best interest.[219] Thus, the discontent with their situation expressed by these deaf adults was handled by using force: hindering escapes, retrieving those who succeeded in their attempts, and transferring the most challenging cases to insane asylums, where they might be kept under an even stricter control.

Wilhelmsdorf

The purpose of the asylum in Wilhelmsdorf was to accept those who were accepted nowhere else. It had been founded by August Friedrich Oßwald, an acquaintance of Heim's who had first worked as a teacher of the deaf at the Paulinenpflege.[220] Although the asylum was designated 'Deaf-mute Asylum', people with normal hearing, but for instance lacking a leg, without arms, or suffering from scoliosis, were also admitted. Inmates were divided in normal pupils, 'feebleminded' pupils, and wards, that is, adults who had either remained there after completing their education, or because of some difficulties been

---

217 Jahresbericht Paulinenpflege zu Winnenden, 1878, StA Ludwigsburg, E 191 Bü 5055; Jahresbericht Paulinenpflege zu Winnenden, 1912, StA Ludwigsburg, E 191 Bü 5058.

218 *Jahresbericht Paulinenpflege zu Winnenden,* 1878, 1886, StA Ludwigsburg, E 191 Bü 5055.

219 Jahresbericht Paulinenpflege zu Winnenden, 1879, 1881, 1883, StA Ludwigsburg, E 191 Bü 5055; Jahresbericht Paulinenpflege zu Winnenden, 1887, 1888, 1891, 1894, StA Ludwigsburg, E 191 Bü 5056; Jahresbericht Paulinenpflege zu Winnenden, 1900, 1901, 1903, 1904, 1909, 1911, StA Ludwigsburg, E 191 Bü 5057.

220 Henninger, Friedrich Jakob Philipp Heim, pp. 145-147.

forced to withdraw to the asylum. The institution had a tailoring shop where the adults worked.[221]

Institutions: Conclusion

All these asylums were confessional initiatives. It is worth noticing that both the catholic and protestant churches were involved in such projects. Seen to the statistics, however, catholic 'deaf-mutes' were over-represented as inmates of asylums.[222]

The motivation for placing deaf people in institutions was concern that the deaf adolescents finishing school might be neglected, become a burden to their families, or lose the skills they had acquired in school. Some of them were orphans, some came from poor families. Especially the young girls were seen as being in great need of protection and support. Many of them went directly from convent school into an asylum, where they then lived and worked. Some catholic schools transferred as many as two-thirds of their female students to asylums. Deaf with learning disabilities and elderly deaf were not being admitted to asylums to the extent that young, educated deaf women were.[223] Institutional life appears not to have differed much between the four institutions. Regulations were strict, work was expected of those who were physically able, and the control lay in the hands of hearing supervisors.

Thus, institutionalisation was not necessarily a last resort for the most helpless and needy individuals. Those who had too many difficulties were unwanted at the Wagner'sche asylums and in the Paulinenpflege. Instead, the educational system apparently failed to offer the kind of preparation that would enable their graduates to live independent lives. By being unable to accommodate them elsewhere, schools produced the target group for the 'deaf-mute asylums.'

---

221 *Bericht und Rechnung, Wilhelmsdorf* 1896/1897-1899/1900, StA Ludwigsburg, E 191 Bü 5299; *Bericht und Rechnung, Wilhelmsdorf* 1900/1901-1902/1903, StA Ludwigsburg E 191 Bü 5300; *Bericht und Rechnung, Wilhelmsdorf* 1906/1907-1913/1914, StA Ludwigsburg, E 191 Bü 5300a.

222 *Cf.* Engelmann, "Die Taubstummen," pp. 21, 30.

223 The Wagner'sche asylums alone, in which young, educated women were admitted, accommodated 270 persons in 1905. The total number of 'uneducable' wards in Bavaria was 108, and the number of inmates admitted after the age of 30 was 62. Pongratz, *Allgemeine Statistik*, pp. 86-89.

Charity: The Royal Trust of King Karl and Queen Olga

The Württembergian royal trust fund "König Karl und Königin Olga-Stiftung" was founded in 1871[224] and paid humble contributions to indigent and worthy deaf. Applications were submitted through the local authorities, mostly the mayor, pastor and/or the parish. Files from this foundation give insight in the lives of 33 deaf individuals, who applied for contributions of 18 to 20 Mk each in 1899, 1904 and 1909.[225] Their applications contained descriptions of their situations, exemplifying the circumstances under which some deaf people in the rural lower classes lived.

Typical of the applications was that the deaf person appeared with a low level of integrity and a limited space of action. No applicant was married, and the majority lived either with their parents, other relatives, in institutions, or as boarders in other households at the expense of the parish. Most either did not state an occupation, or were unable to work, which of course was a reason for their need of support. Furthermore, the deaf persons rarely signed the application themselves. Instead, parents and caregivers cooperated with their mayors, priests and parish councils in preparing the application on behalf of the deaf person.

Although the combined picture is rather bleak, the group had some variation. Many were dependent on their families or on poor relief, but some appeared as industrious and competent. Gottfried Eisenmann, born in 1847, received support all three years studied. He lived with his mother and his disabled brother, both of whom he provided for, in a cottage. In 1899, the mother had applied for the contribution, but as she apparently passed away between then and 1904, Eisenmann himself submitted the following applications together with the pastor and mayor. His situation was certainly not easy; a worker in agriculture and forestry, his physical ability deteriorated over the years. In 1904, he was only partially able to work, and in 1909, he received injury- and disability pension.

---

224 The foundation was founded to comemmorate the 25th wedding anniversary of King Karl and Queen Olga. Its original purpose was to support daughters of deceased Württembergian military servants. *Statut der Karl-Olga-Stiftung vom 13. Juli 1871*, HStA Stuttgart G 314 Bü 4; *Hof- und Staatshandbuch des Königreichs Württemberg*. Vol. 1. (1907): Appendix [II.], p. 1. Although this remained its sole official purpose, it obviously also supported deaf applicants of both sexes.

225 StA Ludwigsburg, F214 II Bü 112.

Nevertheless, he lived in a house of his own, and supported his physically disabled brother.[226]

Philippine Greiner was in her mid-fifties when she applied for support for the first time in 1899. She lived with her sister, and contributed to the household by performing chores and taking on day labour when she could find it. Her earnings were insufficient and she lacked assets, but she did receive disability pension. Greiner also received contributions from the foundation all three years studied.[227] On the other hand, some applications unveiled deplorable situations. Karl and Friedrich Munz, brothers born in, respectively, 1895 and 1896, lived with four other siblings, their stepmother, father, and grandparents on a small farm. Trying to provide for the large family, the father accumulated debts. When the stepmother died, the father was apparently overwhelmed by the situation. Whereas he in 1904 had signed the application, he was five years later described as "mentally abnormal", had left the farmstead, and roamed the country as a railroad worker. According to the mayor, he would soon face total financial ruin. Karl and Friedrich were provided with a legal guardian, probably an older brother or uncle. Friedrich went to school in Gmünd and later worked at a large farmstead, but Karl was labelled "uneducable".[228]

Applicants of both sexes were often described as physically or mentally disabled, in addition to being deaf. Herta Munz, ten years old, could not walk and was in need of "constant attention and care" from her parents, who applied

---

226 Kesine Eisenmann., Pfarrer Leitz, and Kroner to the Oberamt Welzheim 27 Okt and 3 November 1899, Gottfried Eisenmann, Pfarrer Leitz, and Schultheiss Kroner to the Oberamt Welzheim 7 and 17 August 1904, Gottfried Eisenmann, Kalecker, and Schultheiss Kroner to the Oberamt Wertheim 1, 2, and 4 July 1909, StA Ludwigsburg, F214 II, Bü 112.

227 Leitz and Müller, 25 August 1904, Pfarrer Leitz and Schultheiss Kroner to the Oberamt Welzheim, 2 November 1899, Verzeichnis derjenigen *Blinden u. Taubstummen* hies. Gemeinde [Welzheim] welche um Berücksichtigung bei Verteilung von Zinsen aus der *Karl-Olgastiftung* bitten, 3 July 1909, Schultheiss and Pfarrer of Unterschlechtbach to the Oberamt Welzheim, 24 October 1899, Ortsarmenbehörde Unterschlechtbach to the Bezirksrat Welzheim, 3 July 1909, StA Ludwigsburg, F214 II Bü 112.

228 "geistig nicht normal"; "nicht bildungsfähig", Gottlob Munz, Falck, and Kroner to the Oberamt Welzheim, 19 August 1904, Schultheißenamt Kaisersbach 20 June/2 July 1909, Schultheissennamt Kaisersbach to the Oberamt Welzheim 4 November 1915, StA Ludwigsburg, Bestand F214 II Bestellnummer Bü 112.

for a contribution in 1904.[229] Pauline Stettner was ten years old in 1909, when her caregiver received a 20 Mk contribution on her behalf. She was born out of wedlock, and had no contact with her mother, who later had married. Instead, she was taken care of by the basket maker Gottfried Holzmann. He had tried to enrol her in the Paulinenpflege,[230] but she was deemed uneducable. Caring for her was demanding since she was "unclean".[231] Friedrike Schwarz, 33 years old at the time of the application, went to live in the care of a local farmer after losing her parents. She, too, was described as mentally retarded.[232] Gottlob Specht was considered both mentally and physically disabled, and needed constant care from his mother still at the age of 26. Their household was under severe financial strain already in 1899, and was later struck by the death of Gottlob's father.[233]

As we have seen, some key factors can be distinguished in the situation of several beneficiaries of the Karl-Olga-Stiftung. Loss of parents, lack of, or inability to, education and work, together with deafness led to situations that could not be managed without aid. Deafness alone could often be compensated with social networks, education and the opportunity to work, that is, elements keeping the deaf person connected to some community. When these connections were broken, or never established, the language barrier disabled them from coping alone; building new relationships, finding further employment, or even themselves turning to the instances that might be able to assist them.[234]

---

229 "erfordert einer ständigen Wart und Pflege"; She does not seem to have been closely related to Karl and Friedrich Munz. If she received a contribution, and how much, is unclear. Verhandelt vor dem Schultheißenamt Unterschlechtbach, 18 August 1904, StA Ludwigsburg, F214 II Bü 112.
230 V. p. 84.
231 "unreinlich", Gottfried Holzmann through the Kgl. ev. Pfarramt II., Welzheim 30 June 1909, StA Ludwigsburg, F214 II Bü 112.
232 Verhandelt vor dem Schultheißenamt Unterschlechtbach, 18 August 1904, StA Ludwigsburg, F214 II Bü 112.
233 Schultheiss and Pfarrer, Unterschlechtbach, to the Oberamt Welzheim, 24 October 1899; Verhandelt vor dem Schultheißenamt Unterschlechtbach, 18 August 1904, Karolina Specht and Schultheiss, Unterschlechtbach, to the Bezirksrat Welzheim, 3 July 1909, StA Ludwigsburg, F214 II Bü 112.
234 Cf. also the 'unknown deaf-mutes', below pp. 124f.

CONCLUSION OF CHAPTER 1

In the 19th century, the knowledge about 'deaf-mutes' migrated from medicine to demographics. Rather than attempting to cure individuals, physicians cooperated with teachers, clergy, and police to quantify and describe the 'deaf-mutes in general'. The resulting statistical surveys allow us to imagine an 'average deaf-mute' foremost in numerical and socio-economic terms, instead of anatomically. In the course of the century, the German states elaborated the image of this being, describing his social, educational, and vocational situation. The 'average deaf-mute' emerged not at the top, but also not at the very bottom of society. His dependence on others was most typical of his life circumstances.

At the same time as statisticians produced this image, other professionals helped turning the 'average deaf-mute' into flesh. Policies and practices throughout society worked homogenizingly within the deaf group: German law barred deaf people from the very top of society, by prohibiting them from seeking public office. At the opposite end of the scale, the legislators also tried to keep the deaf away from the lowest ranks of society by withholding licences for peddling. Earlier, highly specialized trades like porcelain painting, engraving and calligraphy had offered an alternative to the mainstream apprentice system leading to well-paid jobs for an elite of deaf people. Sign Language based education had also opened the teaching profession to some, and enabled others to pursue careers in intellectual or administrative professions. This was the era of star pupils and famous deaf intellectuals.[235] At the same time, uneducated deaf from rural areas were dependent on their families, and exposed to the risks of poverty, which were enhanced by the language barrier. In short, the deaf had been a most heterogeneous group in regard to class. Some were prominent intellectuals, but most were invisible, isolated beings.

The spread of deaf education, the oral method, industrialization, and the 'deaf-mute bonuses', together resulted in the formation of a more homogenous deaf population. A basic education was offered to increasing numbers of deaf children, and finally became obligatory. Bonuses and efforts from the schools

---

235 Some famous representatives of this era were the French teachers and/or writers Jean Massieu, Laurent Clerc, Roche-Ambroise Bebian, and Pierre Desloges. However, also in Germany there were similar characters, highly talented deaf men with careers in the professions and literature, in the early 19th century. v. Rée, *I See a Voice*, pp. 159-61, 195-204; Lane, *When the Mind Hears;* idem (Ed.), *Deaf Experience;* Groschek, *Unterwegs in eine Welt des Verstehens,* pp. 59-60, 283; *cf.* also below, pp. 54, 223.

helped to place them in vocational training or employment. Since the method turned to "pure" oralism however, the quality of education decreased. It focused on speech, not knowledge, and was ill equipped to produce star pupils, artists, artisans and intellectuals. The teaching profession was also closed to deaf people as a result. Hence, the 'average deaf-mute' was becoming a reality.

2. Deaf Lives in Social Context

The previous chapter was concerned with the frameworks of knowledge, institutions, and interventions surrounding a particular kind of people, the 'deaf-mutes'. The next task is to move closer to the informal structures of the society in which these frameworks existed.

Unlike the previous chapter, this one is not about 'the deaf' as a category, but about deaf people, on two levels. The first is the socio-cultural level. I will ask how certain social, economic and cultural conditions and transformation processes at work in Germany during the study period affected deaf people. The second level is the individual example. I will present a number of deaf persons or events involving deaf persons, to exemplify how deaf people lived inside the formal and informal frameworks of the German Empire.

CLASS AND CULTURE IN 19TH CENTURY GERMANY

Jürgen Kocka summarized the "long" 19th century "as the century of industrialization and prevailing capitalism; as the century of population explosion and great migrations; as the century of national states and nationalism, which began with the French Revolution and Napoleonic Wars and ended in the First World War. In Germany, too, it was the century of the bourgeoisie and bourgeois culture, which was creased by class conflicts and gender inequality, but nevertheless lay the foundations of a civil society [...]."[1] It was, not least in Germany,

---

1   "als das Jahrhundert der Industrialisierung und des sich durchsetzenden Kapitalismus; als das Jahrhundert der Bevölkerungsexplosion und der großen Wanderungen; als das Jahrhundert der Nationalstaaten und des Nationalismus, das mit Französischer Revolution und napoleonischen Kriegen begann und im Ersten Weltkrieg endete. Auch in Deutschland war das neunzehnte das Jahrhundert des Bürgertums

a particularly dynamic century on most levels of society, from the economic and political to the cultural ones.

As Kocka mentions in this quote, Europe experienced significant geo-politic changes. In the multitude of smaller and bigger states in the areas that later became the German Empire, the idea of a national state grew strong during the first half of the century. In association with nationalist sentiments and armed conflict, these states in 1871 united under the crown of the Emperor. As significant to this process as the unification itself, was the change of character to a more modern type of state expressed in a certain degree of democratization and the establishment of an administrative bureaucracy.[2]

A second change in basic conditions was the industrial revolution. Industrialization took off later in Germany than in Western Europe. Remainders of feudalism only gradually disappeared through continual agrarian reform. However, once the industrialization began, the development was rapid. From mid-century to the seventies, the German economy experienced a shift of center, with agriculture losing some of its significance to industry. However, this was paired with strong growth, meaning that the productivity in the agricultural sector still increased in absolute numbers.[3] The growth in the economy continued, although slower during the 'great depression' of 1873-1890, until the First World War.[4]

Through industrialization traditional structures of occupation were shattered. Although the new industries offered many employment, they deprived others of their livelihood. Together with an accelerated growth of the population, this led to a surplus of labourers, which in turn prompted migration – overseas or to the

---

und der dominant werdenden bürgerlichen Kultur, ein bürgerliches Jahrhundert, das von Klassenkonflikten und Geschlechterungleichheit durchfurcht war, aber trotzdem die Fundamente einer Zivilgesellschaft legte [...]." Jürgen Kocka, *Das lange 19. Jahrhundert. Arbeit, Nation und bürgerliche Gesellschaft.* Gebhardt Handbuch der deutschen Geschichte, 10th Ed, vol. 13 (Stuttgart: Klett-Cotta, 2001), p. xv.

2   Kocka, *19. Jahrhundert,* pp. 88-97.

3   Kocka, *19. Jahrhundert*, pp. 141-142; Friedrich Lenger, *Industrielle Revolution und Nationalstaatsgründung (1849-1870er Jahre),* Gebhardt Handbuch der deutschen Geschichte, 10th Ed, Vol. 15 (Stuttgart: Klett-Cotta, 2001), pp. 35-36, 43-45.

4   Volker Berghahn, *Das Kaiserreich 1871-1914. Industriegesellschaft, bürgerliche Kultur und starker Staat,* Gebhardt Handbuch der deutschen Geschichte, 10th Ed, Vol. 16 (Stuttgart: Klett-Cotta, 2001), pp. 41-46.

cities.[5] In 1914, nearly half of the Germans had taken part in the internal migration.[6]

Young people left the countryside and less industrialized regions, especially in the east, for bigger and smaller cities and areas with large industrial sectors such as the Ruhr. Towns grew into cities, so that not only the size, but also the number of urban communities increased. Characteristic of their inhabitants were their youth and their migration background.[7] Their situation was often insecure and unsteady. Some commuted between the industrial centers and their rural home, others were forced to wander from town to town in search of employment. In the city itself, many lacked a living quarter of their own, and instead rented a bed for the night in various apartments. There, away from traditional social structures, in often over-populated, unsanitary apartment buildings, a class emerged with a new sense of groupness – the urban proletariat.[8]

One's position in society, and perhaps to an even greater extent one's self-image and sense of belonging to a certain group, was however not only a matter of class. The life options were to a great extent determined by gender. All women were affected by patriarchal structures, although the effects differed according to social class and type of area. Common to all women were their exclusion from the political life, their limited access to the public sphere, and their restricted civil rights.[9]

Furthermore, many defined themselves more in terms of confession, region, or belonging to a certain ethnic or linguistic minority, than in terms of class. In a summary of the available research, Volker Berghahn concludes that there existed several categories of identification that were potentially as, or more, important than class in building group solidarity. For instance, catholic workers had a tendency to sympathize with the catholic Center party, rather than with the socialists. In the Ruhr area, Polish immigrants preferred to socialize in clubs based on their language and nationality, over assimilating with the rest of the working class.[10] Berghahn nevertheless argues that class was the most important

---

5   Kocka, *19. Jahrhundert*, pp. 61-80.
6   Ibid., p. 76.
7   Berghahn, *Industriegesellschaft*, pp. 96-99; Kocka, *19. Jahrhundert*, pp. 75-80.
8   Berghahn, *Industriegesellschaft*, pp. 96-99; 116-121.
9   Ibid., pp. 121-138; *v.* also below p. 99.
10 *Cf.* also Christoph Klessmann, "Long-Distance Migration, Integration and Segregation of an Ethnic Minority in Industrial Germany: The Case of the 'Ruhr-Poles'," in *Population, Labour and Migration in 19th- and 20th- Century Germany*, ed. Klaus J. Bade (Lemington Spa: Berg, 1987), pp. 101-114.

of the social divisions, and that its significance only grew. The German Empire was, essentially, a class society.[11]

One further aspect of the industrial revolution must be mentioned – the improvement of communications. Most significant of the novelties were of course the railroads, which not only supported the economy, but also transformed the experience of distance and time in everyday lives. The Empire was a vast nation, seen to its surface, but the railroads made it possible to move from one corner to the other relatively comfortably and quickly. The carrying of ideas, in the shape of mail, telegraphs, newspapers, and magazines, was as important as the transportation of people and goods. The quantity of mail increased, and the subscription to newspapers and weekly magazines, most notably the family paper *Gartenlaube,* became widespread.[12] The German Empire possessed a dynamic literary culture. The literacy was high, and there was a wide range of literary products for every interest – political, scientific, moral, entertainment. However, censorship was a constant threat to every publisher, writer, and speaker. Most well known of the repressive measures was the prohibition of socialist organizations and publications that was in effect between 1878 and 1890.[13]

Bürgertum and *Bürgerlichkeit*

One aspect of 19th century German society had such an impact on its culture and values, and relevance for the deaf, that it should be treated separately. This is the notoriously vague concept of the *Bürger*. This word lacks a direct English translation. It began as a judicial designation of the burgher, the class of craftspeople and merchants who possessed certain civil rights in a town or city. It set them apart from farmers, gentry, and clergy, as well as from the lower classes of servants and poor. This category lost significance as the hierarchies of the *ancien régime* dissolved.[14] At the same time, the word *Bürger* and its derivations only gained gravity.

First, this has to do with the changes in class structure associated with the development into a modern, industrial capitalist state. The word became a

---

11 Berghahn, *Industriegesellschaft*, pp. 195-204.
12 Lenger, Industrielle Revolution, pp. 96-103.
13 Berghahn, *Industriegesellschaft*, pp. 240, 273-279.
14 Jürgen Kocka, "Bürgertum und Bürgerlichkeit als Probleme der deutschen Geschichte vom späten 18. zum frühen 20. Jahrhundert," in *Bürger und Bürgerlichkeit im 19. Jahrhundert,* ed. Jürgen Kocka (Munich: dtv, 1988), pp. 21-23.

designation for the class of wealthy industrialists, but also of educated administrators and professionals, both of which at this time grew in size and power.[15] In the course of the 19th century, these categories of people experienced a certain homogenization. For instance, it became increasingly common for university professors and industrialists to send their sons to the same schools. A shared education led to similar values and personal connections, which further reinforced the class formation on a social – if not economic – level.[16]

Thus, the 19th century *Bürger* could have a wide range of different occupations and be more or less wealthy, educated, and influential. Distinctive to them was a system of values and beliefs, rather than a certain position in society or in the production system. Characteristic to the *Bürger* was their orientation towards individual achievement and independence. To them, the autonomous individual was, and should be, the designer of his own life. With this came certain expectations on rewards for achievement and diligence, as well as aversion to outside interventions. Education and cultivation (German: *Bildung*) provided them with a high esteem for science and appreciation for fine arts. As a counterpart to the autonomy of the individual, the ideal-typical *Bürger* also cherished the intimate, emotionally based relationships in the family.[17]

Although the *Bürger* themselves were a minority in the German society, their value system spread to other groups to the extent that it appeared as a mainstream culture. *Bürgerliche* ideals and ideas trickled down to the lower middle- and working classes.[18] While they, in the Marxist sense, were the antagonists of the *Bürger,* "elements of *bürgerlich* life simultaneously entered the world of the workers with the force of a normative model: Orientation towards achievement, work ethos, esteem of cultivation and orientation towards advancement, not least to the legacy of the [18]48 liberalism and strong impulses of enlightenment. [emphasis added]"[19]

---

15   Ibid., pp. 23-25.
16   Hans-Ulrich Wehler, "Wie 'bürgerlich' war das Deutsche Kaiserreich?" in *Bürger und Bürgerlichkeit*, ed. Kocka, pp. 252-253.
17   Kocka "Bürgertum und Bürgerlichkeit," pp. 43-44; M. Rainer Lepsius, "Zur Soziologie des Bürgertums und der Bürgerlichkeit," in *Bürger und Bürgerlichkeit,* ed. Kocka, p. 97.
18   Wehler, "Wie 'bürgerlich' war das Deutsche Kaiserreich?", pp. 252-253, 259-260; Kocka, *19. Jahrhundert,* p. 115.
19   "Elemente des bürgerlichen Lebens währendessen mit der Kraft des normativen Vorbildes in die Welt der Arbeiterschaft eindringen: Leistungsorientierung und Arbeitsdisziplin, Bildungshochschätzung und Aufstiegsorientierung, nicht zuletzt das

Fully adhering to the values of the *Bürger* was not possible for everyone. Both Jürgen Kocka and Hans-Ulrich Wehler point out that even though the *Bürger* were not foremost defined by their economic circumstances, a certain disposable income or capital was required to meet the ideals. For instance, the most of the family must be exempted from gainful labour, and one had to be able to plan ahead and lead a reasonably steady life. There were also boundaries on the immaterial level: Jews, women, and illiterates were examples of groups who had no or limited access to the *Bürger* culture.[20] Unwanted elements such as the insane, paupers, and criminals were kept physically apart from the *bürgerlich* society through institutionalization.[21]

There was one further meaning of the word *Bürger*, which demonstrates the magnitude of the concept –*Bürger* also meant citizen. Civil rights and civil society were both designated *bürgerlich*.[22] This illustrates the supposed universality of the *Bürger* culture, a trait that according to Jürgen Habermas was constitutive to the 'bourgeois public sphere' (*Bürgerliche Öffentlichkeit*). This sphere Habermas defines as "the sphere of private people come together as a public" using a historically unique medium of political engagement: "public reasoning".[23] In the reasoning taking place in the public sphere, only the argument itself is valued, not the social status of its author. Other than the earlier culture of the court, to which only a select number of people had access, anyone could now obtain works of art – literature, music, etc. – on the market. Thus the public was limited by financial assets and education, but not by status.[24] The people populating this public sphere were, as mentioned, "private people". As a complement to the new public sphere, there was also a new sphere of intimacy, centered on the small family unit. The private people who entered the public sphere did so from the shelter of the bourgeois family, which was purportedly based on nothing but human, emotional relationships. In reality, of course, the family was an integral part of the economic system – ideologically, however, it was thought of as independent of the market. As such, it made the head of the

---

    Erbe des 48er Liberalismus und starke Aufklärungsimpulse." Wehler, "Wie 'bürgerlich' war das Deutsche Kaiserreich?" p. 259

20   Wehler, "Wie 'bürgerlich' war das Deutsche Kaiserreich?" p. 254; Kocka, "Bürgertum und Bürgerlichkeit," pp. 46-47; Kocka, *19. Jahrhundert*, p. 127.

21   Wehler, "Wie 'bürgerlich' war das Deutsche Kaiserreich?" pp. 254-255.

22   Kocka, "Bürgertum und Bürgerlichkeit," pp. 28-29.

23   "die Sphäre der zum Publikum versammelten Privatleute"; "das öffentliche Räsonnement", Habermas, *Strukturwandel der Öffentlichkeit*, p. 42.

24   Habermas, Strukturwandel der Öffentlichkeit, pp. 52-53.

household not only an owner of property – *bourgeois*, but also a human being, *homme*.[25] *"The developed bourgeois public sphere rests upon the fictitious identity of the private people come together as a public, in their double roles as property owners and as humans pure and simple."*[26]

Habermas traces the origins of the public sphere back to the emergence of market capitalism in the European High Middle Ages. Its height can be placed somewhere between the Enlightenment and the mid-19th century, when the autonomy of the private person was undermined by public interventions and consumption replaced reasoning in the cultural realm.[27] However, it is questionable if a public sphere in its pure form was ever a historical reality.[28] Even if we imagine that a fully functioning public sphere of this type existed, revisionist historiography has pointed to some weaknesses of the model. The main criticism has to do with the claims to universality and openness of the public sphere. A fact, neither denied nor discussed at length by Habermas, is that large groups were excluded from the public sphere not only due to educational or financial deficits. In an essay on this criticism, Nancy Fraser mentions gender and ethnicity as additional grounds for exclusion from the public sphere. However, exclusion from the bourgeois public sphere did not expel subaltern groups from the field of political discourse and action altogether. Fraser claims that the bourgeois public sphere has always been accompanied by what she calls "subaltern counterpublics" with institutions of their own, where they were able to develop ideas that sometimes entered the mainstream.[29] Other scholars have painted a gloomier picture of such public spheres as resulting from and dependent on the

---

25 Ibid pp. 63-65; 73-74

26 "Die entfaltete bürgerliche Öffentlichkeit beruht auf der fiktiven Identität der zum Publikum versammelten Privatleute in ihren beiden Rollen als Eigentümer und als Menschen schlechthin." [emphasis in original] Habermas, Strukturwandel der Öffentlichkeit, p. 74.

27 Ibid, pp. 28, 46-52; 193-210.

28 Geoff Eley, "Nations, Publics, and Political Cultures: Placing Habermas in the Nineteenth Century," in *Habermas and the Public Sphere,* ed. Craig Calhoun (Cambridge, MA: MIT Press, 1992), pp. 289-290.

29 Nancy Fraser, "Rethinking the Public Sphere: A Contribution to the Critique of Actually Existing Democracy," in *Habermas and the Public Sphere,* ed. Calhoun, pp. 118-142.

bourgeois public sphere, and caught up in a futile struggle for emacipation using the tools invented by their oppressors.[30]

Joseph Murray has used the concept in his dissertation on the web of contacts between deaf individuals and organizations that he calls the "transnational public sphere"[31] of the deaf. Murray views the 19th century deaf community as a counterpublic which neither closed itself off from the mainstream, nor assimilated, but wanted to exist as an alternative but integrated culture, a "co-equal" public sphere. Murray has shown that this transnational public sphere extended also to deaf people in the German Empire.[32]

Nevertheless, the bourgeois public sphere and the culture of the *Bürger* were the dominant ideals and areas for communication in the German Empire. This chapter asks what social spaces deaf people occupied in that context. What was their relationship to the *homme* and the *bourgeois*? What did the *Bürger* ideals of private family life and public autonomy mean to people who were deaf? Were deaf people able to enter the bourgeois public sphere, and if not, on what level did their exclusion take place? Were there deaf 'subaltern counterpublics', and if so, when, how, and where did they emerge, and who was able to enter them?

DEAF NETWORKS

The reader will have noticed that the context outlined above focused on the life in the cities. It was there that the *Bürger* encountered the proletarians, and it was in cities that salons and cafés emerged as parts of the public sphere. The cities also had a particular significance to the forging of relationships between deaf people. This section discusses the evidence of such connections emerging in 19th century Germany.

When viewing the social relationships of a person, we can speak of his or her 'network'. Often used in social sciences, this concept includes all kinds of

---

[30] Geoff Eley holds that this is "open to question", *v.* "Nations, Publics and Political Cultures: Placing Habermas in the Nineteenth Century," in *Habermas and the Public Sphere,* ed. Calhoun, p. 304, whereas Oskar Negt and Alexander Kluge claim that the 'proletarian public sphere' at best reaches a status quo of reasonable comfort by adopting bourgeois values and concepts. V. *Öffentlichkeit und Erfahrung. Zur Organizationsanalyse von bürgerlicher und proletarischer Öffentlichkeit* (Frankfurt a.M.: Suhrkamp, 1972), pp. 108-111.

[31] Murray, *Touch Of Nature*, p. 42.

[32] Ibid, pp. 42-47, 65, 79, 98.

different affiliations someone has – for example those that are given by nature, that is, kinship, those that emerge as a result of affection such as friendship and marriage, and those that evolve in formal settings such as the school or workplace. It also acknowledges, and distinguishes between, contacts with varying degrees of intimacy and frequency, as well as different functions of the relationships.[33] Furthermore, a network does not merely consist of direct person-to-person contact, but also includes people who do not know each other personally, but are nevertheless connected by mutual acquaintances.[34] The purpose here is not to perform a network analysis of relationships between deaf people in the nineteenth century. Nevertheless, the network concept opens up a way of describing these relationships as varying kinds of connections on the social level, as opposed to the conceptual one.

The Question of the 'Deaf Migration'

Not surprisingly, deaf people took part in the processes of urbanisation and internal migration affecting the German population as a whole. The results of the 1900 survey shows that the 'deaf-mutes' moved towards concentration in certain areas: The 48 750 'deaf-mutes' counted were born in 24 992 different parishes, but were at the time of the survey distributed in 18 165 parishes. In particular, it was industrialized areas and larger cities that attracted deaf migrants.[35] In 1880, half of the 'deaf-mute' inhabitants of Berlin were immigrants, mostly from other parts of Germany. In 1910, only one in four 'deaf-mute' men in Berlin were born there.[36] On the other hand, the urban 'deaf-mutes' were a minority, compared to the total number of 'deaf-mutes' in the population.[37] As we shall see, application of perspectives and results from previous research in history to the migration of

---

33 Alain Degenne and Michel Forsé, *Introducing Social Networks,* trans. Arthur Borges (London: Sage Publications, 1999), pp. 28-62; *v.* also Barry Wellmann, Peter J. Carrington, and Alan Hall, "Networks as personal communities," in *Social Structures: A Network Approach*, ed. Barry Wellman and S. D. Berkowitz (Cambridge: Cambridge University Press, 1988), pp. 130-184.
34 Jeremy Boissevain, *Friends of Friends: Networks, Manipulators and Coalitions* (Oxford: Basil Blackwell, 1974), pp. 24-25.
35 Engelmann, "Die Taubstummen," pp. 13-14.
36 Behla, "Die Taubstummen in Preussen," pp. 285, 288-290.
37 21% of the 'deaf-mutes' lived in "Stadtgemeinden", urban parishes, in 1900. Engelmann, "Die Taubstummen," pp. 72*-121*.

deaf people reveals some conditions and effects in the cultural, social, and medical realms unique to 'deaf migration'.

Migration is usually understood as a movement of people from one geographically determined, national, regional, cultural and/or ethnic space to another, geographically determined, space. In their new surroundings, they may integrate or form a minority community.[38] Migration of deaf people often differs from this standard concept.

First, residential schools and school practices contributed to the particular mobility of deaf people. After the mainstreaming movement had failed in the first half of the 19th century, temporary transfer to residential schools or foster families close to the schools were the reality of most deaf children receiving education. Thus, for many deaf people, the move to the city was involuntary and had nothing to do with the labour market. A child migrating is of course nothing unusual, but in the process these children were also separated from their families and integrated either in an institutional setting, or in local households.

Attending a residential school was in the first instance a temporary move that may not fully comply with the usual understanding of migration. However, the relocation was often permanentized after graduation. The practice of the school assisting former pupils in their search for an apprenticeship or employment meant that they had incentives to remain close to the school. Furthermore, asylums for adult deaf and deaf-friendly employers such as Fischer and Walther attracted deaf people to certain localities. Even at this stage, the migration was not necessarily voluntary. The confinement in asylums or, effectively, in a factory such as Fischer and Walther's, was often a decision made by the parents in cooperation with the school or other authorities.[39] Educator Eduard Walther confirmed that deaf people often stayed in the vicinity of their former schools, since masters close to deaf schools generally were more positive towards and familiar with educating deaf apprentices. In these communities, formal and informal structures of support and control of deaf people emerged. Teachers kept in touch with former pupils and deaf newcomers to assist them and supervise their behaviour.[40] Deaf networks formed during the 19th century assisted migrants in formal and informal ways. For instance, clubs sometimes provided

---

38   For a discussion of the definition of migration, see Dirk Hoerder, Jan Lucassen, and Leo Lucassen, "Terminologien und Konzepte in der Migrationsforschung," in *Enzyklopädie Migration in Europa. Vom 17. Jahrhundert bis zur Gegenwart,* eds. Klaus J. Bade et al. (Munich: Wilhelm Fink, 2007), pp. 28-53.

39   *V.* above, pp. 78, 86.

40   Walther, *Handbuch,* p. 711-712, 719, 723.

deaf newcomers with financial support or at least the possibility to find new acquaintances.[41]

Second, a move to the city generally entailed giving up the security of a community, where one was culturally well integrated and enjoyed the right to support, for the financial opportunities of industrial work.[42] Deaf migration often carried the opposite connotations: rural deaf moved from productive integration to communicative integration. Due to the language barrier, deaf people in rural communities, where they lacked contact with other deaf people, had limited possibilities of communication with their immediate surroundings. On the other hand, they may well have had a place in the production, working for instance on the family farmstead. Some scholars have therefore deemed pre-industrial societies as better than capitalist societies with liberalized labour markets at accommodating deaf people, or indeed disabled people in general.[43] This analysis fails to distinguish between integration in the production, and communicative integration. The gravity of this is demonstrated by Habermas' concept of "life-world", and his juxtaposition of this realm with the "system". The life-world is a web of unquestioned presuppositions common to all "sane and normal"[44] adults. As such, it carries the spheres of culture, society, and personality, that is, the basic supply of knowledge and competence that enable individuals to understand each other and the world. This web is reproduced over generations through cultural heritage, social integration, and socialization of the individual. The medium of these processes of reproduction is language. For a single deaf person in a hearing environment, the access to these reproduction processes was therefore severely limited, or completely hindered. Interaction with such a person was only possible by non-communicative means, by power or money – what Habermas calls the "system."[45]

---

41 "Mitteilungen," TsF 7 (1895), p. 28; "Vereinswesen," TsF 11 (1892), p. 42.
42 Which may have made migration unattractive to many people with disabilities. *cf.* Walter Fandrey, *Krüppel, Idioten, Irre: zur Sozialgeschichte behinderter Menschen in Deutschland*, (Stuttgart: Silberburg-Verlag, 1990), p. 97.
43 Jane Berger, "Uncommon Schools. Institutionalizing Deafness in Early-Nineteenth-Century America," in *Foucault and the Government of Disability,* ed. Shelley Tremain (Ann Arbor, MI: University of Michigan Press, 2005), pp. 160, 163-164; Branson and Miller, *Damned for Their Difference*, pp. 3-12.
44 "wache und normale", Alfred Schütz and Thomas Luckmann, *Strukturen der Lebenswelt* (Frankfurt am Main: Suhrkamp, 1979), quoted in Habermas, *Theorie des Kommunikativen Handelns,* Vol. 2., p. 198.
45 Ibid., pp. 198-199, 208-209, 212-213.

This explains why the production integration possibly enjoyed by deaf people in pre-industrial and/or rural societies was unsatisfactory. Inclusion in the production, without access to the reproduction processes of the life-world, is integration only from the perspective of the system of production. From the cultural perspective, the isolation is nearly absolute. Here emerges another motivation specific to the migration of deaf people: In the cities, where there were larger numbers of deaf people, and in and surrounding schools and asylums, a deaf person could engage in signed communication and thereby enjoy cultural integration. Deaf migration can in this sense be understood as an escape from an existence deprived of all but its instrumental value.

Vehicles of Community Formation: The Schools

The key role played by educational institutions, especially residential schools, for the formation of deaf communities has been emphasised by most scholars in Deaf History.[46] From the previous chapter, we are familiar with the outreach of the deaf education system in imperial Germany, as well as with the distribution of residential schools in proportion to day schools. No evidence implies that the schools played a less vital role for the deaf in Germany than elsewhere; to designate them main contributing factors in deaf group formation would most likely be correct.

Still, it does not suffice merely to conclude that schools attracted deaf children and brought them together. To understand the dynamics of the deaf group formations, it must be asked what the specific function of the schools was. Gathering individuals with hearing loss in one locality is not specific to the school system; rather, migration is the decisive factor and the school a mere motive for migration. The role of the schools did, however, go beyond their function as meeting places.

A substantial part of the German deaf shared the experience of deaf school, and their numbers steadily increased. At the end of the 19th century, several generations had passed through special schools for deaf children. The schools were constant locations where a chain of deaf individuals succeeded each other. Opportunity to build a group identity, including the transmission of cultural values and the myths of a shared history, was thus made available to those with access to special schools. The normative function of the education system for the formation of *bürgerliche* values has been touched upon above. The teachers at

---

46   *Cf.* for instance Baynton, *Forbidden Signs,* pp. 3-4; Van Cleve and Crouch, *A Place of their Own,* p. 10; Quartararo, *Deaf Identity and Social Images,* pp. 36, 99-100.

the institutions for deaf education were, even if lower ranking, *Bürger* with a certain cultural capital. Regardless of their individual backgrounds, deaf schoolchildren were brought up in an environment that was ruled by these values. The connections to the church and the state also ensured their socialisation to loyal subjects.

On the other hand, the upbringing in an institution was the opposite of the family ideals of the *Bürger*. The deaf schoolchildren were socialised in a setting built not on emotional ties, but on rational, often ultimately state-governed, policy. There was no intimate sphere at the school, from which the pupils could have emerged as *hommes*. Although the schools provided them with the prerequisites for entering the bourgeois public sphere – they were educated and as a result of school efforts also able to earn a living and acquire property – they were unable to fulfil the requirement of being private people. In the latter part of *Structural Transformation*, Habermas notices that a similar process has undermined the bourgeois public sphere as a whole. Public institutions, especially the state, have increasingly taken over the socialization of children and young people, diminishing the private sphere.[47] This process began earlier for deaf people than for the rest of the population, as the state or semi-public institutions took over the responsibility for their upbringing from the 18th century onward.

Still, the deaf people who were excluded from these institutions most likely outnumbered the educated deaf. Due to lack of sources, it cannot be determined exactly how many deaf people had received special education, but it is certain that the insufficiently educated and uneducated persons remained a substantial fraction of the deaf throughout the period studied.[48] As a rule, physical and mental health and adequate intellectual capability was required of the children entering schools for the deaf. If, at a later date, the child did not fulfil the expectations and failed to benefit from the education, he or she could be sent home.[49] The evaluation of intellectual capability was based above all on the

---

47   Habermas, Strukturwandel der Öffentlichkeit, p. 188.
48   For instance, a mere third of Prussia's deaf children in school-age were taught at special instititions in 1874. One-fifth were taught in mainstream schools, and the rest remained without education. *No 55, Haus der Abgeordneten. 12. Legislaturperiode. II. Session. 1875,* GStA PrK HA 1, Rep. 151 I C 8121, p. 14.
49   *Cf.* statutes of the Prussian deaf-mute asylums in C.W. Saegert, *Das Taubstummen-Bildungswesen in Preußen,* (Berlin: Verlag der Expedition des Taubstummenfreundes, 1874), pp. 42, 54 [GStA PrK I HA Rep. 77, Tit. 3973, Nr. 1, Bd. 1].

children's talent for spoken language.⁵⁰ Thus, deficient oral skills could lead to the deprivation of education.

Some parents were reluctant to send their deaf children to school. The teachers and authorities sometimes interpreted this as an expression of self-interest from parents who exploited their children's labour, or even the compassion they evoked in order to receive benefits. Others were sympathetic with the unwillingness to send children away to spend several years far from the parents. Deaf schools sometimes had the reputation of maltreating the children, which also contributed to some parents' refusal to enrol their children.⁵¹

Scholarships and placements free of charge were available to some children in particularly needy situations. However, families with too high incomes or assets to be covered by these measures could still find the cost of sending a child to boarding school unmanageable, especially when considering the withdrawal of his or her contribution to the household. Children from wealthy families, on the other hand, were sometimes provided with private tutoring instead of being placed in a school alongside other deaf.⁵²

Furthermore, reports of the Royal Deaf-Mute Asylum in Berlin from the first decades of the 19th century displayed a distribution of more than twice as many male as female students, suggesting that parents might be more willing to send their sons to school than their daughters.⁵³ The association of household chores with femininity meant that girls could more easily be accommodated in the parental homes, performing domestic chores. This was a common life option for women with disabilities.⁵⁴ As the century passed, the gender distribution was evened out and by 1901 corresponded with the slight over-representation of men and boys among the 'deaf-mutes.'⁵⁵

---

50   Walther, *Handbuch*, pp. 19-20.
51   Rechenschafts-Bericht des Vereines zur Förderung des Taubstummen-Unterrichtes in Niederbayern für das Kalenderjahr 1877, BayHStA Rep MInn Nr. 46119; Huschens, *Bedeutung der Taubstummenbildung*, p. 111; *Jahresbericht Paulinen-Pflege zu Winnenden*, pp. 19-20, StA Ludwigsburg, E 191, Bü 5055.
52   *Cf.* below, p. on page 209.
53   Grasshoff to the Schulkollegium der Provinz Brandenburg, 20 December 1834, BLHA Rep.34, Nr. 1312.
54   Fandrey, *Krüppel, Idioten, Irre*, p. 96.
55   Josef Radomski, *Statistische Nachrichten über die Taubstummen-Anstalten Deutschlands und deren Lehrkräfte pro 1901*, Vol. V., (Kommissionsverlag Friedrich Ebbeke: Posen, 1901), p. 18; *cf.* Engelmann, "Die Taubstummen," p. 15.

Thus, the socialization that took place at institutions for deaf education was not available to all, and not to just any, deaf children. Several factors co-decided whether or not a child came in question for school enrolment. Gender and class played a part in the decisions, as did school policies that favoured children with no disabilities other than deafness, and those with an aptitude for lip reading and articulation. However, the personal attitudes of parents and the school resources at a particular moment could also be decisive, so that the selection verged on the arbitrary. The main characteristic was that only some were chosen, and many were left out. Exclusion from deaf school was not merely deprivation of an education; it also meant exclusion from the socialization that formed a set of shared experiences among deaf people, beyond their sensory disposition.

Those who remained outside the school system were by no means eligible participants in the bourgeois public sphere. Their possibilities of acquiring education and property were slim. Thus, deaf people were caught up in a catch-22-like dilemma. The only way for them to achieve the educational and financial status expected of the *bourgeois*, deprivatized them so that they could not be *hommes*.

Reactions to 'Deaf Migration'

Although the educational system prompted the probably most significant part of deaf migration, Eduard Walther denounced moves initiated by the deaf persons themselves. He claimed that deaf adults were often prone to migration, which he ascribed to their "wandering drive" (*Wandertrieb*).[56] This concept appeared in psychiatric literature at the end of the 19th century as a pathological explanation for homelessness. The desire to migrate was understood as part of, or symptomatic to, disorders such as psychopathy or dementia.[57] Using the term for describing the mobility of deaf people disconnected them from the socio-economic context of general labour migration and urbanisation. Instead, it appeared as a part of the pathology of 'deaf-mutism'.

Walther did however add that the desire among young people to see the world was understandable, also when it appeared among the deaf. With reference to their difficult situation on the labour market, he nevertheless recommended they be discouraged from migrating. Only few masters were willing to employ

---

56 Walther, *Handbuch*, p. 719.
57 Christoph Kellinghaus, Wohnungslos und psychisch Krank. Eine Problemgruppe zwischen den Systemen. Konzepte – empirische Daten – Hilfsansätze (Münster: Lit Verlag, 2000), pp. 23-24.

deaf assistants, so, in the lack of work, the migration may become wandering and the deaf end up as beggars or criminals. According to Walther, such morally degenerated deaf gathered around the schools in search of assistance, but only seldom could they obtain help from the teachers. In case of necessary migration, he argued, deaf people should not venture on their journey alone, but seek the help of acquaintances or deaf clubs.[58]

At times, deaf authors also denounced the 'wandering drive' of other deaf, although some focused on structural problems, mainly poor education, as important causes of the problem.[59] On the other hand, prominent deaf persons presented as role models often had migrant backgrounds. These include Albin Maria Watzulik, who was of Hungarian origin, G. A. Claudius, who spent several years wandering through Germany and Austria after completing his training as a printer, and August Schenck, who led an inconsistent life, changing places and occupations several times.[60]

Alongside the discouragement from migrating, the deaf organizations tried to ease the situation for those who chose to move anyway. However, assisting migrants put significant pressure on the deaf clubs at times of widespread unemployment. In 1908, the deaf clubs in Berlin joined in a declaration in the TsF, warning deaf people of coming to the city. Due to the high unemployment, the clubs could no longer help newcomers.[61]

Wandering in search of employment was associated with poverty, and the mobile proletariat was often understood as a threat to society and individuals. Teachers and deaf leaders both wanted to keep deaf people away from joining

---

58   Walther, *Handbuch*, p. 719; see also a similar argument in Huschens, *Bedeutung der Taubstummen-Bildung*, pp. 80, 92-93; and in the Hamburg School for the Deaf, as quoted by Groschek, *Unterwegs in eine Welt des Verstehens*, p. 81.

59   "Die Berufswahl der Taubstummen," TC 10 (1887), pp. 109-110; Julius Neuschloss, "Aus dem Berufsleben der Taubstummen," TC 2 (1887), pp. 14-15; Albin Maria Watzulik, "Ein Capitel zum Buchdruckerelend," TC 3 (1888), pp. 26-27; idem, "Noch einmal der Buchdruckerberuf," TC 12 (1901); W. Hollaender, "Das Buchdruckergewerbe," TC 10 (1895), pp. 113-114; P. Junghans, "Das Geschäftsleben der Taubstummen," TC 3 (1894), p. 27.

60   These three gentlemen were all prominent in deaf organizations and/or the deaf press. I shall return to them below. Kurt Laschinsky, "Albin Maria Watzulik," *Deutsche Gehörlosen-Zeitschrift Die Stimme*, 5 (1930), [n.p.]; J. Ernsberger jr., obituary of G. A. Claudius, NZT 2 (1912), p. 9; Obituary of August Schenck, TC 12 (1892), pp. 144-145.

61   "Warnung," TsF 4 (1908), p. 19.

the proletariat and the poor, which explains why they resisted certain types of migration, while contributing to, or engaging in, other kinds.

The Berlin Royal Asylum and its Alumni

Given this context, the question arises if and how networks consisting of deaf people appeared in the urban centers. There are few sources to early group formations by deaf people in Germany. We know that there were schools that brought deaf children together already in the 18th century, but to what extent and how they socialised with each other as adults is difficult to tell. The following section is an attempt to relate the evidence of such a group to the social context of early- and mid 19th century Berlin.

In 1808, French troops ended two years of occupation, and the Prussian court returned to Berlin. This was followed by a cultural upheaval in the city, which vitalized and transformed the public sphere, above all by making it more public. A university was founded, the first daily commercial newspaper went into print, and several more or less formal sociable and intellectual circles emerged, all of these novelties mutually commenting on and affecting each other.[62] The intellectuals and artists, the aristocrats and the *Bürger* had numerous opportunities to engage in convivial and cultured conversation. From the 1820s, cafés opened in the city center offering their guests papers and more or less open debating, in addition to refreshments. Each café had its own character, so that there were meeting places for every grouping, from the leftist to the conservatives, even for women, as long as they were reasonably well off. In the 1830s and -40s, the discussions became increasingly politicised.[63] In the private homes of cultured ladies, the salons, members of the different social groups could join in aesthetic or political conversation. Since the late 18th century, aristocrats, *Bürger*, and artists, not to mention men and women, there experienced a temporary upheaval of the strict hierarchies otherwise separating them. The blending of people of different backgrounds was one of the traits that gave the salons their open and tolerant character.[64]

---

62   Theodore Ziolowski, *Berlin. Aufstieg einer Kulturmetropole um 1810* (Stuttgart: Klett-Cotta, 2002), pp. 22-26; 94-99; 162-175; 221-228.

63   Ilja Mieck, "Von der Reformzeit zur Revolution," in *Geschichte Berlins*. Vol. I.: *Von der Frühgeschichte zur Industrialisierung*, ed. Wolfgang Ribbe, 3rd Ed. (Berlin: Berliner Wissenschafts-Verlag, 2002), pp. 588-590.

64   Petra Wilhelmy, *Der Berliner Salon im 19. Jahrhundert* (Berlin: Walter de Gruyter, 1989), pp. 433-450.

At the same time, Berlin was a city characterized by extreme social differences. Military personnel made up for a significant part of the population, although their relative numbers declined over the first half of the 19th century. The *Bürger* were a minority compared to the many journeymen, servants, and poor. The craftspeople still outnumbered the industrial workers, but the majority of them, including most masters, lived on the verge of poverty. Adaptation to new market structures, specialization, and modernization allowed only a minority to ascend to shop- or manufacture owners.[65] An organized movement of the working class was still non-existent. Craftsmen of a somewhat better position joined to form an organization in 1844, aiming at cultural and vocational improvement of the members.[66]

Centrally located in Berlin was the Royal Deaf-Mute Asylum, founded in 1788 as one of the first educational facilities for deaf children in Germany by none less than Samuel Heinicke's son-in-law Ernst Adolph Eschke. The Royal Asylum played a central part in German deaf education. In addition to educating deaf children from all parts of Prussia, it also trained aspiring teachers of the deaf. Through this assignment, the methods practiced at the Royal Asylum had a normative influence on other institutions. It was supposed to develop and practice a state-of-the-art deaf education. This was later formally regulated, as the Asylum acquired the special status as a model institution for other schools.[67]

Eschke's engagement in deaf education was motivated by philanthropic as well as philological interests, making him a typical representative of the manualist teachers of the deaf in the romantic era.[68] Signs were an unquestioned part of the education. The first teacher he employed was a deaf former pupil, Johann Karl Ludwig Habermaß. After Eschke's death in 1811, the third teacher Ludwig Grasshoff, who was hearing, was promoted to director. Although he introduced the first restrictions to the use of Sign, the school still employed deaf teachers, and articulation played a relatively minor part in the curriculum.[69]

---

65   Mieck, "Von der Reformzeit zur Revolution," pp. 414-419, 487, 542-546.
66   Ibid., pp. 590-592.
67   Eduard Walther, Die Königliche Taubstummenanstalt zu Berlin in ihrer geschichtlichen Entwickelung und gegenwärtigen Verfassung. Ein Beitrag zur Geschichte des Taubstummen-Bildungswesens in Preussen. Festschrift zur Feier des hundertjährigen Bestehen der Anstalt (Berlin: Elwin Staude, 1888), pp. 7-13, 32-34, 65-66, 131, 199.
68   As characterised by Baynton in *Forbidden Signs*, p. 9.
69   Wolff, "Selbstverständlich Gebärdensprache!"; idem, "Die Willkür der Zeichen".

In the first decades of the 19th century, the school expanded each year but could still not accommodate all applicants. Lists of pupils reveal a wide range of social backgrounds: orphans of unknown descent, children of day-labourers, of skilled workers and petty shopkeepers, as well as of bourgeoisie and aristocracy. Most pupils were Protestant, but the school accommodated a smaller number of Jewish and Catholic children as well.[70] With some fluctuation from year to year, male pupils remained in the majority throughout the first half of the century.[71] In addition to the academic subjects, the pupils were also trained in drawing and – in the case of the girls – feminine handicrafts. No large-scale industrial education took place at the Royal Asylum, although individual pupils were trained in lithographing and bookbinding. The qualification in a vocation nevertheless largely remained outside of the school, where the Prussian 'deaf-mute bonus' helped placing the pupils in apprenticeships.[72]

During this period the Royal Asylum distinguished itself by educating several eventually successful deaf professionals and artists. Habermaß, who was mentioned above, was followed by Carl Wilke, who was enrolled as a pupil in 1807, and remained there as a teacher for the rest of his life.[73] Further alumni of

---

70 Between 1845 and 1868, the school employed a rabbi to teach the Jewish pupils in religion. Walther, *Die Königliche Taubstummenanstalt,* p. 188; From 1873, the Israelite Deaf Asylum in Berlin-Weissensee catered to the needs of the Jewish deaf. Vera Bernd and Nicola Gallinger (Eds.), *"Öffne deine Hand für die Stummen." Die Geschichte der israelitischen Taubstummen-Anstalt Berlin-Weissensee 1873 bis 1942* (Berlin: Transit, 1993).

71 Zöglinge und Schüler, pp. 74-75, Sämmtliche Zöglinge und Schüler des Taubstummen Instituts im Jahre 1810, pp. 217-220, BLHA Pr Br. Rep.34 Nr. 1304; Sämmtliche Zöglinge und Schüler des Königlichen Taubstummen Institut im Jahre 1812, Sämmtliche Zöglinge und Schüler des Königlichen Taubstummen Instituts im Jahre 1815, Sämmtliche Zöglinge und Schüler des Taubstummen-Instituts im Jahre 1818, BLHA Pr Br. Rep.34 Nr. 1305; Jahres-Liste der Königlichen Taubstummen-Anstalt, 1822, BLHA Pr Br. Rep.34 Nr. 1307; Jahres Liste der Königl. Zöglinge, Freischüler und Expectanten in dem Königl. Taubstummen-Institute zu Berlin im Jahre 1826, BLHA Pr Br. Rep.34 Nr. 1310; Grasshoff to Schulkollegium der Provinz Brandenburg, 20 December 1834, Grasshoff to Schulkollegium der Provinz Brandenburg, 31 December 1838, BLHA Pr Br. Rep.34 Nr. 1312.

72 Walther, *Die Kgl. Taubstummenanstalt,* pp. 29-30, 46, 164-165, 186-188.

73 Sämmtliche Zöglinge und Schüler des Königlichen Taubstummen Instituts im Jahre 1815, BLHA Pr Br. Rep.34 Nr. 1305; Verleih des Roten Adlerordens an Carl Wilke,

the first half of the 19th century, namely Daniel Senß, Carl Ferdinand von Schulzendorff and Eduard Fürstenberg, pursued careers within civil administration.[74] A handful of former pupils attended the Royal Academy of Arts and later achieved some degree of recognition as artists. This tendency continued over the years, so that a succession of male pupils graduated from the Royal Asylum and proceeded to the Royal Academy of Arts during the first half of the 19th century. The chart below shows how individuals who did not attend the one institution at the same time, might have attended the other together (fig. 5).

Carl Staël von Holstein probably did not encounter Adolph Siebert in the Royal Asylum classroom, but they later studied together under Wach. Wilhelm Devrient, who protrudes as the only one who did not study under Wach, was nevertheless certain to have known Carl von Dunker from school.

Thus, in addition to the Royal Asylum, the Royal Academy offered a further space for deaf men to become acquainted. Through the Royal Asylum, the artists were connected to other successful deaf men. Undeniably, most of them came from privileged backgrounds. Some were aristocrats, others, like Eduard Fürstenberg, came from wealthy families.[75] Wilhelm Devrient belonged to a well-known family with several famous actors, which played a vital role in Berlin's cultural elite during the entire 19th century.[76]

---

gehörloser Taubstummenlehrer in Berlin, GStA PrK 1 HA Rep. 89 22577; Saegert-Heitefuß, "Carl Heinrich Wilke," TsF 3 (1876), p. 9.

74   Johann Samuel Ersch and J. G. Gruber, *Allgemeine Encyclopädie der Wissenschaften und Künste in alphabetischer Folge von genannten Schrifts bearbeitet*, Vol. 38. (Leipzig: Greiditsch, 1843), p. 68; Jochen Muhs, "Eduard Fürstenberg," pp. 422-423; August Schenck, "Daniel Heinrich Senß," TsF 5 (1888), p. 19.

75   Jochen Muhs, "Eduard Fürstenberg," p. 422.

76   *Cf.* Julius Bab, Die Devrients. Geschichte einer deutschen Theaterfamilie (Berlin: Georg Stilke, 1932).

Figure 5: Deaf painters and their stays at the Royal Deaf-Mute Asylum and the Royal Academy of Arts.

Name	Lifetime	Attended the Royal Deaf-Mute Asylum	Studied at the Academy	Professor at the Academy	Participated in Academy exhibitions
Wilhelm Devrient	1799/1800-1871	1805-1815	1815-1821	Buchhorn	1820-1866[77]
Carl von Dunker	1808-1858	1814->1822	1826	Wach	1824-1840[78]
Carl von Staël-Holstein	1809/11-?	1824-?	1829-1840		1834-1840[79]
Wilhelm von Goszycki	1817-?	1823-1836	?		1840-1860[80]
Adolf Siebert	1806-1832	1815->1822	1820-23, 1826-28[81]		-

As artists and civil servants, these deaf men were part of the classes that constituted Berlin's bourgeois public sphere. They were educated and propertied enough to be able to enjoy a visit to one of the many cafés, and with their personal connections and artistic renown would also fit in the circles of the salon guests. However, there is little evidence of them appearing in these contexts.[82]

---

77 Sämmtliche Zöglinge und Schüler des Königlichen Taubstummen Instituts im Jahre 1815, BLHA Pr Br. Rep.34 Nr. 1305; Käte Gläser, *Berliner Porträtisten 1820-1850. Versuch einer Katalogisierung* (Berlin: Verlag für Kunstwissenschaft, 1929), p. 22.

78 Jahres-Liste der Königlichen Taubstummen-Anstalt, 1822, BLHA Pr Br. Rep.34 Nr. 1307; Gläser, *Berliner Porträtisten*, p. 23.

79 Jahres-Liste der Königlichen Taubstummen-Anstalt, 1822, BLHA Pr Br. Rep.34 Nr. 1307; Gläser, *Berliner Porträtisten*, p. 75; Ulrich Thieme and Felix Becker, *Allgemeines Lexikon der bildenden Künstler von der Antike bis zur Gegenwart*, Vol. 31., ed. Hans Vollmer (Leipzig: E.A. Seemann, 1937), p. 442.

80 Goszicki [sic] to the King, 26 December 1825, Altenstein to the King, 24 May 1836, Note, Berlin, 4 June 1836, GStA PrK I. HA Rep.89 Nr. 22577; Gläser, *Berliner Porträtisten*, p. 29.

81 Jahres-Liste der Königlichen Taubstummen-Anstalt, 1822, BLHA Pr Br. Rep.34 Nr. 1307; Gläser, *Berliner Porträtisten*, p. 74.

82 In a necrology of Habermaß, he was claimed to have had "access to the cultured circles of the residence", "Zutritt in die geistreichen Zirkel der Residenz". Friedrich

Visiting cafés leaves few or no traces in written sources, but the visit to salons can often be reconstructed. In a directory of guests to the Berlin salons, none of the men appear.[83]

Through the education at the Royal Asylum, these men were however also connected to members of the lower classes. The Berlin tailor's assistant Johann Friedrich Christoph Hartnuss fathered at least ten children with his wife Maria during the first two decades of the 19th century.[84] This family raised quite a lot of attention, since several of the children were deaf. Exactly how many is uncertain – according to one account, all of the sons, six in number, were deaf.[85] This figure might be slightly overstated, but it is certain that three of Hartnuss's sons, Wilhelm, Heinrich, and Karl, attended the Royal Asylum. The Hartnuss family was under considerable financial strain and received poor relief. After their unusual situation was brought to the attention of the mayor and city council, the boys were taught at the Royal Asylum free of charge.[86] Educating them proved successful, as shown by the annual reports of the school in which the Hartnuss brothers were repeatedly mentioned as especially talented pupils.[87] Through education, not only they, but also the entire family appeared to have improved

---

August Schmidt and Bernhardt Friedrich Voigt, *Neuer Nekrolog des Deutschen*, Vol. 4. (1826), Part 2. (Ilmenau: Bernhard Friedrich Voigt, 1828), p. 847.

83 Wilhelmy, *Berliner Salon*, pp. 892-959.

84 *V.* Taufbuch der Jerusalem-Gemeinde 1800 p. 348 Nr. 305; Taufbuch der Marien-Gemeinde 1802 p. 752 Nr.14; 1805 p. 56 Nr. 220; 1807 p. 133 Nr. 581; 1810 p. 234 Nr. 1371; 1812 p. 63 Nr. 378; 1814 p. 148 Nr. 113; 1816 p. 254 Nr. 127, 128; 1817 p. 327 Nr. 265, ELAB.

85 Paul Elsner, "Ueber Taubstumme und ihre Erziehung," Lecture held on the 16th of March 1861 in the "Ohrenclub", Berlin. *Archiv für Ohrenheilkunde* 5 (1870), p. 174. However, the church records list only five sons born to the couple. *V.* above.

86 Oberbürgermeister, Bürgermeister and Rath, Berlin, 10 October 1809, BLHA Rep. 34 Nr. 1304 Ministerium des Innern, Zweite Abteilung, Sign. Nocolovius, to the Constistorium, 15 August 1816, BLHA Rep. 34 Nr. 1305; Albrecht to Grasshoff, 2 May 1816, Grasshoff to Herr Geheimer Kabinetsrath [Albrecht], 7 May 1816, GStA PrK I.HA Rep.89 Nr. 22577.

87 Zöglinge und Freischüler der Königl. Taubstummen-Anstalt, welche durch Ordnungs-Liebe, Folgsamkeit, Fleiß und Geschicklichkeit im Etatsjahre 1818 vorzüglich ausgezeichnet haben, BLHA Rep.34, Nr. 1305; Zöglinge und Freischüler der Königl. Taubstummen-Anstalt, welche durch Ordnungs-Liebe, Folgsamkeit, Fleiß und Geschicklichkeit im Etatsjahre 1819 vorzüglich ausgezeichnet haben, BLHA Rep.34, Nr. 1306; Grasshoff, Berlin, 3 January 1821, BLHA Rep.34, Nr. 1307.

their social position, at least on the immaterial side. The boys attended school alongside upper-class children and excelled at an education of a higher standard than might have been available to hearing children in their situation.[88] Out of the relationship between the Hartnuss family and the Royal Asylum, the former achieved to build a network in influential circles. When Friedrich Christoph Hartnuss and his wife-to-be christened their first-born in 1802, the godparents and witnesses were two workers, one married woman without any specific title, and one merchant. At the christening of their twin sons in 1816, the witnesses included the Upper Consistory Councillor Nolte, who supervised the administration of the Royal Asylum. Further witnesses were Karolina Eschke, widow of Ernst Adolf Eschke and daughter of Samuel Heinicke, and Mrs. Dunker, mother of one of the Hartnuss brothers' more privileged fellow students.[89] However, there is no evidence that a material levelling of any significance took place at the Royal Asylum. In spite of their remarkable talent, it appears as if none of the Hartnuss brothers reached beyond the class of craftsmen they came from.[90]

At the occasion of the centennial anniversary of the Royal Asylum, August Schenck published a series of biographies on notable alumni in the two leading

---

88 What options would have been available for the Hartnuss brothers, had they been hearing, can of course only be speculated upon. However, their family was obviously disadvantaged. An idea of the limited outreach and strained conditions of the Berlin schools for the working class and the poor can be extracted from Werner Lemm et al., *Schulgeschichte in Berlin* (Berlin: Volk und Wissen, 1987), pp. 58-63; Wilhelm Richter, *Berliner Schulgeschichte. Von den mittelalterlichen Anfängen bis zum Ende der Weimarer Republik* (Berlin: Colloquium Verlag, 1981), pp. 52-55.

89 Taufbuch der Marien-Gemeinde, 1802 p. 752, Nr. 14; 1816, p. 254 Nr. 127, p. 128, ELAB; *cf.* Sämmtliche Zöglinge und Schüler des Taubstummen-Instituts im Jahre 1818, BLHA Rep.34 Nr. 1305; "Heinicke, Samuel," in *Neue Deutsche Biographie,* Vol. 8 (Berlin: Dunker & Humblot, 1968), p. 303; *Handbuch über den Königlich Preussischen Hof und Staat für das Jahr 1805* (Berlin; Johann Friedrich Unger, n. d.), p. 342; Bericht über das Königl. Taubstummen-Institut zu Berlin. Nolte, 7 September 1809, BLHA Rep. 34 Nr. 1304.

90 V. J. W. Boicke (Ed.), Allgemeiner Wohnungsanzeiger für Berlin auf das Jahr 1831: enthaltend: die Wohnungsnachweisungen aller öffentlichen Institute und Privat-Unternehmungen, aller Hausbesitzer, Beamteten, Kaufleute, Künstler, Gewerbetreibenden und einen eigenen Hausstand Führenden, in Alphabetischer Ordnung (Berlin, 1831), p. 241; ibid (1840), p. 139; ibid (1851), p. 171.

deaf periodicals.[91] In this series, he described an intensive sociability between Royal Asylum alumni during the first half of the 19th century. According to Schenck, some of them would regularly gather in the homes of Heinrich Hartnuss and Wilhelm Devrient to fraternize in Sign and thereby satisfy their need for sociability and intellectual stimulation. Apart from the Hartnuss brothers, he mentioned all of the Royal Academy artists listed above except for Siebert – which can be explained by his early emigration and premature death.[92] He also named Carl Wilke, the sculptor von Kalnaffi, Heinrich von Schöning, and the son of the Governor General in Moscow, von Staal.[93] If Schenck's account is correct, this group could be designated a subaltern counterpublic in 19th century Berlin. The bracketing of class boundaries would in that case be remarkable. Not only did it include aristocracy as well as *Bürger* and artists, but even the Hartnuss family, which belonged to the lower ranks of society. However, there are no other sources to this than Schenck's brief articles, written several years after the gatherings had ceased. His description of deaf sociability reminds of his contemporary deaf community, to which he also explicitly compared the Hartnuss and Devrient households.[94] Notwithstanding, it can be confirmed that nearly all of the individuals Schenck mentioned knew each other directly or through common acquaintances. They were part of a network, although it is uncertain how this network was used.

Furthermore, Schenk's texts are in themselves an indication of the importance of this network – apparently, these men left a legacy so strong that Schenck, himself without any immediate personal connection to them, reproduced the memory of their convivial gatherings. There was a collective memory of them and their friendship, which was reproduced not within their social class or their family, but within deaf folklore.

---

91 August Schenck, "Koryphäen einer Jubilarin," TsF 5 (1888), pp. 18-19, TsF 8 (1888), p. 32, TsF 9 (1888), p. 36, TsF 10 (1888), p. 40, TsF 11 (1888), pp. 43-44; idem, "Die taubstummen Koryphäen einer in nächster Zeit jubilierender Anstalt," in TC 5 (1888), pp. 54-56, TC 6 (1888), pp. 66-67; TC 10 (1888), pp. 112-114.

92 Gläser, Berliner Porträtisten, p. 74.

93 August Schenck, "Koryphäen einer Jubilarin," TsF 5 (1888), pp. 18-19, TsF 10 (1888) p. 40, TsF 11 (1888), pp. 43-44.

94 August Schenck, "Koryphäen einer Jubilarin," TsF 10 (1888), p. 40, TsF 11 (1888), p. 43.

A Deaf Topography of the City

Now we shall for a while suspend the examples of individual relationships and instead turn to the city as a setting for deaf group formation. The following section is a survey of urban spaces that could aid this group formation, as well as spaces created as parts of the formation processes.

We have already seen examples of employers and craft masters especially willing to employ deaf workers or apprentices. In such environments, the communication barrier could be overcome. Not only was sociability between deaf colleagues furthered, but the employer and hearing colleagues also had the possibility of learning Sign Language.[95] As mentioned, the bonus system, help from schools in the employment procedure, and lower wages offered incentives to employ and train deaf persons. On the other hand, masters experienced the interaction with deaf apprentices as demanding.[96] Had, however, the communication barrier once been crossed, educating or employing another deaf person would not be as troublesome. Therefore, it is not surprising that there are examples in Berlin of masters training several deaf apprentices over the years.[97]

Some deaf reached the status where they themselves could train or employ others, and then deliberately recruited deaf people. In Hamburg, deaf lithographer John Pacher owned a flourishing printing shop where he employed several deaf workers.[98] As a deaf capitalist, he might be an exceptional example. However, in Berlin, deaf tailor master Johann Lapke applied for and received a bonus for training a deaf boy in 1910.[99] Lapke was not the first deaf master to train a deaf apprentice, but rather an example of what seems to have been a not unusual practice. Already in the second issue of TsF, a deaf shoemaker advertised for a deaf apprentice. Similar notices, offering training or employment,

---

95 Below, the claim by a witness in the case of the Ponholz vagrant, that he had learned to Sign from fellow workers who were deaf, is an individual example showing that working together could be a bridge between hearing-oral and deaf-manual persons. V. p. 129.
96 V. p. 74.
97 See applications from Richard Spindler and Schneider & Ziegler Buchbinderei 1910 and 1911 LA Berlin, A Pr. Br. Rep. 030 Nr. 1886.
98 Fischer, Wempe, Lamprecht, and Seeberger, "John E. Pacher", pp. 126-131, Groschek, *Unterwegs in einer Welt des Verstehens,* pp. 77-78.
99 V. application by Johann Lapke (1910), LA Berlin, A Pr. Br. Rep. 030 Nr. 1886.

would be published frequently over the years.[100] Whether or not they resulted in contracts cannot be proven, but they are evidence that deaf masters could and were willing to train deaf youth in crafts, or to employ other deaf.

Other business owners sometimes advertised in the deaf press looking to attract deaf customers.[101] The declaration that the owner or employees were deaf implied that the reader could conduct his or her business in Sign Language. Alternatively, the choice to advertise in a deaf periodical at least suggested a friendly attitude towards, and some familiarity with, deaf people. This may also have been attractive to deaf consumers.

Through these advertisements, it was possible for the reader to immediately find businesses and meeting places with other deaf, or at least signers, even in an unfamiliar city. From 1908 onward, this type of information was gathered in the *Taubstummenkalender*. This was an address book of German deaf clubs and institutions combined with miscellaneous information such as measurements, a small dictionary, and biographies of famous teachers. In the back, it had several pages with advertisements, mostly of taverns. Equipped with this book, a deaf traveller was able to navigate the German landscape of deaf clubs, deaf-friendly businesses, signed religious services, schools, and asylums.[102]

Taverns formed a special subcategory among the deaf press advertisers. It appears as if in many places, certain establishments would emerge as hubs of sociability between deaf people. How common this was is naturally impossible to determine, since informal gathering places leave few traces in the sources. However, the advertisements in the *Taubstummenkalender* show that such taverns existed not only in metropolises like Berlin, but also in minor towns.[103]

---

100   Advertisement by Hoffmann, TsF 2 (1872), p. 16; *cf.* further advertisements, for instance by Weber, TsF 14 (1878), p. 52; "Offerte für taubst. Mädchen nach Hannover!", TsF 21 (1878), p. 82; advertisement by Otto Vollmar, TsF 25 (1893), p. 100, *cf.* below p. 202.

101   *V.* for instance adverstisements by the deaf ivory carver Rautenstein in TsF 3 (1874) p. 22. [*Cf.* "Taubstummen-Club 'Vorwärts' in Berlin," TsF 4 (1874), p. 24]; the brush maker Haury, TsF 10 (1875), p. 62; and dentist G. Bohne in Berlin, who had a deaf assistant, TsF 2 (1902), p. 8.

102   Max Härdtner (Ed.), *Deutscher Taubstummenkalender auf das Jahr...* (Leipzig: Hugo Dude, 1908-1922).

103   *Taubstummenkalender* (1909), pp. 141, 144.

Figure 6: Advertisements of cafés from the TsF.

From above: "Café Nuck [...] Gathering place for the deaf-mutes of Berlin. Beer 10 Pfennig. Cup of coffee 10 Pfennig. No tips. Particular room is reserved for deaf-mutes. We know the language of signs through long-standing interaction with deaf-mutes." "Club-Room of the deaf-mutes. Family café salon (Café Cirkus.) [...] Ample selection of newspapers. French billiard per hour 40 Pfennig. Chess and salta free of charge. Day and night warm meals." Source: TsF 11 (1900) p. 52; TsF 26 (1892) p. 108.

As with other business owners, some may have advertised simply out of a general sense of good will. Others, however, emphasised features that were supposed to especially attract deaf customers. This included subscribing to deaf periodicals, offering discounts to deaf people, or having deaf or signing staff.[104] These features suggested that deaf people were frequent guests in the establishments, something which was at times explicitly declared. The certainty that one would find other deaf people there was obviously a selling point for the cafés. The advertisements depicted here boast the opportunity to find deaf companions in the localities, even to fraternize in a separate 'deaf room', and to be served by signing staff (fig. 6).

Important was also to clearly state the reasonable prices. The deaf consumer targeted by most advertisements was presumed to have some money to spend on enjoyment, but still have to be careful with his expenses, so that he liked being able to calculate the cost before going. This type of establishments clearly dominated among the advertising taverns, but there were exceptions. In the 1909 *Taubstummenkalender*, not only working-class deaf people were addressed as potential customers. Some restaurants offered fine dining in a family-friendly atmosphere, obviously imagining deaf people with a more *bürgerlich* lifestyle as their target group.[105]

Guesthouses could also have important functions beyond the purely sociable. In the town of Nauen, deaf people frequented a certain tavern for several years. Thereby, the owner acquired the role as an intermediary in their contacts with authorities.[106] Also, many deaf clubs used taverns as their regular meeting places, a practice which was widespread among working-class clubs at the time. The barroom sociability helped constitute a masculine working-class culture, since members of the upper classes did not frequent the bars, and neither did women. Publicly consuming alcohol was regarded as masculine and distinctly working-class.[107]

An 1884 article in the *Illustrirte Zeitung*, a weekly newspaper characterized by its numerous and large illustrations, described the semi-informal meetings of deaf people at the Café Schiller in Vienna. It recommended the reader a visit to this venue on a Sunday afternoon, where he would be able to experience a most

---

104 "Theilnahme der Hörenden gegen Taubstumme," TsF 4 (1874), p. 24; advertisement for the "Café Ambrosius" in Berlin, which had deaf staff, TsF 22 (1876), p. 84; *v.* also fig. 7.

105 *Taubstummenkalender* (1909), pp. 139-152.

106 M. Nigrini, "Das Musterbild eines Taubstummenwirtes. (*Herr Restaurateur Clemens Kunze in Plauen i. V.*)" TC 11 (1897), pp. 121-122.

107 Lynn Abrams, *Worker's Culture in Imperial Germany. Leisure and Recreation in the Rheinland and Westphalia* (London: Routhledge, 1992), pp. 65, 86, 129; cf. *Taubstummenkalender* (1909), pp. 68-112.

extraordinary scene: Deaf people of all ages and diverse vocations met there to read papers, play games, but above all to converse in Sign. The anonymous author especially emphasised the *bürgerliche* characteristics of the guests, namely their compliance with gender stereotypes, nice dress, cleanliness, and apparent wealth. This, of course, matched their typically *bürgerlich* sociability. The etching accompanying the text underlined the impression (fig 7). As far as recognizable, the "deaf-mutes" look like refined ladies and gentlemen. In spite of the reference to the diversity of social positions, the portrayal is thus distinctly *bürgerlich.* Of course, the purpose was to astonish the reader with the existence of such a community, which makes it plausible that the affluence of the Viennese deaf has been overstated. The expectation seems to have been that deaf people *do not* have a *bürgerlich* lifestyle or position, and that is what made this crowd so remarkable.[108]

Figure 7: "Viennese pictures: In the Coffee-House of the Deaf-Mutes."

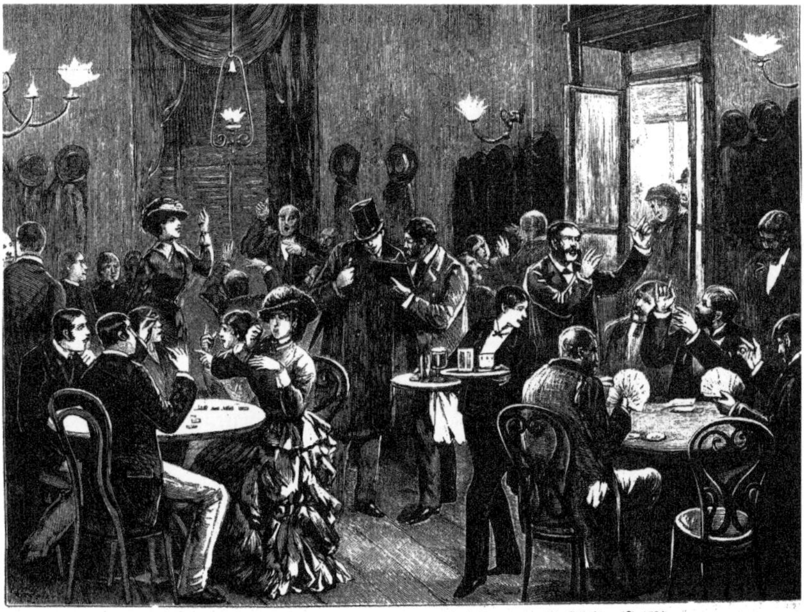

Wiener Bilder: Im Kaffeehaus der Taubstummen. Originalzeichnung von W. Grögler. (S. 173.)

(Source: *Illustrirte Zeitung* No 2122, March 1st 1884, p. 173)

108 "Wiener Bilder. Das Kaffeehaus der Taubstummen," *Illustrirte Zeitung,* No 2122, March 1st 1884, pp. 173, 176, 179.

Religious practice was an exception to the official policy towards Sign Language. In spite of some teacher protest, Sign Language was sanctioned in pastoral care.[109] In Berlin, there were Protestant, Catholic, and Jewish services held especially for deaf people.[110] Apart from the worship, the services were most likely also important meeting-places. They were an alternative to meeting at a tavern, a type of sociability that was open to other groups than the male, working-class clientele dominating the bar. On the other hand, they were less autonomous than the groups of barroom regulars, since they were organized by hearing people with a certain level of authority, often in close association with the education system.[111]

Thus groups of people emerged, who were united not only by deafness or the shared experience of deaf school, but also shared reference points in their trade masters or employers, places of worship, or leisure activities. A sort of 'deaf topography' of the city emerged, with establishments, be it schools, churches or tailor's shops, which carried a meaning particular to this group.[112]

Apart from public places such as these, a semi-public sphere of deaf households appeared. Deaf-deaf marriages were results of deaf sociability, but they were also bases for representation of this sociability. There are no data available on the extent to which deaf people chose deaf spouses, but it is clear that many desired such alliances. A sample of five volumes of the TsF from 1890-1910 contained sixty-five lonely-hearts advertisements. Although most did not explicitly write "deaf man/woman wants to marry deaf woman/man", the act of advertising for a partner in the TsF was a conscious way of finding someone with connections to the deaf community.[113] A couple of advertisements where deaf men requested acquaintance with hearing women added that she should have deaf parents.[114]

Marrying within a deaf network did not necessarily mean marrying a deaf person. The most notable example of this was the marriage between August

---

109 Gutzmann, *Streiflichter*, pp. 12-16.
110 Schorsch, Das Taubstummenwesen der Stadt Berlin, p. 62.
111 A more thorough analysis of the role of religious activities and organizations in the German deaf movement and deaf community had to be omitted here, however, an article on the subject is under preparation.
112 To determine if there were specific areas, in Berlin and in Germany, that can be considered deaf community hubs, further research will be necessary.
113 TsF 1890 (2 advertisements); 1895 (8 ditto); 1900: (26 ditto); 1905: (9 ditto); 1910: (20 ditto).
114 *V.* TsF 15 (1900), p. 72, and also TC 12 (1887), p. 143.

Schenck and Anna Fürstenberg. She was the daughter of Eduard Fürstenberg, the founder of the first deaf club, editor of the TsF, and the most dominant deaf leader in the history of the German Empire. Anna Schenck, née Fürstenberg, was not only a CODA, but also tightly associated with the deaf community and deaf movement by birth, profession and assignment. She acted as a Sign Language interpreter, ran a kindergarten for deaf children, and was herself also a leading figure in the deaf movement. Even before her marriage, she served on the board of a deaf women's club, and later held several high positions in associated organizations.[115] Although she was hearing, her marriage with deaf leader August Schenck undeniably took place within a context of deaf sociability. Another example was a marriage triangle in Dresden. Hugo Dude, Carl von Haase and Carl Theodor Liskowsky were all esteemed members of the local deaf network. Dude had a deaf sister, who was married to Liskowsky. He, in turn, had a hearing sister who was married to von Haase. Mrs. von Haase thus had a deaf brother, husband and sister-in-law, and must be considered fully integrated in a deaf network. She was acknowledged as a "master of Sign Language".[116]

Further advertisements in the TsF suggest that deaf people shared their private domains in other ways than marriage. Offers to let a room or a bed were common, and although these advertisements do not state that the sender is a deaf person looking for a deaf subtenant, the context makes this the most likely scenario.[117]

Parallel to the urban worker's culture then, as it has been described above, similar patterns among deaf people appeared. In the city, there were *deaf* migrant workers, *deaf*-friendly bars, restaurants and cafés, *deaf* employers, masters, and apprentices. There were *deaf* marriages, and apartments overcrowded with *deaf* subtenants. Thus, from a network perspective, connections between deaf people did not form a specific category in themselves. Rather, we can conjecture a pattern in which a deaf individual had acquaintances who were also deaf in several of his or her activity fields – which may or may not overlap.[118]

---

115 "6. Taubstummen-Frauen-Verein," TsF 4 (1873), p. 34; Advertisement for her kindergarten, TsF 10-11-12 (1880), p. 38; Anna Schenck, "Vereinswesen," TsF 11 (1899), p. 55; Obituary of August Schenck, TC 12 (1892), pp. 144-145; Muhs, "Eduard Fürstenberg," p. 422.

116 "Meisterin in der Geberdensprache"Albin Maria Watzulik, "Der Methodenstreit," TC 9 (1896), p. 93.

117 These advertisements were published in most issues of TsF; for examples see TsF 8 (1892), p. 32.

118 *Cf.* Boissevain, *Friends of Friends,* pp. 28-29.

From the workplace and spaces for social communication, to the intimacy of the private home, the relationships between deaf people foremost belonged to the private sphere. However, the path to this private sphere led, in most cases, through the public realm – a residential school. What could be designated the 'subaltern counterpublic' of the deaf had, by necessity, reversed the most basic prerequisite for entering the bourgeois public sphere, that of being a private person.

Exclusion: The Example of the 'Unknown Deaf-Mutes'

The countryside, too, was deeply affected by the transformation into an industrial market economy. Accustomed bonds of support in the local community eroded, while at the same time, the transformation exposed large groups in the population to new risks. Proletarians, recruited from the classes of agricultural workers, petty farmers, domestic manufacture workers, and craftspeople, lived precarious lives exposed to fluctuations in the economy and competition between workers. From the 1860s, the internal migration to industrial centers was a mass phenomenon.[119] Those who were unable to find work risked slipping into poverty and homelessness, and the poor relief laws worsened their desperate situation. Two principles regulated the care for the rural poor, the principle of residence and the principle of nativity, distinguished essentially by their practices of acknowledging residence in a parish. According to the principle of residence, which was used in most of Germany, the municipal poor relief authorities were responsible for supporting anyone who had lived on their territory for at least two years. Frequent movers risked ending up in a situation where no municipality was responsible for them. In that case, the provincial poor relief stepped in.[120] The second principle was that of nativity, according to which a

---

119 Christoph Sachße and Florian Tennstedt, *Geschichte der Armenfürsorge in Deutschland. Vom Spätmittelalter bis zum Ersten Weltkrieg* (Stuttgart: Kohlhammer, 1980), pp. 179-195, 258-259.

120 However, efforts were often made to find a responsible municipality to cover the costs. Katrin Marx-Jaskulski, *Armut und Fürsorge auf dem Land. Vom Ende des 19. Jahrhunderts bis 1933* (Göttingen: Wallstein Verlag, 2008), pp. 74-79.

person only became the responsibility of the parish by birth, marriage, or special appeal. This principle was used in Bavaria.[121]

Travelling people without residence became, at least in the eyes of the police authorities, one of the most severe threats to 19th century German society. As a solution to the problem with vagrants, the police controlled the borders and supervised the travellers in the native population. Much effort was devoted to keeping mobile people under observation, for example circulating their names and descriptions in police papers. It was commonly assumed that vagrants intentionally withheld their true identity and their residency from the authorities.[122] Shelters for wanderers were also founded as an attempted solution. They were intended for workers who migrated in the search for employment, but were in reality mostly populated by people unable to work. Detention in workhouses was another, equally ineffective, means of tackling the problem. Merely keeping the nuisance away from the rest of society for a period of time, workhouses offered no rehabilitation. Former inmates had difficulties integrating in society, and were limited to employers offering poor conditions.[123]

Deaf people were viewed by the police as especially prone to vagrancy, and were therefore objects of special surveillance. For example, the Württemberg police issued a printed register of the "mute, deaf, deaf-mute, feeble-minded and insane persons roaming the country" in 1856.[124] In the register, 264 'deaf-mutes' were described with name, age and appearance. All of them were not vagrants. Some were persons from which it was expected that they might leave their homes. The purpose of the publication was to facilitate the identification of beggars and vagrants who could not or would not give the authorities their name.[125]

---

121 Susanne Hauser, *Die Geschichte der Fürsorgegesetzgebung in Bayern*, Inaugural dissertation, Ludwig-Maximilian University, Munich, (1986), pp. 131-132, 171-182.

122 Leo Lucassen, "Eternal Vagrants? State Formation, Migration, and Travelling Groups in Western-Europe, 1350-1914," in *Migration, Migration History, History. Old Paradigms and New Perspectives*, eds. Jan Lucassen and Leo Lucassen (Bern: Peter Lang, 1997), pp. 242, 246-247.

123 Karl Wilmanns, "Das Landstreichertum, seine Abhilfe und Bekämpfung," *Monatsschrift für Kriminalpsychologie und Strafrechtsreform*. 1 (1904/5), pp. 606-607, 614-615.

124 Högg (Ed.), Polizeiliches Verzeichnis der im Lande umherziehenden stummen, tauben, blödsinnigen und geisteskranken Personen (Knittlingen: Beesenmayer, 1856).

125 Ibid., pp. 3-4.

Such cases appear to have been relatively common in some parts of Germany during the 19th and well into the 20th century. Unemployed wanderers were the responsibility of the authorities in two ways. First, vagrancy and begging were illegal, which meant that they were arrested by the police and put in prison. Second, caring for indigents was a municipal duty towards the state.[126] In Prussia, where the principle of residence ruled, regional poor relief authorities (*Landesarmenverbände*) were obliged to care for the deaf who were otherwise not supported.[127] Bavaria, however, kept the principle of nativity until 1916. Support of the poor was thereby in the hands of the parishes, but only encompassed those belonging to the parish by birth, marriage, long-term residency or employment in civil and military service.[128] This might explain why files on deaf vagrants appear relatively frequently in Bavarian archives, but not in in Württemberg or Berlin: In each case of unknown deaf individuals appearing on the countryside, the first priority of the local authorities was to determine where the person came from, since this might enable them to deport the person and thus rid them of the cost. If this was not possible, the county office was required to assign the vagrant with interim citizenship in a parish.[129] This parish, in turn, had to find a suitable occupation and shelter for the person in question. Investigations of this kind were severely complicated by the language barrier, and sometimes encompassed several hundred pages. In other parts of Germany, the principle of residence and the support of the *Landesarmenverbände* perceivably made such investigations less complicated or even unnecessary, making the phenomenon marginal in, for instance, Württemberg and Berlin.[130]

---

126 Sachße and Tennstedt, Geschichte der Armenfürsorge in Deutschland, p. 204; Marx-Jaskulski, Armut und Fürsorge auf dem Land, p. 92; Georg Steinmetz, Regulating the Social. The Welfare State and Local Politics in Wilhelmine Germany (Princeton: Princeton University Press, 1993), p. 168.

127 Marx-Jaskulski, Armut und Fürsorge auf dem Land, pp. 74-76.

128 Hauser, Geschichte der Fürsorgegesetzgebung in Bayern, pp. 151-153, 165.

129 Ibid., pp. 153-154.

130 Furthermore, Bavarian archives list these files as a special category, stating in the title that the subject is a 'deaf-mute' vagrant. This facilitates the identification, whereas any files on unidentified deaf vagrants that may exist in Württemberg, and possibly in Berlin, do not contain the word 'taubstumm' in their title. Finding them would require an inventory of thousands of files on other kinds of police investigations and poor relief cases, which unfortunately would be too time-consuming for this study.

Below, twenty-two investigations of 'unknown deaf-mutes' [*unbekannte Taubstumme*] from the state archives in Munich, Amberg, and Landshut will be analyzed with the aspects of communication and interaction between the deaf individual and the authorities, the background of those who ended up in this situation, and their social conditions after the arrest in focus. The purpose is to balance the image of the urban, educated deaf, showing that the society that produced a class of comfortable, deaf quasi-*Bürger* also left some in isolation and poverty.

The Files

In the records of files relating to deaf people requested from the German state archives for this study, four Bavarian archives listed cases of "unknown deaf-mutes" ("unbekannte Taubstumme"). These files turned out to contain descriptions, decisions and investigations into the background of homeless deaf persons without proper identification, who had appeared in rural parishes. The Munich Hauptstaatsarchiv kept four such cases, the Munich Staatsarchiv seven; the Staatsarchiv in Landshut recorded six cases, and the Staatsarchiv in Amberg five cases. I have selected files that, at least in part, stem from the Imperial era, but considered each case in its entirety even if it extended outside of this period. The earliest entry dates back to 1852, and the last case was closed in 1910.[131] This shall not be interpreted to the effect that "unknown deaf-mutes" did not appear before or after this period.[132] The aim is not to determine the extent of deaf vagrancy either at a given moment or over time, but to gain access to a number of life stories from this period. Therefore, I also chose not to consider some of the cases that contained too little information.[133]

The files contain documents from what was essentially a police investigation, but involved also the authorities responsible for poor relief and local administration. Depending on the individual circumstances, they may contain questionings, expert statements, and correspondence with other parishes or institutions. The stated goal of identifying the person meant that investigators had an urgent

---

131   StA Landshut BezA/LRA Pfarrkirchen Rep. 164/14 512; StA Munich LRA Laufen 141728.

132   An earlier case was, for instance, StA Amberg Reg. d. Obf. Kammer d. Innern, from the years 1835-1838; *cf.* also Ylva Söderfeldt, "Lebenswelt eines 'taubstummen Vaganten' – Die Befragung eines gehörlosen Bettlers als Ego-Dokument zur Geschichte der Gehörlosen," *Das Zeichen* 83 (2009), pp. 375-379.

133   *V.* for instance StA Amberg, BezA Tirschenreuth 1766.

interest in his or her life story. The task of caring for him or her meant that the further fate of the person was also documented.

The 'unknown deaf-mutes' were mostly male – only three of them were women.[134] The youngest at the time of arrest were two boys of 16, the oldest was 63 years old.[135] The average age was 30.

Arrest and Investigation

Typical of the cases studied is that a deaf person was arrested by gendarmes and brought into custody. Where details on the circumstances of the arrest were given, it appears that locals encountered the stranger first, and notified the authorities.[136] When the person was in custody, the county office started an investigation to determine who the person was and where he or she came from. Since investigation could proceed for years, the unknown deaf were sometimes confined for lengthy periods of time.[137] An anonymous deaf man found in Holnstein in 1879 exemplifies how such detention could be experienced. On the third day in prison, he attempted to commit suicide. One month later, he still conveyed in pantomime that he intended to take his own life if he was not set free.[138]

A minority of the unidentified deaf could read and write well enough to allow communication through this medium. Josef Maier for instance, found in Waldkirchen in 1905, had merely been able to write his name,[139] but other files

---

134 A woman found in Sonthofen in 1883, BayHstA MInn 46180; and two further cases, StA Landshut BezA/LRA Pfarrkirchen Rep. 164/14 512; StA Landshut BezA/LRA Passau Rep. 164/13 8458.

135 Karl Burger, found in Tittmoning in 1902, a boy found in Laufen in 1905, StA Munich LRA Laufen 141728, and a man found in Wolfstein in 1905, StA Landshut BezA Rep164/22 1203.

136 Gendarmerie-Brigade Laufen to the Kgl. Bez. A.. Laufen, 6 December 1905, Gendarmeiestation Waging to Bez. A.. Laufen, 16 November 1908, StA Munich, LRA Laufen, 141728; Gendarmerie-Station Tittling to Bez. A.. Passau, 25 September 1875, StA Landshut, BezA/LRA Passau Rep 164/13 8458.

137 *Cf.* StA Munich, LRA Weilheim LRA 3181, an investigation that went on for two years.

138 Bez. A.. Sulzbach to the Reg. der Oberpfalz und von Regensburg, Kammer des Innern, 5 March and 8 April 1879, BayHStA MInn 46180.

139 Report by the Gendarmerie-Station Waldkirchen, 13 November 1905, StA Landshut BezA/LRA Wolfstein Rep 164/22, 1204.

contain elaborate written questionings.[140] In most cases, however, no communication took place between authorities and the object of their investigation. Standard procedure was instead to post a search warrant in the police paper or to request information from other administrative instances.[141]

A rare case was a deaf man was arrested in Ponholz, Bavaria, in 1885. Without identification and illiterate, he was questioned several times in Sign about his background. The unidentified man claimed to be a glassblower, who had worked in a glassworks together with his father. In the Franco-Prussian war (1870-71) his father had been drafted and subsequently killed. When the mother died, apparently shortly thereafter, the boy was left to himself. The factory closed, and driven by hunger he began his wandering.[142] This story was recaptured by no less than three signers: His hearing fellow prisoner Thomas Hluzek, who had learned Sign through deaf former colleagues, and the hearing teacher of the deaf Johann Döring submitted information they had gained through conversation with him in prison. A third prisoner, the deaf Conrad Reiter, reported from prison in Schirnding in Upper Franconia that he knew the stranger, and confirmed some of the information offered by the other two.[143]

---

140 St Munich LRA Garmisch-Partenkichen 105814 contains written questionings with Anton N., who was found in 1890, awarded citizenship in Garmisch, and repeatedly arrested and detained by the authorities until 1907. Karl List, who was arrested for begging, violence against police and other crimes several times between 1886 and 1896, was also questioned in writing, StA Amberg, BezA Neustadt 3354.

141 Bayerisches Zentral-Polizei-Blatt 154 (1905), p. 643; Bayerisches Zentral-Polizei-Blatt 35 (1890), p. 149; Bayerisches Zentral-Polizei-Blatt 99 (1909), p. 419; Bayerisches Zentral-Polizei-Blatt 108 (1905), p. 453; other warrants: Bez. A. Pfarrkirchen to Polizeipräsidium Berlin, 22 August 1871, StA Landshut BezA/LRA Pfarrkirchen Rep. 164/14 1711; Bez. A. Passau to the Bezirkshauptmannschaft Rohrbach 11 October 1900, StA Landshut BezA/LRA Passau Rep. 164/13 8457.

142 The story varies slightly in different questionings. Protokoll, 23 June 1885 [statement by co-prisoner Thomas Hluzek] StA Amberg, Bez. A. Stadtamhof 4023; Bescheid im Namen Seiner Majestät des Königs von Bayern. In der Sache: Anweisung einer vorsorglichen Heimat... 12 December 1885, Statement by Johann Döring, Vorstand of the Kreistaubstummenanstalt, 12 December 1885, StA Amberg, Reg. d. Obf. Kammer d. Innern 17289.

143 K. B. Gendarmerie Corpes, Station Schirnding, to the Kgl. Bez. A. Stadtamhof, 21 July 1885, Protokoll betreffend der Feststellung der Identität.., Thiemheim 25 July 1885, StA Amberg, BezA Stadtamhof 4023.

Instead of attempts to communicate in idiomatic Sign Language, some investigators used other types of visual communication. A man found in Schleswig in 1875 was assumed to be Bavarian, since he appeared familiar with Bavarian military uniforms and the Catholic mass.[144] Josef Maier, arrested in Waldkirchen in 1905, could, apart from writing his name, state his profession, his age, and relate previous events in his life through pantomimic signs.[145]

Measures and Consequences

Although vagrancy and begging were illegal, and in most cases had been the reason for arrest, prosecution and punishment were rarely used in the cases studied. Deaf beggars were not considered responsible for their actions, but, on the other hand, could not be released to continue their wandering and begging.[146] Different practices were used to resolve the situation. Most convenient for the authorities was deportation. However, only two of the 'unknown deaf' were identified and could be sent to their homes.[147] Josef Maier was assessed to have been in touch with the authorities in another area before, and therefore belonged to that municipality, even though his origin was unknown.[148] Instead of positive identification, decisions were often made based on assumption. It was common to assume that the deaf person was foreign, sometimes due to the possession of coins or other objects, sometimes without giving any reason for this belief. Thus, little evidence was required to allow the gendarmes to bring deaf strangers over the national or municipal border and out of the responsibility of the community.[149] If this type of deportation was not carried out immediately, problems could

---

144 Ministerium des Innern to all Kgl. Regierungen, 18 July 1876, BayHStA MInn 46180.

145 Report by the Gendarmerie-Station Waldkirchen, 13 November 1905; Protocoll In Sachen Aufgreifen einer taubstummen Mannsperson... Waldkirchen 9 December 1905, StA Landshut, Bez.A./LRA Wolfstein Rep. 164/22 1204.

146 *V.* Report by Christoph Fick, Stationscommandant Gendarmerie-Station Waging, 27 February 1906, StA Munich, LRA Laufen 141728

147 Stadtmagistrat Tittmoning, 23 October 1902, StA Munich LRA Laufen 141728; Bez. A. Cham to the Kgl. Reg. der Obf. u. v. Regensburg, Kammer des Innern, 23 November 1867, StA Amberg, Reg. d. Obf. Kammer des Innern. 15779.

148 Bez. A. Wolfstein to the Bez. A. Erding 31 December 1905, StA Landshut BezA/LRA Wolfstein Rep 164/22 1204.

149 Report by Ludwig Stockbauer, Gendarmerie-Station Waging, 24 February 1906, Gendarmeriestation Waging to the Bez. A. Laufen, 16 November 1908, Gendar-

arise. A man arrested in Leoprechting in September 1900 was, according to all authorities involved, from Bohemia. He was reported to already have been brought over the border several times, but returned to Bavaria and was this time taken into custody. An investigation was commenced. After three months, the government of Lower Bavaria decided that deportation would be the proper action, but that it was impossible due to the cold season. The Ministry of the Interior was still not prepared to grant him interim citizenship or to accommodate him in an institution, but decided to give him shelter in the poorhouse in Leoprechting. Shortly after the implementation of this decision, the man escaped and no longer posed a problem to the parish.[150]

Awaiting results of the investigation, or when the efforts to identify the person failed, the local authorites had to find an accommodation for him or her. Institutional care was a considerable cost and therefore avoided when possible.[151] For instance, the county office of Passau suggested that the unidentified man in Leoprechting be brought to an institution, but the Ministry of the Interior declined this request. Bavarian citizens were not accommodated in institutions on the expense of the state, the Ministry argued, and foreigners should not be given better treatment than Bavarians.[152] Similar cases confirm the unwillingness at the higher level of authority to place vagabonds in institutions unless it was absolutely necessary.[153] Additional disabilities or illness prompted institutional care in three cases: A woman suffering from epilepsy who was found in Sonthofen in 1883, a man who appeared in Mannersberg in 1898 and could not be

---

merie-Brigade Laufen to the Kgl. Bez. A. Laufen, 6 December 1905, StA Munich, LRA Laufen, 141728.

150 StA Landshut, BezA/LRA Passau, Rep 164/13 8457.
151 *Cf.* Marx-Jaskulski, Armut und Fürsorge auf dem Land, p. 120-121.
152 Bez. A. Passau to the Kreisfiskalat vom Niederbayern, 17 November 1900, Reg. von Niederbayern, Kammer des Innern, to the Bez. A. Passau, 11 December 1900, StA Landshut, BezA/LRA Passau, Rep 164/13, 8457
153 Kgl, Reg. von Oberbayern, Kammer des Innern to Kgl. Bez. A. Weilheim, 25 January 1902, StA Munich LRA Weilheim 3181; Gemeindeverwaltung and Armenpflege Waldhof to Bez. A. Pfarrkirchen, 19 December 1871, StA Landshut BezA/LRA Pfarrkirchen Rep. 164/14 1711, in which they ask for the institutionalization of an unknown deaf man, a request that was, as it appears from the rest of the file, not granted.

kept in the poorhouse due to his uncleanliness, and a man who was ill when he was arrested in Bassdorf in 1909.[154]

When deportation was impossible and institutional care not necessary, the deaf vagrants were assigned to local families who received financial support from the local administration to feed and shelter them. In 1875, a farmer in Witzmannsberg found a deaf woman wandering the fields. Since she appeared helpless, he took her in. When she complained about pain in her stomach, the farmer sought the assistance of the gendarmerie. A medical examination was performed by the district physician, who stated that the woman was healthy and probably simulated her pain to evoke compassion. She was in no need of hospitalization, but although she appeared to have been in good care until recently her identity could not be determined. Thus this woman, who was about 25 years old, fell under the responsibility of the parish. Although there were no criminal charges, the gendarmerie placed her in prison, which prompted a protest from the fiscal of Lower Bavaria. If she was able to work, the fiscal argued, her support was no concern of the authorities. Only if she was partially of totally unable to work, she was the responsibility of the parish. Once again the district physician made a statement: Except for her deafness, she was fully able. However, since she could not read lips, and her ability to understand signs and mimic was limited, she could neither find work nor understand instructions. Thus the woman was brought to the mayor of Witzmannsberg, but immediately escaped from his premises. Shortly thereafter she reappeared, under similar circumstances as before, in the parish Aicha von Wald. There she was placed in the care of a succession of local farmers.[155]

Arrangements of this kind appear in the material as the usual way of handling those unidentified deaf persons who could not be deported.[156] In their history

---

154 The case of the woman in Sonthofen appears in BayHstA MInn 46180; the uncleanly man in Mannersberg in StA Amberg Reg. d. Obf. Kammer des Innern, 16231; the Bassdorf case is contained in StA Munich LRA Laufen 141728; Also, Anton Neurre, who will be discussed below, was sent to an institution, although not for medical reasons. v. below p. 139.

155 StA Landshut, BezA/LRA Passau, Rep. 164/13 8458.

156 Boarding with local families appears also in the files on the man in Holnstein in 1879, BayHstA MInn 46180; the man in Ponholz in 1885-1886, StA Amberg Reg. d. Obf. Kammer d. Innern 17289, Bez. A. Stadtamhof 4023; the man in Eglsee in 1866-1871, StA Amberg, Bez. A. Amberg, 779; the man in Laab in 1871-1875, StA Landshut BezA/LRA Pfarrkirchen Rep. 164/14 1711; and the woman in Schaldorf, 1852-1880, StA Landshut BezA/LRA Pfarrkirchen Rep. 164/14 512.

of German poor relief, Christoph Sachße and Florian Tennstedt have argued that mass-migration caused immense costs for rural parishes, which left them with scarce funds for impoverished inhabitants. To manage the situation, many parishes turned to inhumane policies and deportations of poor or potentially needy people. Although poorhouses and workhouses offered the possibility of controlling the poor and maintaining them for relatively low costs, a such establishment appears only once in the files on 'unknown deaf'.[157]

Sachße and Tennstedt described *Reihenpflege*, a rotation system where the parishioners took turns in caring for the local poor, as forced labour without any regard to the ability of the subject, and impossible for third parties to control.[158] Although no *Reihenpflege* appears in the files in question here – the former vagrants were permanently assigned to local households – Sachße and Tennstedt's analysis may still apply. Whether the conditions were decent for the deaf individuals we encounter in this material most likely varied between individual cases. Striking is, however, that several of them escaped, not only from the authorities, but also from their private caregivers.[159] The most noticeable case was an unidentified deaf man in Eglsee, who was assigned to a farmer in the parish in 1866 or 1867.[160] Between then and 1871, he escaped a total of twelve times. He returned on his own accord at some occasions, at others, he was arrested and brought back to Eglsee. As a reaction to this, the local authorities suggested that he be placed in an institution, but the royal government denied this request. At the twelfth occasion, the Ministry of the Interior questioned the conditions in the family where the man lived. Since, this time, the man appears not to have returned, no action followed.[161]

---

157 Sachße and Tennstedt, *Geschichte der Armenfürsorge in Deutschland*, pp. 250-251, cf. the man in Mannersberg, who was brought to the poorhouse, but found to be too uncleanly to be kept there. Kgl. Bez. A. Neumarkt i. Obpf to the KGL. Reg. d. Obpf. und Regensburg, 26 May 1898, StA Amberg Reg. d. Obf. Kammer des Innern, 16231.

158 Sachße and Tennstedt, Geschichte der Armenfürsorge in Deutschland, pp. 250-251.

159 Apart from those discussed below, such cases appear also in the case of the unknown deaf man in Sulzbach, 1879 BayHsta MInn 46180; and the one in Laab in 1871-1875, StA Landshut BezA/LRA Pfarrkirchen Rep. 164/14 1711.

160 Neither the decision to place him with the farmer, nor any information on exactly when the decision was made are included in the file. The first mentioning of the arrangement occured in March 1867. StA Amberg, BezA Amberg 779, p. 41.

161 StA Amberg, BezA Amberg, 779, p. 179.

This case was extreme in the number of escapes, perhaps due to the fact that the authorities were rather successful in retrieving him and that he sometimes was able and willing to return by himself. Other deaf boarders did not return: After the man in Ponholz had been granted temporary citizenship there, he was brought to the farmer Georg Pirzer in Hagenau. Two weeks later, the prison guard Michael Ott, who knew the man from his previous detention, reported that the latter had approached him and complained that Pirzer treated him unkindly. The allegations were repudiated by the local poor relievers, who stated that the man received the same food as the other members of the Pirzer family, that he had a bed, and was not forced to work.[162] Ott had claimed that another parishioner was able and willing to care for the deaf man, but that he could not name him. It is possible that he made his statement with some scheme in mind. Cases where people attempted to use the poor relief as a tool in private conflicts have been found elsewhere.[163] Even if this was the case, the deaf man appears to have been less than satisfied with his situation, since he left Pirzer's household three months later and did not return.[164]

Communication and Interaction: At the Mercy of the System

Faced with the files on deaf vagrants, the questions arise of where these individuals came from, and what led to their desperate situation. Here, it needs to be distinguished between reasons connected to their deafness, and factors affecting the population in general. Historical studies on vagrancy in the late 19th and early 20th centuries are scarce. However, research from the time on the backgrounds of vagrants gives some valuable insights. In the early 20th century, psychiatrist Karl Wilmanns surveyed the inhabitants of a workhouse in Baden, and his colleague Moritz Tramer studied the occupants of a Zurich shelter. The resulting studies of the physical, mental, and social states of vagrants offer reference points for comparing the 'unknown deaf-mutes' with other vagrants.

Both Willmans and Tramer concluded that, in most cases, several reasons contributed to the social decline of the vagrants. Wilmanns decided that persons with severe physical or intellectual disabilities were dependent on the good will of others, foremost the family, lest they were forced to beg for their living. Also,

---

162 Statement from Michael Ott, Stadtamhof, 4 January 1886, Lokalarmenpflege, Beschluß vom 10 January 1886, StA Amberg, Reg. d. Obf., Kammer d. Innern 17289.
163 Marx-Jaskulski: Armut und Fürsorge auf dem Land, pp. 405-410.
164 Gemeindeverwaltung Ponholz to the Bez. A. Stadtamhof, 7 March 1886, StA Amberg, Reg. d. Obf. Kammer d. Innern 17289

multiple disabilities caused exclusion from the labour market, whereas a mere intellectual disorder could be compensated with physical fitness.[165] Tramer differentiated between fourteen reasons for vagrancy, divided into two main groups: environmental factors and personal factors. 'Physical defects' belonged to the latter category, and according to Tramer often appeared together with other factors. His list of environmental factors correlates with the information we have about the 'unknown deaf-mutes': he noticed early loss of parents, illegitimate birth, and change in work opportunities as more or less common elements in the history of the vagrants.[166] All these factors appear among the deaf vagrants, but to what extent cannot be determined, since most could not describe, or were not asked to describe, their background.[167] Personal factors that according to Tramer could lead to vagrancy were, apart from physical disease and disabilities, old age, alcoholism, wandering drive, reluctance to work and mental illness or disability.[168] Every factor in this category is represented in the descriptions of deaf vagrants.[169] Thus, a relatively wide range of possible reasons appears, of which deafness was the common denominator. Tramer's conclusion that physical, or, in this case, sensory, 'deficits' were not sole reasons, but rather could cause vagrancy if combined with other factors, therefore appears

---

165   Wilmanns, "Das Landstreichertum, seine Abhilfe und Bekämpfung." pp. 612-613.
166   Moritz Tramer, "Vaganten (Arbeitswanderer, Wanderarbeiter, Arbeitsmeider) einer 'Herberge zur Heimat' in der Schweiz," *Zeitschrift für die gesamte Neurologie und Psychiatrie* 35/1 (1916), pp. 9-34.
167   Early loss of parents and change in work opportunities: The Ponholz case, Statement by Johann Döring, Vorstand of the Kreistaubstummenanstalt, 12 December 1885, StA Amberg, Reg. d. Obf. Kammer d. Innern 17289. Illegitimate birth: Franz Hehs, BezA Cham to the Reg. d. Obf. u. v. Regensburg, Kammer des Innern, 23 November 1867, StA Amberg, Reg. d. Obf. Kammer des Innern 15779.
168   Tramer, "Vaganten," pp. 42-89.
169   Old age: *Bayerisches Zentral-Polizei-Blatt* 108 (1905), p. 643. Alcoholism: Gemeindeverwaltung and Armenpflege Waldhof to the Bez. A. Pfarrkirchen, 19 December 1871, StA Landshut BezA/LRA Pfarrkirchen Rep. 164/14 1711. Wandering drive: Bez. A. Erding to the Bez. A. Wolfstein, 16 December 1905, StA Landshut BezA/LRA Wolfstein Rep 164/22 1204. Reluctance to work: Court protocol, Amtsgericht Schongau, 22 February 1907, StA Munich LRA Garmisch-Partenkirchen 105814. Mental illness/disability: Bez. A. Neumarkt i. Obpf. to the Reg. d. Obpf. u. v. Regensburg, Kammer des Innern, 21 May 1898, StA Amberg Reg. d. Obf. Kammer des Innern, 16231.

plausible.[170] Another reason, applying especially to deaf people, might be escape from institutional care; at least the authorities sometimes assumed that this was the case.[171] This might be a mere assumption, but it is certain that three out of the four deaf vagrants above who were placed in institutions escaped.[172]

The files on unidentified deaf vagrants in Bavarian archives give the question of deaf people's 'wandering drive' another dimension. Several of the vagrants voluntarily deserted the relative safety of boarding families or institutions to wander, which was interpreted as an urge to migrate. However, another possible explanation is the conditions for the inmates of institutions and boarders of rural families. The poor state of some of the vagrants on their arrest indicates that life was exceptionally hard for the group.[173] If we acknowledge them as rational minds, the choice to wander and to beg for their living, rather than remaining in the safety of an institution or boarding family, implies that deaf inmates and boarders experienced inadequate treatment.

This does not apply to all cases, however: When Josef Maier was arrested in Waldkirchen in 1905, he was relatively well dressed and stated his vocation as shoemaker. He recounted in Sign that he had stayed in an institution run by nuns, and that the experience of arrest and investigation was not new to him. It emerged that he had been given temporary citizenship in Erding some twenty years earlier. The county office in Erding was contacted, and suggested that Maier was simply set free. Due to his 'wandering drive', they argued, he was impossible to keep in an institution, but by himself, he would be free to go back to his beloved nuns. This argument did not impress the county office in Wolfstein, and Maier was brought to Erding.[174] He might correspond with the type of

---

170 Tramer, "Vaganten," pp. 48-49.
171 Gendarmerie-Brig. Laufen to the Kgl. Bez. A. Laufen 6 December 1905, Bez. A. Laufen to the Verwaltung der Anstalt Ottl., 9 July 1909, StA Munich LRA Laufen 141728.
172 Kgl. Reg. von Schwaben und Neuburg, Kammer des Innern, to the Staats-Ministerium des Innern, 22 December 1883, BayHsta MInn 46180; Marktgemeindeverwaltung Teisendorf to the Bez. A. Laufen, 10 May 1910, StA Munich, LRA Laufen 141728; Amtsgericht Brunnberg, Strafsache gegen N.N., namenloser Taubstummen von Garmisch, 21 April 1892, StA Munich, LRA Garmisch-Partenkirchen 105814.
173 For example the woman in Aicha v. Wald, Gendarmerie-Station Tittling to Bez. A. Passau, 25 September 1875, StA StA Landshut, BezA/LRA Passau, Rep. 164/13, 8458, the boy in Laufen and the man in Bassdorf, StA Munich LRA Laufen 141728.
174 StA Landshut BezA/LRA Wolfstein Rep 164/22 1204.

deaf wanderer described by teachers and, in some cases, deaf writers.[175] He had a vocation, was in relatively good shape, and was to some extent able to communicate with his hearing surroundings, although his literacy appears to have been limited to writing his name. Thus his wanderings seems to some extent voluntary.

One case allows us to follow the biography of a deaf vagrant from childhood. Karl List has a file in the Staatsarchiv in Amberg, which goes back to the financing of his education. He attended the Kreistaubstummeninstitut in Regensburg from 1877. Only ten years later, he was arrested in Tischenreuth for begging. Following this occasion, a career of crime and begging unfolded. List travelled over great distance in the German Empire, and was frequently arrested for begging, vagrancy, impecuniosity, and even violent resistance against a police officer. During the course of his life, he appears to have undergone a process of proletarianization. When he was first arrested for begging, he was registered as shoemaker. On later occasions, he was titled 'worker' or 'day labourer.' List corresponded with the standard image of craftspeople turned into proletarians, forced by poverty to migrate, and descended to crime due to lack of work. He was, however, not treated as fully responsible for his actions, but considered feebleminded and provided with a legal guardian. In the written interrogations of him, he was repeatedly asked if he understood that begging and using violence against a police officer were illegal acts. Instead it was his father, Michael List, who was threatened with prosecution if he did not control his son and keep him at home. Also the Mayor of Kohlberg received a reprimand from the local authority in Neustadt for allowing Karl List to run wild. It was expected, the county office in Neustadt emphasised, that the parents acted in a way adequate to the efforts put into List's education.[176]

Karl List had a family to which he could return, which made him unusual. Most of the other deaf vagrants appeared as disconnected. None of them travelled with others. Relations with other mobile or stationary persons were rarely mentioned. Karl Burger, found in Tittmoning in 1902, had a legal guardian and a master, to whom he was returned.[177] Witnesses recognized the man in Ponholz and the woman in Schaldorf.[178] She and the woman in Aicha von

---

175   V. above p. 107.
176   StA Amberg, BezA Neustadt 3354.
177   Karl Burger's case is contained in StA Munich LRA Laufen 141728.
178   Interview with Conrad Reiter, 25 July 1886, StA Amberg Bez. A. Stadtamhof 4023; Testimony of Johanna Strasburger to the Landgericht Pfarrkirchen, 10 June 1854, StA Landshut BezA/LRA Pfarrkirchen Rep. 164/14 512.

Wald both later gave birth to children while they were in the care of local farmers.[179]

Most of the time, the authorities and the unidentified deaf persons were unable to communicate. Some cases do not contain any evidence that communication was at all attempted.[180] Instead, investigations were performed without regard to the information offered by some of the subjects. Franz Hehs, arrested in Cham in 1866, was able to write his name and claimed to be from Wolschan nearby Prague. Regardless of this, he was identified as Johann Enzinger from Schwabach. The mistake was realized only after Hehs had been deported to Schwabach. Enzinger had been at home in Schwabach when Hehs was arrested, and therefore it was impossible for the two to be identical, noted the Mittelfranken Chamber of the Interior. After his release, Hehs was again arrested and once more deported – this time to Wolschan.[181]

Often, the authorities doubted that the vagrants were really deaf. The assumption that they were simulating complied both with the general mistrust against vagrants and the interests of the officials, since hearing beggars were less difficult to handle. Today, it is impossible to determine if these allegations were justified. All who were labelled 'deaf-mutes', 'alleged' or not, have been included in this analysis.[182] An elderly man found in Wolfstein in 1905 was first

---

179 The woman in Schalldorf had also alledgedly had another child before she was arrested. Gemeindeverwaltung and Lokalarmenpflege Schalldorf to the Bez. A. Pfarrkirchen, 1 July 1862, Testimony of Johanna Strasburger to the Landgericht Pfarrkirchen, 10 June 1854, StA Landshut BezA/LRA Pfarrkirchen Rep. 164/14 512; Landesgemeindeverwaltung Aicha v. Wald to the Bez. A. Passau, 5 November 1882, StA Landshut BezA/LRA Passau Rep. 164/13 8458.

180 The man in Sonthofen, Reg. von Schwaben and Neuburg, Kammer des Innern, and the Staats-Ministerium des Innern, 22 December 1883, BayHSta Rep. MInn 46180; an unknown deaf boy, Laufen 1905, St Munich LRA Laufen 141728; the man in Mannersberg, StA Amberg Reg. d. Obf. Kammer des Innern, 16231; StA Landshut BezA/LRA Pfarrkirchen Rep. 164/14 1711; StA Landshut BezA/LRA Passau Rep. 164/13 8457.

181 Reg. von Mittelfranken, Kammer des Innern, to the Reg. der Obf. und von Regensburg, Kammer des Innern, 15 September 1867; Bez. A. Cham to the Kgl. Reg. von Oberpfalz und von Regensburg, 23 November 1867 StA Amberg Reg. d. Obf. Kammer des Innern 15779.

182 "Alleged deaf-mute", "angeblich taubstumme", was the label given to Franz Hehs in the description of his file in the StA Amberg, Reg. d. Obf. Kammer des Innern 15779.

thought to be deaf. He had shown through pantomime that his hearing and speech was lost though an accident in the military, thus he was no proper 'deaf-mute' in the contemporary definition of the concept. Nevertheless, he was labelled as such, but later identified as the hearing Johann Marouschek, a notorious vagrant and beggar from Bohemia, and deported.[183] With Franz Hehs, unsuccessful attempts at oral communication in different languages were made.[184] Anton Neurre, who will be discussed below, was also believed to be simulating his deafness. Two gendarmes stated under oath that they had heard him shout obscenities at them, which could imply that he was able to hear.[185] However, regardless of whether he could hear or not, he evidently acted as if he was deaf in his contact with authorities for 17 years.[186]

The reason for the inability of authorities and deaf vagrants to communicate was not only the language barrier. Literate deaf stood no better chance than illiterate ones to successfully convey their identity to the interrogators. The use of Sign Language interpreters also had little significance, as shown by the Ponholz case. There, the unidentified man had been able to describe his background in detail, but had not offered the authorities what they needed: A name and a place of origin. Narratives had little value in the search of a judically valid identity, as had a mere mentioning of name and origin made by a deaf vagrant. The investigators needed documents of identification, or confirmation by some authority, to determine their identity. Thus communication in the true sense of the word between authorities and deaf vagrants practically never took place, regardless of the language mode.

The voluminous file of a man first arrested in Garmisch in 1890 exemplifies deficits in communication between authorities and unidentified deaf. Here, I will call him Anton Neurre, since that was the name he gave on his first arrest. Over the years, he was to be arrested and questioned several times, the last documents deriving from 1907. Compared to the other unidentified deaf, he was an unusual case. He received citizenship in Garmisch after less than a month in prison, and after another two months he was brought to the Asylum for Deaf-Mutes in Ursberg. He remained there for about a year, but his violent resistance and

---

183   StA Landshut BezA/LRA Wolfstein Rep. 164/22 Nr. 1203.
184   Report by Bez. A. Cham, 18 March 1867, StA Amberg Reg. d. Obf. Kammer des Innern 15779.
185   Öffentliche Sitzung des Kgl. Schöffengerichts Wippersfürth, 4 November 1903, StA Munich LRA Garmisch-Partenkirchen 105814.
186   V. below.

attempts to escape caused problems. Finally, in March 1892, he managed to run away.

Following this escape, he appears to have travelled across Europe and made his living as a wandering salesman of miscellaneous products. He had no permission to perform such trade, and was therefore repeatedly arrested. Neurre could read and write fairly well, thus enabling the authorities to interview him in writing. Mostly they asked him his name and place of origin, questions he seldom answered. Already in the first interrogation protocol from 1891, he claimed: "I am really without home".[187] His statement that he was from Petersburg appears to have been ignored. After calling himself Anton Neurre in 1890, he later signed documents with the name Jossepf, and on a further occasion called himself Josef Mayer. None of these identities were given any consideration from the authorities.[188]

Instead of acting on the information gained through questioning him, the authorities in the different parts of Germany, Belgium and Switzerland where he was arrested interacted with him through the means of power and money. He was forcibly placed in institutional care, arrested and detained in prison, and spent six months in the workhouse in Rebdorf.[189] At other occasions, the officials equipped him with the funds to go back to Garmisch, or sentenced him to pay fines for his behaviour.[190] When Neurre asked for documents that would enable him to find work, he was told that this was impossible unless he gave his 'real name'. To this he once replied that he would have told them his name if he had one, but since his mother died before she could tell him his name, he did not

---

187 "Ich bin würklich [sic] ohne Heimat", Interrogation with Neurre, Garmisch 9 January 1891, Munich LRA Garmisch-Partenkirchen 105814.

188 Interrogation with Neurre, 2 May 1892, Kgl. Reg. von Oberbayern. Kammer des Innern to the Bez. A. Garmisch, 13 February 1900, StA Munich LRA Garmisch-Partenkirchen 105814.

189 Öffentliche Sitzung des Kgl. Schöffungsgerichts Wippersfürth den 4 November 1903, Kgl. Schöffengericht Schongau in der Strafsache gegen Unbekannte Mannsperson, angeblich taubstumm, 22 February 1907, Verwaltung des Arbeitshauses Rebsdorf to the Bez. A. Garmisch, 6 May 1907, StA Munich LRA Garmisch-Partenkirchen 105814.

190 Eröffnungsnachweis Nr. 2238, 16 March 1903, Öffentliche Sitzung des Kgl. Schöffensgerichts Wippersfürth, 4 November 1903, StA Munich LRA Garmisch-Partenkirchen 105814.

know.[191] His desire was to be allowed to conduct trade as a wandering salesman, but the Garmisch authorities denied him this due to his deafness,[192] and suggested he seek employment. "No master will take me",[193] Neurre replied. Papers of identification bearing the designation 'unknown deaf-mute' were issued instead, and he was, this time, set free.[194] Without networks – "you are the only one I have", [195] Neurre once told his interrogators – and without permission to perform the only work he considered himself able to, he was destined to fall in the hands of the police again.

This vicious circle was repeated for seventeen years. Neurre tried to make a living by playing a portable organ, selling tobacco and printed pamphlets, and letting people pay for looking into his stereoscope.[196] If this provided him with a sufficient income, and whether or not he was content with his life as a wanderer, is unknown. Be that as it may, he never complained in the questionings, only asked for the documents that would enable him to carry on his trade. Since he never obtained them, he persistently ended up in the hands of the police. When he was arrested, the mechanisms of the system only allowed a limited number of options of handling him: Confinement in prison, institutional care, or sending him to Garmisch.

Nevertheless, the case of Anton Neurre stands out by the relatively high level of dialogue between him and the authorities. Since he was literate, he was potentially able to hold conversations not only with them, but also with others in his surroundings. Uneducated, illiterate vagrants made up for the majority of the unidentified deaf. Some of them might have spent their lives cut off from all linguistic communication, be it Sign, speech or writing.[197] These persons existed

---

191 Interrogation with Neurre, Garmisch 9 April 1904, StA Munich LRA Garmisch-Partenkirchen 105814.
192 *Cf.* above p. 56.
193 "es nimt [sic] mich kein Meister an", Interrogation with Neurre, Garmisch 16 March 1904, StA Munich LRA Garmisch-Partenkirchen 105814.
194 Ibid.
195 Interrogation with Neurre, 4 May 1893, StA Munich LRA Garmisch-Partenkirchen 105814.
196 Bez. A. Garmisch to the Bez. A. Füssen, 22 December 1890, Interrogation 4 May 1893, Interrogation with Neurre, Garmisch 16 March 1904, Öffentliche Sitzung des Kgl. Schöffengerichts Wippersfürth 4 November 1903, StA Munich LRA Garmisch-Partenkirchen 105814.
197 For instance the unidentified deaf man in Seeshaupt, with whom communcation through an interpreter was attempted, but without success: He did not know Sign.

in a vacuum, disconnected from the hearing world as well as from deaf networks. Incapable of communication, they were excluded from the processes and spheres of culture, society and even personality. As such, they were helplessly left at the mercy of the system, the spheres of economy and administration, since they could only be interacted with by means of power and money.[198]

With Anton Neurre the authorities could engage in dialogue. He was able to roughly explain his wishes and intentions. This was likely the reason why he and Karl List, who also was literate, were prosecuted for their actions, and set free after serving their punishments. Other deaf vagrants were treated as objects. No responsibility for their actions was acknowledged to them, which made it necessary to assign them to others.

Uneducated, disconnected deaf on the margins of society were also unable to apply for support, however not primarily because they were illiterate, but since they were shut out from communication. The conditions for receiving support, laws and regulations, even the possibility of obtaining poor relief, was knowledge passed on through communication and was thus beyond reach to these persons.[199] Perhaps this had contributed to their original exclusion from society: Loss of their parents, as experienced by the man in Ponholz, meant losing their link to the shared life-world of others. Lack, not only of communication, but of basic understanding of society made them unable to find employment or support from those authorities that originally would have been responsible for them.

Report to the Regierung von Oberbayern, by the Bez. A. Weilheim, 9 December 1901, StA Munich LRA 3181. Also with an unidentified man in Sulzbach, fruitless attempts to communicate were undertaken by the teachers and students at the deaf school in Nuremberg. Bez. A. Sulzbach to the Reg. d. Obf. u. v. Regensburg, Kammer des Innern, 5 May 1879, BayHsta MInn 46180.

198 Habermas, *Theorie des kommunikativen Handelns* II, pp. 191-192, 198-199; 208-209, 272. Interestingly, neurologist Oliver Sacks comes close to this analysis in his thesis that deprivation of language – regardless of its mode – in childhood might cause retardation of celebral development, although he refers to medical facts and makes no reference to Habermas. Sacks argues that congenitally deaf with no access to language resemble patients with left hemisphere brain damage; their language is limited to the "this-here-now". Oliver Sacks, *Seeing Voices. A Journey into the World of the Deaf* [Berkeley, CA: University of California Press, 1989] (London: Picador, 2000), pp. 85-88.

199 Katrin Marx-Jaskulski has shown how recipients of poor relief were aware of the conditions and argued for their cases accordingly. Marx-Jaskulski, *Armut und Fürsorge auf dem Land*, pp. 23-25, 140-162.

Their identity, even the very concept of an identity in the administrative sense, remained as obscure to them as to the authorities. Consequently, we see none of the deaf vagrants applying for or receiving poor relief directly and for themselves. When the parish fed and sheltered them, it was by assigning them to either local families or institutions, where they could be kept under control. One individual, the man in Ponholz, allegedly complained about his situation, but that was given no consideration. To him, and several other boarders and inmates, reaching a solution by communication was impossible, leaving escape as sole option to influence their situation.

CONCLUSION OF CHAPTER 2

Traditionally, the criteria for becoming a private person who could enter the public sphere were unattainable for deaf people. They lacked education, and therefore also the possibility to obtain an autonomous occupational status so that they could become owners of property. From the 18th century onward, public efforts, mainly the establishment of special education, enabled increasing numbers of deaf people to escape this situation. They received an education, which introduced them to *bürgerliche* values. Through this education and additional measures by the schools and the state, they were able to learn manual trades or in some cases even become recognized artists and professionals. This enabled them to marry and become heads of their own households, creating a sphere of intimacy coupled with a certain level of autonomy. It would seem as if institutional deaf education had the potential of creating a class of deaf *Bürger*, of private people. However, even these fortunate individuals were the objects of state intervention. Not the private sphere, but the public, allowed them to emerge as educated and propertied. Thus, they were no private people.

What the institutional education did was not to allow deaf people to be *Bürger*, but instead to provide an alternative set of criteria for them as a class. Thus, the deaf people who populated the growing cities shared more than their sensory disposition: they also to a great extent had been socialized within the same system, or even the same institutions. In this setting, additional places for encounters and types of relationships between deaf people emerged. This sociability cannot be ascribed to one particular social class. There were examples of deaf group formation within typical working class- as well as *Bürger* contexts. However, it was particular to the urban, educated deaf.

Other deaf people remained socially and communicatively isolated, without access even to the most basic cultural knowledge. Illiterate and impoverished vagrants were subjects to the most explicit and thorough interventions by the system. In the absence of communication, and thereby without access to a shared life-world to act within, physical power and monetary transactions were the only means of interaction with them. They, of course, did not fulfil any of the requirements for entering the bourgeois public sphere. However, lacking the alternative socialization and the competences of the educated deaf, neither did they fulfil the requirements that enabled some deaf people to build and enter a subaltern counterpublic.

3. Ways to be Deaf

The fact that deaf people in Imperial Germany formed friendships, that they married each other, and that there was a range of different spaces, private and public, for them to socialize with each other leads to the question if these people can be labelled a 'deaf community'.

The meaning of the concept deaf community varies in the available literature. There is no generally accepted definition of the term. Sociologist Paul C. Higgins has used it for the groups that Deaf signers form, based on their shared experiences and their identification as Deaf, the core of which are the Deaf clubs. According to Higgins, entering a Deaf community is always an active choice, entailing certain effort in order to be achieved. Thus, Deaf communities offer a volitional way of being Deaf, as opposed to deafness as a stigma ascribed by others.[1]

Other scholars have set the threshold lower, accepting any distinguishable demographic concentrations of deaf people as Deaf communities.[2] This approach implies the equivalence of a certain sensory disposition, or indeed, a certain

---

1   Paul C. Higgins, *Outsiders in a Hearing World. A Sociology of Deafness* (Beverly Hills, CA: Sage Publications, 1980), pp. 38-47. Higgins does not capitalize deaf, but since he does discuss modern Deaf communities, I have nevertheless chosen to use the capital D when referring to his results.

2   Nicholas Mirzoeff, *Silent Poetry. Deafness, Sign, and Visual Culture in Modern France* (Princeton, NJ: Princeton University Press, 1995), p. 64; Harlan Lane, Richard C. Pillard, and Mary French, "Origins of the American Deaf-World: Assimilating and Differentiating Societies and Their Relation to Genetic Patterning," pp. 47-73; Harry G. Lang, "Genesis of a Community: The American Deaf Experience in the Seventeenth and Eighteenth Centuries," pp. 1-23, both in *The Deaf History Reader*, ed. John Vickrey Van Cleve (Washington D. C.: Gallaudet University Press, 2007).

genetic profile, to a community of Deaf people. While it is intriguing to consider the cultural significance of hereditary deafness – the most eminent example is, of course, Nora Ellen Groce's study of Martha's Vineyard[3] – the demographic approach alone usually has little potential to offer valuable information for historical analysis of deaf group formations. From official statistics, we can extract the information that at least fourteen German cities had over 100 adult deaf inhabitants in 1900.[4] We also know that epidemic meningitis, known to cause deafness in children, spread in Bavaria during the 1860s and -70s, which resulted in unusually high numbers of deaf people in certain areas.[5] However, this information leads no further. It does not tell us if these people were acquainted, nor what their language mode was. Attempting to analyze deaf communities in these places based merely on this knowledge is futile. It can only lead to imposing on the past observations from present Deaf communities.

Carol Padden offers a third interpretation of Deaf community, which transfers some of its significance to what she instead calls Deaf culture. A Deaf community, she argues, is plainly a local, interest-oriented group of like-minded people. Values and traditions, folklore, and the shared language she locates in Deaf culture. This culture connects the local Deaf communities to each other, encompassing a larger area (in Padden's case, the United States). At the same time, as Deaf culture is wider, it is also more exclusive, since it according to Padden only accepts those who actively and openly embrace its values: "Members of the Deaf culture behave as Deaf people do, use the language of Deaf people, and share the beliefs of Deaf people toward themselves and other people who are not Deaf." [6] Thus, Padden's description of Deaf culture overlaps with the Deaf community according to Higgins, where membership must be achieved through internalising and expressing a particular self-image.

Both Higgins and Padden describe Deaf communities as essentially local groups of face-to-face encounters. In the previous chapter we already encountered such groups, and this chapter will offer more examples. However, it

---

3   Where, noticeably, there was no Deaf community, since the deaf were completely integrated in the community, in which everyone could sign. Nora Ellen Groce, *Everyone Here Spoke Sign Language. Hereditary Deafness on Martha's Vineyard* (Cambridge, MA: Harvard University Press, 1985).
4   Those cities were Berlin, Breslau, Königsberg, Dresden, Posen, Stettin, Leipzig, Munich, Nuremberg, Danzig, Cologne, Frankfurt a. M., Hamburg, and Hanover. Engelmann, "Die Taubstummen", pp. 159*-179*.
5   Pongratz, *Allgemeine Statistik,* pp. 59-62.
6   Padden, "The Deaf Community," pp. 89-104 [quote from p. 93].

also becomes clear that this was not the only type of interchange between deaf people in Germany at the time. There were also organizations, publications, and events that were common to deaf people from different regions and even from different countries. The web of connections between deaf people in different European countries and in the United States constituted another level of deaf groupness than the local sociability.[7] The question becomes, what is the relationship between this level, and the local deaf groups? Are they both parts of the same "community"?

Benedict Anderson has argued that most, perhaps all, communities do not consist of personal contact, or any other type of natural connectedness, but that they are imagined. This, he emphasises, does not mean that they are false, but it allows us to interpret their ideological components: "Communities are to be distinguished, not by their falsity/genuineness, but by the style in which they are imagined."[8] The tools for creating imagined communities in the last centuries have foremost been literary culture and education. Anderson points out how newspapers create the impression of a succession of somehow related events – and by the ritual of reading the news, these events are also related to the reading public.[9] He also notes how the educational system has made people in Sumatra regard their neighbours in Malaysia as foreign, but the remote Ambonese as fellow-Indonesians. By distributing the same knowledge, by the same means, to youth from all parts of the vast colony but to no one from outside its territory, the government schools consolidated the borders of an imagined community.[10]

The personal ties between deaf people who lived or worked together, socialized with or married each other, have a different quality. It might be more suitable to think of them as networks, rather than as communities. This opens for a wider understanding of these relationships by allowing one to consider the connectedness of individuals in its own right. Network analysis puts the relationships first, and categories such as class, ethnicity, or gender second.[11] When using this approach to the local-personal level of deaf sociability, we are liberated from the strict but hard-to-define admission criteria of the Deaf communities as they appear in the studies cited above. The question of an elusive 'deaf identity' is separated from the tangible social ties.

---

7   *Cf.* Murray, *Touch of Nature*.
8   Anderson, *Imagined Communities*, p. 6.
9   Ibid., pp. 32-46, 62.
10 Ibid., pp. 120-122.
11 Stanley Wasserman and Katherine Faust, *Social Network Analysis: Methods and Applications* (Cambridge, England: Cambridge University Press, 1994), pp. 7-8.

This chapter looks at the formal organizations created by deaf people in Germany. The first part compares the emergence and early history of the first deaf clubs in Berlin with that in Württemberg and Bavaria, to find differences and similarities in the organizational patterns. Together with an overview of the club activities as they appear in the deaf press, this helps to place the deaf movement in the social and political landscape of German associations and clubs. The aim is on one hand to describe the form and function of these formalized networks of deaf people, on the other to analyze their conceptual superstructure. The second part of the chapter is devoted to biographies of and by deaf people. Here, the self-image of the deaf community is elucidated.

PRACTICING DEAF COMMUNITY

In the summer of the revolutionary year 1848, two men addressed a letter to Friedrich Wilhelm IV. of Prussia, declaring that they had founded a club of 'deaf-mutes' in Berlin. The purpose of the *Taubstummen-Verein in Berlin*, they stated, was

"the ethical vitalization and further spiritual education of its members, the recreational gathering of the up until now solitarily living companions-in-suffering to edifying messages and conversations, support of the individual through advice and action, as well as awakening of every gregarious virtue."[12]

This was, as far as known, the first formal manifestation of the German deaf movement. By forming a club, a *Verein,* these two – Eduard Fürstenberg, a trainee at the crown land bursary, and Wilhelm Twele, a basket maker – were part of a trend which had begun in the second half of the 18th century, and would during the course of the 19th only gain in significance: the association movement. Reader's clubs, freemason lodges, and patriotic associations at first brought mostly academics and civil servants together for an egalitarian and sociable exchange of ideas. This was one of the foundations of the bourgeois public

---

12   "die sittliche Belebung und geistige Fortbildung seiner Mitglieder, gesellige Vereinigung der bis jetzt vereinzelt lebende Leidensgefährten zu belehrenden Mittheilungen und Unterhaltungen, Unterstützung der Einzelnen durch Rath und That, sowie Weckung jeder geselligen Tugend." E. Fürstenberg and W. Twele to the King, 11 July 1848, GStA PrK, HA I., Rep. 89, 22575.

sphere.¹³ The early clubs and associations were distinctly *bürgerlich* considering their membership. By forming clubs that engaged in cultural and social issues, the *Bürger* manifested their aspiration to power. It opened up a door to influence besides the rigid structures of the estate system. Furthermore, joining a club meant gaining access to important contacts that could favour the individual's progress to influence and wealth. Membership in a club or society was fashionable and could enhance one's prestige.¹⁴

During the first half of the 19th century, the size and number of clubs and societies multiplied, so that they encompassed all regions and all fields of interest and activity belonging to the *Bürger*. Especially in the 1840s, social and charitable motives grew strong within the associations. On one hand, the *Bürger* thereby shouldered some of the public efforts concerning the care of the poor and the sick, and the solving of social problems. On the other hand, it also meant that the working classes encountered the associations, and soon not only entered the charitable and edifying clubs headed by *bürgerlich* patrons, but gained control over them, or formed their own organizations.¹⁵

However, although the club membership spread in all social strata, *bürgerliche* values still defined the character of the associations. The principle of the association is simultaneously that of the bourgeois public sphere: anyone (any private person with assets and education) can enter it. The members act as equals, make decisions by rational, open, and democratic deliberation. They engage in issues of public concern, for the common good. Although in reality, the clubs often were elitist, had explicit or implicit restrictions on membership, developed their own bureaucracy over time, or were commercialized, they opened a space for their members to unfold and practice egalitarian, democratic values.¹⁶ By assuming social responsibilities and acting as lobby and referral

---

13   Klaus Nathaus, Organizierte Geselligkeit. Deutsche und britische Vereine im 19. und 20. Jahrhundert. (Göttingen: Vandenhoeck & Ruprecht, 2009), pp. 31-33.

14   Ulrich Im Hof, Das gesellige Jahrhundert. Gesellschaft und Gesellschaften im Zeitalter der Aufklärung (Munich: C. H. Beck, 1982), pp. 201-203, 216.

15   Nathaus, *Organizierte Geselligkeit,* pp. 35-36; Thomas Nipperdey, "Verein als soziale Struktur in Deutschland im späten 18. und frühen 19. Jahrhundert. Eine Fallstudie zur Modernisierung I.," in *Gesellschaft, Kultur, Theorie. Gesammelte Aufsätze zur neueren Geschichte* (Göttingen: Vanderhoeck & Ruprecht, 1976), pp. 175-176.

16   Nipperdey, "Verein als soziale Struktur," pp. 183-190; Otto Dann, "Conclusion. Sociabilité und Vereinsbildung," in Sociabilité et société bourgeoise et France, en Allemagne et en Suisse, 1750-1850. Geselligkeit, Vereinswesen und bürgerliche

instances, the association movement carried the *Bürger* to the former ranks of society. Thus, clubs and associations were among the most important actors in transforming Germany into a civil and fundamentally *bürgerlich* society.[17]

This development did not occur without conflict. Throughout the 19th century, clubs and associations were objects of supervision or suppression by the state. If they had political ambitions, there were many restrictions, if not total prohibition. The definition of political aims in the Prussian legislation was wide, banning any associations striving for "changes in the constitution or administration."[18] On the other hand, the attitude towards associations was in many other cases favourable and the relationship between them and the state sometimes even symbiotic, that is, if the association was considered beneficent to the common good, or harmless.[19]

From the mid-19th century, the spread of the association movement gained momentum. The exclusiveness of the earlier clubs dissolved, as the classes below the *Bürger*, and *bürgerlich* women, formed and entered organizations. The dominant types of associations were the singer-, sharpshooter-, and gymnastic clubs, which were typically based in a local community, and had a wide social basis in their membership. These clubs were much more than what their official designation suggested. Rather than just groups of amateur gymnasts, sharpshooters, or singers, they functioned as pivots of the local public and sociable life. As had been the case with earlier, more socially exclusive clubs, these broader organizations were also bases for building a potentially profitable network. Local shopkeepers and craftspeople, not least also barkeepers, reached a prospective clientele through the clubs. Supporting a club could be a sort of

---

Gesellschaft in Frankreich, Deutschland und der Schweiz, 1750-1850, ed. Étienne François (Paris: Editions Recherche sur les Civilisations, 1986), pp. 313-316; Klaus Tenfelde, "Die Entfaltung des Vereinswesens während der industriellen Revolution in Deutschland (1850-1873)," in Vereinswesen und bürgerliche Gesellschaft in Deutschland. Historische Zeitschrift, Beiheft 9. Ed. Otto Dann (Munich: R. Oldenburg Verlag, 1984), pp. 111-112.

17 Tenfelde, "Entfaltung des Vereinswesens," pp. 110-111; Nipperdey, "Verein als soziale Struktur," pp. 195-204.

18 "Veränderungen in der Verfassung oder in der Verwaltung" Alfons Hueber, "Das Vereinsrecht in Deutschland des 19. Jahrhunderts," in *Vereinswesen und bürgerliche Gesellschaft in Deutschland*, ed. Dann, p. 117.

19 Nipperdey, "Verein als soziale Struktur," pp. 196-200.

marketing, for instance through advertising in its print material.[20] Gradually, more groups thus encountered and internalised *bürgerliche* and democratic values in the *Verein*. The association movement became a space and instrument for emancipation and influence common for many different social groups. By forming and joining a club, they could unfold their personality by accessing cultural goods and shouldering responsibility, as well as gain prestige by constructing and formalizing hierarchies and elites.[21] Although the association movement eventually encompassed the entire nation, it was in the cities that it began and continued to have its core. Not least was this because clubs in urban communities offered a replacement for the traditional bonds of the rural society.[22] Women did enter clubs and also formed their own, but as a whole, the association movement was a predominantly male domain.[23]

The implications of this context for an analysis of the German deaf movement are seemingly contradictory: On the one hand, it is only to be expected that deafness be made an object of club formation. No interest, opinion, activity or attribute appears to have been too trivial for its possessors to gather, elect a board, and pass statutes.[24] The particular characteristics of deaf clubs were neither unusual nor new: Cultural belonging and language had been the basis of associations as early as in the 16th century, and continued to give rise to clubs in the imperial era.[25] On the other hand, many of the needs satisfied by deaf clubs would appear possible to cater to in conventional clubs. Saving money, fencing, or riding a bike seem on a basic level to be activities deaf and hearing people

---

20 Nathaus, *Organizierte Geselligkeit*, pp. 105, 108-112,115, 130-131; *cf.* above pp. 118-118.
21 Tenfelde, "Entfaltung des Vereinswesens," pp. 110-114.
22 Ibid., pp. 71-77.
23 Geoff Eley, "Nations, Publics and Political Cultures," pp. 311-312; Tenfelde, "Entfaltung des Vereinswesens," pp. 76-77.
24 V. the diverse examples given in Herbert Freudenthal, *Vereine in Hamburg. Ein Beitrag zur Geschichte und Volkskunde der Geselligkeit* (Hamburg: Museum für Hamburgische Geschichte, 1968), pp. 244-287.
25 Ibid., p. 238; Christoph Klessmann, Polnische Bergarbeiter im Ruhrgebiet 1870-1945. Soziale Integration und nationale Subkultur einer Minderheit in der deutschen Industriegesellschaft (Göttingen: Vanderhoeck & Ruprecht, 1978), pp. 94-105.

would be able to engage in together. Nevertheless, special cycling-, fencing-, and mutual savings clubs for deaf people were eventually formed.[26]

The First Deaf Club

We return now to the letter to the King in July 1848. Berlin at this time was caught up in a wave of political unrest, which had come from France, and affected all of Germany. The background to the revolution was a widespread sense of discontent with social as well as political conditions. What caused the discontent varied according to social and geographical position. The peasants rose against the remnants of the feudal system – taxation, hunting- and land rights. Liberal professionals were losing their patience with the unfulfilled promise of a constitution and the suppression of the public sphere. Craftspeople saw their existence threatened by proletarianization, as industrialization and population increase created growing lower classes.[27] News of the Paris revolution in February 1848 gave the spark to the built-up frustration. Berlin soon became one of the main scenes of the events. With its wide social cleavages and profound fear of material want, an 'academic proletariat' of journalists, writers, actors, and similar educated, but socially insecure, persons, and a popular but highly restricted association movement, Berlin was susceptible to revolutionary impulses.[28] A brief sketch of the most important developments shall give an idea of the climate in which the first German deaf club was constituted.

In the beginning of March, a group mainly made up of students started to hold public meetings in a Tiergarten beer garden, demanding above all democratic reform.[29] They were soon joined by craftspeople and workers, mobilized by the financial and industrial crisis that resulted from the political unrest, and by the refusal by the city council to heed the demands for reform.[30] In order to protect the state, military and militia were deployed around the city, which further provoked the protesters. From the 13th of March, there were recurrent

---

26 These are examples of special interest deaf clubs listed in the *Taubstummenkalender* (1913), p. 55, and in "Verwaltungen und Versammlungen der Taubstummen-Vereine," TC 8 (1891), p. 95.

27 Thomas Nipperdey, *Deutsche Geschichte 1800-1866. Bürgerwelt und starker Staat* (Munich: C. H. Beck, 1987), pp. 396-402, 600-604.

28 Rüdiger Hachtmann, Berlin 1848. Eine Politik- und Gesellschaftsgeschichte der Revolution (Bonn: Dietz, 1997), pp. 68-86, 94-103.

29 Ibid., pp. 127-128.

30 Hachtmann, *Berlin 1848*, pp. 131-138.

violent confrontations between the people and the military. Despite attempts by the city council to cool the public by meeting some of their demands, the fighting escalated and on the 18th, Berlin saw regular barricade battles.[31] The following day, an order of a cease-fire came from the Prussian King. The revolutionaries had, for the time being, sieged over the military.[32]

In the following days, the King asserted his dedication to a national state, with himself as the leader of the German people. A state funeral for the fallen revolutionaries was arranged. Although the King clearly spoke of an absolute monarchy, the audience interpreted his performance quite differently: They saw themselves as having arrived at their goal of a constitutional monarchy in an imperial nation. Thus, the monarchy gained time to deliberate the next move.[33] Speedily, elections for a National Assembly in Frankfurt, as well as local parliaments, were declared. The National Assembly would then negotiate changes in the Prussian constitution with the crown.[34]

In connection with the elections and the spirit of freedom and fellowship, all kinds of communities and interests groups organized. For a brief period, the repression of overtly political clubs was lifted. Thousands of petitions were addressed to the newly formed parliament.[35] It was in the midst of these efforts that also a group of 'deaf-mutes' formed an organization for the first time in Germany.

Geographically and chronologically, the founders of the *Taubstummenverein* (TsV) *in Berlin* could hardly have been closer to the center of events. A later account has it that the founders used to gather in a restaurant in the Taubenstrasse.[36] This street is located by the Gendarmenmarkt in the very heart of Berlin. In March 1848, it was blocked by several barricades.[37] The club statutes

---

31   Ibid., pp. 137-159.
32   Ibid., pp. 188-202.
33   Ibid., pp. 208-213.
34   However, the elections were indirect, and, in the case of local elections, only allowed those possessing burgher rights to participate. Hachtmann, *Revolution,* pp. 295, 300-308.
35   Nipperdey, *Deutsche Geschichte,* pp. 601, 617-622; Dieter Langewiesche, "Vereins- und Parteibildung in der Revolution von 1848/49 – ein Diskussionsbeitrag," in *Vereinswesen und bürgerliche Gesellschaft in Deutschland,* ed. Dann, pp. 51-54.
36   August Schenck, obituary of Joseph Ludwig Karl Beck, TsF 5 (1886), p. 19. The choice of location seems to be a pun, since "Taubenstraße" in German could mean both "Dove Street", and "Deaf Street".
37   *Cf.* map of Berlin with barricades in Hachtmann, *Revolution,* inside of book cover.

had been submitted to the police on May 3rd, only weeks after the revolt.[38] A connection between the club and the political and social turmoil thus seems likely, at least at first glance. Earlier in the year, the Paris deaf, who had organized already in the 1830s, associated their emancipation with the revolution. There, deaf people took part in the uprising on all levels, from barricades to candidacy for the Constituent Assembly.[39] For the relationship between the Berlin deaf, the TsV, and the revolution, the sources are scarcer. The only direct accounts are the statutes and the letter to the King, where the ideological foundations of the club were laid out. Later histories of the club associated its emergence with the revolution, but rather vaguely, as we shall see below.[40] Finally, at least one deaf person, the young Albert Leitzke, took part in the barricade fights, and was killed.[41] There is, however, no closer information about the circumstances surrounding his death, neither can any connection between him and the TsV be determined.

In the multitude of hopes and demands associated with the revolution, three basic themes can be distinguished, although they should not be understood as unanimously embraced by the revolutionaries. Indeed, all three were the causes of division between different social and political groups. Nevertheless, these main themes help to understand the ideological context of the deaf club. The first theme was constitutional reform: few went as far as insisting on a republic, but there was a general call for constitutional monarchy. Then, there was the question of the nation state, a 'Germany' united under one government, as it shared language and culture. Finally, the 'social question', the material need and the distribution of resources was central, above all to the lower classes.[42]

As described in the statutes, the TsV appeared as charitable, mainly sociable, and with a tendency towards moral discipline. The members must obey the board, and were obligated to several restrictions to their socializing: no smoking or disturbing the lectures, end of the get-together at 10 pm, attendance only

---

38 *Statuten des Taubstummen-Vereins in Berlin.* (Berlin: E. Feister, n.d.), p. 8, GStA PrK HA I., Rep. 89 Nr. 22575.
39 Quartararo, Deaf Identity and Social Images, pp. 118-123.
40 *V.* below p. 171.
41 *V.* the list of fallen revolutionaries in Walter Schmidt et al., *Illustrierte Geschichte der deutschen Revolution 1848/49* (Berlin: Dietz, 1988), p. 89.
42 Dieter Langewiesche, "Republik, konstitutionelle Monarchie und 'soziale Frage.' Grundprobleme der deutschen Revolution von 1848/49," in *Die deutsche Revolution von 1848/49,* ed. Dieter Langewiesche (Darmstadt: Wissenschaftliche Buchgesellschaft, 1983), pp. 341-361; Nipperdey, *Deutsche Geschichte,* pp. 600-604.

allowed for members or for those who have been previously approved by the president.[43] In contrast to later deaf movement organizations, no reference was made to a progressive agenda, particular group interests, or discontent. In the accompanying letter, the founders expressed their great loyalty to the King, strongly positioning themselves as supporters of the monarchy:

> "So be it that the power of speech is withheld from us, but not so the sentiment of love to the King, to Your Royal Majesty, that our parents implanted in our chests[. T]he most esteemed country father we will keep with faithfulness, and if there is something that comforts us for lacking the noble sense, the hearing, it is the thought of not hearing all that is excogitated to undermine faithfulness and love to his ancestral Monarch.
> Were we to be called to manifest our faithfulness through manor and blood, we would not hesitate to sacrifice it all for Your Royal Majesty."[44]

Devotion to the King was nothing unusual, not even among the revolutionaries. Anger was not directed towards him, but towards the military, the administration, and the advisors surrounding him.[45] However, Fürstenberg and Twele did not confine themselves to personal loyalty to the King, but explicitly declared their support for an ancestral, that is, not constitutional, monarchy. They also made a reference to anti-royalist agitation, declaring that they were unconditionally loyal.

As it seems, they made no attempt at grasping the opportunity of a more liberal society, but instead chose to officially seek permission from, and declare commitment to, the old regime at the very moment when this would not have been necessary. Neither would the legal limitations imposed on associations and clubs before the revolution have been an obstacle to them, since they clearly had

---

43   Statuten des Taubstummen-Vereins in Berlin, GStA PrK HA I., Rep. 89 Nr. 22575.
44   "Ist uns auch die Macht der Rede versagt, so doch nicht das Gefühl, die von unseren Eltern in unsere Brust gelegte Liebe zum Könige, zu Ew Königl. Majestät, den allerwerthen Landesvater werden wir mit Treue bewahre[n] und wenn irgend etwas ist, was uns über den Mangel des edelen Sinnes, des Gehörs tröstet, so ist es der Gedanke nicht hören zu dürfen, was alles ersonnen wird, um Treue und Liebe zu seinem angestammten Monarchen zu untergraben. // Sollten wir berufen sein, unsere Treue dur[ch] Gut und Blut zu bekunden, so würden wir nich[t] zögern, dies alles für Ew Königl. Majestät hinzugeben." E. Fürstenberg and W. Twele to the King, 11 July 1848, GStA PrK, HA I., Rep. 89, 22575.
45   Hachtmann, *Revolution,* pp. 183-184, 207, 217.

no political aim in any sense.⁴⁶ Considering these aspects, the connection between the TsV Berlin and the revolution seems weak. Fürstenberg and Twele were neither dependent on the new freedom to form their club, nor did they associate themselves with the movement for political and social change.

Nevertheless, revolutionary sentiments do echo in their letter and statutes. The idea of Germany as a nation, a German people united by their language and culture, but scattered across the geographical space, received its pendant in the situation of the deaf as they described it. 'Up until now' the deaf had been 'solitarily living', but in the club, they were unified. Fürstenberg and Twele did not see their club as merely a circle of friends, but as a union of 'the deaf': "The male deaf-mutes living in Berlin join together in an association, which shall carry the name Taubstummen-Verein."⁴⁷

Membership was restricted to deaf men with a certain occupational position. They must "either run a business, or as assistants, artists, [or] civil servants have an independent position."⁴⁸ Furthermore, teachers at the Royal Asylum were allowed to be members, but no other hearing people. Thus, the TsV in reality only organized a minority of the deaf, but by introducing itself as the union of 'the' Berlin deaf men, it made a claim to universality. A new classification of the deaf, coming not from physicians or statisticians, but from people who themselves were deaf, had thus entered the stage, and it defined them as *Bürger* in the wider sense. They could be either craftsmen or professionals, but must have at least a standard of living that made them 'independent'.

The further political developments in 1848 and 1849 were too complex to be described at length here. The remark will have to suffice that the parliament was unable to implement its mission, and in spring 1849, it was dissolved.⁴⁹ It followed the so-called reactionary era. Liberal reforms such as electoral laws, freedom of press, association- and military laws were withdrawn. Censorship, police authority, and suppression and persecution of the opposition once again became Prussian trademarks. The German states took, to a greater or lesser

---

46 *Cf.* Hueber, "Vereinsrecht" pp. 116-117.
47 "Die in Berlin lebenden männlichen Taubstummen treten in einen Verein, welcher den Namen 'Taubstummen-Verein' führen soll, zusammen." *Statuten des Taubstummen-Vereins in Berlin*, p. 3, GStA PrK HA I., Rep. 89 Nr. 22575.
48 "entweder ein Gewerbe betreibt, oder als Gehülfe, Künstler, Beamter eine unabhängige Stellung einnimmt" *Statuten des Taubstummen-Vereins in Berlin*, p. 3, GStA PrK HA I., Rep. 89 Nr. 22575.
49 Nipperdey, *Deutsche Geschichte*, pp. 647-663.

extent, a conservative political course.⁵⁰ During this period, the TsV Berlin appears to have had a quiet and uncontroversial existence. For more than twenty years, until 1872, the club left no further traces in the sources.

The Spread of the Deaf Movement

It was, however, only a few years later that Eduard Fürstenberg for a brief moment again caught the attention of the Prussian authorities. In 1851, the principal Carl Wilhelm Saegert at the Royal Asylum reported a case of alleged fraud to the police. He had come across advertisements for a theatre play, which was to be performed "on behalf of the deaf-mutes."⁵¹ Saegert, however, had nothing to do with the play, and considered it a way of tricking the audience into thinking they attended a charity event, when in fact the profits never reached the asylum. As Saegert was well aware, it was Eduard Fürstenberg who stood behind the advertisements. The latter was made to apologize and explain to the school council that the show was in fact on behalf of the *Centralverein für das Wohl der Taubstummen* (CVWT). The phrase "on behalf of the deaf-mutes" had been used merely as a simplification, instead of the full name of the organization.⁵²

This was a different club than the 1848 *Taubstummenverein*. From its early years, only these letters remain as sources, so that we can at best guess what the reasons were for forming another organization. Judging by the name, the CVWT was different from the TsV Berlin by being 'central', as opposed to local, and charitable ("für das Wohl", "for the wellbeing of", the deaf). There was obviously an ambition to gather funds for the organization, and this was thought of as an activity 'on behalf of the deaf', but how the funds were used is obscure. The club entered the public sphere with the assertion to act 'on behalf of the deaf,' which challenged the claim made by the hearing managers of the education system of being the sole benefactors of 'the deaf-mutes'. The CVWT thus transferred the designation 'the deaf-mutes' from the educational, state administered realm, to a space that lay outside of the institutions. Who populated this realm, who the 'deaf-mutes' on whose behalf the CVWT acted in 1851

---

50 Ibid., pp. 674-683.
51 "zum Besten der Taubstummen" Saegert to the Provenzial-Schul-Kollegium, 5 April 1851, BLHA Rep. 34 Nr. 1314.
52 Saegert to the Provenzial-Schul-Kollegium, 5 April 1851, Saegert to the Polizei-Präsidium 5 April 1851; E. Fürstenberg/ CVWT to the Schul-Kollegium der Provinz Brandenburg, 5 April 1851, BLHA Rep. 34 Nr. 1314; "Vereinswesen," TsF 9 (1899) p. 43; *cf.* below p. 246.

were, neither we, nor Saegert knew. We only know from his letter that it was not those 'deaf-mutes' who stood under his protection.

Then, in October 1872, Eduard Fürstenberg and the CVWT launched the periodical *Taubstummenfreund*. The address on the front page of the first issue explained the motive of this undertaking: Deaf people from the entire monarchy – Prussia – came together once each year for the 'church feast', a three-day event arranged by the CVWT. "Thus you remain for an entire year disconnected and quiet and without any message from the central point of the deaf-mutes here."[53] With the *Taubstummenfreund*, this isolation was to be remedied. The *Taubstummenfreund* "will liberate you from the quiet and sad condition and offer pleasant entertainment, edification and encouragement."[54] Once again, Fürstenberg, who was most likely the author of the text, referred to 'the deaf mutes', or rather, 'you deaf-mutes', in general. Those who came together in Berlin for the church feast were not 'many deaf-mutes', but simply 'the deaf-mutes'. 'The deaf-mutes' lived in different places, but they had a central point, which was located in Berlin. The role of the TsF was to distribute messages from this central point to the periphery.

Through the issuing of the TsF, an imagined community of deaf people emerged more clearly. Fürstenberg had expressed the idea of uniting the 'up until now solitarily living companions-in-suffering' already in 1848, but with the TsF, there was, for the first time, an infrastructure beyond the local-personal network for this movement. Print media are crucial vehicles for the imagining of communities, as noted by Benedict Anderson. Printed texts, especially newspapers, have the power of making a certain group of unacquainted people feel that they are connected to each other and to certain events. Of early American newspapers, Anderson writes:

"Early gazettes contained – aside from news about the metropole – commercial news (when ships would arrive and depart, what prices were current for what commodities in what ports), as well as colonial political appointments, marriages of the wealthy, and so forth. In other words, what brought together, on the same page, *this* marriage with *that* ship, *this* price with *that* bishop, was the very structure of the colonial administration and market-system itself. In this way, the newspaper of Caracas quite naturally, and even

---

53 "So bleibt Ihr dann ein ganzes Jahr ganz abgeschlossen und still und ohne alle Mittheilungen von dem hiesigen Centralpunkt der Taubstummen." TsF 1 (1872), p. 1.

54 "Euch von der stillen traurigen Lage befreien und Euch eine angenehme Unterhaltung, Belehrung und Ermunterung darbieten wird." TsF 1 (1872), p. 1.

apolitically, created an imagined community among a specific assemblage of fellow-readers, to whom *these* ships, brides, bishops and prices belonged."[55]

In a similar way, the TsF brought together personal news, current events, and the activities in deaf clubs, and distributed them to a readership, to whom, then, *these* personal news, current events, and club activities belonged.[56] Although personally unacquainted, deaf people living in different places were now able to "visualize in a general way the existence of thousands and thousands like themselves through print-language."[57]

A further result of the publication of the TsF was that, from this moment on, activities in the deaf clubs in Berlin and elsewhere were regularly advertised and reported, so that the available sources are suddenly plentiful. As we shall see, the silence between mid-century and the 1870s had concealed the ongoing existence of the Berlin clubs, as well as the emergence of several others, both there and in other German cities. With the TsF, they obtained a forum for publicly announcing their existence and activity. Through the lists of clubs published on a few occasions by the TsF and its successors, and the notices of club activity, an idea of the extent and character of the movement can be gained.

The first list of deaf clubs was published in the TsF in 1873; the next appeared in the *Taubstummencourier* in 1891. For a third overview, I have selected the 1913 *Taubstummenkalender* (which was based on information from 1912), since this was the publication available closest to the end of the study period. (fig. 8)

Due to the type of the sources and the necessarily inconsistent selection, the lists should not be understood as a representation of activity in deaf clubs, but as three statements on the extent of deaf organization in Germany.[58] However, all three publications, and especially the *Taubstummenkalender,* had a practical function beyond the discursive one: They assisted the communication between deaf individuals and clubs. Deaf migrants could easily initiate contact with local deaf. Travellers could include a visit to a deaf club in their sojourns in unfamiliar cities. It was also possible to extend one's local network by extracting information about the activity taking place in the surrounding area.

---

55 Anderson, *Imagined Communities,* p. 62 [emphasis in original].
56 A mixture between trivial stories from the lives of deaf individuals with news with a more general significance was typical for 19th century deaf press. V. Murray, *Touch of Nature,* p. 27.
57 Anderson, *Imagined Communities,* p. 77.
58 *Cf.* above, pp. 19f.

Figure 8: Number of deaf clubs in Germany, their locations and representatives, as listed in 1873, 1891, and 1913.

Source	Number of clubs	Individual locations	Representatives	Thereof: women	clergymen	teachers	other authorities
Taubstummen-freund 1873[59]	20	13	86	4	2	3	1
Taubstummen-courier 1891[60]	37	23	137	3	0	0	0
Taubstummen-kalender 1913[61]	281	145	907	24	21	27	11

Viewing the three lists together, it appears as if the deaf movement had embraced the German nation in an ever-denser net over the years. Complying with the tendency observed in other types of organizations, the last of the three lists displays a differentiated movement.[62] Clubs for different sports received their own sections in the *Taubstummenkalender*, as did central and regional organizations and political, that is, social democratic, clubs.[63]

Each of the three publications had their own characteristics, which of course impacted the impression they gave of the totality of the deaf movement. The strong position of the CVWT and Fürstenberg displayed in the 1873 overview cannot be considered without regard to the fact that Fürstenberg compiled the list. The publication of such a list in the TC implied its desired status as an organ for deaf people all over Germany, and its agenda of uniting them in a lobby. Further, it was an opportunity to define the borders of the deaf movement in the internal discourse. Through publishing a list of deaf clubs, the TC was able to influence the information deaf individuals had about deaf clubs, and what the clubs knew about each other. Significantly, no teachers or other hearing authority figures, such as clergy or officials, were named as deaf club representatives in

---

59 "Verzeichnis," TsF 4 (1873), pp. 33-34; TsF 5 (1873), pp. 49-50; TsF 6 (1873), p. 61; TsF 7 (1873), p. 71.
60 "Verwaltungen und Versammlungen der Taubstummen-Vereine," TC 8 (1891), pp. 94-96.
61 *Taubstummenkalender* (1913), pp. 50-78, 92-95, 101-103, 107-108, 113.
62 Nathaus, Organizierte Geselligkeit, pp 124-125.
63 *Taubstummenkalender* (1913), pp. 50-53, 78, 92-95, 101-103, 107-108.

the TC; more so than the TsF, the TC was openly critical to the education system and to policy.[64]

Most significant, however, is the leap from the lists in the TsF and the TC to the *Taubstummenkalender*. TsF and the TC had both issued their lists as series, which were completed through cooperation with the readers. Thus, they were not only directories, but also surveys. Both publications issued their lists as a part of a communication with their readers, who were asked to submit information to complete the picture.[65] The *Taubstummenkalender*, on the other hand, appeared as a finalized product. Of course, clubs reported their addresses to the editor for publishing, but the result was a booklet meant to spread, not gather, information. The existence of deaf clubs all over Germany had shifted from a novelty being surveyed, into an unquestioned certainty, which needed only to be broadcast. The interest in the clubs and other establishments for the deaf was obviously widespread enough to sustain a commercial product such as the *Taubstummen–kalender*.

Due to the diverse contexts of the three lists, differences are inevitable in the images of the deaf movement they offer. Instead, the similarities are more interesting. In all of the publications, the number of women mentioned as representatives of the clubs was extremely low. When they appeared, it was mostly on the boards of women's clubs.[66] Hearing men in esteemed positions – teachers, clergymen and other authority figures – were featured as representatives of the deaf more frequently than women. Greater differentiation and spread of the movement was not matched by internal diversity. Rather, it seems as if the male dominance reproduced itself whenever the movement grew, regardless of its transformation from the small number of 'deaf-mute-clubs' scattered across Germany in 1873, to the elaborate network of 1912. This

---

64   Grötz, "Taubstummen-Courier", *cf.* also below p. 232.
65   "Verzeichnis," TsF 4 (1873), p. 34; "Verwaltungen und Versammlungen der Taubstummen-Vereine," TC 4 (1891), p. 48.
66   A women's club existed in Berlin already in 1873. It had four women on the board, although supervised by Eduard Fürstenberg. "Verzeichnis," TsF 4 (1873), p. 34. In 1891, this club was still the only one listed with women on the board. "Verwaltungen und Versammlungen der Taubstummen-Vereine," TC 8 (1891), p. 94. In 1913, the greater number of women's clubs accounted for the majority of the women board members, although there were exceptions. Thekla Faust in Dresden was on the board of the central organization *Arbeitsausschuß für die Allgemeinheit der Taubstummen Deutschlands* and the regional *Sächsischer Taubstummen-Bund*. *Taubstummenkalender* (1913), p. 50, 52 *cf.* also pp. 56, 58, 68-69.

complied with the general trend; throughout the 19th century, the administrative level of clubs and associations remained a predominantly male domain.[67]

Getting Together: Event Announcements

Most likely, the greater part of deaf club activities were organized without any paperwork. It was common for deaf clubs to have taverns as their regular meeting places, suggesting that informal sociability had an important place in their activities.[68] Participants in such groups knew when and where the meetings took place and needed no invitation, nor documented decisions. Only when the club had charitable or financial aspirations, documentation was required. Furthermore, only when the clubs wished to display their activities or invite others than the regulars, there was a need to advertise. A comprehensive survey of the totality of deaf associations is therefore impossible. It is plausible that many activities and groups were not mentioned in the available sources, and that the most common types of activities that were advertised were not necessarily the most common activities that took place.

Instead of an inventory of the totality of deaf organizations, the following is a portrait of the dominant expressions of deaf group formation.[69] The TsF is an excellent source for this purpose. It was one of the inventions of Eduard Fürstenberg, and remained in his family for its entire publication span. In the first years of its distribution, Fürstenberg made explicit efforts to position it as a central institution of the deaf. He actively sought contact with deaf people in other parts of Germany and Europe, and published overviews of the deaf movement and the deaf population. In 1873, the first congress accepted it as the official organ of the deaf.[70]

Many deaf clubs used the TsF to advertise and report from their activities. Such notices had two immediate functions: First, potential participants learned about upcoming events. Second, readers everywhere were involved in the activities, even if they were unable to take part in them. Even in the absence of any formal or informal deaf group formations nearby, one could enjoy the

---

67 Tenfelde, "Entfaltung des Vereinswesens," p. 76.
68 *Cf. Taubstummenkalender* (1913), pp. 54-77, also above p. 120.
69 *Cf.* above pp. 19f.
70 Fürstenberg, "Bekanntmachung," TsF 4 (1874), p. 33; "Verhandelt im Saale des evangelischen Vereins," TsF 9-10 (1873), p. 94; "Uebersicht," TsF 2 (1873), pp. 13-15; "Uebersicht," TsF 11 (1873), pp. 114-115; "A nos lecteurs! To our readers!" TsF 19 (1878), p. 76; above p. 160.

accounts of what went on in other localities. It is foremost this experience that we can access today by reading the TsF.

A sample of three volumes of the TsF, 1873, 1892 and 1911, shows that the paper was successful in connecting to deaf clubs and have them advertise their activities. (fig. 9) During the first two decades of issuance, the number of clubs reporting to the TsF fivefolded and the number of referred activities tenfolded. Thereafter, they appear to have reached a plateau and remained at approximately the same level in 1911, the last year of issuance. As the table below shows, administrative meetings was the most common single type of event. Some clubs used the TsF to announce all their meetings, or at least the annual conference, to their members. The rest of the activities were more sociable in nature: Feasts, often at public holidays, or the anniversary of the club formation, were typical parts of German associational life also enjoyed in deaf clubs.

Figure 9: Number and type of deaf club activities as advertised in the TsF in 1873, 1892, and 1911.

Year	1873	1892	1911
Regular meetings	6	93	76
Seasonal feasts	3	20	13
Internal celebration	4	27	27
Other social events	2	35	42
Religious events	3	10	11
Excursions	0	21	15
Sport	0	2	10
Lecture, education	0	3	1
Other	5	21	18
Sum			
Total number of activities	23	232	213
Number of clubs	12	59	67
Average number of activities per club and year	2	4	3

In fact, all events were sociable in the sense that they brought groups of deaf people physically together. Less convivial activities, for instance distributing support, collecting funds, and lobbying, were part of the purpose of some clubs, but were rarely mentioned in the TsF. Activism in the political sense was completely absent, and charity or mutual support seldom a topic. Consequently, the deaf movement as presented in the TsF was foremost centered on conviviality, not on campaigning or aid.

Another side of the Deaf movement: Württemberg and Bavaria

Since Eduard Fürstenberg and his relatives dominated the sources to the deaf clubs and their activities, the history of the German deaf movement threatens to become the history of the Fürstenberg/Schenck family. In their history, Berlin is the center. Other parts of Germany did not, however, lack vivid deaf communities and organizations, although they tend to be overshadowed by the Fürstenberg-related structures and events. Previous research has described the flourishing deaf community of Hamburg, with its deaf bourgeoisie and rather heady relations between deaf clubs.[71] In order to balance the presentation, the following offers a brief history of some deaf clubs in Württemberg and Bavaria. No publication comparable to the TsF was issued in these areas, whence the analysis has been based on other types of sources. Instead of periodicals, the available narratives of origins and activities of deaf clubs in these areas derive mainly from correspondence with the authorities. Thus, this section portrays another side of the deaf movement geographically, as well as regarding the type of sources.

The history of deaf organizations in Württemberg appears differently depending on the source. The first proof of its existence dates from 1884, when the *Allgemeiner Taubstummenverein* (ATV) in Stuttgart sent a birthday greeting to King Karl I. of Württemberg. During the following decades, the club continued to send greetings and submitted its annual reports at irregular intervals.[72] Otherwise, the ATV attracted little attention until the King received a cryptic letter from the president, Friedrich Grözinger, in 1887. In this letter, Grözinger turned to the King to explain that he had seen himself forced to resign from his office due to "unworthy members".[73] He expressed no request in the letter, but simply informed of his resignation and declared his devotion and gratitude to the King. This message prompted an investigation by the city director Hermann Wilhelm von Hoser to determine its purpose. He presented a comprehensive report on the history of and relations within the club, in which he dated its origin to 1881. Grözinger had been its president from that date, and according to von Hoser he had exercised a strict control over its members. Himself a well-educated and established craftsman, Grözinger had a high self-esteem as

---

71   Hannen, *Von der Fürsorge zur Barrierefreiheit*, pp. 3-32; Fischer et al., "John E. Pacher"; Iris Groschek, "John Pacher."
72   V. HStA Stuttgart E 14 Bü1388.
73   "unwürdige Mitglieder" Grözinger to the King, 10 February 1888, HStA Stuttgart, E 14, Bü1388.

president of the club. He had turned to "high and highest personalities"[74] with requests on behalf of the club – likely, the sending of annual reports to the King was an example of this habit. In later years, according to von Hoser, other members had criticized Grözinger's style of leadership, which they experienced as meddling in private matters. The club took a "freer direction, perhaps somewhat coloured by social democracy."[75] Nevertheless, von Hoser asserted, it posed no threat to society but was at the present day headed by a decent man, the bookbinder Karl Krieger. Grözinger, concluded von Hoser, was likely disappointed that he had not been able to split the club and take part of its assets with him into a new organization. This, and not any implicit demand for personal favours, was probably the true motive of the letter.[76]

The purpose of the club, as von Hoser derived from the statutes, was similar to that of the 1848 Berlin club: bringing deaf people together to socialize and learn, as well as support of needy members. This remained in the statutes adopted in 1899 by the club, which by then had changed its name to *Württembergischer Taubstummen-Verein* (WTV). The statutes of the WTV put the emphasis on support rather than on sociability. Social and educational gatherings were part of the activities, but motivated by the need to collect funds for the club. These were then used to support old, physically disabled, or ill members. How this support should be distributed was tightly regulated in the statutes. Rules such as the duty to report illness and recovery within three days, membership fees rising according to age, and the requirement that members join before reaching the age of 50, made it similar to an insurance association.[77]

These statutes were written to provide for registration as an incorporated society. Included was a brief history of the club. In this version, the origins were dated to 1852, when the paper *Blätter für Taubstumme* was published at the expense of the royal government. This was the first German periodical for deaf people and was edited by a succession of hearing teachers. It mainly consisted of religious, moral, and edifying texts, serving the purpose of maintaining the contact with former pupils. Occasionally, brief notices on the personal lives of

---

74   "hohe und höchste Persönlichkeiten", Report by von Hoser, 20 February 1888, HStA Stuttgart, E 14 Bü1388.
75   "eine freiere, vielleicht auch etwas sozialdemokratisch gefärbte Richtung", ibid.
76   Ibid.
77   Württembergischer Taubstummen-Verein, *Satzung beraten und angenommen in den außerordentlichen General-Versammlungen vom 5. Nov. 1899 und 1. April 1900* (Ludwigshafen a. R.: Josef Huber, 1911), pp. 3-11, StA Ludwigsburg E 191 Bü 3938.

the readers were included. Apparently, the author of the 1899 history of the Württembergian deaf movement considered this rudimentary formal forum for adult deaf crucial to their eventual organization. From 1869, lectures for deaf adults were held by teachers at the deaf schools, also financed by the government. At last, so the statutes had it, the deaf adults of Stuttgart formed a club in "connection with these efforts of the High Royal Government".[78]

When the WTV, once again renamed *Württembergischer Taubstummen-Fürsorge-Verein* (WTFV), celebrated its 50th anniversary in 1931, it offered two other versions of the origin of the club. According to the jubilee annual report, the club originated in gatherings organized by the superintendent Wilhelm Hirzel of the deaf asylum in Gmünd.[79] The second narrative, a Festschrift, explained that Grözinger, Krieger, and the jeweler Paul Junghans had been inspired to form a club on their visit to the 1880 church feast in Berlin.[80]

Thus, efforts by authorities – the government and the school – and influence from outside – the Berlin church feast – appeared as more important for the founding of the WTV/WTFV in those narratives that derived from the club itself. von Hoser's account did not mention any such affiliations, but described the club as an entity independent of government and transregional control. Displaying itself as independent was not desirable for the WTV/WTFV. When it could, it claimed to have connections to powerful, or at least more notable, institutions. The club also sought to align itself with the monarchy by sending addresses to the King. In the words of von Hoser, Grözinger "has displayed a very high esteem of the dignity of the presidency of the, in itself, quite insignificant club."[81] From von Hoser's viewpoint, the club was so unimportant that not even its social-democratic tendencies were reason for concern. The declarations of affiliation with the government and the school should be understood in this

---

78 "Im Anschluß an diese Bestrebungen der hohen K. Staatsregierung", Württembergischer Taubstummen-Verein, *Satzung beraten und angenommen in den außerordentlichen General-Versammlungen vom 5. Nov. 1899 und 1. April 1900* (Ludwigshafen a. R.: Josef Huber, 1911), p. 3, StA Ludwigsburg E 191, Bü 3938.

79 Württ. Taubstummen-Fürsorgeverein e.V., *Jubiläums-Jahresbericht 1881-1931*, p. 1, StA Ludwigsburg, E 191 Bü 3938.

80 Festschrift des Württemberg. Taubstummen-Fürsorge-Vereins in Stuttgart e. V., p. 9, StA Ludwigsburg, E 191 Bü 3938.

81 "eine sehr hohe Meinung von der Würde der Vorstandsschaft und von der Wichtigkeit des an sich unbedeutenden Vereins an den Tag gelegt" Report by von Hoser, 20 February 1888, HStA Stuttgart, E 14 Bü1388.

context. By claiming to have originated in initiatives from outside, the club may have appeared to be dependent, but that was preferable to insignificance.

According to the first of the 1931 narratives, arrangements by the teacher Hirzel and his colleagues in other places had led to the emergence of local clubs outside of Stuttgart. These had, however, gathered in one organization and thus together formed the WTV. As far as I have been able to find, no traces of any parallel clubs are available in Württembergian archives, so that the WTFV and its predecessors stand alone, at least in the communications with the authorities.

The sources to the deaf movement in Bavaria kept in state archives give the impression of a more pluralistic organizational pattern. Four Munich deaf clubs reported their statutes and activities to the police in the late 19th and early 20th centuries. Oldest of these was the *Taubstummenbrüderbund München,* later renamed *Münchener Taubstummenverein,* and finally *Taubstummenklub Monarchia-Gruß.* It first appeared in 1880 with fourteen members, all men. The board consisted of a gilder, a carpenter's assistant, and a tailor, and had its clubroom in a Munich tavern.[82] The club remained stable over the years, with roughly the same number of members and with few changes in the statutes. Their purpose was, too, sociable gatherings and reciprocal support. Later lists submitted by the club reveal a membership base with a somewhat elevated social status. Several performed finer artisanry such as gilding, goldsmithery, or engraving. Others were artists, one of them the well-known painter Erwin Spindler. A couple were listed as 'academics'. There was, nevertheless, no lack of humble craftsmen such as brush makers and mechanics.[83] The club appears to have had no outward activity. They held regular meetings, excursions, and parties, taking care not to cause offence among the hearing. The statutes proscribed that "Whoever disturbs the hearing through screaming, speaking, stomping, or otherwise inappropriate noise, as if fighting, in the club or other public places, must pay a penalty of 20 [Pfennig] to 1 Mk."[84]

---

82   Statutes, 1880, Rottmann to the Polizei-Direktion, 21 February 1882, StA Munich Pol. Dir. 3675.
83   Müller, Rottmann, and Illing to the Polizei-Direktion, 4 March 1883, Rottman, Kinzinger, and Illing to the Polizei-Direktion 16 March 1884, The Club to the Polizei-Direktion, 4 March 1886, StA Munich Pol. Dir. 3675; *cf.* Joachim Winkler, "Der gehörlose Leipziger Maler Erwin Spindler," *Das Zeichen* 41 (1997), pp. 334-344; idem (Ed.), *Erwin Spindler. 1860-1926. Werkverzeichnis* (Hamburg: Signum Verlag, 1998).
84   "Wer durch Schreien, Reden, Aufstampfen oder sonstwie durch ungebührliches Lärmen, wie beim Streiten, die Hörenden, sei es im Verein oder in anderen öffentlichen

Alongside this club, the more short-lived *Zwanglosen*, a convivial society, and *Friedenspalme*, a mutual savings club, corresponded with the police in the years around the turn of the century. The *Zwanglosen* submitted statutes scrabbled in irregular, sloping writing and incorrect German declaring its purpose to be purely sociable. Ten men were named as members in the society, which met each Saturday in a tavern.[85] The *Friedenspalme* had saving as its main purpose, but also arranged parties for its carefully selected, "able-bodied, proper and peace-loving"[86] members. As far as their occupations were listed, they were all craftsmen or manual workers.

The artists' club *Totenkopf*, which existed between 1902 and 1937, created more controversy. It first denominated itself a 'group of regulars', suggesting that it was a rather informal gathering of deaf men in artistic professions.[87] When they went on to organize art shows in the City Hall, however, this sparked a conflict with a group of deaf artists who were not members. They found it unfair and "almost deceitful"[88] of the club to arrange an exhibition to which not all deaf artists were invited. The complainants contended that a show advertised as an exhibition of works by 'deaf-mutes' should include all deaf artists, not just the members of a certain club. According to some rumours, there were even works by hearing artists, they claimed. Thereby, the buyers were deceived into thinking that they supported needy deaf artists, whereas in fact the members of *Totenkopf* were all wealthy – so they argued. The police investigated the matter but found no evidence of crime.[89]

The information about the number of members, their names, and occupations is unique to these documents on Munich deaf clubs. There was not a single woman in any of the clubs, although the annual 'family feast' arranged by the *Friedenspalme* suggested a possibility for women to take part in at least some

---

Lokalen belästigt, der wird zur Strafe von 20 .. – 1 MK verurtheilt." Statutes 1885, § 3, StA Munich Pol. Dir. 3675.

85   Statutes 1895, Johann Selze to the Polizei-Direktion, 28 January 1895, Pol. Dir. Munich, Revision des im Adreßbuch angefürten Vereine 17 March-3 July 1900, StA Munich Pol. Dir. 1445.

86   "arbeitsfähige, ordentliche und friedensliebende" Statutes, 1901, StA Munich, Pol. Dir. 2688.

87   Anmeldung des freien Taubstummen-Künstler-Klub "Totenkopf" als Verein, 5 January 1903, StA Munich Pol. Dir. 3674.

88   "fast betrüglicher Weise", Josef Oberndorfer, Ernst Kohlmajer, and Kamper to the Polizei-Direktion, 18 November 1905, StA Munich Pol. Dir. 3674.

89   Aktenvermerk., Munich 23 April 1906, StA Munich Pol. Dir. 3674.

activities.[90] All four had their clubrooms in taverns, an environment which may have contributed to the exclusion of women. As for the social structure of the membership, craftsmen made up for the most part, but there were a few day labourers, as well as academics. Striking is that several of the members were artists or artisans. The Munich deaf movement thus appears to have largely been carried by an elite of free professionals and highly skilled craftsmen. Yet, occupations such as these were no guarantee for a good material standard. A 1903 letter to the King from the xylographer Joseph Oberndorfer, a member of *Zwanglosen,* demonstrates this. In the letter, he asked for support to open a secondary school and teach other deaf in legal matters. He thought of this as a possibility for a new career, since the spread of photography had put his services out of demand. At the moment, his deaf wife supported the family by peddling religious prints he made. The request was denied with reference to the expert opinion of the principal Koller of the Munich Central Royal Deaf-Mute Institute, who claimed that Oberndorfer was unqualified for this work – not least because he was deaf.[91]

Mutual Support

As we have seen, the less sociable activities were also important parts of the purpose of many clubs. Not least, this applies to saving money together, and collecting funds for comrades in need. This becomes evident in other types of sources. Rather than in periodicals, charitable and financial motives and activities appear in statutes, annual reports, and correspondence. How common this was is not possible to determine, but of the few clubs already discussed, most had some sort of charitable or mutual aid purpose. In some cases, as with the 1848 Berlin club, the statement was a rather vague reference to helping the individual "with words and deeds".[92] The WTFV on their hand had a statute that regulated exactly how the aid should be distributed. Documents from the WTFV show that they paid modest contributions, ranging between five and seven Mk, to

---

90 Statutes, 1901, StA Munich, Pol. Dir. 2688.
91 Pol. Dir. Munich, Revision der im Adreßbuch angefürten Vereine 17 March- 3 July 1900, StA Munich, Pol. Dir. 1445; BayHStA, Kultusministerium Rep. MK, Nr. 17542.
92 *Statuten des Taubstummen-Vereins in Berlin,* GStA PrK 1 HA Rep. 89 22575,; *cf.* Statuten, 1880, StA Munich Pol. Dir. 3675.

members in need well into the 20th century.[93] There were numerous clubs with mutual savings banks, as shown not least in the directory in the *Taubstummenkalender*.[94] Yet others engaged in charity, rather than reciprocal aid. This applied to the *Totenkopf*, which donated part of the profit from their exhibitions to poor deaf children, and to a sewing club on behalf of needy deaf in Berlin.[95] A further type of social engagement by the deaf clubs were the asylum projects, undertakings by some clubs to build and run their own asylums for elderly, disabled, or poor deaf. These projects will be discussed at length in the next chapter.[96]

The social insurances introduced in the last decades of the 19th century have been observed to have had an inhibiting effect on societies for mutual support and charity in general.[97] In the available sources, there appears no obvious effect of the welfare laws on deaf movement activity. Sociability and support were no opposites and could be tightly associated with each other to the point where it cannot be determined which was more important. When a mutual savings bank for deaf people advertised weekly meetings, they offered not only an opportunity of depositing money, but of course of getting together with other deaf.[98] Their significance may have been more one of building self-confidence and a sense of independence. Being an object of official measures and of charity was an experience shared by many deaf. Therefore, the ability to support each other instead of turning to instances representing the hearing majority was possibly a way of manifesting the integrity of the deaf community. Not being confronted with cultural and communication barriers might also have made the support from a deaf club more accessible for the needy. Furthermore, investing in a mutual

---

93 Paul Junghans to the Zentralleitung des Wohlthätigkeitsvereins, Stuttgart 10. January 1910; 29 December 1910; 15 December 1912; 26 September 1912; 26 September 1913; 11 February 1914; 30 September 1914, StA Ludwigsburg, E 191 Bü 3938.
94 *Taubstummenkalender* (1913), for instance pp. 55-56, 68-71, 74, 76.
95 Fritsch, Erlaubniserteilung, 30 November 1904, StA Munich Pol. Dir. 3674; *Taubstummenkalender* 1913 p. 56.
96 *V.* below p. 246.
97 Ingo Tornow, *Das Münchner Vereinswesen in der ersten Hälfte des 19. Jahrhunderts, mit einem Ausblick auf die zweite Jahrhunderthälfte*. Neue Schriftenreihe des Stadtarchivs München (Munich: Kommissionsbuchhandlung R. Wölfle, 1977), p. 270; Im Hof, *Das gesellige Jahrhundert*, p. 234.
98 *Cf.* notice on the Berlin mutual savings society *Einigkeit*, TsF 21 (1911), p. 116.

support fund tied the members to the club, and therefore had the additional function of consolidating the social network.[99]

Practicing Deaf Community: Conclusion

The association movement channelled popular desires for egalitarian ways of interaction, sociability and leisure, and public manifestation and influence in 19th century Germany. As a part of this general trend, deaf people also organized – as deaf people – in clubs of various kinds. They thus created their own institutions for encounters between people who were deaf, and started to collectively and independently manage their social needs. These organizations served all the purposes of the mainstream association movement: leisure, networking, support, internalisation of democratic and civic values and skills, and lending social status.

IMAGINED DEAF COMMUNITIES

In addition to being formalized forms of deaf networks, the deaf association movement also crystallized a new meaning of the category 'the deaf-mutes', as we shall see. Whereas governments, statisticians, and educators were concerned with identifying and managing the deaf as a demographic subgroup and an educational challenge, the clubs imagined the deaf as a community.

Birth of a Legend: Eduard Fürstenberg and his Legacy

For the previous account of how the first deaf clubs in Germany were formed, the ambition was to use only what could be considered 'first-hand' sources. The correspondence with authorities and club statutes were part of the constitution of the clubs. It was only much later, in the deaf press, that narratives of how the clubs formed appeared. The earliest of these is from 1873, twenty-five years after the founding of the Berlin TsV. Since they have likely been polished over the years, such stories are more telling of their contemporary context than of the actual events they claim to account for. The recollections in the late 19th century

---

99 *Cf.* Klaus Tenfelde, "Bergmännisches Vereinswesen im Ruhrgebiet während der Industrialiserung," in *Fabrik, Familie, Feierabend. Beiträge zur Sozialgeschichte des Alltags im Industriezeitalter*, eds. Jürgen Reulecke and Wolfgang Weber (Wuppertal: Peter Hammer Verlag, 1978), p. 323.

of how the Berlin TsV came to be indicate above all the great influence of one of its founders, Eduard Fürstenberg.

Fürstenberg was born into a wealthy and well-connected Berlin family in 1827. Allegedly deafened at the age of four, he was enrolled at the Royal Asylum. Following his education there, he commenced autodidactic studies and began a career in the Prussian administration, bringing him to the position of secretary at the Finance Ministry. He married the hearing schoolteacher Malvine Pasch and had six hearing children. One of his sons, Paul Fürstenberg, became a teacher of the deaf; his eldest daughter, Anna Schenck, a Sign Language interpreter.[100] As we have seen, Fürstenberg in 1848, aged twenty-one, became president of the TsV Berlin, soon thereafter also of the CVWT, and from 1872 he edited the TsF. As president of the CVWT, he was effectively the leader of all Berlin deaf clubs, published what was for a long time the only periodical owned by the deaf movement, and organized the first deaf congresses.[101] Thus, he undoubtedly had a great influence over the early deaf movement. From the 'first-hand' documentation, however, we cannot extract much about his leadership style, or organizational and ideological legacy. It was later on, when references to and narratives of the early history of the deaf movement started to appear, that the image of Fürstenberg received the characteristics that will be discussed below.

After the Berlin TsV celebrated its 25th anniversary in 1873, the festivities were described in detail in the TsF. It was a double anniversary, both of the club and of Fürstenberg as its president. To the occasion, the club arranged a dinner and dance in a banquet hall at Unter den Linden. Fürstenberg opened the event with a speech – in Sign – on the club's history. He used a stylized story of the coming of age of a young deaf man to explain the role of the TsV: the school was the first rescuer of the deaf child, equipping him with skills and knowledge and turning his parents' grief over his deafness into joy over his achievements. After school, however, there was nowhere for the young man to turn. In spite of his education, he was at risk of choosing an immoral path. Then and there, he encountered the deaf club. "A community of deaf-mutes",[102] which to Fürstenberg was equivalent to the TsV, prodded the young man onto the right path. Following this symbolic tale, Fürstenberg recalled how the club was formed, according to him over twenty-five years ago. It was from the beginning an

---

100 Muhs, "Eduard Fürstenberg," p. 422; "Eduard Fürstenberg," TC 2 (1885), pp. 13-15.
101 V. above/below pp. 158, 178, 186.
102 "Eine Gesellschaft Taubstummer", "Doppel-Jubiläum," TsF 5 (1873), p. 43.

informal circle of deaf friends, who due to "the unrest prevailing in Europe in those days"[103] could not formalize their group until April 30th, 1848. The activity of the TsV Berlin from then on was described as follows:

"Under the gracious protection of the Good Lord [the club] quietly, through instructions, advice, and deeds endeavoured to steadily urge its members to a proper and decent life. The board is constantly prepared to help every deaf-mute in any direction, and stands by its members and other companions-in-suffering as advisor, leader, and mediator in civil [bürgerlich] life."[104]

Finally, Fürstenberg explained that the CVWT had been formed in association with the TsV Berlin with the main purpose of founding an asylum for elderly deaf. His lecture was accompanied with three tableaux vivants, depicting the constitutive meeting, the purposes of the club, and finally a vision of the future, where an elderly deaf couple joyously await the visit of a young deaf man in the projected asylum.[105]

In connection with the anniversary, Fürstenberg received numerous gifts from the club members as a sign of their gratitude and appreciation. The eldest members of the club were honoured with commemorative silver plates. Several addresses from other clubs were also received. At the end of the banquet, a Mr. Meißner from the club board made a toast in Fürstenberg's honour, calling the members to address the latter "no longer as president, but from now on as father of all deaf-mutes".[106]

The club and Fürstenberg could hardly be distinguished from one another at the celebration. To honour the club was to honour Fürstenberg, and vice versa. The role of the club that was emphasised was above all that of a moral guide and benevolent helper. It did not appear as a place for public deliberation, and only to

---

103 "die damals in Europa herrschenden Unruhen", "Doppel-Jubiläum," TsF 5 (1873), p. 44.
104 "In aller Stille war derselbe unter dem gnädigen Schutze des lieben Gottes bemüht, seine Mitglieder allmählig durch Belehrung, Rathschläge und That zum ordentlichen und sittlichen Leben anzuhalten. Der Vorstand ist jedem Taubstummen stets bereit zur Hülfe in jeder Richtung und steht auch als Rathgeber, Führer und Vermittler seiner Mitglieder und anderer Leidensgefährten im bürgerlichen Leben zur Seite." "Doppel-Jubiläum," TsF 5 (1873), p. 44.
105 Ibid., p. 44.
106 "nicht mehr als Vorsitzenden, sondern nunmehr als Vater sämmtlicher Taubstummen" ibid., p. 46.

a degree sociable – the latter impression came foremost from the buoyant mood of the evening itself, not from the description of club activities. Fürstenberg, as the personification of the club, was celebrated as a father figure, not as an emancipator.

In early 1885, Eduard Fürstenberg died at the age of 58. Over 300 deaf people and several elevated personalities from government and military attended his funeral, which was conducted in Sign by the preacher Schönberner. The coffin was carried by the other members of the club board, and the banner of the TsV Berlin headed the cortège. The obituaries in the TsF and the new deaf periodical *Taubstummencourier* remembered him much in the same tone as he had been honoured at the 25th anniversary. The TsF emphasised his reputation as a servant to the common good.[107] In the *Taubstummencourier,* he was called the father of the deaf, described as an indefatigable organizer, helper, and guide, and a captivating although strict signer.[108] The founding of the first deaf club was described as a personal impulse of Fürstenberg's, who was inspired by the liberal ideas of the time to unite the deaf:

"It was in the days of the spring of nations, a freer striving animated the awakened spirits, people everywhere sought to give the new ideas form and figure, people everywhere strode towards associations with eagerness and agile will. Could then Fürstenberg's clear gaze overlook the social isolation of his companions-in-suffering? Must not his eager heart have felt stimulated to the foundation of beneficial associations?"[109]

The next account of deaf movement history appearing in the deaf press was written by August Schenck, a deaf teacher, sculptor, secretary and photographer, and son-in-law of Eduard Fürstenberg. He was married to the Sign Language interpreter Anna Schenck, née Fürstenberg.[110] The context was an obituary of Joseph Ludwig Karl Beck, born in 1822, who had been a founding member of

---

107 Obituary of Eduard Fürstenberg, TsF 1 (1885), pp. 1-2.

108 "Eduard Fürstenberg," TC 2 (1885), pp. 13-15.

109 "Es war die Zeit des Völkerfrühlings, ein freieres Streben belebte die erwachten Geister, überall suchte man den neuen Ideen Form und Gestalt zu geben, überall schritt man mit Eifer und regem Willen zu Vereinigungen. Konnte da der klare Blick Fürstenberg's die gesellschaftliche Isolirtheit seiner Leidensgefährten übersehen? Musste sich da nicht sein thatbereites Herz zur Gründung von heilsamen Vereinigungen angeregt fühlen?", "Eduard Fürstenberg," TC 2 (1885), p. 13.

110 Albin Maria Watzulik, obituary of August Schenck, TsF 46 (1892), p. 195, *cf.* above p. 123.

the TsV Berlin. Beck had arrived in Berlin in 1840, and attended classes at the Royal Asylum although already a grown man and trained carpenter. "In the evenings after completing his day's work, he enjoyed a pleasant gathering with different comrades-in-fate in a certain restaurant in the Taubenstrasse. Here stood the cradle of the first deaf-mute-club".[111] In this circle of friends, ten in number, the idea of forming a club for the purpose of saving for old age emerged. This was, according to Schenck, in 1847. Lacking a formal statute and permission, the club was shaken by the social turmoil in the following year. At this point in Schenck's account, Eduard Fürstenberg appeared as a *deus ex machina*. He had not been part of the original group, but when learning about its existence, he initiated contact, "averted the collapse of the club, was elected president, devised the club-statutes".[112]

At the 50th anniversary of the Berlin club, the TsF, now edited by Anna Schenck, printed Fürstenberg's portrait on the front page. It was accompanied by a short text, recalling the origins of the TsV Berlin as an informal group of 29 deaf friends. Fürstenberg and the subsequent presidents were listed, and the paper expressed the hope that the club might continue its valuable service to its members.[113] The *Taubstummencourier* used the same occasion to evaluate and celebrate the whole German deaf movement. The theme from Fürstenberg's obituary was repeated. He stood as the originator of the movement, driven by the emancipatory ideals of the *Vormärz*.[114] As a sign of the success, not only of Fürstenberg's endeavour, but in a wider context of the entire project of deaf education, the TC took the reader on a journey through six German cities and displayed a stylized image of the present status of the clubs and deaf communities. Focus lay rather on the elite of each local deaf community, than on the actual clubs. In each city, the TC encountered successful deaf entrepreneurs

---

111 "Abends nach vollbrachtem Tagewerk hatte er mit verschiedenen Schicksalsgenossen eine gemüthliche Zusammenkunft in einer gewissen Restauration in der Taubenstraße. Hier stand die Wiege des ersten Taubstummen-Vereins." August Schenck, obituary of Joseph Ludwig Karl Beck, TsF 5 (1886), p. 19, *cf.* above p. 153.

112 "verhinderte das Eingehen des Vereins, wurde zum Vorsitzenden gewählt, schuf die Vereins-Statuten" August Schenck, obituary of Joseph Ludwig Karl Beck, TsF 5 (1886), p. 19.

113 "Das 50jährige Jubiläum des ältesten deutschen Taubstummen-Vereins," TsF 9 (1898), p. 41.

114 "Der älteste deutsche Taubstummenverein," TC 4 (1898), p. 37.

and skilled craftsmen.[115] Families were emphasised, including the description of the deaf women of Hanover as the "paragons of devoted wives".[116] The present state of the deaf movement was not described in terms of benevolence or moral guidance, but of independence and co-equal sociability. Deaf self-sufficiency, talent, and success were celebrated parallel to the proud mentioning of hearing supporters of the movement, hearing employees and family members.[117] Fürstenberg's legacy was that of a figure symbolizing the origins of the community. In Berlin, the TsV celebrated its anniversary by commissioning a portrait bust of him, their "unforgettable founder".[118]

After Fürstenberg

Fürstenberg was involved in most deaf club activities reported in the TsF in 1873.[119] Thus, he was in charge of both the media and its contents, a position that made him an unparalleled force in administrating the deaf community. The pillars of the deaf movement in Germany – the club, the periodical, the church feast, and the congress – all count their histories back to his initiative. Thus, he was unquestionably a creative and capable force in the development of the movement. On the other hand, the concentration of power had the disadvantage of making his inventions, such as the TsF, highly dependent on him as a person. He struggled with an excessive workload, which, especially in combination with his declining health, meant that the TsF at times had to be downscaled or cancelled.[120] Given this problem, it could have been expected that Fürstenberg's death would lead to a serious crisis for the German deaf movement. This was, however, not the case. As we shall see, the movement was transformed, but only grew stronger, after 1885.

---

115 "Das 50jährige Jubiläum des Localvereines in Berlin," TC 6 (1898), pp. 53-58.
116 "Muster ergebener Gattinnen", "Das 50jährige Jubiläum des Localvereines in Berlin," TC 6 (1898), p. 57.
117 "Das 50jährige Jubiläum des Localvereines in Berlin," TC 6 (1898), pp. 53, 55-56.
118 "unvergesslichen Gründers", "Das 50jährige Jubiläum des Localvereines in Berlin," TC 6 (1898), p. 54.
119 Twelwe out of twenty-three activities were organized by clubs that he headed. *Cf.* above p. 163.
120 "Liebe Leser des Taubstummen-Freundes!" TsF 8 (1873), pp. 79-80; announcements on delayed or downscaled publication, TsF 17 (1875), p. 89; and TsF 13-14 (1880), p. 41; "An unsere geehrten Abonnenten!" TsF 1 (1883), p. 2.

Friedrich Fürstenberg, son of the deceased, inherited the TsF and published it more regularly than before, which suggests that his father at the end of his life had been more of a hindrance than an asset. Only after his death, a new generation could proceed to take on his earlier responsibilities. Carl Rumpf, formerly one of the curators, succeeded Eduard Fürstenberg as president of the CVWT. A second son, Paul Fürstenberg, also joined the board.[121] Thus the Fürstenberg family remained influential in the deaf community. Worth noticing is also that this meant that some of the most important positions in the movement were now held by hearing CODAs.[122] Altogether, it soon became evident that the deaf movement without Eduard Fürstenberg entered a new phase.

Coinciding with Fürstenberg's death, the *Taubstummencourier* was first issued in Vienna. This new forum shifted the central point of the deaf movement's communicative infrastructure away from Berlin and the Fürstenberg family. It made it possible to follow the deaf movement and issues concerning deaf people without relying on the body of organizations built around Fürstenberg. The TC was well-connected with the deaf movement in southern and eastern Germany. Deaf authors and reports from Saxony and Württemberg, and of course Austria, gave perspectives that had been absent or rare in the TsF. Furthermore, the TC contained less moral lessons and more debate than the TsF. The attentive reader would notice a change in the TsF as well, as it ceased to be the official organ of the CVWT. Instead, Eduard Fürstenberg's hearing sons continued the publication at their own expense.[123] The focus on current events in deaf clubs, combined with religious, royalist, and moral texts, remained unaltered.

A further development was that the asylum project drifted from attention after Fürstenberg's death. Instead, another of CVWT's issues gained in topicality: the central organization. In a sense, Fürstenberg had personified the unity of the movement. His personal network had replaced a central organization. Internal conflicts never appeared on the surface of discourse during his years as a leader. Following his death, the deaf movement needed to find a formal interregional structure.

---

121 "An unsere geehrten Leser," TsF 1 (1885), p. 2; "Vereinswesen," TsF 3 (1885), p. 9, *cf.* "Kassen-Bericht," TsF 1 (1884), p. 4.

122 The first example of this was Anna Schenck, at that time Fürstenberg, who was part of the Berlin deaf women's club board already in 1873. "Verzeichnis," TsF 4 (1873), p. 34.

123 "An unsere geehrten Leser," TsF 1 (1885), p. 2.

Unification part I: A Central Organization

The idea of a central organization accompanied the deaf movement from its beginning and throughout the period studied here. In the 1848 letter from the Berlin club to the King, Eduard Fürstenberg's concept of an association for all of Prussia and Germany was mentioned.[124] In the following year, the CVWT reported its address to the police department in Berlin.[125] The original concept of the organization is unknown, since its early statutes do not remain. The scarcity of sources makes it difficult to distinguish the activities of the CVWT from those of the local deaf club. It was not until the issuing of the TsF in 1872 that the CVWT entered a written discourse more elaborate than this brief correspondence.

From this point, it is also possible to determine a difference between the organizations, which can suggest Fürstenberg's motives for founding a second organization so shortly after the first. The CVWT and the local club had a parallel existence and had separate boards, except for Fürstenberg who was the president of both. Alongside these two clubs, there were already in 1873 a further five deaf clubs in Berlin. All were supervised by the CVWT, which thereby functioned as a central administration for the Berlin deaf movement.[126] In that sense, then, the CVWT was 'central', and assured that the Berlin deaf clubs were united as well as concentrating the power over them to Fürstenberg. However, in the list of clubs from 1873, Stettin in Pomerania was the only city except Berlin where the local deaf club described itself as standing under the administration of the CVWT.[127] Thus, Fürstenberg's idea to unite the German deaf in one organization had not yet been fulfilled. The CVWT clearly had a dominant position, but most clubs remained formally independent.

Deaf people could turn to the CVWT for assistance with matters such as translations, contact with officials, and writing letters.[128] In addition, the CVWT engaged in activities with distinctly interregional components: It issued the first

---

124 E. Fürstenberg and W. Twele to the King, 11 July 1848, GStA PrK, HA I., Rep. 89, 22575.
125 An das Kgl. Polizei Präsidium, 10 September 1849, p. 1, Minister des Innern und der geistlichen, Unterrichts- und Medizinal-Angelegenheiten to the Polizeipräsident, 1 December 1849, p. 2, LA Berlin, A Rep. 030-04 Nr. 3008.
126 "Verzeichnis," TsF 4 (1873), pp. 33-34.
127 "Verzeichnis," TsF 5 (1873), p. 49.
128 As recalled by August Schenck, "Der Centralverein für das Wohl der Taubstummen einst und jetzt," TC 4 (1888), p. 40.

periodical in German by and for deaf people and with focus on the deaf movement, which made it possible for deaf people in different regions to communicate more effectively than before. For the first time, deaf activists scattered across the German-speaking world (and beyond, provided they could read German) could enter a shared public sphere. At the same time, their expressions were made available to passive readers. Individuals who were deaf and literate obtained the possibility of identifying with a larger group of people who were also deaf and literate. This created a level of deaf community that was not bound to the physical encounter or to the local network of acquaintances. The readers of the TsF imagined a group of fellow-readers, who, although anonymous, were still known to them as people of the same kind as themselves. Later, the CVWT completed this course by organizing events that brought German deaf from different regions physically together, the church feasts and the congresses.[129] The TsF reader could then heed the call to visit one of these gatherings, where he or she would be able to incorporate into his or her personal network people who were also members of the imagined deaf community.

However, the CVWT had not fulfilled its purpose to be a formal organization for all deaf in Germany. Although the club still existed, deaf activists perceived of their situation as lacking a nation-wide organization. Forming one, however, turned out to be a difficult task, which was not sustainably solved until 1927.[130] The interregional forums for debate within the deaf community, the press and the congresses, were used to discuss if and how such an organization should be formed, and what it should look like. Conflicts arose over numerous questions regarding the central organization issue. Some of these stand out as especially controversial and enduring.

First was a formal question of whether it should be an association with individual members, or an umbrella organization of deaf clubs. Second, the opinions were diverse on what a central organization could and should achieve. For example, there were suggestions to start a labour bureau and a college, or to provide health insurance.[131] The essential point here was whether the central organization was to be social/charitable or ideological/lobbyist. In a debate in the

---

129 V. below pp. 183, 186.
130 In 1927 a "Reichsverband" was founded in Weimar, which the current German-wide Deaf association counts as its predecessor. Cf. *Allgemeine Deutsche Gehör-losen-Zeitschrift* 3 (1927), pp. 11-12, and the homepage of the Deutscher Gehör-losen-Bund e. V., www. gehoerlosen-bund.de .
131 Carl Bente, "Der Taubstummen-Kongreß zu Hannover am 5., 6. und 7. Juni 1892," TsF 25 (1892), pp. 101-102.

TC, the recent formation of a German association of teachers of the deaf was mentioned as a reason why the deaf must unite.[132] A central lobby organization would, in the minds of its proponents, pen petitions and leaflets that could be distributed to press and authorities.[133] The suggestions for a college, health insurance, and labour bueraus are rather signs of a desire for a sort of parallel welfare system for deaf people, with separate-but-equal, self-governed institutions.

For decades, the congresses were unable to settle between the conflicting concepts of the central organization. The solution was each time to elect a committee to process the question. Franz Bossong of Wiesbaden, a hearing publisher and bookstore owner, chaired the first committee.[134] According to the rest of the debaters, both in the TC and at the congresses, Bossong's committee achieved practically nothing. Dissatisfaction with this lead to a new approach at the Nuremberg congress in 1896: As suggested by Albin Maria Watzulik, printer from Altenburg and a prominent figure in the deaf movement, the congress decided that there was no need for a special committee. Instead, the boards of the existing deaf clubs should deliber the issue and try to reach an agreement.[135] This strategy was apparently more effective, as a new organization was founded at the next congress in 1899. It was named *Central-Verband für die Wohlfahrt und die Interessen der Taubstummen Deutschlands,* Central League for the Wellbeing and the Interests of the German Deaf-Mutes (CVWITD).

CVWITD was independent of the existing clubs and therefore required individuals to apply and pay for membership. The capital was to be used for supporting local deaf clubs, which made the organization the opposite of the social support system proposed by some. Instead of deaf individuals receiving support from their organizations, this was an organization that transferred finances from the individual to the movement. The expectation was, of course, that this would strengthen them as a group, or in other words, further their interests and wellbeing. With its seat in Berlin, the CVWITD was linked to the existing deaf clubs there. It appeared almost as a repetition of the CVWT: The

---

132 Max Birnbaum, "Offene Frage an Herrn Franz Bossong in Wiesbaden," TC 1 (1895), pp. 11-12.

133 "Bericht über die Verhandlungen des VI. Allgemeinen Deutschen Taubstummen-Kongreß zu Leipzig am 12.-13. Juni 1905," TsF 14 (1905), p. 72-73.

134 Carl Bente, "Vom zweiten deutschen Taubstummen-Kongreß," TsF 22-23 (1894), p. 73.

135 *Protokoll der Verhandlungen des dritten Deutschen Taubstummen-Kongresses zu Nürnberg* [Appendix to the TsF 1896], p. 2; Max Birnbaum, "Offene Frage an Herrn Franz Bossong in Wiesbaden," TC 1 (1895), pp. 11-12.

organizations shared the same president, Carl Rumpf, and the vice-president was Eduard Fürstenberg' daughter, Anna Schenck. The third board member, Hermann Michelson, was president of the TsV Berlin. As the CVWT before, the CVWITD had the TsF as its official organ.[136] Its editor was at this point Anna Schenck, so that considerable power was once again concentrated in the hands of a member of the Fürstenberg family.

This was, however, only a brief phase in the history of the German deaf movement. It was not until the congress in Leipzig in 1905 that the statutes of the CVWITD were presented and ratified. From the debate at this congress, it was clear that the old conflicts had not been resolved, and that the CVWITD did not live up to the expectations. At the time of the following congress, which was held in Munich in 1908, the organization still appeared to have come no further than discussing basic administrative matters.[137] In Hamburg, where the next congress was held in 1911, the CVWITD was no longer mentioned. A new central organization was formed instead, in the shape of an executive committee with the assignment to carry out the decisions made at the congresses.[138] It was named *Arbeitsausschuss für die Allgemeinheit der Taubstummen Deutschlands* (AATD).[139] This decision settled the conflict between lobbyism and social welfare to the benefit of the former, by formally appointing a group of people to advocate the interests of the deaf.

Other than the CVWITD, which was hardly ever mentioned even in its own official organ,[140] the new executive committee openly and actively sought communication with diverse partners. The editor and the publisher of the deaf periodical *Neue Zeitschrift für Taubstumme* (NZT), were both committee

---

136 "Kassenbericht," TsF 12 (1899), p. 63, "Aufruf," ibid., p. 64.

137 "Bericht über die Verhandlungen des VI. Allgemeinen Deutschen Taubstummen-Kongreß zu Leipzig am 12.-13. Juni 1905," TsF 14 (1905), pp. 72-73; Julius Heinrich, "7. Deutscher Taubstummen-Congreß in München," TsF 19 (1908), pp. 107-108.

138 "Achter Deutscher Taubstummen-Kongreß," TsF 17 (1911), p. 90.

139 Later, it was apparently renamed *Arbeitsausschuss für das Wohl der deutschen Taubstummen* (AAWdT). Wilhelm Gottweiß, "Bericht des Arbeits-Ausschusses für das Wohl der deutschen Taubstummen e. V." ATZ 3 (1917), pp. 13-14.

140 The congress reports and a bulletin declaring that it had been constituted were the only traces it left in the TsF. "Aufruf," TsF 12 (1899), p. 64; "Bericht über die Verhandlungen des VI. Allgemeinen Deutschen Taubstummen-Kongreß zu Leipzig am 12.-13. Juni 1905," TsF 14 (1905), pp. 72-73; Julius Heinrich, "7. Deutscher Taubstummen-Congreß in München," TsF 19 (1908), pp. 107-108.

members.[141] Through this paper, the committee reported its activities. During 1912, it turned to each German state demanding better care of the deaf-and-blind, and obligatory schooling and secondary school classes for deaf children and youth. It also addressed a petition to the Emperor to withdraw new regulations on railroad ticket discounts, achieved a declaration of support from the *Bund Deutscher Taubstummenlehrer* in the issues of obligatory and secondary schooling, and initiated a survey among readers on whether agriculture should be recommended as a line of work for deaf people.[142] Simultaneously, the NZT reported the official disbandment of the CVWITD. They described themselves as outdated by local organizations for social support, and left their remaining funds to the executive committee.[143]

The outcome of the attempts to unify the deaf movement was a formalized deaf elite with the mandate to act on behalf of the group on the political level. A deaf elite had existed for at least a century,[144] but not until the AATD, there was an official mandate for it to enter discourse on behalf of the deaf. As a project aiming at formal representation, not sociability, the roots of the executive committee can be traced back to 1849, when Eduard Fürstenberg created an organization claiming to represent deaf people in the entire German nation. The idea of an imagined deaf community was, however, at that point too weak to support such an organization. Furthermore, the CVWT and the CVWITD both concentrated on the distribution of monetary support, in the shape of aid to the individual or to clubs, or through projects such as the asylum campaign. The dull reality of money transactions did not fit in the abstract sphere of the imagined deaf community. Such needs were better catered to in local networks. However, the question of what a central organization should be concerned with continued

---

141 *Taubstummenkalender* (1913), p. 50; *cf.* NZT 1 (1912), p. 1.
142 "Vom Kongreß-Arbeitsausschuß," NZT 1 (1912), pp. 2-3; "Die Immediateingabe an Se. Majestät den Kaiser," NZT 5 (1912), pp. 35-36; Wilhelm Gottweiss, "Vom Arbeits-Ausschuß des Deutschen Taubstummen-Kongresses," NZT 10 (1912), p. 78; Wilhelm Gottweiss and Ludwig Neubauer, "Zweiter Bericht des Arbeits-Ausschusses für die Taubstummen Deutschlands," 14 (1912), p. 108.
143 "Der Zentralverband für die Wohlfahrt und die Interessen der Taubstummen Deutschlands," NZT 17 (1912), p. 136.
144 If we decide to consider the educated deaf as such an elite.

to be debated throughout the years of the First World War, without any decision being reached.[145]

Unification part II: Church Feasts

In a number of ways, the imagined deaf community created spaces for face-to-face interaction between deaf people. The development of the deaf movement can be viewed as a mutually enforcing circular process between the personal bonds connecting people who were deaf, and the imagined deaf community. The origin of the movement was a small, local circle of friends in Berlin. Among them, the idea emerged of a larger community of deaf people, connected although not necessarily acquainted. This was a supporting idea behind the formal deaf organizations. They then created spaces for deaf people with no personal connection, except subscribing to the idea of an imagined deaf community, to come together. There, the members of the imagined deaf community could form concrete personal relationships with each other.

Kirchenfeste or church feasts were services held in Sign and connected to other activities, to which deaf people were invited from the surrounding regions. The concept was established by the CVWT, and the first and most notable church feasts were held in Berlin. The accounts on exactly how they began vary in different sources. According to the TsF, the origin was an 1855 initiative on the part of the organization to reward successful pupils at the Royal Asylum with bibles.[146] After Reinhold Schönberner was assigned to the pastoral care of the Berlin deaf in 1866, the tradition apparently developed into a yearly signed service at Trinity 12, on which Mark 7:31-37, the healing of a deaf man, was read.[147] The word spread, and in the following years, they drew increasing numbers of visitors from outside Berlin. This was facilitated by free tickets and discounts for deaf visitors to the annual church feast issued by private and state

---

145 *Cf.* Wilhelm Gottweiß, "Reichsverband," ATZ 15 (1916), pp. 85-86; Mertens, "Was ich mir über den Reichsverband denke!" ATZ 23 (1917), pp. 105-106, ATZ 24 (1917), pp. 109-110, *cf.* below p. 270.
146 "Das Taubstummen-Kirchenfest," TsF *Fest-Nummer* (1883), [n.p.].
147 Maybach and Gohsler to the Emperor, 28 February 1882, Pag. 38, GStA PrK I HA Rep. 89 Nr. 22575; *cf.* Karl-Heinrich Bieritz, *Das Kirchenjahr. Feste, Gedenk- und Feiertage in Geschichte und Gegenwart* (Munich: Beck, 2001), p. 172.

railroads from 1872.[148] In the 1870s, about 1000 people came to the church feasts each year. Apart from the service, the participants gathered for lectures, went sightseeing, and socialized during the evenings. Guests were provided with accommodation in garrisons or asylums.[149] Altogether, the events were mostly sociable rather than religious in character. For the deaf community, they were vital. With the considerable number of participants, otherwise solitary deaf could for a couple of days experience belonging to a group where their sensory disposition, and more importantly, mode of communication, was the rule. Furthermore, the gatherings were arranged by people who were deaf. This was novel, since previous efforts to gather deaf people had been initiated and controlled by the hearing. Thus, large, albeit temporary, groups of people who were deaf now appeared on a self-determined, voluntary basis, not only as results of social- and educational policy. The connection of the church feast with other CVWT events, such as the first deaf congress in 1873, or the laying of the corner stone of the prospected deaf asylum in 1876, ensured a connection to the formalized deaf movement.[150] The church feasts were not separatist; there was a close connection to the educational sector and to the state, but the CVWT was the organizer that brought the actors together.

In spite of worship being the central activity, the gathering of large numbers of deaf people was not uncontroversial. By 1882, the ministers of education, Gustav von Goßler, and trade, Albert von Maybach, had been reached by complaints from teachers of the deaf about the sociable character of the church feasts, and reacted with concern. The criticism was that there was close to no gain on the religious side, whereas the participants did indulge in the many amusements available in the city. Deaf people of both sexes got acquainted, which also made the feasts inappropriate in the eyes of Maybach and von Goßler. Instead, the ministers suggested that deaf persons who wished to visit smaller services held at the regional schools should be allowed a discount on the

---

148 Maybach and Gohsler to the Emperor, 28 February 1882, Pag. 38, GStA PrK I HA Rep. 89 Nr. 22575; "Das Taubstummen-Kirchenfest," TsF *Fest-Nummer* (1883), [n.p.] .
149 "Programm des Kirchenfestes für Taubstumme," TsF 8 (1873), p. 80; "Das Kirchenfest der Taubstummen im Jahre 1873," 9-10 (1873), pp. 82-84; August Schenck, "Das jährliche Kirchenfest der Taubstummen in Berlin," TsF 18 (1875), pp. 99-100; "Das diesjährige Kirchenfest," TsF 17 (1877), pp. 65-66; "Mittheilungen," TsF 20 (1878), p. 77.
150 Eduard Fürstenberg, notice on forthcoming congress, TsF 6 (1873), p. 62; "An die Leser," TsF 18 (1876), p. 66.

railroad fare. The Emperor approved this suggestion, and the ticket discount for the church feast in Berlin was cancelled.[151] Fürstenberg objected to the decision with reference to the language barrier between contemporary oralist teachers and older, manually educated deaf, but without success.[152] If the 1870s had been the height of the Berlin church feasts, the following decades saw their importance decline. They were continued throughout the period at issue here, but only deaf people from Brandenburg could travel at the reduced price. Over the years, they received less attention in the TsF, and the number of participants decreased.[153]

Governmental concern about mass events such as the church feasts was not restricted to the deaf. Probable models for the church feasts were the *Kirmes* feasts, celebrated in Rhineland-Westphalia. These, too, had originated as religious events, but, during the late 19th century, took on a more secular character. This raised moral concern and lead to measures to limit their number, duration, and size.[154]

Through the decision to sanction regional services, deaf people, especially those with low incomes, were directed to events controlled by hearing educators. Those with sufficient funds were still able to travel to Berlin, if they wished. Likely, however, it also enabled those previously unable to travel as far as Berlin to get together with other deaf people in their area. Berlin had been the center and dominated the deaf movement from its beginning, but the expansion of the movement produced new centers across the nation. In fact, this tendency was already underway when the government decided to break up the Berlin church feasts. For example, the deaf in Hanover saw themselves equally affected by the decision, since they already had their own church feast with external guests. A protest in 1883 led to a dispensation for older deaf to visit the services with a signing preacher in Hanover.[155]

The church feasts were the first events that on a larger scale anchored the imagined deaf community in concrete relationships. People who had earlier only been able to vaguely imagine the existence of each other as deaf people like

---

151 Maybach and Gohsler to the Emperor, 28 February 1882, Pag. 38-45, Statement by Emperor Wilhelm, 8 March 1882, GStA PrK I HA Rep. 89 Nr. 22575.
152 "Das Taubstummen-Kirchenfest," TsF *Fest-Nummer* (1883), p. 2.
153 K. Kr., "Das Kriegs-Kirchenfest in Berlin," ATZ 18 (1914), pp. 135-137; "Vereinswesen," TsF 34 (1892), p. 146; "Vereinswesen," TsF 17 (1899), p. 85; notice on the next church feast, TsF 17 (1905), p. 87.
154 Nathaus, Organizierte Geselligkeit, p. 118.
155 Maybach and Goßler to the Emperor, 11 April 1883, pp. 46-50, GStA PrK I HA Rep. 89 Nr. 22575.

themselves, now came together and turned that sense of affinity into a lived experience. The sexual relationships the ministers implied turned the symbolic solidarity into kinship. The harsh reactions from teachers and the government suggest that this was not desired by the hearing establishment. The protests against the decision to restrict the practice, and the persistence of many deaf to continue celebrating church feast, were the deaf movement's first acts of public and collective opposition to policy.

Unification, part III: Congresses

A further invention of Fürstenberg's were the deaf congresses, which were commenced in 1873. Again, the idea – recurrent international or national meetings for discussing a certain issue – fit well into the general tendencies of the time. Above all, the railroads were an important precondition for such events, as they revolutionized individual travel.[156] By train, participants from far away could relatively easily make the trip to the meeting. Above we have seen the close connection between railroads and church feasts, to the extent that the latter appeared as dependent on rail fare discounts to exist. This point was also at times made in relation to congresses, but was less crucial.[157] The reason for this was the character, especially in regard to class, of the congresses. A comparison between the reports from church feasts and congresses show that they were displayed in markedly different terms. Whereas the TsF discussed the need for hay and buckets for the accommodation of church feast visitors, the congress participants mentioned the hotels they stayed at; after the church feast, visitors received soup and coffee from a shelter, whereas the congress participants enjoyed their champagne.[158]

---

156 Nipperdey, *Deutsche Geschichte*, p. 139.
157 *V.* the discussion on rail fare in connection with the planned congress in Hamburg 1899. "Erklärung," TC 2 (1889), p. 13; "Nochmals der Taubstummencongress," TC 3 (1889), p. 25, *v.* also below p. 187.
158 The hay had to be provided by the CVWT, whereas the buckets were available at the military quarters where the men were accomodated in 1884. *V.* "Das Taubstummen-Kirchenfest," TsF *Fest-Nummer* (1884), [n.p.]; *cf.* "Das Große Kirchenfest in Berlin," and Bernhard Brill: "Der zweite Taubstummen-Kongreß in Wien 1874," TsF 7-8-9 (1874), pp. 52-55; "Die Fahrt zum III. deutschen Taubstummen-Kongreß in Nürnberg, Pfingsten 1896," TsF 11 (1896), p. 55; "Das diesjährige Kirchenfest," TsF 17 (1877), pp. 65-66; Carl Bente, "Vom zweiten deutschen Taubstummen-Kongreß," TsF 26-27 (1894), p. 89.

Deaf leaders of the 19th century were aware that the absence of a ticket discount excluded low-income deaf people from the congresses, but this was not necessarily seen as a problem. In a contribution to the TC, which admittedly drew criticism, the Swedish deaf teacher Gerhard Titze stated "A discount for the congress participants on the fares of state railroads and steamboats should not be strived for, since only poor deaf-mutes, who visit the church feasts, need such a reduction."[159] Thus, the congress participants were distinguished from the church feasts visitors by their financial assets. However, there were reports in the deaf press that people lacking funds of their own received discounts to visit the services held as a part of the congress program, which may well have been part of the motive to hold such services.[160] Another option was joint saving in local deaf clubs to send one or more delegates to the meeting.[161]

The first congress was held in connection with the Berlin church feast in 1873. Thirty-five men from three countries – Germany, Sweden, and Austria-Hungary – attended the one-day meeting. The assembly was designated a 'Congress of the Boards of the Deaf-Mute Associations', and eighteen of the men were delegates sent by deaf clubs. According to the protocol printed in the TsF, they discussed matters concerning the educational and social situation for deaf people and organizational issues, then had dinner and attended church.[162] In the following years, five more congresses were held in direct succession to this meeting. Although the congresses were international, Germany was the dominant nation, hosting three out of six congresses, and with strong representation at each event. (Fig. 10)

---

159 "Eine Fahrpreisermässigung für die Theilnehmer des Congresses auf Staatsbahnen und Dampfschiffen ist nicht anzustreben, weil nur arme Taubstumme, welche die Kirchenfeste besuchen, diese Begünstigung benöthigen." Gerhard Titze, a Swedish deaf teacher, quoted in "Nochmals der Taubstummencongress," TC 3 (1889), p. 25; H. Martens, "Titze oder Pacher-Claudius?" TC 6 (1889), p. 62.
160 "Der IV. deutsche Taubstummen-Congreß in Leipzig," TsF 12 (1878), p. 44; "Die Fahrpreis-Ermäßigung für Taubstumme im Reichstag," ATZ 10 (1913), p. 81; "Nochmals Fahrtausweise," 19 (1914), pp. 141-142.
161 *Cf.* invitation to the 1894 congress in Wiesbaden, TsF 14-15 (1894), p. 52; "Neunter Allgemeiner Deutscher Taubstummen-Kongreß zu Breslau 1914," ATZ 8 (1913), p. 66.
162 "Der erste Congreß der Vorstände der Taubstummen-Vereine"; "Verhandelt im Saale des evangelischen Vereins," TsF 9-10 (1873), pp. 84-86, 88-95.

Figure 10: The first wave of international deaf congresses (shaded) and the German deaf congresses until 1914.

Year	Location	Year	Location
1873	Berlin[163]	1894	Wiesbaden[164]
1874	Vienna[165]	1896	Nuremberg[166]
1875	Dresden[167]	1899	Stuttgart[168]
1878	Leipzig[169]	1902	Berlin[170]
1881	Prague[171]	1905	Leipzig[172]
1884	Stockholm[173]	1908	Munich[174]
1892	Hanover[175]	1911	Hamburg[176]
		1914	Breslau[177]

---

163   Eduard Fürstenberg, notice on forthcoming congress, TsF 6 (1873), p. 62.
164   Invitation to the 1894 congress in Wiesbaden, TsF 14-15 (1894), p. 52.
165   Bernhard Brill: "Der zweite Taubstummen-Kongreß in Wien 1874," TsF 7-8-9 (1874), pp. 53-55.
166   "Aufruf zum III. Deutschen Taubstummen-Kongreß in Nürnberg," TsF 7 (1896), p. 37.
167   August Lehmann, "Der dritte Taubstummen-Congreß in Dresden 1875," TsF 18 (1875), pp. 100-102.
168   Anna Schenck, "Vereinswesen," TsF 11 (1899), pp. 53-55.
169   "Tages-Ordnung," TsF 11 (1878), p. 41.
170   "Deutscher Taubstummen-Congreß in Berlin," TsF 7 (1902), p. 29; Carl Krüger, "Das Kirchenfest und der V. Deutsche Taubstummen-Congreß zu Berlin (15.-20 August.)" TsF 17 (1902), pp. 83-84.
171   "Der Taubstummen-Kongreß zu Hannover," TsF 23 (1892), p. 90.
172   Advertisement, TsF 9 (1905), p. 48; "Der VI. Allgemeine Deutsche Taubstummen-Kongreß zu Leipzig," TsF 13 (1905), pp. 63-65.
173   "Der 6. internationale Taubstummen-Congreß am 1. bis 3. Juli 1884 zu Stockholm," TsF 2 (1885), pp. 6-7.
174   Advertisement, TsF 12 (1908), p. 72; Julius Heinrich, "7. Deutscher Taubstummen-Congreß in München," TsF 17 (1908), pp. 95-96, TsF 18 (1908), pp. 104-105, TsF 19 (1908), pp. 107-109; TsF 20 (1908) pp. 113-115.
175   "Der Taubstummen-Kongreß zu Hannover am 5., 6. und 7. Juni 1892," TsF 24 (1892), p. 97.
176   "Achter Deutscher Taubstummen-Kongreß," TsF 17 (1911), pp. 89-91.
177   Advertisement for the 9th congress in Breslau, ATZ 6 (1914), p. 48.

In 1889, the last in the first wave of congresses failed to be realized, at the same time as the first congress independent of the original series was arranged in Paris. It is unclear why the congress planned for Hamburg in 1889 never came to be. The arrangers blamed above all the denial of railroad ticket discounts. However, it is hard to imagine that this was grave enough to cancel the entire meeting. An additional cause may have been the organizational vacuum left behind by Fürstenberg. He had been instrumental in arranging all previous congresses, and after he died, conflicts emerged between the other deaf leaders. The Hamburg congress was debated in harsh terms in the TC. Especially provoking to the German deaf leaders was the summon to a congress in Paris the same year, an event some refused to attend with reference to their patriotic sentiments.[178]

From this point, international deaf congresses were no longer bound to a succession of events, but were pluralistic to the extent that they become difficult to categorize.[179] In Germany, however, a new series of congresses was launched in 1892. A committee of seven deaf men had formed, apparently out of informal contacts, and invited the German deaf to attend a congress in Hanover. This was the first in a series, which continued until 1914.[180] This time, the congresses were unmistakably 'German', always taking place within the nation, advertising themselves as 'German Deaf-Mute Congresses', and dealing with German issues, although the participants were not exclusively German.[181]

Both the early, 'international', and the later, 'German', congresses were always held in connection with social events of some sort. At the first congress, the social gathering appeared to be of marginal significance compared to the

---

178 "Erklärung," TC 2 (1889), pp. 13-14; "Nochmals der Taubstummencongress," TC 3 (1889), pp. 25-26; "Nachklänge zum Hamburger Beschlusse," TC 4 (1889), pp. 38-40; "Der Taubstummen-Congress in Paris," "Titze oder Pacher-Claudius?", TC 6 (1889), pp. 61-63.

179 *Cf.* Murray, *Touch of Nature,* pp. 59-65.

180 "Mitteilungen," TsF 2 (1892), p. 6; Another congress was planned for Königsberg in 1917. However, it had to be cancelled due to the war and replaced with a "War meeting" ("Kriegstagung")in Berlin in 1916. The AATD and the presidents on German deaf clubs discussed a number of issues, and in connection to the meeting there was a service and a larger meeting of deaf people. *Cf.* Wilhelm Gottweiß, "Zur gefl. Beachtung!" ATZ 13 (1916), p. 75; Max Lummert, "Kriegstagung in Berlin," ATZ 17 (1916), pp. 95-96, ATZ 18 (1916), pp. 99-100.

181 *Cf.* "Der VI. Allgemeine Deutsche Taubstummen-Kongreß zu Leipzig," TsF 13 (1905), pp. 63-65; Max Lummert, "IX. Deutscher Taubstummen-Kongreß zu Breslau," ATZ 12 (1914), p. 91.

negotiations.[182] However, this was to change. What types of reports were published varied from year to year. Some set focus on the personal experience of the congress trip, others on the discussions, yet others on the sights of the host city.[183] Over time, lengthy narratives of the congress and especially the events surrounding it became the typical aftermath of a congress in the deaf press. Together with the schedules, they convey the image of congresses as foremost sociable events. The time devoted to sessions was sometimes no more than six hours, whereas the rest of the congress, often lasting several days, consisted of excursions, banquets, theatre performances and religious services.[184] Apart from the wide variety of entertainments arranged by the hosts, the congresses were scenes for informal sociability. This aspect of the congresses, practiced on the side of and in between scheduled events, may have been just as important as the official deliberations. Owen Wrigley has claimed that what happens behind the scenes and beside the schedule contains the true value of deaf organizations to the average deaf person. The formal, hierarchical structures of the associations, and their lobbying activity, have less impact on the lives of deaf people than their roles as meeting places do, Wrigley argues.[185] Descriptions of informal evenings enjoyed in larger or smaller groups underlined the jovial mood conveyed in congress reports. Reconnecting with old friends and making new acquaintances was obviously seen as one of the great thrills of the congress experience, whereas the official entertainment program was sometimes deemed tedious.[186] An advertisement in the ATZ anticipating the Breslau congress in

---

182 "Der erste Congreß der Vorstände der Taubstummen-Vereine." TsF 8-9 (1873), pp. 84-86.

183 A few contrasting examples: Fritz Mehle "Wie es auf dem Kongreß war!", ATZ 13 (1914), pp. 100-101; Julius Heinrich, "7. Deutscher Taubstummen-Congreß in München" TsF 17 (1908), pp. 95-96, 18 (1908), pp. 104-105, 19 (1908), pp. 107-109; 20 (1908) pp. 113-115; "Die Fahrt zum III. deutschen Taubstummen-Kongreß in Nürnberg, Pfingsten 1896.", TsF 11 (1896), p. 55.

184 Advertisement for the 1905 Leipzig congress, with schedule, TsF 9 (1905), p. 48; ditto for the 1914 Breslau congress, ATZ 6 (1914), p. 48.

185 Wrigley, *The Politics of Deafness*, pp. 100-102.

186 Carl Bente, "Vom zweiten deutschen Taubstummen-Kongreß," TsF 26-27 (1894), p. 89; "Die Fahrt zum III. deutschen Taubstummen-Kongreß in Nürnberg, Pfingsten 1896," TsF 12 (1896), p. 59; Anna Schenck, "Vereinswesen," TsF 11 (1899), pp. 53-55; Lina Scherzer, "Kongreß-Erinnerungen," ATZ 16 (1914), pp. 124-125.

1914, in which a "congress groom" requested contact with a prospective "congress bride",[187] illustrates yet another aspect of the networking. Compared to the early church feasts, the number of congress participants was rather modest for most of the period. Numbers between 150 and 300 people appear to have been average. Exceptions were the congresses in Berlin, Munich and Hamburg in the early 20th century, which according to the TsF were visited by between 700 and 1000 people.[188] Anthropologist Hilde Haualand has described events where considerable numbers of deaf people gather as temporary Deaf cities. Under such circumstances, "deaf people were visible and many enough to gain rights and services they often can't claim or experience at home without being viewed as demanding or 'difficult'."[189] The presence of many Deaf people in a city, she argues, transforms the visual and communicative landscape, as a high density of signers is noticed, and the hearing locals need to adapt to visual communication.[190] At events with as few participants as most congresses, however, the increased number of deaf people may not have been more than a marginal phenomenon in the eyes of the outsider. To the deaf themselves, there was a greater significance. Some congress narratives comment on the hearing gaze at the deaf participants, or the space taken over by deaf people in connection to the congress. In a report on the Vienna congress in 1874, Bernhard Brill jokingly speculated on the thoughts that hearing people may have had when seeing groups of deaf people in the streets: "All of the philistines looked at us

---

187 "Kongreßbräutigam", "Kongreßbraut", ATZ 10 (1914), p. 81.
188 Paul Müller, "Mittheilungen vom dritten Taubstummen-Congreß zu Dresden," TsF 22 (1875), pp. 118-119; "Der IV. deutsche Taubstummen-Congreß in Leipzig," TsF 12 (1878), p. 43; "Der 6. internationale Taubstummen-Congreß am 1. bis 3. Juli 1884 zu Stockholm," TsF 1 (1885), pp. 6-7; "Der Taubstummen-Kongreß zu Hannover am 5., 6. und 7. Juni 1892," TsF 24 (1892), p. 97; "Der VI. Allgemeine Deutsche Taubstummen-Kongreß zu Leipzig," TsF 13 (1905), p. 63; "Deutscher Taubstummen-Congreß in Berlin," TsF 7 (1902), p. 29; Julius Heinrich, "7. Deutscher Taubstummen-Congreß in München," TsF 17 (1908), p. 95; "Achter Deutscher Taubstummen-Kongreß" TsF 17 (1911), p. 89.
189 Jan Kåre Breivik, Hilde Haualand, and Per Solvang, *Rome – a Temporary Deaf City! Deaflympics 2001*, Stein Rokkan Centre for Social Studies, Bergen University Research Foundation, 2002. Working paper from the project *"Transnational Connections in Deaf Worlds"*, p. 21.
190 Ibid pp. 19-21.

with saucer eyes and asked themselves: who could this curious crowd be?"[191] Fritz Mehle struck a similar tone in his account on his and his wife's trip to Breslau in 1914. They spent an evening in a restaurant together with deaf friends. After a while, Mehle looked around him: "Everywhere I looked I saw: The Breslau congress pin! The hearing had been gradually swept outside."[192]

However, this should not be seen as rejection of hearing people. Instead, congress reports often included reference to the support and appraisal of the congress by notable hearing persons. Teachers of the deaf were regular participants.[193] Furthermore, religious leaders, representatives of the city, of the education authorities, and of charity organizations attended the meetings.[194] An obligatory component of the congress was sending a telegram to the Emperor.[195] Honouring the father of German oralism, Samuel Heinicke, was also a popular part of the programs, as was a visit to the local deaf school.[196] The arrangers sought to obtain recognition from those in power, rather than positioning themselves in opposition.

---

191 Brill used the work "Völkchen", which translates to "crowd", but is also the diminutive of "people". "Alle Spießbürger schauten uns mit Glotzaugen an und fragten sich: wer möchte wohl dieses sonderbare Völkchen sein?" Bernhard Brill: "Der zweite Taubstummen-Kongreß in Wien 1874," TsF 7-8-9 (1874), p. 53.

192 "Ueberall, wohin ich sah: Das Breslauer Kongreßabzeichen! Die Hörenden waren allmählich hinausgefegt worden." ATZ 14 (1914), p. 108.

193 "Protocoll," TsF 17 (1875), pp. 89, 93, 95; "Der IV. deutsche Taubstummen-Congreß in Leipzig," 12 (1878), pp. 43-45; "Verzeichnis der Mitglieder des Taubstummen-Kongresses in Hannover," TsF 27 (1892), p. 109; "Der VI. Allgemeine Deutsche Taubstummen-Kongreß zu Leipzig," TsF 13 (1905), p. 63.

194 Carl Krüger, "Das Kirchenfest und der V. Deutsche Taubstummen-Congreß zu Berlin (15.-20 August.)" TsF 17 (1902), p. 83; Julius Heinrich, "7. Deutscher Taubstummen-Congreß in München," TsF 17 (1908), p. 95; Max Lummert, "IX. Deutscher Taubstummen-Kongreß zu Breslau," ATZ 12 (1914), p. 91.

195 V. for instance Max Lummert, "IX. Deutscher Taubstummen-Kongreß zu Breslau," ATZ 12 (1914), p. 91; Carl Bente,"Der Taubstummen-Kongreß zu Hannover am 5., 6. und 7. Juni 1892," TsF 25 (1892), p. 100; Anna Schenck, "Vereinswesen," TsF 11 (1899), p. 54; v. also the telegrams in the file GStA PrK I. HA Rep. 89 22575.

196 "Lebensbild Samuel Heinicke's aufgeführt im Thalia-Theater in Leipzig," TsF 12 (1878), pp. 45-47; "Achter Deutscher Taubstummen-Kongreß," TsF 17 (1911), pp. 89-90; "Der VI. Allgemeine Deutsche Taubstummen-Kongreß zu Leipzig," TsF 13 (1905), p. 63.

In the face of the many amusements and social events, the networking, and the positioning in relation to authorities, it is reasonable to ask what standing the actual sessions had. Criticism expressed during the debates of the teaching methods and policies affecting deaf people was compensated for with displays of respect for the very institutions that were criticized. This may well been a strategic decision, since an overtly rebellious deaf movement could have faced considerable difficulties in the repressive climate of Wilhelmine Germany. However, if this was a strategy to get through to the authorities with their demands, it failed. Apart from the prolonged process of forming a central organization depicted above, concrete results were practically inexistent. The people within the movement were aware of this, and it caused some distress, but was not to change within the period studied here.[197] As with the church feasts, the subversive element of the congresses was not the official program, but the socializing that surrounded it.

THE INDIVIDUAL IN IMAGINED AND LOCAL DEAF COMMUNITIES: A NEW WAY OF BEING DEAF

Historians of the deaf have, surely due to the limitations given by the source material, almost exclusively been concerned with educated, urban men from the middle or upper classes. This minority has come to represent 'the deaf'. Paradoxically, it is nevertheless presumed that deaf communities consist of both men and women, and that they have members from different social classes. This is due to two intertwined assumptions. First, the supposition that a number of privileged deaf men constituted a sort of tip of the iceberg, the iceberg being a larger group of deaf, who due to their gender, ethnicity, place of residence, vocational or educational status did not enter the public sphere. In other words, a base is imagined by subtracting the elite from the mass of 'the deaf-mutes', whom we know existed, but almost never hear from.[198] Second, the charac-

---

197 "Titze oder Pacher-Claudius?" TC 6 (1889), p. 62; Carl Bente, "Vom zweiten deutschen Taubstummen-Kongreß," TsF 22-23 (1894), p. 73; Fritz Mehle, "Taubstummen-Kongreß zu Breslau!" ATZ 8 (1914), p. 59.

198 See the comparison between members of the French National Union of the Societies of the Deaf and the total number of deaf in France in Quartararo, *Deaf Identity and Social Images*, p. 193, or the discussion on the statutes of of the New England Gallaudet Association in Van Cleve and Crouch, *A Place of Their Own*, pp. 90-91, and Murray, *Touch Of Nature*, pp. 38-40, 85-96.

teristics of this silent majority is deduced from notions expressed by the elite. This construct is performed based on the assumption that power structures symmetrical to the mainstream ones can simply be superimposed on the deaf community. By modifying the statements made by the deaf elite according to social conventions, historians attempt to construct an image of the subaltern of the deaf community. Thus, in the absence of sources, the imagined base of the deaf community is provided with a constructed "identity-in-differential".[199]

Resulting from the model of the 'iceberg'-model of deaf community is a potential misinterpretation of deaf movement ideas. "The deaf" are supposed to encompass people of both sexes, of different ethnicities and classes, at the same time as it is noted that the ideas of the movement come from a distinctly Western, white, masculine, bourgeois perspective.[200] The conclusion would have to be that the leaders dominated the subalterns through values derived from the mainstream, thus misrepresenting the community. Before making such a statement, however, one should carefully examine whom the leaders of the movement actually represented. In order to do that, the following sections are devoted to the way deaf people were presented in media associated with the deaf elite.

With the emergence of print media related to deaf people not principally as educational or medical objects, above all texts written by deaf people, a rich material of life stories of deaf individuals also appeared. What distinguishes these texts from those produced within the educational, medical, and administrative realms are their focus on deaf adults and on the lives of particular deaf people. Although together, the texts can give an impression of 'deaf people in general', the main concern of the deaf authors was always the individual.

Most of these narratives appeared in the deaf press. The occasions were typically the death of the person in question, his or her birthday, or other significant events such as professional anniversaries or weddings. In some cases, deaf criminals or missing persons were the subjects of warrants and warnings, also offering some biographical data. Furthermore, two deaf authors – Otto Kruse and Heinrich Lingelmann – published collections of biographies on deaf people, and two others – August Schenck and Albin Maria Watzulik – compiled series of biographies of notable deaf for the deaf press.

---

199 *Cf.* Gayatri Chakravorty Spivak, "Can the Subaltern Speak?" in *Colonial Discourse and Post-Colonial Theory. A Reader.* eds. Patrick Williams and Laura Chrisman (New York: Harvester/Wheatsheaf, 1994), p. 79-80.

200 *Cf.* Robert Buchanan, "The *Silent Worker* Newspaper and the Building of a Deaf Community 1890-1929" in *Deaf History Unveiled,* ed. Van Cleve, pp. 178-179; idem, *Illusions of Equality,* p. 18; Murray, *Touch of Nature,* pp. 38-40.

The object of this section is to analyze the image of deaf people as they appeared in these texts. So far, the deaf movement and the deaf community have been described as organizations and ideas. It remains to determine what kind of people carried this movement. The hypothesis of an imagined deaf community includes readers of the *Taubstummenfreund* or *Taubstummencourier* who imagined "thousands and thousands like themselves"[201] when reading these papers. The question is, what kind of people did they thereby envision? As we have seen, Fürstenberg repeatedly referred to 'the deaf-mutes' when writing about the members of deaf clubs or the visitors to their events. Concrete examples of some of the people he meant will help to define what this elusive category meant in the deaf community context.

'Peculiar deaf-mutes'

Before exploring the many obituaries and similar texts in the deaf press, we turn to four biographical compilations by 19th century deaf authors. These show how the use of biographies on deaf persons developed during the course of the century. In 1832, *Der Taubstumme im uncultivierten Zustande nebst Blicken in das Leben merkwürdiger Taubstummen* ["The Deaf-Mute in the Uncultivated State besides Gazes at the Lives of Peculiar Deaf-Mutes"] by Otto Friedrich Kruse was published. Kruse was a teacher at the deaf school in Schleswig, and an author of several works on deaf education. This volume was his second book, and also one of the earliest books ever to be published written in German by a deaf person.[202]

Heinrich Lingelmann, a deaf printer from Berlin, collected facts and anecdotes about deaf people and deaf education in the booklet *Aus der Taubstummen-Welt. Biographien, Charakterzüge und Erzählungen aus dem Leben der Gehörlosen für Leser jeden Standes,* first published in 1876. The title translates "From the Deaf-Mute World. Biographies, Characteristics, and Stories from the Lives of the Deaf for Readers of any Estate." It contained the biographies of eleven famous deaf, intended as examples of the success achieved by well-educated deaf persons, and as role models for younger deaf.[203]

---

201 Anderson, Imagined Communities, p. 77.
202 Vogel, "Otto Friedrich Kruse", (Part 1), pp. 198-207; *cf.* below p. 223.
203 Lingelmann, Aus der Taubstummen-Welt, (1876), pp. 30-35; cf. Heinrich Lingelmann, Aus der Taubstummen-Welt. Biographien, Charakterzüge und Erzählungen aus dem Leben der Gehörlosen für Leser jeden Standes 2nd Ed. (Berlin, 1878); cf. advertisements for his shop, TsF 10-11-12 (1880), p. 38.

August Schenck wrote a series of biographies of 21 former students of the Royal Asylum in Berlin to the centennial anniversary of the institution. They were published in the TsF and the TC in 1888.[204] Schenck explained in his introduction to the series: "Due to the upcoming centennial celebration of the Royal Deaf-Mute Asylum in Berlin I feel obliged to bring the deaf geniuses, i.e. the former pupils of this institute who have distinguished themselves, to the eyes of the readers minds."[205] In the eyes of Schenck, thus, these twenty-one were the most eminent alumnae of the institute.

In 1894, finally, the printer and prominent deaf leader Albin Maria Watzulik declared his intention to compile a treatise on deaf education by collecting texts by deaf writers of different nationalities describing the disadvantages of oralism and the value of Sign Language. The project never resulted in a book, but was eventually published as a series in the TC. Each letter was accompanied by a brief biography of the author.[206]

Authorship has not been used as an exclusive category in this analysis, which means that the ascribing of one group of texts to Kruse, one to Lingelmann, one to Schenck, or one to Watzulik is a means of distinguishing their physically distinct form as being published together and on separate occasions. In fact, Kruse was not the author of all biographies, Schenck and Lingelmann obviously copied some of their texts from Kruse, and Watzulik relied on and sometimes quoted personal descriptions submitted by the subjects themselves. Still, this web of texts being copied and edited, with sentences reappearing as parts of new statements, stayed within a deaf community discourse.[207] Only a couple of texts in Kruse's collection, which differed markedly from the rest, have been excluded

---

204 August Schenck: "Koryphäen einer Jubilarin" TsF 5 (1888), pp. 18-19, 8 (1888), p. 32, 9 (1888), p. 36, 10 (1888) p. 40, 11 (1888) pp. 43-44; idem, "Die taubstummen Koryphäen einer in nächster Zeit jubilierender Anstalt." in TC 5 (1888) pp. 54-56, 6 (1888) pp. 66-67; 10 (1888) pp. 112-114.

205 "Angesiches [sic] der bevorstehenden Säkularfeier der Königlichen Taubstummenanstalt zu Berlin fühle ich mich gedrungen, die gehörlosen Koryphäen, d. h. die ehemaligen Zöglinge dieses Instituts, die sich hervorgethan haben, den geistigen Augen des Lesers vorzuführeu [sic]." August Schenck, "Koryphäen einer Jubilarin," TsF 5 (1888), p. 18.

206 Albin Maria Watzulik, "Die von mir angekündigte Streitschrift in Buchform," TC 4 (1894), p. 47; Albin Maria Watzulik, "Aufforderung," TC 1 (1895), pp. 8-9.

207 *Cf.* above pp. 19f.

from the discussion.[208] Furthermore, the discussion focuses on biographies of German deaf. All except Schenck included biographies of deaf people of other nationalities in their series. While this fact is important to note, the analysis of the biographical presentations is concerned mainly with those who came from, or lived in, the German states.

From Wonders to Working Men

Kruse's work was intended as a psychology of the 'deaf-mutes', which would give the general public, and especially teachers of the deaf, better knowledge about, and more understanding for, the deaf. Kruse considered the existing literature on the subject contradictory and incomplete, and thought himself better suited to write about the deaf, since he was deaf himself.[209] In an appendix to the treatise on the nature of the 'deaf-mutes', he compiled twenty-six biographies of "peculiar deaf-mutes."[210] What made them peculiar were their remarkable talent, cultivation, and/or careers. Famous deaf such as the teachers Jean Massieu and Laurent Clerc appeared, as did the legendary Comte de Solar, and Kruse himself.[211] Some were aristocrats, others came from in other ways prominent families.[212]

In each of the sixteen biographies of German deaf, Kruse reflected on their education in deaf school, or, in a few cases, their lack of such education.[213] He

---

208 The first was about an anonymous woman, and is serving as a moral caution rather than a biography. The second was an appendix written by Kruse's hearing colleague David Christian Ortgies, and is a case study, rather than a biography. Otto Friedrich Kruse, *Der Taubstumme im uncultivierten Zustande nebst Blicken in das Leben merkwürdiger Taubstummen* (Bremen: Kaiser, 1832), pp. 157, 177-199.
209 Ibid., pp. ix-xi.
210 "merkwürdiger Taubstummen" ibid., p. 109.
211 Ibid., pp 114-116, 119-122, 138-147, 150-155.
212 Ibid.: de Solar pp. 119-122 , de Fontenai, pp. 123-124; Habermaß, pp. 126-133, von Schulzendorff p. 158, Siebert p. 166. *Cf.* Lane, *Deaf Experience*, pp. 73-80; idem, *When the Mind Hears*.
213 The Germans were, in Kruse, *Der Taubstumme*: Boving pp. 111-112, Grimm p. 125, Habermaß pp. 126-133, Hüttman pp. 134-136, Köster pp. 137, Kruse, pp. 138-147, Löper p. 148, Lüders p. 149, von Schulzendorf p. 158, von Schütz pp. 159-160, Senß pp. 161-162, Siebert p. 166, Sven pp. 167-168, Teutscher pp. 169-170, Wilke pp. 171-172, Willig pp. 173-176. Additionally, *v.* the two excluded texts: Ibid., pp. 157, 177-199, *cf.* above, p. 197.

was precise in his information about which school the person had attended, and sometimes also described the education in detail.[214] When it came to their adult life, Kruse focused on their occupations. Here, we see a clear bias in favour of professionals. The subjects were in eight cases teachers, in one case an artist, and in two cases civil servants. The remaining five were craftsmen.

Apart from background and career, Kruse paid much attention to the characteristics of the persons as deaf, starting with their deafness in its physical form, and its consequences. Typical is his tendency to describe the causes of deafness and sometimes its degree in the individual, at times in physical detail.[215] He also devoted much attention to the role of Sign Language. He described where his subject learned to sign, that they were able to sign, in some cases their particular use of signed communication, or that they were especially proficient in Sign Language.[216]

Another characteristic of Kruse's biographies was his focus on religion and morals. He consistently assured the reader of the devotion to Christianity and the moral behaviour of his subjects.[217] Here, and in his comments on their physical deafness, Sign Language and speech, he relates to the main issues in the discourse on deafness since the 17th century. Hearing society's discovery of Sign Language disproved the assumption that deaf people were incapable of language and knowledge, thus opening the possibility of educating 'deaf-mutes'. Speaking 'deaf-mutes' have been called one of the greatest revelations of the 17th century, and altered the entire concept of the 'deaf-mute' and, to some extent, of language.[218] Deriving from the discovery that 'deaf-mutes' were capable of understanding, the early institutional deaf education aimed chiefly at bringing them to develop as human beings and reach religious salvation. This ambition still dominated in Kruse's period.[219] Thus, his literary display of several speaking

---

214 Ibid., pp. 126-128, 161.
215 Ibid., biographies of: Otto Friedrich Kruse, p. 138, Anton Köster p. 137. Most distinctive is the detail in Kruse's description of the French Pierre Desloges' illness and following loss of hearing and speech. Ibid., p. 117.
216 For example, in ibid.: von Schütz, pp. 159-160, Margaretha Hüttman p. 134, Habermaß, p. 126.
217 This applies to almost all biographies in the collection. V. especially, in ibid., Hüttmann pp. 134-135, Teutscher p. 169, Willig pp. 173-174.
218 Rée, *I See a Voice,* pp. 97-117.
219 Branson and Miller, *Damned for Their Difference,* pp. 17, 68-79; Baynton, *Forbidden Signs,* pp. 15, 49-50; Wolff, "Selbstverständlich Gebärdensprache!" pp. 24-25.

and pious 'deaf-mutes' corresponds with the state of the art of deaf education at the time.

Heinrich Lingelmann's booklet from 1876 contained miscellaneous facts and anecdotes concerning deaf people. They included the biographies of Samuel Heinicke and the Abbé de l'Epée, a juxtaposition of "[t]he deaf mute in the natural (uncultivated) condition" with "[t]he deaf-mute in the cultivated condition",[220] and statistics of the 'deaf-mutes' in Prussia. The texts had been, he asserted, "[w]ritten, set, and illustrated by deaf-mutes",[221] and the publication marked the laying of the cornerstone of CVWT's prospected deaf asylum in Königs-Wusterhausen, an event that was also described at length in the appendix. In the foreword, Lingelmann appealed for contributions to the CVWT and promoted the *Taubstummenfreund*.[222]

Of interest here are the twelve biographies of 'famous deaf-mutes' included in the booklet.[223] Most had been featured already in Kruse's book. Again, we find Laurent Clerc and Jean Massieu, the German teachers Karl Wilke and Johann Habermaß, and the artist Adolph Siebert, all of which were mentioned by Kruse.[224] The only new addition to this presentation of famous deaf was Eduard Fürstenberg. Otherwise, the biographies are an abbreviated selection from Kruse, with few new additions. For instance, the author seems unaware that Siebert had died in 1832, appropriating the information available to Kruse.[225] Through his selection, Lingelmann focused even stronger than Kruse on teachers and other professionals. Only one manual worker was included, the mechanic Andreas Grimm.[226]

Since most of the texts were reproductions of Kruse's work, it is not surprising that they occasionally repeat his phrases on the onset and cause of deafness.[227] To a greater extent than Kruse, however, Lingelmann emphasised

---

220 Probably derived from Kruse: "Der Taubstumme im natürlichen (unkultivierten) Zustande", "Der Taubstumme im kultivierten Zustande" Lingelmann, *Aus der Taubstummen-Welt* (1876), pp. 16, 19.
221 "Verfaßt, gesetzt und illustrirt durch Taubstumme." ibid, title page.
222 Ibid., pp. iii-iv, 47-56.
223 Ibid., pp. 26-35.
224 Lingelmann, *Aus der Taubstummen-Welt*, (1876) pp. 30-34; cf. Kruse, *Der Taubstumme*, pp. 114-116, 126-133, 150-155, 166, 171-172.
225 Lingelmann, *Aus der Taubstummen-Welt* (1876), p. 34, cf. Kruse, *Der Taubstumme*, p. 166, Gläser, , *Berliner Porträtisten*, p. 74.
226 Lingelmann, *Aus der Taubstummen-Welt* (1876), p. 34.
227 Ibid., pp. 26-27, 30.

talent, culture and knowledge instead of morals and language mode. He never discussed the role of Sign Language, but on occasion mentioned the skills of a certain individual in other languages. Intellectual achievements played an important part in his description of deaf role models. In particular, he emphasised autodidactic studies as desirable and advantageous.[228]

The contrast is striking between the statistics of the Berlin deaf that were included in Lingelmann's booklet, and the biographies of famous deaf. According to the text, most deaf in Berlin performed manual work. Many were illiterate. Only very few – eleven out of a total 627 – were professionals or artists. In the gallery of famous deaf, the distribution was the opposite, with only one manual worker and ten professionals.[229]

Kruse and Lingelmann both juxtaposed their biographies of successful and talented deaf with descriptions of 'uncultivated deaf-mutes'. The message to the reader was clear: those deaf who had not received special education were wretched, not due to their deafness, but due to their lack of education. Given the proper resources, deaf people could excel in a range of different areas. Furthermore, the 'peculiar' or 'famous' deaf were clearly not the rule, but accompanied by a mass of less fortunate "comrades-in-suffering."[230]

The deaf press biography series of 1888 and 1895-97 differ considerably in context from Kruse's and Lingelmann's compilations. Schenck and Watzulik wrote above all for an audience within the deaf community, and by publishing in the deaf press, the biographies were made parts of an ongoing dialogue within that community. Nevertheless, especially Schenck's biographies display similarities to the previously discussed two. His selection was based on other criteria, since his object was to present the most prominent former pupils of the Berlin Royal Asylum. However, several of these were the same people that Kruse and Lingelmann had written about. Like Lingelmann, he obviously relied on Kruse as a source to much of his material. The passage on how Eschke taught Johann Habermaß in articulation, and the biographies of Carl Ferdinand von Schulzendorff and Daniel Senß were almost copies of Kruse's texts.[231] Other subjects

---

228 Ibid., pp. 28, 35.
229 Lingelmann, *Aus der Taubstummen-Welt* (1876), pp. 30-38.
230 "Leidensgenossen" Kruse, *Der Taubstumme*, p. 148.
231 August Schenck, "Die taubstummen Koryphäen einer in nächster Zeit jubilierender Anstalt," TC 5 (1888), p. 55, TC 6 (1888), p. 66; *cf.* Kruse, *Der Taubstumme*, pp. 127, 158, 161-162.

were new, for instance the brothers Georg and Ferdinand Stucken, the engineer Wilhelm Naglo, and the artisan Andreas Schubert.[232]

In his biographies, Schenck built in a description of a sociable deaf network.[233] He also emphasised other relationships between deaf people, for instance the friendship between Habermaß and von Schulzendorf in the late 18th century, the Stucken brothers being the boarders of Karl Wilke, and Joseph Beck's marriage to a deaf woman. Furthermore, he mentioned the positions some of his subjects held in deaf clubs.[234]

Concerning occupation, which was one of the main themes also in Schenck's biographies, he conveyed a balanced picture between different kinds of trades. He included seven craftsmen, but also three teachers, five artists, one merchant, three civil servants, and one engineer. They distinguished themselves in diverse ways – some through their intellectual power, others through talent for craftsmanship, or service in the deaf clubs.[235]

Watzulik's series, finally, was, as already mentioned, not primarily intended as a compilation of biographies. The presentations of twenty-six deaf men and one woman accompanied their letters in support of Sign Language use in deaf education. Like the others, Watzulik selected "the most eminent"[236] deaf for the series, but due to the character of the compilation, they were of course all his contemporaries. This resulted in a selection significantly different from that in the three earlier compilations. Of the eight German contributors, none was a teacher. Neither were there any civil servants or other professionals among them, except for one artist.[237] The baron Rudolph von und zu Buttlar may partly qualify as a learned professional, since he allegedly had written several books, but this was strictly speaking more of a hobby, since von und zu Buttlar was a landowning aristocrat.[238] Bertha Landecker, the only woman in the series, was married

---

232 August Schenck, "Die taubstummen Koryphäen einer in nächster Zeit jubilierender Anstalt," TC 6 (1888), p. 67, TC 10 (1888), pp. 112-113.
233 V. above, p. 116.
234 August Schenck, "Die taubstummen Koryphäen einer in nächster Zeit jubilierender Anstalt," TC 5 (1888), p. 54, TC 6 (1888) pp. 66-67, TC 10 (1888), pp. 112-114.
235 Ibid., TC 5 (1888), p. 54, TC 6 (1888) pp. 66-67, TC 10 (1888), pp. 112-114.
236 "die hervorragendsten", Albin Maria Watzulik, "Aufforderung," TC 1 (1895), p. 8.
237 The artist was Carl von Haase, Albin Maria Watzulik, "Der Methodenstreit," TC 9 (1896), pp. 92-93.
238 Ibid., TC 9 (1896), p. 92. It has not been possible to confirm the information on his authorship.

and did not perform gainful work.²³⁹ The remaining five Germans were all craftsmen, which however does not mean that they were described as any less talented and prominent than the professionals in the earlier series. Two of them performed more advanced crafts, on the verge to art, namely lithography and engraving.²⁴⁰ The mechanic Heinrich Buchheim ran his own business, and the shoemaker Otto Vollmar was a purveyor to the court. Theodor Liskowsky, of a distinguished Leipzig family, was comfortably retired from his work making fine leather articles.²⁴¹

Other characteristics Watzulik emphasised were engagement in deaf associations, and personal affiliations with other deaf people, especially marriage.²⁴² He also made a point of the exquisite skills in Sign Language of some of his subjects.²⁴³

A Discursive Shift

Teaching had always been a rare occupation among deaf people, available only to a handful of each generation since the beginnings of institutional deaf education. Other professions with higher status, in administration, science or business, were also marginal phenomena as far as the statistics were concerned. There, white-collar professions appeared in such small numbers that a statistically definable change over time cannot be determined with any certainty.²⁴⁴

The biographies compiled by four deaf authors in the course of the 19th century give another impression. As examples of the most successful and remarkable deaf of the century, it is hardly surprising that most had impressive

---

239 Ibid., TC 7 (1896), p.76.
240 Ibid., TC 8 (1896), p. 84, TC 9 (1896), p. 92.
241 Ibid., TC 8 (1896), p. 84, TC 9 (1896), pp. 93-94.
242 Ibid., TC 7 (1896), p.76, 8 (1896), p.84; TC 9 (1896), p. 94.
243 Ibid., TC 8 (1896), p. 84, TC 9 (1896), p. 93.
244 Statistics on this subject are unreliable, but perhaps it gives some idea of the matter that Bavaria in 1840 noted 4,9% of the deaf as working in "Business, art and science" ("Berufsgeschäften, Künsten und Wissenschaften") as compared to 3% in the "free professions" ("Freie Berufe") in 1900. Hermann (ed.) *Beiträge*, Vol. 1., p. 230; However, according to Pongratz all of them were artists. Pongratz, *Allgemeine Statistik*, pp. 94-95;108 According to the 1900 nation-wide survey, only 3‰ of the' deaf-mutes' belonged to the category "Military- court- civil and clerical service including so-called free professions" ("Militär-, Hof-, bürgerlicher und kirchlicher Dienst, auch sogenannte freie Berufsarten") Engelmann, "Die Taubstummen," p. 29.

careers. As we have seen, half of the persons Kruse selected were teachers, most of them his contemporaries. Lingelmann and Schenck, although writing much later, chose to mainly portray people from the same period – that is, before mid-century. Their collections also included several teachers, and a few professionals of other kinds. However, this tendency changed.

Watzulik wrote about his contemporaries just before the turn of the 19th century. He used largely the same means of accentuating the prominence of his objects: talent, achievement, and a successful career. Nevertheless, he did not include any German teachers or other professionals. Since he did write about a few such persons from other countries, it seems unlikely that this was due to any unwillingness on his part.[245] Rather, he was unable to find any deaf teachers or professionals in late 19th century Germany. Remaining for him as objects in his display of deaf people's achievements were self-made men in manual trades. Successful craftsmen, who had achieved their middle-class status by manual work, took the place of educated professionals such as teachers and bureaucrats. Persons such as Kruse, Wilke, Habermaß, and Fürstenberg remained in the memory of the deaf community and were occasionally mentioned throughout the period.[246] As individuals, they did not disappear as objects of discourse. What ceased to exist in discourse was the contemporary German deaf professional. Although the structure of the 'deaf-mute' workforce had changed only moderately, a significant discursive shift appeared regarding objects.

Considering the rhetoric used by the four authors, another change appears. Kruse took efforts to underline the human qualities of the deaf people he described. In the first part of his book, he repeatedly compared 'uncultivated deaf-mutes' to animals.[247] In the second part, he emphasised that these 'peculiar' deaf were pious, had high moral standards, and that they were capable of language. Their skills in spoken, written, and signed languages were close to

---

245 For instance the Swedish teacher Gerhard Titze, the French journalist Eugène Née, Albin Maria Watzulik, "Der Methodenstreit," TC 2 (1896), pp. 13-15, the American preacher Austin Ward Mann and chemist George T. Dougherty, Albin Maria Watzulik, "Der Methodenstreit," TC 6 (1895), pp. 64-65, 67.

246 Also in the deaf press, for instance: Wilke: M. K., "Vereinswesen," TsF 22 (1899), p. 112; Habermaß: Otto Kruse, "Erzählungen," TsF 9-10 (1873), p. 88; Kruse: "Zum 77jährigen Geburtstage des Otto Friedrich Kruse am 29. März 1878," TsF 6 (1878), pp. 24-25; "Das Reisen der Taubstummen," TC 7 (1891), pp. 77-78; Fürstenberg: "Der Taubstummen-Kongreß zu Hannover," TsF 23 (1892), pp. 89-90.

247 Kruse, *Der Taubstumme*, pp. 5, 7, 9.

obligatory parts of each biography. Kruse also described their moral character, and especially pointed out religious devotion.[248]

The questions whether 'deaf-mutes' were capable of learning language, of their moral character, and relationship to God were typical of the early 19th century. Training in articulation was still a rarity to be marvelled at. Throughout the 19th century, deaf education was expanded. At the end of the century, it was an every-day practice in almost 100 schools in Germany. To the readers of the TsF and TC it constituted a very familiar, shared experience. The novelty of teaching the deaf to speak was gone, especially so to the deaf themselves. It had moved to another level, or rather been transformed into another object: instead of marvelling at its possibility, its usefulness was being questioned.[249]

Schenck and Watzulik wrote for an audience that did not doubt that deaf people are human. Religion and moral could therefore be expelled to the periphery of discourse and appear only as personal characteristics of certain individuals, not as an obligatory assurance.[250] Instead of proving the human nature of their subjects, Schenck and Watzulik asserted their status as responsible, independent *Bürger,* with careers, families, and sociable networks.

Obituaries in the Deaf Press

Although their history as a genre goes back to antiquity, obituaries as a means of bourgeois self-representation emerged in newspapers around 1850. In an aesthetics of obituaries, Thomas Goetz uses three criteria to define the genre: its contents concern the life and death of a deceased person, it is written or spoken shortly after the death of the person in question, and it is directed at the public sphere. Characteristic is the uncritical praise or at least forgiving attitude towards the subject, which distinguishes obituaries from scientific biographies and makes them unsuitable as sources to the actual lives of the deceased. Instead, they

---

248 All of his biographies contain at least one of these verdicts. See for instance the "chastity" ("Keuschheit") of Margaretha Hüttmann, Kruse, *Der Taubstumme,* p. 135, and the "immaculate morals" ("untadelhaften Sitten") of Teutscher, ibid., p. 169; the religious Lüders ibid., p. 149, and Willig, ibid., pp. 173-174, the speaking skills of Senß, ibid., p. 162, and von Schütz's Sign Language, ibid., pp. 159-160

249 *Cf.* below p. 233.

250 Schenck noticed the especially moral and pious nature of Karl Wilke, but regretted the "religious frenzy" ("religiöse Schwärmerei") of Heinrich Karnatz. August Schenck, "Die taubstummen Koryphäen einer in nächster Zeit jubilirenden Anstalt.", TC 6 (1888), p. 66, TC 10 (1888), p. 113.

function as transmitters of collective memory, confirm the identity of groups, spread political messages, and present models for the living. At the same time as the collective memory of deceased persons affirms a group, argues Goetz, the group determines the legacy of the deceased by the way it chooses to remember them. When a deceased person is made subject of an obituary, this individual is separated from the whole and made into a person of special meaning.[251]

Obituaries were featured in the German deaf press from the beginning. The first two, that of a joiner named Langner and the mechanic Gustav Matthewes, both appeared in the third issue of the TsF in 1872.[252] Until 1914, the TsF and the TC together published fifty-five obituaries on forty-seven people. Other deaf periodicals also contained obituaries, but, in order to limit the number of sources, only the TsF and the TC have been considered in this analysis. Both had long and consistent publication spans, but differed considerably in character.[253] In the following, I will ask what kind of people, and what parts of their lives, were collectively recalled, and what this tells us about the style in which the deaf community was imagined. A complete list of the obituaries and other deaf press biographies can be found in the appendix.[254]

Diligence and Success: Working Lives of the Deceased

The vocational life of the deceased was the most common topic of obituaries. When one examines which occupations were mentioned, the distribution of trades differs greatly from what previously emerged from statistics. Deaf people working in agriculture were virtually invisible. Out of the forty-seven persons, only one was said to have worked in agriculture, whereas nearly half of all subjects were artists or professionals, mainly teachers.[255] None of the obituaries mentioned any of the vocations of the group 'Clothing and Cleaning'. Instead, crafts verging to art, such as lithography, photography and engraving, were strikingly common. In addition, the exclusive crafts silver artisan and goldsmith were each mentioned once. Thus, highly specialized and high-status trades

---

251 Thomas Goetz, Poetik des Nachrufs. Zur Kultur der Nekrologie und zur Nachrufszene auf dem Theater (Wien: Böhlau Verlag, 2008), pp. 21-24, 34-42, 51-54, 57-88.
252 TsF 3 (1872), pp. 20-21.
253 *V.* above, p. 177.
254 *V.* below, p. 281.
255 H. Lübbers was the only person working in agriculture, *v.* below and his obituary, TsF 3 (1873) p. 24.

frequently appeared also in those obituaries that depicted deaf people in manual occupations. The bias towards occupations with a higher status does not, however, mean that deaf people from the lower classes of society were entirely absent. One cigar maker and one cork- and cigar maker represent relatively unprofitable trades, diminished by industries and/or associated with the lower classes.[256] In both of these cases, further detail on the career of the subject completed the picture: H. Lübbers manufactured corks and cigars, but due to his peculiar lack of finger- and toenails could, according to his obituary, hardly perform any craft. After the death of his father, he helped his family tending the farm, where he himself died only a couple of years later at the age of 26.[257] With the image of 'the deaf-mutes' from the statistics in mind, Lübbers biography appears to be typical. We have seen that dependency on the family or on others for their sustenance was common among 'deaf-mutes' as they appear in statistics.

In the self-image conveyed by the deaf community, on the other hand, Lübbers was atypical, a fact that the author seemed aware of. Christian Riekenberg, who wrote the text, emphasised Lübbers physical, as opposed to sensory, disability and its effect on his career: Due to his lack of fingernails "he was not suitable for business".[258] Thus, the only representative of the statistically largest group of deaf people was apologized for: First, he had at one point performed crafts, before helping out on the family farmstead. Second, he had a physical disability, which affected his ability to work. Not deafness, but lack of fingernails, was understood as an obstacle to his career. The other cigar manufacturer, Carl Haar, was treated in a similar way. His obituary was one of the few that described deafness as having negative consequences for the life of the subject: he resigned to this trade since, "due to his organic flaw",[259] he was only poorly

---

256   Karl-Friedrich Bohler, Regionale Gesellschaftsentwicklung und Schichtungsmuster in Deutschland (Frankfurt a. M.: Peter Lang, 1995) pp. 101-102; Wilhelm Heinz Schröder, Arbeitergeschichte und Arbeiterbewegung. Industriearbeit und Organizationsverhalten im 19. und frühen 20. Jahrhundert. (Frankfurt a. M.: Campus Verlag, 1978), p. 237; Ludwig Hoerner, Agenten, Bader und Copisten. Hannoversches Gewerbe-ABC 1800-1900 (Hanover: Reichold Verlag, 1995), p. 257.

257   Obituary of H. Lübbers, TsF 3 (1873), p. 24, cf. "Druckfehler-Berichtigungen," TsF 5 (1873) p. 36.

258   "so taugte er nicht zu Geschäften", Obituary of H. Lübbers, TsF 3 (1873), p. 24.

259   "seines organizchen Fehlers wegen", obituary of Carl Haar, TsF 17 (1896), p. 85.

educated. Still, the author emphasised, he managed to make a good living and left behind the substantial inheritance of $ 3000.[260]

Regardless of their social stratum, descriptions of the working lives of the subjects emphasised skill, talent and success. Reliability and industriousness, exemplified by remaining for longer periods of time with the same employer, or having had only a few masters, were praised in the obituaries of manual workers Michaelis Lichtenstein, Alexander Dräge, and Langner.[261] Carl Heinrich Wilke's and Otto Friedrich Kruse's long services in deaf education had earned them recognition from royalty. The obituary over Kruse also mentioned academic merits, including a Master's degree, which composed a picture of a truly impressive career.[262]

Side by side with success, there was also hardship and misfortune in the narratives. Several of the people were described as having succeeded against all odds. Samuel Collin, who died in 1897, was uneducated and illiterate, finding himself in deepest poverty and even (wrongfully accused) in jail, but also had his own business with several employees.[263] Michael Schmaler had been unable to find an apprenticeship in the vocation he wanted, lithography. Instead, he was offered the opportunity to become an engraver, and was later awarded a medal for his successful performance in this craft. Misfortune struck again, however, and his aspiration to run his own business proved difficult.[264] Joseph Ludwig Karl Beck had similar problems, although he, too, was an accomplished craftsman who had created pieces of furniture bought by the King. Author August Schenck blamed Beck's insufficient schooling and exploitation by "conscienceless furniture merchants"[265] for his only being able to remain in business for two

---

260 Carl Haar died in the United States. TsF 17 (1896), p. 85.
261 Obituary of Langner, TsF 3 (1872), pp. 20-21; obituary of Alexander Dräge, TsF 3 (1873), p. 25; obituary of Michaelis Lichtenstein, TsF 22 (1892), p. 86.
262 Kruse was awarded an honorary Master of Arts degree from the National Deaf-Mutes College in Washington, D.C., United States, in 1878. Kruse to Edward Miner Gallaudet, 11 July 1878, Gallaudet University Archives, Presidential Papers of Edward Miner Gallaudet, Box 10, Folder 18, Letter # 174; Saegert-Heitefuß, "Carl Heinrich Wilke," TsF 3 (1876), p. 9, "Aufruf!" TsF 8-9 (1880), p. 30.
263 Adam Brehler, obituaries of Samuel Collin, TsF 11 (1897), s. 51, and TC 6 (1897), p. 66.
264 Obituary of Michael Schmaler, TC 7 (1885), p. 80.
265 "gewissenlosen Möbelhändler", August Schenck, obituary of Joseph Ludwig Karl Beck, TsF 5 (1886), pp. 19-20.

years. After this failure, Beck was employed by a colleague, whose shop he brought to flourish.

Common to these narratives was that the obstacles came from outside, in the shape of discrimination, mere bad luck, or from disabilities other than deafness. Only on two occasions did the authors describe deafness as a disability, and in both cases it was understood as an obstacle that could and should be overcome: Carl Haar had been able to achieve some wealth in spite of the low-skilled labour his deafness confined him to.[266] Gustav Schubert, explained August Schenck, refrained from a position as teacher at the Royal Academy of Arts with reference to his deafness. Schenck depicted this as an expression of Schubert's personality, which lacked fortitude and ambition. To underline that deafness posed no objective obstacle to such a career, he mentioned "the deaf professor Baron Teobald von Oer", who had held a position at the Dresden Academy.[267] Other disabilities, such as blindness, mental illness and physical impairments, were described as inflictive to the person's ability to work and quality of life: Lübbers' physical disability and its effects have been discussed above. Another example was August Winckler, lamented for his acquired blindness, which had prompted deaf friends to support him. Wilhelm Naglo became mentally ill, which cut his career and deaf movement activities short.[268]

Some subjects depending on their parents or on other relatives, socially or financially, can be found in the obituaries. However, this was not necessarily understood as a sign of dependence. Friedrike Bosse, for instance, was described as offering faithful support to her elderly father.[269] Joseph Schäfer and Karl Krieger worked in their family businesses and were described as competent craftsmen.[270]

---

266 Obituary of Carl Haar, TsF 17 (1896), p. 85.
267 "der taube Professor Freiherr Teobald von Oer", August Schenck, obituary of Gustav Schubert, TsF 9 (1885), p. 36, cf. Ulrich Thieme and Felix Becker, *Allgemeines Lexikon der bildenden Künstler von der Antike bis zur Gegenwart.* Vol. 25. Ed. Hans Vollmer (Leipzig: E.A. Seemann, 1931), p. 569.
268 Obituary of H. Lübbers, TsF 3 (1873), pp. 24-25; obituary of August Winckler, TsF 1 (1874), p. 2; August Schenck, obituary of Wilhelm Naglo, TsF 1 (1886), p. 3, TC 1 (1886), pp. 2-3.
269 Obituarity of Friedrike Bosse, TsF 12 (1873), p. 128.
270 Obituary of Karl Krieger, TC 1 (1902), pp. 2-5; Obituary of Josef Schäfer, TsF 15 (1906), p. 72.

Deaf Movement and Deaf Community in the Obituaries

A majority of the obituaries commented on the subject's education, which in most cases had taken place at an institution for deaf education. Private education and attending mainstream school seldom appeared.[271] Typically, the name of the institution they had attended was given. The *alma mater* seems to have functioned as a point of reference, which helped the reader to place the deceased in a deaf community context.[272] Also, mentioning the role of the person in a club or at least his or her membership therein was common in the obituaries. They were sometimes named simply as 'member of the deaf club X'.[273] Of course, their affiliation with the movement was a decisive reason for the papers to publish their obituaries. At the same time, as the number of deaf clubs increased, the number of individuals that were occupying a position on their administrative level multiplied. Thus, being the president of a club, a long-time member, or a frequent participant of deaf congresses, to a greater extent became ways to be deaf. By emphasising this in the obituaries, the authors helped making deaf movement engagement into a status provider.

As we have seen, the deaf taking a prominent role in, for instance, administration or education were losing significance as ways to be deaf. Just like in the collections of 'peculiar' deaf, obituaries over deaf white-collar professionals became increasingly rare as time progressed. Not counting the artists, eight professionals, most of them teachers, appeared.[274] The last was the teacher

---

271 Wilhelm Naglo, Carl Bente and Karl Fuchs had had private teachers. Obituaries of Wilhelm Naglo, TC 1 (1886), pp. 2-3; Karl Fuchs, TC 2 (1896), pp. 16-17; Albin Maria Watzulik, obituary of Carl Bente, TC 3 (1895), p. 26; Ernst Batterman attended the village school. TsF 5 (1874), p. 37.

272 This information appeared in almost every obituary. A few examples are Friederike Bosse, TsF 12 (1873), p. 128; Ludwig Wolff, TC 6 (1895), pp. 78-79; and Moritz Schubert TsF 21 (1906), p. 107.

273 The designation appeared in the obituaries of Michael Schmaler, TC 7 (1885), p. 80, Gustav Büchting, TsF 1 (1911), p. 3, and Moritz Lederer, TsF 7 (1908), p. 37. A few other obituaries emphasizing deaf movement activity were those of Alfred Steinthal, TsF 12 (1901), pp. 53-54, Michaelis Lichtenstein, TsF 22 (1892), p. 86; Wilhelm Vogt, TsF 6 (1892), p. 22, August Winckler TsF 1 (1874), p. 2.

274 The teachers were 'Widow' Harstrick, TsF 5 (1874), p. 34; Wilke: Saegert-Heitefuß, "Carl Heinrich Wilke," TsF 3 (1876), p. 9; Kruse: "Aufruf!" TsF 8-9 (1880), p. 30; Ferdinand Rasch TC 7 (1885), p. 74-75; Albin Maria Watzulik, obituary of August Schenck, TsF 46 (1892), p. 195, TC 12 (1892) pp. 144-145; idem, obituary of

Karl Max Löwe, who died in 1893.[275] After that, all obituaries were about craftsmen, or, in some cases, artisans or even artists, but no professionals. For the writers of obituaries, a void was opened in terms of emphasising the importance of their subjects, offering role models, and thereby reproducing group identity. This void could in part be filled by positions held and achievements made within the deaf movement.

Independence, Ableness, Masculinity: The Deaf in Obituaries

The distribution of persons appearing in obituaries of deaf people gives an impression of a group distinctly separate from the 'deaf-mutes' of statistics and professional literature. The latter genres presented a group of people consisting of peasants, depending on family members and relatives for their sustenance; of deaf women, often living in institutions; of people unlikely to marry and very rarely found in occupations of a higher status. In the deaf press obituaries, the deaf appeared as competent workers and professionals, although at times in cumbersome situations. Dependence on others was rarely explicitly mentioned, but rather, the dependence of others on the deaf individual was emphasised: Friedrike Bosse had cared for her father, and the death of Alexander Dräge was described as a great loss for his master.[276] Remaining in the home of one's parents or other relatives was never described as typical for deaf people, although at times as a resort for those with other disabilities. Confinement in institutions was treated in a similar manner: Wilhelm Naglo ended his life in an lunatic asylum, thus not institutionalized due to his deafness but because he was afflicted with mental illness. A Herr Marsch died in the asylum run by the CVWT where he had moved in his old age, as a continuation of his life-long engagement in the deaf movement.[277]

Obituaries elevate individual lives into the collective memory, but they do so by integrating their singularity into a superior context, where certain attributes of

---

Carl Max Löwe TsF 51 (1893), p. 207; the civil servant Fürstenberg TsF 1 (1885), p. 2 and TC 2 (1885), pp. 13-15, and the engineer and factory owner Wilhelm Naglo, obituary by August Schenck, TsF 1 (1886), p. 3; TC 1 (1886), pp. 2-3.

275 Albin Maria Watzulik, obituary of Carl Max Löwe TsF 51 (1893), p. 207; Carl von Haase, obituary of max Löwe, TC 1 (1894), pp. 4-5.

276 Obituary of Alexander Dräge, TsF 3 (1873), p. 25.

277 "Berliner Chronik," TsF 4 (1911), p. 17; August Schenck, obituary of Wilhelm Naglo, TsF 1 (1886), p. 3, TC 1 (1886), pp. 2-3.

the deceased, namely those suitable as examples, are emphasised.[278] The great achievements of Carl Heinrich Wilke and Otto Kruse, the exquisite talent of Joseph Ludwig Karl Beck, the business Samuel Collin ran against all odds, were all subjects the deaf reader could understand as models. Gustav Schubert, who had believed himself to be unable to teach hearing people due to his deafness, had this belief posthumously falsified in his obituary: August Schenck presented a counter-example proving to the reader that this path would, in fact, have been possible.

Obituaries may serve other purposes than honouring the dead, which makes the genre, in the words of Ralf Georg Bogner, "a surface of projection for the selfish literary, political or religious interests of the necrologist."[279] Altogether, all obituaries of deaf people in the deaf press can be said to serve the interests of the movement by highlighting diligent, successful and talented deaf people. Thus, the deaf press challenged the established view of the deaf as defective and disadvantaged. In addition, the medical view on deafness was undermined through largely ignoring the sensory and disabling side of deafness but instead lamenting other disabilities and emphasising the deaf community.

The construction of the deaf as a fairly well off and socially independent group applied foremost to deaf men. Whereas in statistics, deaf women had appeared as even more dependent than their male counterparts, in deaf press obituaries they hardly appeared at all. Only three women were paid tribute at their death: Friederike Bosse, the teacher 'Widow' Harstrick, and Klara Hötzold. Compared to the bleak impression gained from statistical averages, Mrs. Harstrick stood out as having been not only married, but also as pursuing a career as a teacher in Hildesheim.[280] Bosse and Hötzold apparently spent much of their adult lives in their parental households, but their biographies offer alternative interpretations of the conditions for deaf women remaining at home. As mentioned above, Bosse's relationship to her father appeared in the obituary as one of his dependence on his deaf daughter, rather than her inability to build an independent life. Klara Hötzold lived with her foster mother for 33 years, yet she, after the death of the latter, married the deaf teacher Moritz Hötzold. In the obituary, she appeared as a highly independent woman, as a benefactress of the

---

278 Goetz, *Poetik des Nachrufs* pp. 30, 34-35, 60-61.
279 "Projektionsfeld für die eigennützigen poetologischen, politischen oder religiösen Interessen der Nekrologisten," Ralf Georg Bogner, *Der Autor im Nachruf. Formen und Funktionen der literarischen Memorialkultur von der Reformation bis zum Vormärz* (Tübingen: Max Niemeyer Verlag, 2006), p. 4.
280 Obituary of Harstrick, TsF 5 (1874), p. 34.

deaf movement, and of deaf people in need.[281] The obituaries of her and Bosse thus countered the assumption that deaf women were left with few options. They showed that dependence in terms of formal status in the household did not have to be a permanent state, nor did it necessarily imply that the deaf woman was incapable. On the other hand, only three examples of this during forty years indicate the low status of the group. The main alternative the deaf press offered to the description of the dependent and indigent 'deaf-mute' woman was silence.

Special Occasions: Other Personal Stories in the Deaf Press

Stories and news about deaf individuals appeared also in other shapes than obituaries. Birthdays, anniversaries, and the awarding of scholarships and decorations could, like deaths and funerals, prompt the publication of biographical texts. As a genre, these texts were in some aspects similar to obituaries: they had a positive attitude towards the subject, contained some information on his or her life, emerged in direct connection with an event in the life of the subject, and may, as the obituaries, have served the purpose of transmitting a certain image both of the individual and the group. Both the narratives and the type of occasions selected reflected the way that the deaf press wished to present deaf people.

In many cases, the occasions that caught the attention of the deaf press were related to work. Vocational anniversaries, scholarships, long and faithful service, or exceptional achievements motivated the publication of biographies. Craftspeople and domestic servants were used as examples of diligence and loyalty. Remarkable careers in art, business or professions were displayed as examples of what deaf people could achieve.

Being from 25 up to 60 years in a vocation or at the same workplace prompted celebrations, which were sometimes remarkably elaborate. The 25th anniversary of John Pacher's business – he was the owner of a printing factory on the outskirts of Hamburg – occupied the first five pages of TC 3:1890. Most of the article was devoted to describing the festivity, which had included 200 guests, many of them elevated personalities from the government and military, the performance of a theatre play about Pacher's life, numerous greetings from around the country, and the awarding of a Persian order.[282]

---

281 Obituary of Klara Hötzold, TC 4 (1891), p. 39.
282 Ernsberger, "Das 25jährige Geschäftsjubiläum des Herrn Comissionsrath John Pacher," TC 3 (1890), pp. 25-29.

John Pacher was a self-made man, and his life a true success story. He was unquestionably a member of the bourgeoisie, he had even married into a wealthy, noble family,[283] and the celebration of his 25th year in business showed that he was well established in hearing society as well as highly important to the self-image of the deaf community. TC began the article by declaring him a role model and a proof of what deaf people can achieve.[284] However, also diligent workers of lower social status celebrated their professional anniversaries on the pages of deaf periodicals. At her 25th professional anniversary, the tailor Ernestine Collier in Stettin was congratulated by a teacher, representatives of the deaf movement, and her employer.[285] Others who were celebrated for their long service were the domestic servant Borschitz and lithographer Löwenberg.[286]

The teachers Otto Kruse and Moritz Hötzold were paid tribute on their birthdays, as was the exceptionally successful artist Paul Ritter.[287] Their birthdays gave the opportunity to remind the readers of especially important deaf people.

Deaf movement engagement prompted the publication of one of the biographies. Albert Edel in Berlin celebrated his 50th anniversary as a member of the local deaf society in 1908. Edel's line of work was not specified, rather his career within the club. Earlier, he had served as a member of the board, but in old age he instead received its support.[288]

Weddings and wedding anniversaries where both parties were deaf received special attention. The TsF declared, as it published a story on a wedding anniversary in 1873, that the purpose was to spread knowledge about "peculiarities

---

283 Fischer, Wempe, Lamprecht, and Seeberger, "John E. Pacher", p. 125; his 25th business anniversary is also described in ibid, pp. 129-131.
284 Not the word "taubstumm" – "deaf-mute" was used, but the word "gehörlos", "hearing-less", a relatively uncommon term at this point, but in contemporary German the usual word for "deaf". Ernsberger, "Das 25jährige Geschäftsjubiläum des Herrn Comissionsrath John Pacher," TC 3 (1890), p. 25.
285 Notice on the Collier anniversary, TsF 1 (1902), p. 3.
286 "Ein langer Dienst," TsF 4 (1875), p. 23; "Jubiläum," TsF 18 (1877), p. 70.
287 "Zum 77jährigen Geburtstage des Otto Friedrich Kruse am 29. März 1878," TsF 6 (1878), pp. 24-25; "Professor Paul Ritter's 70. Geburtstag," TsF 4 (1899), pp. 16-17; "Vereinswesen," TsF 6 (1899), pp. 29-30; L. H., "Professor Paul Ritter," TC 3 (1899), pp. 25-26; Birthday greeting to Moritz Hötzold, TC 3 (1903), pp. 25-26, cf. Ursula Kubach-Reutter (Ed.), *Spätromantik im Industriezeitalter. Die Nürnberger Künstlerfamilie Ritter* (Nuremberg: Museum Industriekultur, 2007).
288 W. Gottweiss, notice on the Lederer anniversary, TsF 3 (1908) p. 13.

from the lives and fates of deaf-mutes".[289] Short notices and advertisements about weddings were most common, but in some cases brief articles on the celebrations and biographical data on one or both spouses also appeared. Apparently, deaf-deaf couples were perceived as especially important to report about.[290] Thanks to the weddings and wedding anniversaries, where both sexes were always represented among the leading characters, a few more women were brought to the readers' attention. Still, the focus was on the groom, or husband, in all articles, and at times the female part was more or less ignored.[291]

The debate about marriages between deaf people was not as active in Germany as it was in America at the time. Both the TsF and the TC did print excerpts from Alexander Graham Bell's essay "Upon the Formation of a Deaf-Mute Variety of the Human Race", but it failed to cause many reactions.[292] When the issue was debated, it was more about whether deaf people were intellectually and socially mature enough to have families, than about genetics.[293] Through the

---

289 "Merkwürdigkeiten aus dem Leben und Schicksale Taubstummer", Ferdinand Rasch, "Erzählungen [...] 2.," TsF 1 (1873), p. 6.

290 Ferdinand Rasch, "Erzählungen [...] 2.," TsF 1 (1873), p. 6; "Die silberne Hochzeit", TsF 12 (1877), p. 45; "Mitteilungen.", TsF 39 (1893), p. 158; Reach/Kramper wedding, TsF 12 (1905), p. 62.

291 The Beck Wedding anniversary, "Die silberne Hochzeit", TsF 12 (1877), p. 45, and the Reach/Kramper wedding, TsF 12 (1905), p. 62, are examples of this.

292 Alexander Graham Bell, "Die Ehe," TsF 42 (1892), pp. 180-182, continued in subsequent issues; ibid., TC 9 (1892), pp. 105-107, continued in subsequent issues. In the German deaf movement, Bell was more controversial when it came to his resistance to deaf clubs. A series of TC articles in 1886 argued against his positions. "Winke und Rathschläge für Taubstummen-Vereine," TC 5 (1886), pp. 49-50, TC 6 (1886), pp. 61-62, TC 7 (1886), pp. 73-74, TC 8 (1886), pp. 85-86; Franz Rotter criticized Bell's positions in "Sollen taubstumme einander heiraten?" TC 12 (1890), pp. 133-134, TC 1 (1891), pp. 2-3.

293 Joseph Oblidahl, "Ein Wort an die heiratslustigen Taubstummen," TC 10 (1886), pp. 113-115; Moritz Friedländer, "Dürfen Taubstumme heiraten?" TC 11 (1886), pp. 123-124; In the brief notice "Dürfen Taubstumme heirathen?", a review of a recent medical article, genetics were the focus, TsF 19 (1898), p. 92; Eugen Sutermeister, "Über Taubstummen-Heiraten," TC 1 (1900), pp. 6-8; Hans Silberbauer, "Über Taubstummen-Heiraten," TC 2 (1900), pp. 13-14; Therese Heilborn, "Offener Brief an Herrn Sutermeister," TC 3 (1900), p. 27; Emil Schönthaler, "Die Ehe. Mit besonderer Berücksichtigung der Taubstummen," TC 8 (1894), pp. 88-89.

reports on long deaf-deaf marriages, the papers proved that it was indeed possible for such alliances to succeed.

Warrants, Criminals, and Vagrants

Apart from the attention paid to certain deaf people at the event of their death, birthday, or other anniversaries, or merely because they were 'peculiar', the periodicals also contained stories about deaf individuals who distinguished themselves in less honourable ways. Deaf people who had committed crimes appeared in news reports, accounts of court proceedings, or notices of warning. In addition, descriptions were sometimes published of unknown deaf individuals found by the authorities, or missing deaf persons. These categories of texts widened the range of narratives on concrete lives of deaf people in the deaf press. In this section, I will ask which role these malefactors and unfortunates played in the self-image of the deaf community.

Over the years, the TsF published texts on altogether nineteen deaf individuals who were either reported missing, found but unidentified, wanted or arrested for crimes, or who were considered dangerous and therefore named and described as a warning.[294] These texts have in common that they were concerned not with honouring in some way prominent deaf, as were obituaries and other celebrations. Still, they contained biographical information covering some of the same aspects of life as we have seen above.

In those cases where their vocation was mentioned, the combined picture is not entirely dissimilar from that of the previous types of biographies. For the most part, they were craftsmen. However, no white-collar professionals appeared among them. Contrasting with the other biographies, they were hardly ever described as talented, diligent, and loyal workers. In a letter to the editor of TsF, a former employer of August Rautenberg stated that he was quite satisfied with his employee until Rautenberg left without notice, taking with him a pocket watch.[295] Others were explicitly described as work-shy: con man Andreas Bitz and thief August Boyry were both designated as skilled workers, who in spite of their talent did not work.[296]

The most obvious difference was, however, that those appearing in warnings, crime stories and missing person reports were described as solitary. References

---

294 A list of all these articles and notices can be found in the appendix.
295 A. Obst, letter to the editor, TsF 38-39 (1894), p. 128.
296 "Diebstahl," TsF 5 (1875), pp. 27-28; ; Report on Andreas Bitz, TsF 5 (1877), pp. 18-19; "Ein taubstummer Hochstapler," TsF 11 (1906), p. 53.

to their family of origin, marriage, children, or deaf networks were seldom made, and the schools they had attended were rarely mentioned.[297] If and where deaf criminals and vagrants had gone to school was in most cases not specified, leaving the reader without this means of identifying with the subject. In some cases, they were described as uneducated.[298] Mentioning their lack of education could be used as a means of evoking sympathy with impoverished deaf, but at the same time it set them apart from the reader. When the deaf community was mentioned, it was as being exploited by ruthless deaf con men. To the list of crimes Friedrich Bude was accused of, leaving Halberstadt without officially cancelling his membership in the deaf society was added in a notice of warning directed at "all German Deaf-Mute-Presidents."[299]

Such warnings were advocated in a 1903 article in the DTZ, in which Bruno Schott expressed concern that deaf criminals hurt the reputation of the deaf as a group. Due to the complicated court procedures when prosecuting deaf people, and that deaf defendants were sometimes declared having unsound minds and therefore not convicted, Schott argued that the measures taken by the legal system were not sufficient. In order to save the reputation of the deaf, he argued that the deaf movement should warn the general public against such individuals.[300]

For the most part, the respectable and the disreputable appeared to belong to the same class of manual workers. The difference was located on the level of personality and individual ability, rather than on social structures. Diligent and skilled deaf men overcame obstacles, and were proudly presented as members of the deaf community. The work-shy, the immoral, and the desolate were separated from the community. They were mentioned, but with a different purpose than in obituaries. If obituaries served the wish of the group to claim the memory of an individual and to gain strength by identifying with that person, the notices of warning were the opposite. They were means of officially excluding certain individuals from the group, and encouraging all deaf people to do the same.

---

297 Information about the school was only given about an unidentified boy possibly named Kunze (who lacked education), "Ein 14 jähriger taubstummer Unbekannter," TsF 3 (1874), pp. 15-16, the convict Andreas Bitz, "Diebstahl," TsF 5 (1875), pp. 27-28, and the missing person Margerethe Duckert, TsF 4 (1908), p. 19.

298 "Ein 14 jähriger taubstummer Unbekannter," TsF 3 (1874), pp. 15-16; "Mitteilungen," TsF 18 (1890), p. 95.

299 "An alle deutschen Taubstummen-Vorstände," TsF 22-23 (1894), p. 78.

300 Bruno Schott, "Recht und Gesetz," DTZ 4 (1903) [n. p.].

CONCLUSION OF CHAPTER 3

The formation of organizations for people who were deaf was based on the imagining of a deaf community. Other than mere personal networks, the formal clubs and associations, and their expressions, rested on an idea of 'thousands like themselves'.

This idea proved remarkably powerful. The size of the movement increased significantly from the last decades of the 19th century. The organizations were also able to create a variety of print media, institutions, and smaller and larger events. Through the periodicals and the public places that were permanently or temporarily claimed by deaf people, it can be said that the German deaf created a public sphere of their own. There, in turn, personal acquaintances were made, and networks built.

However, with the average of a few hundred visitors, those enjoying a few days in a deaf space during church feasts and congresses were a tiny minority. Compared to living the rest of the year in isolation, the duration of the temporary deaf space was also very short. These phenomena shall not lead us to believe that life had changed for 'the deaf-mutes', but rather that a new and different group was taking shape under the same name.

The biographies of people belonging to this group offer a fairly consistent set of characteristics, which crucially differed from those set up for 'the deaf-mutes' in official accounts. That the editors of deaf periodicals and writers compiling biographies of deaf people chose to present the most remarkable, those with especially successful careers, and unusual achievements, is not surprising. The exceptional is often the most interesting to the reader. However, it were not only business owners, renowned artists, and polyglots who appeared. Several people with more humble lives were also honoured with obituaries or other biographical texts. Still, they were not just any people, and the things they had in common presented to the reader a way to imagine those other 'thousands like himself.'

Characteristic were petty bourgeoisie vocations – crafts, mostly – and virtues such as independence, diligence, loyalty. There was hardly any trace of the indigent, rural, dependent 'deaf-mutes' that the government found when performing surveys. These kinds of people were not relevant to the construction of a self-image of the deaf community. At times, the boundaries of the community were explicitly defended against unwanted elements. But these, too, belonged to the same social classes as those who were included. Disregard is more powerful than denouncement and warning. This is what happened to deaf women, to inmates of institutions, to rural deaf people, and to those who were indigent and dependent on others.

The new kind of deaf people joined deaf clubs, travelled to congresses, and read deaf periodicals. They may well also have frequented bars with other deaf clients, bought their shoes from deaf shoemakers, let a room to a deaf person, and married deaf women.[301] Together, the classification and the practices made the educated, middle-class deaf man "a way to be a person, to experience oneself, to live in society."[302]

---

301 *Cf.* above, pp. 117ff.
302 Ian Hacking, "Kinds of People: Moving Targets," p. 303.

4. Conflicts: The Debate in the Deaf Movement

This chapter explores the ways in which deaf people collectively tried to influence their situation. The subjects appearing, and the space in which they appeared, were parts of the imagined deaf community, a sphere dominated by relatively well-educated and –situated men. The reader will notice that the number of people cited in this chapter is relatively small. A handful of individuals together produced the majority of the statements in the Silent press, in related print media, and in the formalized public debate, such as congress presentations, official statements, and petitions. However, these sources represent only one part of the public sphere. For this period, we can only access sources where the thoughts and opinions of deaf people have made their way into writing. Most statements will come from the authors themselves, using written German to express their ideas. Some are translations or transcripts of statements that were originally signed or spoken. The inaccesability of debates that took place in other language modes than writing is of course not unique to the deaf context. Spoken debates in the 19th century that were not recorded in writing also remain obscure. However, the deaf public sphere was to a great extent founded on a language which had no writing at all. Signed expressions and debates could not be recorded before film technology. Due to the language barrier, literacy in German was most likely less common among deaf Germans than among their hearing counterparts, enabling a smaller group of people to take part in the debate which will be the object of analysis here.

Furthermore, it is plausible that the leap into written German not only excluded those persons who were unable to write fluently enough, but also excluded certain expressions from the debate. As for excluded people, we can presume that they were those who had no or poor education, or for some reason had been unable to benefit from it. Even such individuals did, occationally, have the possibility to enter print media by having signed congress presentations translated and included in protocols.¹ Concerning excluded kinds of statements, on the other hand, it is considerably harder to determine if they existed, and, in that case, what they contained. Nevertheless, we need to be aware of the probability of their existence, as well as conscious of the impact they may have had on the written debate. Compared to the readers and writers of the deaf press and the participants of deaf congresses, what we can read today is only one side of the story. In the bilingual space in which they lived, the center may have been located somewhere completely different than in the coordinates we can obtain from the printed sources. Some were only able to access the one or the other mode: an illiterate deaf person may have been familiar only with what was signed in his or her local club, whereas others may have had little or no contact with a signing network, but followed the affairs of other deaf people by subscribing to a periodical. Many, however, had access to both realms. The articles in the deaf press were to a great extent written by and for people who were integrated into signing networks, so that there was an interchange between what went on in signed and written realms. At times, this left traces in the shape of reactions to views that are not to be found in the written sources.² It seems likely that those were views that circulated in Sign Language. However, the evidence is too sparse to allow any consistent reconstruction of the Sign Language idea debate. It merely acts as a reminder of what has been lost.

Therefore, the image obtained from periodicals, petitions and protocols is in one sense necessarily fragmentary. In another sense, however, it did possess contiguity. Although a representation of speech, text is, as Christopher Krentz has

---

1 How often this occurred is unknown. There is one mention of an illiterate deaf man participating in a congress debate, which proves that this was possible: "Der fünfte Deutsche Taubstummen-Congreß in Berlin," TC 9 (1902), p. 99.

2 For instance, the signature H. Zech defended the habit of sending addresses to the Emperor against the "many" deaf who opposed it for being politically charged. I have been unable to find such claims in the written sources, which would suggest that Zech refers to opinions he encountered in a signing environment. "Keine Politik in den Taubstummen-Vereinen." ATZ 14 (1913) p. 114; another example is a declaration of support of Anna Schenck that appeared in the TsF in 1899 after she and the CVWT had been criticized for their handling of funds at a club meeting. The exact contents of the criticism remains unknown, since only the replies appeared in print. Carl Rumpf and Hermann Michelson, "Erklärung," TsF 15 (1899), p. 74; "Protest-Erklärung," TsF 16 (1899), p. 83; "Protest-Erklärung," TsF 17 (1899), p. 90; *v.* also Krentz, *Writing Deafness,* pp. 132-134.

pointed out, a "silent, visual space",[3] where borders between hearing and deaf lose significance. Since Sign Language-based networks in the absence of modern technology are necessarily local, written exchange was the only vehicle for a continuous interregional exchange. If we are to study the ideas of 'the German deaf', and not only the sum of ideas circulating in different local networks, texts are the proper sources. This makes the protocols from congresses in a way more relevant than the signed debates they are translations of. The latter reached only those immediately present, whereas the protocols were circulated among members of a wider audience.

Thus demarcated, the following chapter will be dedicated to the structure and contents of the discussions that took place in the written realm of the German deaf community. In the first section, the issues they addressed, and the channels used to discuss and advocate these issues, will be presented. Following this summary of the debate, the next section analyzes the reactions to deaf movement requests and opinions among those at whom they were directed: educators and administrators. In the final section, the strategies used by deaf leaders when faced with these responses are outlined and evaluated. The questions are in what areas the deaf movement tried to gain influence, what they hoped to achieve, how they undertook this task, and what the consequences were.

THE ISSUES AND THE CHANNELS

During the eighty years studied, the public discussions of the deaf movement covered a wide range of individual issues: anything from dog tax, cycling, and alcohol consumption, to the Dreyfus-process.[4] Here is not the place for an index

---

3   Krentz, *Writing Deafness*, p. 22; *cf.* also Lennard J. Davis, *Enforcing Normalcy: Disability, Deafness, and the Body* (New York: Verso, 1995), p. 4. It needs, however, to be stressed that this is true only for the sensory aspect of deafness. The socio-linguistic reality is that pre-lingual deafness often is a barrier also to literacy. *Cf.* Brenda Jo Brueggeman, "Introduction: Reframing Deaf People's Literacy," in *Literacy and Deaf People. Cultural and contextual Perspectives,* ed. Brenda Jo Brueggeman (Washington, D. C.: Gallaudet University Press, 2004), pp. 1-4.

4   *Protokoll über die Verhandlungen des IX. Allgemeinen Deutschen Taubstummen-Kongresses zu Breslau, am 31. Mai und 1. Juni 1914* (n.pl.: AATD, 1915), p. 26; "Dämon Alkohol und die Taubstummen," TC 10 (1903), pp. 110-112; "Dürfen Schwerhörige und Taube Radfahren?" TC 10 (1898), pp. 108-109; Josef Obhlidal, "Eine französische Stimme über die deutschen Taubstummen," TC 7 (1899), p. 77.

of the debate in its totality; rather, this section will give an orientation in the dominant tendencies and their transformation over time. In accordance with Foucault' model of discourse analysis, the focus will be set on the structure of the debate, rather than the contents. The moment when deaf people appeared as 'speakers' in the public sphere will be traced, and the development of channels for this discourse explored. The analysis of the contents of the debate concentrates on their structural function in the demarcation of deaf groupness and positioning towards allies and opponents.

Meetings and Media: The Channels of the Deaf Movement

Considering the types of print media where deaf people expressed and discussed their opinions, and the intensity of this activity, a fourfold division of the time 1828-1914 can be made: One of sparse publications by singular authors, followed in 1873 by the formalization and recording of occasional face-to-face discussions between deaf men; from 1885 a more continuous debate, and from 1903 onward a diversified landscape of several regular publications with different profiles. Thus, it becomes clear that most of the 19th century was characterized by a remarkable silence. Deaf persons with a good command of written German and a relatively solid education had existed for half a century before any of them entered the public sphere of print media. Contrastingly, works by deaf men appeared in France already in the 18th century. By the mid-19th century, the United States had a handful of deaf writers.[5]

The complete absence of any German deaf authors before 1828 means that an intellectual history of the German deaf at the very earliest can start in this year. Other kinds of sources can and have been used to reconstruct certain 'Deaf experiences' from before this date.[6] Deaf people most certainly had ideas and opinions, and discussed these with each other and with hearing people, before 1828. If this took place in Sign, the contents have been lost to us. When it took

---

5   For France, *v.* "Chronology", in *The Deaf Experience,* ed. Lane, p. ix; in America, a public debate between several deaf men on the prospect of forming a 'deaf state' unfolded during the 1850s, *v.* Van Cleve and Crouch, *A Place of Their Own,* pp. 60-70.

6   Historian Hans-Uwe Feige has published several essays on late 18th- and early 19th century deaf lives, using mainly school records and letters as sources. *v.* Feige, "Lebenswirklichkeit gehörloser Kinder"; idem, "Gehörlose Handwerker vor 200 Jahren"; idem: "Samuel Heinickes Eppendorfer ‚Muellersohn'," *Das Zeichen* 48 (1999), pp. 188–193; idem, *Gehörlosen-Biografien.*

place in writing (e.g. in letters), it was not intended for, or never reached, an audience and was thus not part of the public sphere.

The first texts to be published in the German language written by a deaf author appeared in 1828. Carl Wilhelm Teuscher (1803-1835), a teacher at the Royal Deaf-Mute Asylum in Leipzig, contributed to *Blicke auf die Taubstummenbildung*, the main work of his former teacher, by then colleague, Carl Gottlob Reich. In this essay, Teuscher described the way he used different communicative modes for his cognitive activity.[7] In the same year, Teuscher also published a small tractate on deaf education. The latter work does not seem to have received much attention, but the essay in *Blicke auf die Taubstummenbildung* probably reached a considerable number of readers, as this work was widely used by instructors. However, Teuscher's early death put an end to his literary production.[8]

Slightly later, in 1832, the young teacher Otto Friedrich Kruse (1801-1880) began what was to be a more enduring authorship. Kruse was born hearing in Altona, a town in Schleswig-Holstein on what is today the Danish-German border.[9] He learned Low German as his first language and briefly attended a village school, before becoming deaf at age six. The following year he was enrolled in the deaf school in Schleswig, where he was subsequently hired as a teacher and spent most of his career. Apart from teaching, Kruse independently studied pedagogy and, particularly, deaf education in literature and by travelling to different European institutions.[10] This enabled him to develop a method for

---

7   "Bemerkungen über meines Denkens Form," in Carl Gottlob Reich, Blicke auf die Taubstummenbildung und Nachricht über die Taubstummenanstalt zu Leipzig seit ihren 50jährigen Bestehen, nebst einem Anhange über die Articulation, 2nd. ed. (Leipzig: Leopold Voß, 1828), pp. 93-99.

8   In addition to this, several unpublished manuscripts and letters written by Teuscher exist. However, these never reached an audience. *Cf.* Hans Uwe Feige, "Carl Friedrich Wilhelm Teuscher und Carl Gottlob Reich. Der gehörlose Schüler und sein hörender Mentor," *Das Zeichen* 59 (2002), pp. 8-22.

9   This area was a linguistic melting pot, where Danish, Frisian and Low German were the vernacular, whereas High German or Danish were the administrative and educational languages. Olaf Klose and Christian Degn, *Die Herzogtümer im Gesamtstaat. 1721-1830. Geschichte Schleswig-Holsteins* Vol. 6. (Neumünster: Karl Wahholtz, 1960), pp. 114-124.

10 Otto Friedrich Kruse, *Bilder aus dem Leben eines Taubstummen. Eine Autobiographie des Taubstummen* (Altona: Self-published by the author, 1877), pp. 1-13, 19; Helmut Vogel, "Otto Friedrich Kruse" [Part 1.], pp. 198-207.

deaf education, which was to a great extent an implication of Pestalozzian ideas in the particular setting of a deaf school. Until 1877, Kruse published more than a dozen books, most about deaf education.[11]

Although Kruse was a productive writer, he and Teuscher being the sole deaf persons involved in public discussion before the 1870s makes publications by deaf authors very rare for most of the century. Furthermore, there was no such thing as a public exchange between deaf people. Kruse did not write for a deaf audience, nor did he ever claim to be speaking for a group of deaf people, real or imagined. He wrote about deaf people, but did not represent them. Foremost, his work is that of a teacher of the deaf, not of a deaf man. On the other hand, he incorporated his own experience of being deaf in the texts: his communicative situation in his family after losing his hearing, the experience of deaf school, coping with exclusion, prejudice and communicative barriers are all mentioned.[12] Kruse's books without doubt contain a deaf 'I', and certainly a deaf 'they', but never a deaf 'we'.[13]

The deaf 'we' entered German print with the 1848 statutes of the TsV Berlin, but it took another quarter-century until this deaf 'we' started to record and spread its ideas via print media on any significant scale. When they did, a new structural phase of deaf movement debate was commenced. Compared to Kruse's and Teuscher's sparse publications from 1828 and onward, the issuing of the TsF in 1872 meant an avalanche of printed text by deaf authors. However,

---

11   A list of his publications is attached to Kruse, Bilder aus dem Leben eines Taubstummen, pp. 184-186. His pedagogic ideas are laid out in Otto Friedrich Kruse, Über Taubstumme, Taubstummenbildung und Taubstummenanstalten; nebst Notizen aus meinem Reisetagebuche (Schleswig: Published by the author under commission of the Prussian administration, 1853), pp. 112-295; cf. also Groschek, Unterwegs in eine Welt des Verstehens, pp. 55-56.

12   Especially, of course, in his 1877 autobiography, but also in Kruse, *Der Taubstumme*, pp. 138-147. In Kruse, *Über Taubstumme*, he declared that he was "himself deaf-mute" ("selbst taubstumm") on the title page.

13   The only 'we' that appears in his texts refers to the teaching community. Cf. Otto Friedrich Kruse, Zur Vermittlung der Extreme in der sogenannten deutschen und französischen Taubstummen-Bildungs-Methode. Ein Versuch zur Vereinigung beider, (Schleswig: Verlag der Schulbuchhandlung Hermann Heiberg, 1869), p. 1. Teuscher at one point in his 1828 essay used the word 'we' to designate deaf people, and mentioned having contact with other deaf. However, he seems rather to use the 'we' as a rhetoric tool when referring to himself, than meaning a group of deaf individuals. Cf. Teuscher, "Bemerkungen über meines Denkens Form," pp. 93, 96.

the TsF was never a forum for debate. What opinions deaf people might have had, what they considered to be their interests, and how they viewed themselves, can at best be guessed at, based on the TsF. More important for articulating concrete ideas and for posing demands were the congresses commenced in 1873. Through the protocols – which survive from most congresses – we can access the concrete statements made by a number of deaf men. Through them, also, the contemporaries of these men could access their statements. What earlier had been uttered in Sign, therefore only reaching the circle of people immediately present in time and space, was now translated into written German and could be spread and preserved. The potential audience instantly multiplied.

Discussions within small groups of educated deaf men was nothing new; they had probably gone on in Germany for about a century.[14] From 1873 onward, however, they were formalized, recorded, and broadcast. In short, they entered the mainstream public sphere. The architect behind this was Eduard Fürstenberg. He took part in organizing the six congresses from 1873 until 1884 that represent the first phase of public discussion between deaf people. When he died in 1885, the first series of congresses was interrupted, which meant a significant structural change.

Coincidently, the first issue of the TC was issued shortly after Fürstenberg's death. Unlike the TsF, which continued in the hands of Fürstenberg's hearing children, this new publication was focused on debate. Topical and often opinionated articles accounted for the greater part of its contents, whereas less space was devoted to the every-day activities of deaf clubs and religious and moral lectures. The TC could be enjoyed by anyone who took interest in deafness, deaf people, and deaf education, whereas the TsF had mostly been useful to keep track of events. Consequently, the deaf community debate entered a third structural phase. Since the congresses had been discontinued, the debate was for a while detached from the physical encounter of deaf men. Instead, thanks to the TC, it now took place continuously, not only at fixed intervals, and independently of face-to-face contact. In 1892, the deaf congresses were also reintroduced, this time as purely German events. In addition, international deaf congresses were held in different Western countries from 1889 onward.[15] The period 1885-1903 thus represents an intensive phase for the German deaf community debate.

---

14   At least since the introduction of institutional deaf education; possibly longer.
15   Murray, *Touch of Nature*, p. 60; *v.* also above p. 189.

In the early 1900s, the TC struggled with financial difficulties.[16] The sudden death of its editor, Bernhard Brill, in 1904 was the final blow. Others made efforts to continue issuance, but the TC was unable to keep its position as a leading paper.[17] With the end of the TC, the comprehensiveness of *the* pan-German deaf movement debate was lost. The writers who had formerly contributed to the TC were now published in a number of different papers. No single publication, but a combination of several, replaced the TC. The TsF was published until 1912, but publications that did not play any significant part in the debate on ideas were by the 20th century perceived as dated.[18] *Neue Zeitschrift für Taubstumme* was founded in 1905 as the official organ of the deaf associations in Hamburg and Hanover and the deaf section of the gymnastics association *Deutsche Turnerschaft*. In 1913 it merged with the TsF to form the *Allgemeine Deutsche Taubstummenzeitschrift*.[19] *Deutsche Taubstummen-Korrespondenz* was founded by the Leipzig teacher Hermann Lehm and since 1903 edited by "a union of Leipzig deaf-mutes".[20] *Deutsche Taubstummen-Zeitung* was issued between 1898 and 1914 by a union of deaf associations from Silesia, the Rhineland, and Mecklenburg. Furthermore, there were a number of other more or less short-lived and local papers, which have not been possible to take into consideration here.[21] The German congresses continued to be held at regular intervals but were more and more reduced to sociable events.[22] As a result of the outbreak of the First World War, the congresses had to be cancelled, and the deaf

---

16   Albin Maria Watzulik to Edward Miner Gallaudet, 17 November 1902, Gallaudet University Archives: Presidential Papers of Edward Miner Gallaudet, Box 39a, Folder 04, Letter # 808.

17   Albin Maria Watzulik, obituary of Bernhard Brill, TK 8 (1904), pp. 63-64; Heinrich Buchheim: "Zur Richtigstellung," TK 7 (1905), p. 57; Benno Voigt, "Eine Ehren- und Dankesschuld!" TK 24 (1905), p. 201; "Neue Neujahrsgedanken eines Taubstummenlehrers," TK 2 (1910), pp. 13-14.

18   Albin Maria Watzulik, "Noch Eins ins Album des Herrn Heinrichs," TK 8 (1909), p. 62; "Der Redakteur," TK 19 (1913), pp. 145-146.

19   "An die Leser," NZT 24 (1912), p. 189.

20   "einer Vereinigung Leipziger Taubstummen", "Zum Jahreswechsel," TK 1 (1903), p. 1; *cf.* "Neuere Neujahrsgedanken eines Taubstummenlehrers," TK 1 (1912), p. 2.

21   For instance, there was the *Chronik*, published by the Berlin Swimming club 1905-1909, the sport paper *Deutsches Turnblatt für Taubstumme* between 1911 and 1914, the local papers *Märkischer Taubstummenbote* (1906-1926), *Rheinisch-Westfälische Taubstummenzeitschrift* (1912-1913), and the *Sächsisches Blatt* (1900-1902).

22   *Cf.* above pp. 186ff.

movement as a whole came out of the war and the following revolution transformed in both structure and context.[23] Therefore, the period between the cancellation of TC and the outbreak of the Great War constitutes a distinct phase in the structure of German deaf movement debate, signified by its diversity and multitude of channels.

From Language to Labour:
The Issues in the Deaf Movement Debate

The dominance of well-educated and relatively well-off men in the sources has been emphasised throughout this study. To this general rule, there were occasional exceptions. However, a trait shared by all participants in the debate without exception, was that they were adults. This means that the methods in education immediately affected almost none of those who discussed the issue. Only the few who were teachers of the deaf could claim direct involvement in the conflict. It could be argued that this very core issue for so much of the history of the deaf movement, actually lay outside of their immediate interest. Even if Sign was not used in the classroom, a community of signing deaf adults would still be able to flourish. There seems to be no imperative reason for them to be bothered with how deaf children – who were in most cases not related to the deaf adults – were currently educated at a point in time when they themselves had left school. The objections to this point of view seem obvious to the modern reader; as will be shown, however, this was exactly the way the German deaf community approached the issue during its first decades of public existence.

Discussions on Sign Language appeared at congresses and in the deaf press from the start, and education was always a central issue. However, the two were clearly distinguished from one another. Sign Language in the schools was not discussed at length, but instead its use outside of this setting was in focus. A common demand was its internationalization, so that the communication between deaf people from different nations would be facilitated.[24] On other

---

23   Cf. "Das Ergebnis von Weimar," *Allgemeine Deutsche Gehörlosen-Zeitschrift* 3 (1927), pp. 11-12.

24   This was on the agenda at the first three deaf congresses. "Verhandelt im Saale des evangelischen Vereins," TsF 9-10 (1873), p. 94; "Protokoll," TsF 7-8-9 (1874), p. 58; "Protocoll," 17 (1875), p. 95.

occasions, writers complained about the etiquette of signers and the manner in which certain deaf signed.[25]

The demands posed on education concerned for the most part the outreach of the schools, not the methods used within them. Presenters at the early congresses advocated obligatory schooling, secondary education, pre-schooling, and longer duration of school attendance. The main objective was to extend education to as many deaf people as possible.[26] Thus, the deaf activists positioned themselves more as allies of the educational system, than as critics of the teachers and methods. Occasional disapproval did emerge – but at least in the printed records of the debate, it appears as unspecific or relatively mild.[27] In the initial volumes of the TC, criticism of teachers was also rare. Rather, the authors pleaded for their help to better the situation of the deaf. Education was not debated as a matter of different methods, but as a matter of access. The martyrdom of the deaf was lack of education, not methods nor contents of the education provided.[28]

Apart from education, the structure, outreach, and activities of deaf organizations, and the sociability between deaf people were common topics. The tendency in these issues mirrored that in the debate on education: the main concern was to expand the informal and formal deaf networks to include a larger portion of the deaf population. Furthermore, existing deaf networks strived for unity, for

---

25 Julius Neuschloss, "Der Taubstumme in öffentlichen Localen," TC 8 (1888), pp. 86-87; Albin Maria Watzulik, "Leipzig und die Mimik," TC 9 (1889), pp. 98-99.

26 "Verhandelt im Saale des evangelischen Vereins," TsF 9-10 (1873), pp. 91-92; "Protokoll," TsF 7-8-9 (1874), pp. 55-58; "Protocoll," TsF 17 (1875), pp. 91-94, 96-97; "Der IV. deutsche Taubstummen-Congreß in Leipzig," TsF 12 (1878), p. 44.

27 A Mr. Wolfsram of Stettin mentioned the "flawed method of teaching" ["mangelhafte Unterrichtsmethode"] used in schools at the 1873 congress; at the 1875 congress, Ferdinand Stucken of Minden claimed that many teachers had insufficient competence, especially in Sign Language, and that they used arbitrary methods. He received support from several other participants, but also opposition from Wilhelm Naglo, Berlin, who found the tone of the debate disrespectful against the teachers present. "Verhandelt im Saale des evangelischen Vereins," TsF 9-10 (1873), p. 92; "Protocoll," TsF 17 (1875), pp. 92-93.

28 "Rathschläge zur Fortbildung der Taubstummen," TC 5 (1885), pp. 49-50; August Schenck, "Im Wissen ist Macht!" TC 12 (1886), pp. 135-137; "Etwas aus der Taubstummenwelt. Abhilfe tut Noth," TC 3 (1887), p. 30; Josef Gläsner, "Der Taubstumme ohne Bildung und Erziehung," TC 10 (1887), pp. 111-112; "Neujahr!" TC 1 (1888), p. 1; Wilhelm Gans, "Der bildungslose Taubstumme," TC 1 (1889) pp. 5-6.

instance to standardise Sign Language, as mentioned above. The idea of unifying all deaf people can be found already in the 1848 Berlin TsV statutes, and in Eduard Fürstenberg's attempts to form a 'central' organization. At the congresses he co-arranged, unification was one of the main themes. For instance, the issuance of one periodical for all deaf clubs was repeatedly proposed. Another common demand was the offering of a certain activity or facility, such as a mutual savings bank or religious services, in *all* deaf clubs. Achieving unity through regulation and official decisions gradually lost the dominance and unanimous acceptance it enjoyed at the first congress, but the idea of extending and consolidating deaf networks still persisted in the TC debate.[29]

Altogether, the early congresses and the deaf press gave no reason for concern about any challenge to the people and structures in power. Congress presenters and Silent press writers used a number of different means to assert their gratefulness towards and loyalty with authority figures. At the 1875 Dresden congress, where the first cautious criticism against educators surfaced, another speaker demanded that the teachers of the deaf receive better pay.[30] The TC repeatedly expressed confidence in the educators.[31] Celebration of more distant authorities was integrated as parts of celebrating and manifesting the own community and organizations: addresses and narratives that displayed deaf people and deaf organizations as devoted to the monarch were regularly featured in the press.[32] The historical figure of Samuel Heinicke could also be evoked to lend

---

29 "Verhandelt im Saale des evangelischen Vereins," TsF 9-10 (1873), pp. 90-95; "Protokoll," TsF 7-8-9 (1874), pp. 55, 57-58; "Der 6. internationale Taubstummen-Congreß am 1. bis 3. Juli 1884 zu Stockholm," TsF 2 (1885), pp. 6-7; "Programm und Pränumerations-Einladung," TC 1 (1885), p. 2; "Winke und Rathschläge für Taubstummen-Vereine," TC 6 (1886), p. 61; "Seid einig ein Volk von Brüdern!" TC 11 (1888), pp. 121-122, *cf.* also above p. 178.

30 The speaker, Moritz Hötzold, was himself both deaf and a teacher by profession, thus he spoke in his own interest. However, his suggestion received no opposition and was accepted as a resolution. "Protocoll," TsF 17 (1875), p. 95.

31 Editor's footnote to "Rathschläge zur Fortbildung der Taubstummen," TC 5 (1885), p. 49; "Neujahr!" TC 1 (1888), p. 1; "Etwas aus der Taubstummenwelt. Abhilfe tut Noth," TC 3 (1887) p. 30.

32 "Friedrich Wilhelm II. und Elisabeth," TsF 12 (1873), pp. 126-127; Address to the Emperor and Empress, TsF 11 (1879), p. 41; "Kaiser Friedrich und die Taubstummen," TC 7 (1888), pp. 73-74.

splendour and gravity to the deaf community.[33] In case there was still any doubt as to whether the deaf elites intended to take issue with the educational system, a few articles in the TC explicitly rejected such tendencies. In an editorial from 1886, the paper expressed satisfaction with the triumph of the German method and called for its readers to use their oral skills. That being said, the article went on to justify the use of Sign in the communication between deaf people, thus drawing a clear line between school practice and sociability between adults.[34] "To each their own!"[35] exclaimed a further editorial in 1888, declaring full acceptance of the Milan decisions.[36] As in the previous example, the consent to oral education was paired with a pledge to signing as the mode of communication between adult deaf. In connection to the 1889 international deaf congress in Paris, the TC distanced itself from any discussion on pedagogic issues, by calling it 'meddling in the affairs of the teachers'.[37]

These remarks were made at the end of the era of which they are so telling. They convey the essence of the period up until 1889, which was characterized by the almost complete absence of a methods debate in the deaf elite. Which language modes were used in the classroom was left to the teachers to decide. Outside of the schools, members of deaf communities apparently perceived of themselves as uninhibited by educational methods, and instead focused on extending and refining their sociable and formal networks.

When the methods debate took off in the German deaf community, the initiative came from outside. In 1889, Johann Heidsiek, a hearing teacher at the

---

33   For instance, his name was used for a foundation to the benefit of poor deaf in need of education. "Protocoll," TsF 17 (1875), p. 95; Also, he was remembered at the 100th anniversary of his death: "100jähriger Todestag des Samuel Heinicke," TC 4 (1890), p. 47.

34   "Surdophone," TC 4 (1886), pp. 37-38.

35   "Jedem das seine!", "Ist die Geberdensprache im geselligen Umgange der Taubstummen unter sich nothwendig?" TC 10 (1888), p. 110.

36   In 1880, a congress of teachers of the deaf in Milan, Italy, voted for pure oralism as the superior method in deaf education. This decision had a great symbolic significance to both sides in the methods debate, and is often referred to as the direst turning point in the history of the deaf. cf. Lane *When the Mind Hears,* pp. 376-414; Rée. *I See a Voice,* pp. 227-231; Van Cleve and Crouch, *A Place of Their Own,* pp. 108-111; others, however, argue that the significance of Milan has been overstated: cf. Branson and Miller, *Damned for their Difference,* p. 154.

37   "Stimmen über den nächsten internationalen Taubstummencongress," TC 6 (1888), p. 65; "Der Taubstummencongress in Paris," TC 8 (1889), p. 85.

Deaf Asylum in Breslau, published a book titled *Der Taubstumme und seine Sprache. Erneute Untersuchungen über das methodologische Fundamentalprinzip der Taubstummenbildung*, "The Deaf-Mute and His Language. New Studies on the Fundamental Methodological Principle of the Education of Deaf-Mutes."[38] In it, Heidsiek accused his colleagues of ignoring the basic prerequisite of their service: that deaf people cannot hear. He claimed that the oral method set unrealistic goals, which resulted in abusive practices. Instead of oralism, which, according to Heidsiek, was an obvious failure, he envisioned a school for the deaf based on their sensory disposition. If the pupils were allowed to fully use their vision, including communication in Sign, more of them would be able to get a good command of German, which would allow them to live independent lives, he argued.

These were indeed unusual views in Germany at this point. However, the book initially received only modest attention in the Silent press. The TC published a positive review, welcoming Heidsiek as a breath of fresh air after a long period of dogmatism.[39] In the teachers' periodicals on the other hand, Heidsiek received negative response.[40] In the following decades, he continued to be an active writer both in the teachers' magazines, the deaf press, and of independent books and pamphlets.[41]

Although the reactions to his work were relatively cautious at first, Heidsiek's entrance into the public debate proved to be a turning point for the rhetoric of the deaf elites. An editorial in the TC looked back at 1889 as a year defined by three events: the Paris deaf congress, a German congress of teachers of the deaf, and the issuing of *Der Taubstumme und seine Sprache*. The two congresses had made it clear that there was a divide between those who advocate Sign and those who defend articulation:

"Then came in the nick of time J. Heidsiek's word of deliverance. He appears to have eavesdropped on the most concealed traits in the lives and feelings of the deaf-mute and also to have found the key to his soul [...]. We intend to move into real life and scurry back to the golden years of youth on the wings of reminiscence. It has been a long time since we were introduced to the glorious secrets of articulation, but still we vividly think

---

38   Breslau: Max Woywood, 1889.
39   "Literatur," TC 10 (1889), pp. 116-117.
40   K. E. Sch., Review of *Der Taubstumme und seine Sprache*, Organ Vol. 35. No. 9 (1889), pp. 280-286; G. Sch.: Review of *Der Taubstumme und seine Sprache*, *Blätter* Vol. 2. No. 17 (1889), pp. 268-272.
41   For an overview of Heidsiek's *oeuvre*, v. Muhs, *Johann Heidsiek*.

of the effort the process of articulation cost us and our brave teachers. [...] In Sign, the deaf-mute is like a king, for he has all signs at his service; in spoken language on the other hand, he is like a slave, who cannot move freely."[42]

This article thus suggests that opposition to oralism had been present among the deaf all the time, but that the expressions had been suppressed as an act of self-censorship. Judging by the following debate, this seems plausible. Quite suddenly, what Brenda Jo Brueggemann has called a 'rhetoric reversal', occurred in the TC.[43] The writers now took pride in Sign Language, and directed harsh criticism at those they had earlier mentioned with devotion: the teachers. A completely new, critical, and even fierce tone appeared in the texts about education. Whereas only months earlier, the TC editor had declared that deaf people should not meddle with the teachers' business, in the 1889 December issue he quoted Albin Maria Watzulik saying that he "shook [his] head in disbelief"[44] at the teachers' congress. Instead of reassuring the teachers that the methods in education was their domain, the TC now claimed that deaf people knew best about their own needs.[45] Hand in hand with the new rhetoric, the methods debate in the TC rapidly gained intensity during the early 1890s. A new, positive understanding of deafness became manifest. Some articles praised the sense of sight and the visual experience of the world. Expressions of what might be labelled deaf culture were celebrated, instead of being disciplined. Intelligence was disconnected from skills in German, and could just as well be paired with

---

42 "Inzwischen kam zur rechten Zeit das erlösende Wort des J. Heidsiek. Derselbe scheint dem Leben und Fühlen des Taubstummen die verborgensten Züge abgelauscht und gleichsam den Schlüssel zu seiner Seele gefunden zu haben [...]. Wir wollen ins volle Leben hineingreifen und auf den Flügeln der Erinnerung zur goldenen Jugendzeit zurückeilen. Es ist schon lange her, seitdem wir in die segensreichen Geheimnisse der Lautarticulation eingeweiht wurden, doch lebhaft denken wir daran, welche Mühe der Articulationsprocess uns und unseren braven Lehrern kostete. [...] In der Geberde ist der Taubstumme wie ein König, denn er macht sich alle Zeichen dienstbar; in der Lautsprache aber ist er wie ein Sklave, der sich nicht frei bewegen kann." "Noch ein Wort über die Geberdensprache." TC 11 (1889) pp. 121-122

43 Brueggemann, *Lend Me Your Ear*, p. 182

44 "schüttelte ich ungläubig den Kopf", "Der II. Taubstummenlehrer-Congress in Köln," TC 12 (1889), p. 134.

45 "Ein sonderbares Veto," TC 2 (1891), pp. 13-14; Albin Maria Watzulik, "Die Vereine und die Presse der gebildeten Taubstummen," TC 3 (1891), pp. 26-27.

Sign Language.[46] The suddenness of this transformation suggests that these sentiments were actually present before Heidsiek, but that they entered print media only after he had initiated the debate.

Negative views were instead attached to hearing people and spoken language. Earlier, signing and groups of deaf people in public had been considered inappropriate. Now, the staring and comments of hearing spectators were described as expressions of their ignorance and lack of cultivation.[47] Watzulik modified complaints he had earlier made about ugly Saxon signing: the disagreeable habits of some signers were, he explained, caused by the oralist schools.[48] One of the American contributors to Watzulik's series of letters against oralism, Oscar H. Regensburg, discredited the usefulness of lipreading: "Lipreading is, like playing the piano, a mere skill. Although it may be a means to further the deaf-mute socially, it is nevertheless not alone suitable to further him intellectually, just like the plunking of a hearing lady cannot remedy an insufficient literary cultivation."[49] This quote lets lipreading appear superficial and feminine, making the great significance awarded to it by oralists ridiculous – not least through a footnote where Watzulik stated that Regensburg was indeed a very proficient lipreader. Apparently, this skill was so trivial that he had no reason to pride himself with it. By shrugging their shoulders at an art so central to the reputation of oralists, the writers undermined the authority of the teachers.

Whereas the tone towards teachers previously had been devout, deaf writers now took the liberty of ridiculing them. The former authorities were scrutinized in detail, and not only their conduct, but also their physical appearance were matters of debate: The long beards sported by, among others, Eduard Walther

---

46 "Charakter und Charakterbildung des Taubstummen," TC 6 (1891), pp. 61-63; "Das Reisen der Taubstummen," TC (1891), pp. 77-78; "Bilder und Geschichten aus der Taubstummenwelt," TC 10 (1891), pp. 112-113; "In eigener Sache," TC 5 (1893), p. 49.

47 "Wodurch können die gegen die Taubstummen bestehenden Vorurtheile bekämpft werden?" TC 12 (1893), pp. 133-134.

48 Albin Maria Watzulik, "Zur Aufklärung," TC 4 (1890), pp. 39-40; *cf.* idem, "Leipzig und die Mimik," TC 9 (1889), pp. 98-99.

49 "Lippenablesung ist wie Clavierspiel nur eine Fertigkeit. Während sie ein Mittel sein mag, den Taubstummen gesellschaftlich zu fördern, ist sie doch nicht ausschliesslich geeignet, ihn geistig zu fördern, ebensowenig wie bei einer hörenden Dame das Geklimper eine mangelhafte literarische Bildung ersetzen kann." Oscar H. Regensburg, quoted by Albin Maria Watzulik in "Der Methodenstreit," TC 6 (1895), p. 66; *cf.* above p. 196.

must undeniably have been an obstacle to their teaching.[50] Nevertheless, the act of publicly reviewing the grooming of well-respected civil servants – sometimes even in their presence – must be considered quite bold.

Ridicule and outspoken conflicts with the teachers did not, however, originate in the deaf press. Heidsiek's work had been a powerful trigger, but just as important were repeated attacks on 'the adult deaf' by oralist teacher Eduard Walther in Berlin during 1891. When commenting on a recently issued deaf paper in the teachers' periodical *Blätter für Taubstummenbildung,* he made the following statement, which seems to address the entire Silent press:

"Oh, the writing deaf-mutes! As much as we are inclined to feel joy about some of our former students being brought so far that they are able to clearly and comprehensively express their thoughts, we also know that those who consider themselves to have reached a somewhat higher level of cultivation than their comrades-in-fate are unpleasantly presumptuous and act with the pretensions of great men."[51]

Walther went on claiming that the deaf simply cannot understand the value of speech, and therefore should not interfere in educational matters. The reaction in the TC was outraged. An editorial commented that Walther, although he had devoted his professional life to de-mute the deaf, now obviously wanted to silence them.[52]

Later that year, Walther used the same patronizing tone when referring to an article in the TC. In the article, where August Schenck described his first encounter with Johann Heidsiek, a quite unusual scene was portrayed. The

---

50   C. Rumpf, quoted by Albin Maria Watzulik in "Der Methodenstreit," TC 8 (1896), p. 83; "Der fünfte Deutsche Taubstummenkongreß in Berlin," TC 9 (1902), p. 100, *cf.* photographs in Paul Pettke, "25 Jahre Taubstummen-Anstaltsdirektor," TK 12 (1904), p. 102, and "Herrn Direktor Vatter zu seinem 50jährigen Lehrerjubiläum gewidmet," TK 23 (1911), p. 181.

51   "Ach- die schriftstellernden Taubstummen! So viel Ursache wir auch haben mögen, uns darüber zu freuen, dass einzelne unserer ehemaligen Schüler so weit gefördert sind, dass sie ihre Gedanken klar und fliessend auszudrücken vermögen, so wissen wir doch auch, dass diejenigen, welche meinen, in etwas über die Bildungsniveau ihrer Schicksalsgenossen hinauszuragen, sich in unangenehmer Weise überheben und mit den Prätensionen grosser Männer auftreten." Eduard Walther: "Rückblick." in: *Blätter* Vol. 4. No. 1. (1891), p. 7. The paper in question was the *Taubstummen-Welt-Blatt,* "Deaf-Mute's World Paper", a title Walther found presumtuous.

52   "Ein sonderbares Veto." TC 2 (1891) p. 14.

meeting had taken place without previous announcement in the offices of the CVWT. Schenck described how a stranger entered the room and introduced himself with his name-sign. Although Heidsiek proved to him that he could both speak and hear, Schenck only realized he was Hearing[53] when he scrabbled his name on a piece of paper so that he understood whom the stranger was. For the rest of Heidsiek's brief stay in Berlin, Schenck accompanied him and engaged with him in discussions on Sign Language and speech. The encounter, as it was described in the TC, was one of equals.[54] It seems as if Schenck could not believe that Heidsiek was Hearing, much less a well-known educator and writer, because of the way he had entered the 'deaf world' of the CVWT office. Apparently, this was provocative to Walther, who reacted with a contemptuous comment in the *Blätter*, calling the article "touching".[55] He explained that Schenck, thanks to the Berlin Asylum, was a very good speaker, but unfortunately had weak eyesight and therefore may be excused for preferring Sign. Thus Walther reduced Schenck to a former pupil at his institution, and took the liberty of publicly discussing his physical features. As had been the case after the previous attack from Walther, the TC reacted in a more aggressive tone than before. Schenck was infuriated, and replied by calling Walther a "biased speech fanatic",[56] among several other accusations. Together with Heidsiek, then, Walther played a not insignificant part in radicalising the debate. Julius Neuschloss, another semi-frequent contributor to the TC, reflected on this in 1892: "maybe we should thank [Walther] for revealing the true state of things to us, and thus spurring us to eradicate the prejudice!"[57] As is implied in this quote, the loyalty towards the educators previously displayed by deaf elites had been a one-way street. Walther's remarks had made it clear to the deaf writers that their

---

53 As a parallel to the term Deaf, Hearing means belonging to hearing culture rather than being able to hear. It seems appropriate to use this term here, since Schenck at first did not consider Heidsiek as a 'Hearing person' although he obviously could hear.

54 August Schenck, "Nachrichten aus Berlin," TC 8 (1891), pp. 89-90.

55 "in so rührender Weise geschilderte" Eduard Walther, "Agitation erwachsener Taubstummer gegen die deutsche Methode," *Blätter* Vol. 4. No. 17 (1891), p. 268.

56 "parteiischer Lautsprachfanatiker," August Schenck, "Nachwehen des Berliner Kirchenfestes – Kritik der 'Blätter für Taubstummenbildung' über dasselbe – Abwehr und Berichtigung," TC 10 (1891), pp. 110-112, quote from p. 110.

57 "vielleicht haben wir's ihm noch zu danken, dass er uns einen Einblick in die wahre Sachlage verschaffte und uns dadurch aneiferte die Vorurtheile auszumerzen!" Julius Neuschloss, letter to the editor, TC 2 (1892), p. 15.

assertions of allegiance to the teachers had been useless – the deaf received no regard in return.

The result was a new positioning vis-à-vis the teachers. A renewed series of congresses was begun in 1892. Debates and commentaries on these congresses drew a clear line between the teachers and the deaf. They now appeared not as allies, nor as givers and recipients of aid, but as opponents.[58] Although some regretted it, there was obviously a sense among the deaf congress participants that the relationship to the educators had drastically changed over the last few years.[59] Also, the positioning of deaf elites and teachers as opponents was at the same time an indication of their equal status. In a commentary on the 1902 congress, Walther Syrutschöck suggested that an independent investigation should resolve the issue. Both sides – teachers and deaf – would have to accept the results of such a survey, he argued, conceptualizing the teachers and the deaf adults as equal parties in the conflict.[60] This polarization even went as far as to court processes, when the Leipzig mechanic Heinrich Buchheim had to answer to allegations of defamation against Eduard Walther. Provoked by Walther's demeaning statements, Buchheim had in a TC article accused him of seing his profession as 'a milking cow'. The sentence, a minor fine, was less important than the proceedings as a public event, which was followed by many deaf, but also by the mainstream media. An article in the local paper *Leipziger Gerichtszeitung*, quoted in the TC, clearly took Buchheims side in the matter. In a comment, Buchheim himself thanked the school board for filing charges, since this had made public opinion turn in favour of the deaf.[61]

Loyalty and gratitude had been signs of subordination, as had the reluctance to at all having an opinion about deaf education. During the 1890s, this sense of inferiority gave way to an atmosphere where deaf people felt entitled to discuss

---

58 Carl Bente, "Der Taubstummen-Kongreß zu Hannover am 5., 6. und 7. Juni 1892," TsF 27 (1892), pp. 109-111, TsF 29 (1892), pp. 117-119, TsF 30 (1892), pp. 124-125; "Aufruf zum III. deutschen Taubstummen-Kongreß in Nürnberg," TsF 7 (1896), p. 37; J. Heinrich, Letter to the editor, TsF 23 (1902), pp. 121-122.

59 *Cf.* Protokoll der Verhandlungen des Dritten Deutschen Taubstummen-Kongresses in Nürnberg am 24. und 25. Mai 1896 [appendix to the TsF 1896], p. 7; cf. also Albin Maria Watzulik, "Der Methodenstreit," TC 5 (1896), p. 55.

60 Walter Syrutschöck, "Einige Worte an den Taubstummenkongreß Berlin 1902," TC 7 (1902), p. 75.

61 "Process Walther-Buchheim," TC 10 (1893), pp. 112-113; Johann Heidsiek, too, was fined for defamation due to statements in his books. "Der Process Heidsiek," TC 12 (1892), pp. 141-144.

education, and to be listened to. In this new climate there was also room for conflicting views. Not all deaf authors embraced the manual or combined methods. Eugen Sutermeister, a deaf lay preacher and poet from Switzerland, was the most vehement deaf advocate of oralism. He went further than many oralist educators, rejecting Sign Language altogether except for use with children and the feeble-minded, and openly supported a ban on signs in the schools.[62] However, those who used articles and congresses to defend the oral method were also part of something new. Before the methods debate had started in the TC, no deaf people made the effort to promote oral education through print media or at congresses. The deaf pro-oralist views emerged as reactions to the defence of Sign Language and the criticism of deaf education. Sutermeister mostly published his contributions in the teachers' press instead of the TC, and gave his lengthy lecture at the IV. German deaf congress in spoken language. He thus partly distanced himself from the deaf community by not using their channels, and by using a mode of communication that hindered most congress participants from understanding his presentation. On the other hand, his polemics were directed at the deaf advocates of Sign, and he reacted to their replies although he did not, like some other pro-oralists, contribute directly to the TC in this debate.[63] He and other deaf pro-oralists were the other side of a coin, which had only recently been tossed.

Around the turn of the 19th century, the methods debate in the deaf press and at congresses gradually lost its intensity. The discontinuation of the TC meant the loss of the main media for anti-oralist campaigning by deaf people. The publications that replaced it tended to be somewhat less focused on the methods. Even though language and education remained among the central issues, the tone was generally less confrontational than in the TC, and the contributions on the topic more irregular. There may also have been a sense of the debate having

---

62 "Aus der Schule gechwatzt," TC 7 (1895), pp. 73-74; "Ein taubstummer Dichter über die Taubstummen," TC 10 (1897), pp. 105-109; Eugen Sutermeister, "Hie Lautsprache, hie Gebärden!" TC 1 (1898), pp. 2-4; *Protokoll der Verhandlungen des Vierten Deutschen Taubstummen-Kongresses zu Stuttgart (21. und 22. Mai 1899)* [appendix to the TC 1899], pp. 7-13.

63 *Cf.* Josef Obhlidal, letter to the editor, TC 5 (1892), pp. 52-54; E.H. Martens, "Kritik des Streites um die Laut- und Geberdensprache," TC 7 (1892), pp. 81-83, TC 8 (1892) pp. 93-94; W. Schill, "Eine Stimme für die reinorale Methode," TC 6 (1896), pp. 66-68; Eugen Sutermeister, "Wider die Gebärdensprache," *Blätter* Vol. 10. No. 12. (1897), pp. 183-187; idem, "Hie Lautsprache – hie Gebärden!" *Blätter* Vol. 10. No. 22. (1897), pp. 349-351.

reached a dead end. Deaf organizations, congresses and individuals had put great effort into a campaign for Sign Language in the schools, but their petition had been turned down, the court had ruled against them, and there is not much evidence that they had influenced the teachers in any significant way.[64] Thus, the attention turned towards other issues.

As the congresses acquired the function of organizing and centralizing the deaf movement, more and more time was devoted to discussing administrative issues. Centralised mass-organizations of the type attempted at the second-wave deaf congresses may be better suited to pursue concrete demands such as better pay and working conditions, than to ponder on visual versus audial languages. Also, as we have seen, the plenary debates shrunk to give way to social events, which might also have favoured simpler issues over the more philosophical ones. Finally, the surge of the social democrats after the abolishment of the anti-socialist laws may have played its part in bringing labour issues, rather than education, to the front of the deaf movement agenda as we shall see.

In the decade before the outbreak of the Great War, the main concern of the deaf elite was the social position of deaf people. This means that attention once again turned mainly towards deaf adults, rather than children. In other words, the writers and congress petitioners discussed issues directly affecting themselves, instead of acting as advocates for others who shared their sensory disposition.

At this point, the position the deaf elite had settled on, for themselves and for the deaf as a group, was that of the upper working class. There were occasional glances at the United States and the National College of Deaf-Mutes, which suggested a wish to elevate oneself above manual labour, but the realization of such wishes was distant.[65] More frequently, writers and petitioners were concerned with maintaining and extending a deaf labour aristocracy. At the core of this aspiration was the printer's trade. Printing has been a typical 'deaf vocation'

---

64 "Der Process Heidsiek," "Ein abschlägiger Bescheid," TC 12 (1892), pp. 141-144, 147-148; "Process Walther-Buchheim," TC 10 (1893), pp. 112-113. However, Albin Maria Watzulik claimed in 1910 that the debate had ended with the victory of the deaf, and that the teachers now proposed Sign: "Wieder eine Lanze für die Gebärden- und Fingersprache," TK 9 (1910), p. 70; I have been unable to find anything supporting this argument; deaf education in Germany remained explicitly oralist, although it accepted the use of pantomime and gestures. Cf. Schumann (ed.), Handbuch, pp. 139-172; 198-393, esp. pp. 231-235; cf. also below p. 252.

65 Protokoll des VI. Allgemeinen Deutschen Taubstummen-Kongresses zu Leipzig im Saale des Krystallpalastes. Pfingsten 1905 [Print, Leipzig, 1905], pp. 20-21; Thekla Faust, "Ein Wort zum Internationalen Taubst.-Kongress," TK 13 (1904), p. 113.

across the Western world since the 19th century, and deaf printers could often be found in central functions in the deaf organizations as well as in the debate on ideas.[66] This was the case in Germany as well: Albin Maria Watzulik, John Pacher, and G. A. Claudius were all printers, only to mention some of the most prominent examples.[67] As the print shops became increasingly mechanized, Watzulik raised alarm about the future of the trade. The linotype machines, he believed, would put many printers out of work, and this would strike deaf printers particularly hard.[68] He, and most of the other writers on the subject, therefore warned deaf youth of choosing the trade, especially if they had a less than perfect command of German.[69] Mingling with concerns caused by mechanization, the advice also reinforced the image of printing as a high-status trade. A suggestion that deaf women would be able to pursue the vocation threatened this image, and was categorically rejected by Watzulik. In the same article, he argued that a printer needed not only good skills in German, but also some familiarity with Hebrew, Arabic, and other foreign languages. Thus, it appeared almost as a learned profession.[70]

In 1913, the gravity of the issue was further enhanced by a decision by the printers' union not to admit deaf members. This ruling was made considering a perceived risk of injury involved with deaf printers operating machines. Reactions in the deaf press were upset and worried that other unions might

---

66 *Cf.* for France: Quartararo, *Deaf Identity and Social Images*, pp. 145, 158-159; for the United States, Van Cleve and Crouch, *A Place of their Own*, pp. 164-168.

67 Kurt Laschinsky, "Albin Maria Watzulik," *Deutsche Gehörlosen-Zeitschrift Die Stimme*, 5 (1930), [n.p.]; Ernsberger, "Das 25jährige Geschäftsjubiläum des Herrn Comissionsrath John Pacher," TC 3 (1890), pp. 25-29; J. Ernsberger jr., obituary of G. A. Claudius, NZT 2 (1912), p. 9.

68 The first warning appeared in an 1886 TC editorial, "Besser bewahrt als beklagt!" TC 3 (1886), pp. 25-26. Albin Maria Watzulik then brought up the issue in "Ein Capitel zum Buchdruckerelend," TC 3 (1888), pp. 26-27; and repeatedly in the 1890s and early 1900s, e. g.: "Etwas zum Buchdruckerberuf," TC 5 (1895) p. 53; "Noch ein Nothschrei!" TC 10 (1898), pp. 107-108; "Noch einmal der Buchdruckerberuf," TC 12 (1901); *cf.* Gannon, *Deaf Heritage*, p. 83.

69 W. Hollaender, "Das Buchdruckergewerbe," TC 10 (1895), pp. 113-114; Gustav Hoffer, "Ueber die Berufswahl der Taubstummen," TC 7 (1898), pp. 65-66; Ernst Barth, "Vom Buchdruckerberuf," TK 9 (1903), pp. 57-58, TK 10 (1903), pp. 65-66, TK 11 (1903), pp. 70-71.

70 Albin Maria Watzulik, "Über die Verwendung taubstummer Mädchen als Schriftsetzerinnen," TK 5 (1906), pp. 38-39.

follow the example. To make matters worse, it was not just any deaf people who were deemed unfit, but those who were seen as the elite of the deaf community. Nevertheless, their protests remained unsuccessful.[71]

Although the contradiction between deafness and working a linotype machine turned out to be fictitious,[72] to the turn-of-the-19th-century deaf community printing appeared as a trade on its way out. A replacement was sought in dentistry, more specifically, in the speciality of the dental technician. This suggestion was brought forth by the dentist association as a solution to their problem of keeping dental technicians as employees. According to the dentists, dental technicians were hard to keep since they often preferred to open their own practices, where they offered patients a low-budget alternative to treatment by actual dentists. Deaf dental technicians, the dentists presumed, would due to the communicative barrier be unable to make this leap. Thus, they would stay as employees in the dentists' practices. Presented as a craft closely associated with both science and art, dental technology appeared to be a potential new vocation for a deaf labour aristocracy, at a time when the deaf community desperately needed one. Teaching, the traditional high-status deaf profession, had been lost a generation ago, and printing, the literary craft, appeared to be losing ground. Dental technicians, both deaf and hearing, however rejected this idea and claimed that their trade was an unprofitable one – possibly to avoid competition. The most enthusiastic proponent was Christian Schweiker, who offered training for aspiring deaf dental technicians for a relatively high price.[73]

When the discussion turned from education to the situation on the labour market, it entered politically more controversial ground. A suggestion such as the one from the dentists' association confronted the debaters with the conflict between labour and capital. "The exquisite plan", wrote the TK ironically, "to exploit the infirmity of deaf-mutism to create a helotage in the vocation of the

---

71 Ludwig Neubauer, "Aufgepaßt, gehörlose Buchdrucker!" ATZ 8 (1913), p. 65; Carl Bohlmann, "Nochmals die taubstummen Buchdrucker!" ATZ 10 (1913), pp. 80-81; L[udwig] N[eubauer], "Taubstumme Buchdrucker," ATZ 15 (1913), pp. 120-121, v. also "Ein Notschrei der taubstummen Kollegen," TK 8 (1913), pp. 57-58.

72 In America, the number of deaf printers actually increased as a result of the mechanization of printing. Gannon, *Deaf Heritage*, p. 83.

73 "Taubstumme als Zahnarztgehilfen," ATZ 13 (1913), p. 105; "Die 'Befreiung' der Zahntechniker," TK 11 (1913), pp. 82-83; Christian Schweiker, "Zur Berufsfrage der Taubstummen," TK 5 (1911), p. 38; Paul Kroner and Ernst Löwenstein, "Entgegnung," TK 6 (1911), p. 46; Loorber, "Zur Berufsfrage der Gehörlosen," and Christian Schweiker, "Erwiderung," TK 7 (1911), pp. 55-56.

dental technician, no philanthropist can accept, much less support."[74] Debate on unemployment, mechanization, and wages inevitably brought deaf leaders to positions where they must take a stand for or against unions, and ultimately, social democracy. Since the anti-socialist laws were lifted, it had become possible for deaf clubs and individuals to openly express social democratic ideas. As the power of the labour movement grew, it may have appeared less risky, or even tactically wise, to direct one's loyalty to the SPD rather than to traditional authorities such as the church or monarchy. Leading in this tendency was the TK. Although its editors were cautious not to openly affiliate with any party, it frequently featured articles expressing social democratic ideas, and refrained from the typical celebrations of the Emperor.[75] It by no means excluded opinions negative to the SPD and the unions, but the fact that it so generously published social democrats contrasts with the more conservative ATZ. The latter only published contributions that were negative to social democracy or political involvement in general, when it at all paid attention to the issue.[76]

The DTZ also took a negative attitude against social democracy, repeatedly warning its readers of the SPD, whom they blamed for exploiting the deaf in their quest for more voters.[77] Especially the founding of a deaf section of the

---

74 "Den raffinierten Plan, das Gebrechen der Taubstummheit zur Organization einer Helotenschar im Zahntechniker-Beruf zu mißbrauchen, kann kein Menschenfreund billigen oder gar unterstützen." "Taubstumme als Zahnarztgehilfen"; "Die 'Befreiung' der Zahntechniker," TK 11 (1913), pp. 82-83.

75 Cf. Alfred Scholz, "Lebenskampf! Ein soziales Bild," TK 17 (1912), p. 133-134; Karl Puich, "Religion, Politik und Taubstummen-Kongresse," TK 18 (1913), p. 138 (v. also the editorial footnotes). Also, the TK repeatedly quoted or reprinted entire articles from the SPD organ Vorwärts and Die Arbeit: Dr. Wassielieff, "An die sogenannten 'Arbeitswilligen!'" TK 13 (1907), pp. 105-106; "Eine politische Versammlung Taubstummer Groß-Berlins," TK 13 (1911), p. 101; "Sozialdemokratischer Terrorismus gegen Taubstumme," TK 1 (1914), pp. 1-2; The lack of attention paid to the Emperor provoked some criticism: "Rückblick," TK 2 (1914), pp. 10-11.

76 Cf. Ludwig Neubauer: "Keine Politik in den Taubstummen-Vereinen." ATZ 12 (1913), p. 97; H. Zech: "Keine Politik in den Taubstummen-Vereinen." ATZ 14 (1913), p. 114; "Berlin. (Sozialdemokratischer Terrorismus gegen Taubstumme.)" ATZ 23 (1913), p. 189.

77 Editorial comment to "Zur Frage der politischen Taubstummenvereine," DTZ 50 (1911), [n.p.].

SPD in Berlin in 1911 caused outrage.[78] Gustav Schmeller pointed out that the teachers, the state, and the church had done much for the deaf, and that the SPD was the enemy of these institutions. The deaf should, he insisted, be loyal to their benefactors.[79] However, the editors did allow the social democrats to respond to the criticism, by reprinting their reactions from the SPD paper *Vorwärts*.[80]

The question of union- and party affiliation was not only a political one, but also part of a re-identification of the deaf collective. Concepts of class solidarity and class divisions offered a sense of belonging, going along with the social democratic ideas. At this point, we see how the identification of deaf people as *Bildungsbürger* of the type that Otto Kruse or Eduard Fürstenberg represented was becoming obsolete. Educated deaf people were no longer a rarity or a marvel, but a demographic subgroup, for the most part socio-economically belonging to the working classes. It was within that framework that a new kind of respectability could be claimed. Articles in the deaf press encouraged the readers to strive for manual skills, to be diligent and provident, and to take pride in mutual support rather than accepting handouts.[81] Readers were informed about the tax-deductibility of union fees – a fact that would be of interest to the economical organized worker.[82] This new positioning not only coincided with labour movement ideals, but could also be aided and enhanced by SPD affiliation. Part of being the respectable skilled workers that many now argued that the deaf ought to be, was to be unionized. Furthermore, by claiming to belong to the working class and offering their solidarity with hearing workers in labour conflicts, deaf people could obtain the organized social democrats as their allies.

---

78 Barthold, "Warnung!"; "Der Kongreß der Ärmsten" [from Leipziger Neue Nachrichten], both in DTZ 46 (1911), [n.p.]; "Sozialdemokratische Gewerkschaften," DTZ 66 (1911), [n.p.]; *cf.* also Ylva Söderfeldt, "Taubstumme Genossen. Vor 100 Jahren wurde eine spezielle Sektion der SPD gegründet," *junge Welt*, supplement *Behindertenpolitik*, 24. August 2011, p. 6.

79 Gustav Schmeller, "Taubstumme und Sozialdemokratie," DTZ 53 (1911), [n.p.].

80 "Sozialdemokratische Taubstummenvereine" [from *Vorwärts*], DTZ 53 (1911), [n.p.]; "Als Heiland der Taubstummen" [from *Vorwärts*], DTZ 54 (1911), [n.p.].

81 "Die Lehrlingsfrage," TK 20 (1906), pp. 160-161; Curt Laschinsky, "Der Taubstumme im wirtschaftlichen Kampfe. Ein Mahnwort an den Schicksalsgenossen," TK 2 (1911), p. 13; Hermann Lehm, "Der arbeitslose Taubstumme," TK 4 (1911), pp. 29-30.

82 "Gewerkschaftsbeiträge sind bei der Steuer-Erklärung abzugsfähig," TK 19 (1912), pp. 151-152; *cf.* "Ein Mahnwort in Sachen der Invalidenversicherung," DTZ 20 (1906), [n.p.], on social insurance rules.

In return, they reassured their hearing colleagues that they would not compete with them by underbidding.[83] On the other hand, being a social democrat meant being in opposition to the establishment, i.e. the state and the church, which maintained such a firm grip of many deaf people's lives. Not only gratitude towards and identification with the institutions that had provided them with education, but also a real sense of dependence in their every-day lives, gave many deaf people good reason to instead oppose social democracy. Resulting from this, new divisions appeared in the debate.[84] The teacher-deaf cleavage lost some of its significance to social democrats and their opponents.

The second issue where the social position of the deaf was defended was that of the *Lumpenproletariat*, foremost in the shape of the deaf peddler. Peddling as a 'deaf occupation' may be considered the antithesis of printing. It doubtlessly played an important part in sustaining the livelihoods of many deaf people in the 19th century as well as it does today, but it remains controversial within the deaf community.[85] Deaf peddlers convey to the general public the image of deafness as a misfortune, and of deaf people as indigent. The difference between peddling and begging is not always clear, as deaf peddlers may plead to the sympathy of their customers to make sales. Such behaviour, and perhaps also the nomadic lifestyle associated with peddling, certainly conflicts with an image of the deaf as well-established, educated *Bürger*, or respectable workers. This contrast appeared at its perhaps most drastic at the 1896 congress, when a Mr. Stünkel complained that deaf peddlers "do not even leave one be with the family in the evening."[86] Stünkel thus positioned himself in a stereotypical image of

---

83 C[urt Laschinsk]y, "Werde ich Gewerkschaftsmitglied oder nicht?" TK 4 (1913), p. 25; Gustav Adolf Teuber, "Taubstumme und freie Gewerkschaften," TK 4 (1913), pp. 35-36; "Berlin. Die Taubstummen und die freien Gewerkschaften," TK 2 (1913), p. 14.

84 *Cf.* for instance Gustav Schneller, "Taubstumme und Sozialdemokratie," TK 14 (1911), pp. 109-110; Karl Müller, "Taubstumme und die freien Gewerkschaften," TK 3 (1913), p. 19 (*cf.* with Teuber, above, footnote 83); Ludwig Neubauer, "Keine Politik in den Taubstummenvereinen," ATZ 12 (1913), p. 97.

85 Carol Padden and Tom Humphries, "Deaf People. A Different Center," in *The Disability Studies Reader*, ed. Lennard J. Davis, 3rd Edition. (New York: Routledge, 2010), pp. 396-397; Higgins, *Outsiders in a Hearing World*, pp. 105-119.

86 "einem sogar des Abends in seiner Familie keine Ruhe liessen." Protokoll der Verhandlungen des Dritten Deutschen Taubstummen-Kongresses in Nürnberg am 24. und 25. Mai 1896 [appendix to the TsF 1896], p. 5.

bürgerlich family seclusion, which was disturbed by the deaf peddler – literally and symbolically. Deaf as peddlers were no more compatible with the respectable skilled worker with whom deaf elites increasingly identified. Hence, the attitudes towards peddling were overwhelmingly negative, even hostile, in the forums dominated by the elite: the deaf press and the congress debates. The question first appeared at the 1884 congress in Stockholm, but it was not until the late 1890s that it became more intensively debated.[87] Some would argue that peddling was a legitimate way of earning a living, at least for certain groups of deaf people, or if conducted in a certain way.[88] For the most part however, it represented the ultimate failure, either of the system or of the deaf individual. Wherever the blame was put, the general consensus was that peddling was harmful and should be "abolished".[89] By taking this position, the deaf elites demarcated the range of social positions where they wanted to be co-equal. Even though they demanded equal opportunities for deaf and hearing people in most cases, they here in fact argued that the deaf should be denied something that was granted the hearing, that is, the licence to be a peddler. This shows the limits of co-equality set up from within the deaf community: it was not a matter of simply having equal rights and possibilities with hearing people. Instead, deaf leaders tried to position the deaf as co-equal with certain, but not all, categories of hearing people.

Deaf subalterns could, in other cases, aid the more respectable deaf in their identity politics. Deaf people with additional disabilities, especially the deaf-and-

---

87 "Der 6. Internationale Taubstummen-Congreß am 1. bis 3. Juli 1884 in Stockholm," TsF 2 (1885), pp. 6-7.

88 V. "Das neue Preßgesetz," TC 7 (1902), p. 73; "Der fünfte Deutsche Taubstummenkongreß in Berlin," TC 9 (1902), p. 104; Robert Steiner, "Zum Kapitel: Taubstumme Hausierer," TK 15 (1913), pp. 116-117; *cf.* also Albin Matia Watzuliks praise of a certain brand of fingerspelling cards, a traditionally popular merchandise of deaf peddlers: Albin Maria Watzulik, "Ein neues Handalphabet," TC 6 (1897), pp. 64-65.

89 "abgeschafft", Protokoll über die Verhandlungen des IX. Allgemeinen Deutschen Taubstummen-Kongresses zu Breslau, am 31. Mai und 1. Juni 1914 (n.pl.: AATD, 1915), pp. 26-27; cf. also Protokoll der Verhandlungen des Dritten Deutschen Taubstummen-Kongresses in Nürnberg am 24. und 25. Mai 1896 [appendix to the TsF 1896], pp. 4-5; "Schutz den bedruckten Taubstummen!" TC 11 (1896), pp. 113-114; Protokoll des VI. Allgemeinen Deutschen Taubstummen-Kongresses zu Leipzig im Saale des Krystallpalastes. Pfingsten 1905 [Print, Leipzig, 1905], p. 9; "Vom Kongreß-Arbeitsausschuss," NZT 1 (1912), p. 2.

blind, were used as objects of pity and charity. Furthermore, comparison between 'the blind' and 'the deaf' had been a recurrent theme in the deaf press during the 1880s and -90s.[90] In the early 20th century the interest in people with other disabilities than deafness noticeably increased. The great number of articles on the deaf-and-blind and the hard of hearing published in the deaf press during the pre-war years is striking. It can in part be ascribed to processes outside of the deaf community. Helen Keller's rise to fame could hardly be ignored by anyone who took interest in deaf people and deafness, and so she and deaf-and-blind people in general became regular features in the Silent press.[91] Recent technology and medical knowledge had differentiated between different degrees of deafness, making the partially hearing appear as a distinct group, which was also noticed in the deaf press.[92] However, the attention paid by the deaf community to deaf-and-blind, deafened, and hard of hearing people went beyond mere curiosity. Writers, congress petitioners, and even the officially elected Executive Committee actively engaged in lobbyism and charity on behalf of these groups.[93] Making themselves advocates for deaf people with additional disabilities, or people with disabilities other than deafness, the 'able-bodied deaf'

---

90 V. for instance: "Die von der Natur stiefmütterlich bedachten Viersinnigen," TC 1 (1885), pp. 2-3, TC 2 (1885), pp. 15-16; Wilhelm Gans, "Der bildungslose Taubstumme," TC 1 (1889), pp. 5-6; N.P.J., "Traumleben der Blinden und Taubstummen," TC 4 (1893), pp. 37-39.

91 A few examples: Helen Keller, "Menschenhände," TK 4 (1910), pp. 29-30; "Wie unterrichtet man einen Taubblinden oder wie verkehrt man mit ihm?" TK 8 (1910), p. 63; "Ein Experiment mit Helen Keller," TK 12 (1910), pp. 95-96; "Taubstumme, Blinde und menschliches Denken," TK 21 (1912), pp. 165-166; Ludwig Cohn, "Taub-blind," TK 18 (1913), pp. 138-139.

92 Cf. Friedrich Drebusch, letter to the editor, TsF 17 (1904), pp. 84-85; "Schwerhörigkeit und Sehhören. Von einem Leidenden," TK 20 (1910), pp. 158-159; "Das neue Mittel gegen Schwerhörigkeit," TK 18 (1913), pp. 139-140; "Hilfe für Schwerhörige," TK 12 (1906), pp. 94-95.

93 Lina Scherzer, "Von einem Tage, welcher den Taubstummblinden gehörte," TK 16 (1909), p. 126; "Die Blinden und die Taubstummblinden," TK 17 (1909), p. 136; Protokoll über die Verhandlungen des VII. Allgemeinen Deutschen Taubstummen-Kongresses zu Hamburg. (21. und 22. August 1911), (n.pl.: AATD, 1911), p. 17; "Vom Kongreß-Arbeitsausschuss," NZT 1 (1912), p. 2; Josef Gebel, "Ist der Blinde schlimmer dran als wir?" DTZ 38 (1907), [n.p.]; "Eine wichtige sozialpädagogische und sozialwirtschaftliche Aufgabe. Hilfe den Schwerhörigen!" DTZ 62 (1912), [n.p.].

displayed themselves as superior and capable. As one participant of the 1911 Hamburg congress put it, caring for the deaf-and-blind was "a beautiful task"[94] for the deaf. By acting as givers, the deaf elites ruled out the perception of themselves as receivers. In the following section, the methods used to reach this end will be further analyzed using the example of the club-owned asylum.

A Deaf Space: Three Asylum Campaigns

An enterprise typical to 19th and 20th century deaf organizations was the asylum project. The building and maintaining of club-owned homes for elderly or otherwise needy or disadvantaged deaf are highly complex phenomena. Chronologically, these campaigns went on during most of the period studied in this chapter. Although they were, essentially, practical and administrative ventures, they were also carriers of some of the ideas characteristic of the deaf elites, and they prompted contact between this group and the authorities. Realizing the project of an institution by and for deaf people developed into an essential issue for the deaf movement as a whole. This was not unique to Germany; American deaf also strived to found homes for the elderly as a way of coping with isolation in old age and physically manifesting the power of the movement.[95]

To a great extent, these projects belonged to the realm of practical, concrete action, which does not leave many traces in the written sources. The history of their inceptions will often remain incomplete. Based on deaf press reports and correspondence, I have however been able to outline the particular histories of three of these projects, in Berlin, Württemberg, and Bavaria.

In some of the advertisements that prompted Carl Wilhelm Saegert to report, as he put it, the "deaf-mute secretary" Eduard Fürstenberg to the Berlin police authorities on charges of fraud, there was the formulation "on behalf of the deaf-mute asylum".[96] Establishing of a home for elderly and indigent deaf later

---

94 "eine schöne Aufgabe", *Protokoll über die Verhandlungen des VII. Allgemeinen Deutschen Taubstummen-Kongresses zu Hamburg. (21. und 22. August 1911)*, (n.pl.: AATD, 1911), p. 17;, for a description of similar efforts by an American deaf association in the 1880s, *cf.* Boyd and Van Cleve, "Deaf Autonomy," pp. 160-161.

95 Burch, *Signs of Resistance,* pp. 83-88; Boyd and Van Cleve, "Deaf Autonomy," pp. 164-167.

96 "taubstummen Secretair", "zum besten der Taubstummen-Anstalt", Saegert to the Provinzial-Schul-Kollegium 5 April 1851, Saegert to the Polizei-Präsidium 5 April 1851, Fürstenberg/ CVWT to the Schul-Kollegium der Provinz Brandenburg, 5 April 1851, BLHA Rep.34, Nr. 1314; *cf.* above p. 157.

appeared as one of the main purposes of this organization. Thus, the designation 'on behalf of the deaf-mute asylum' may not have been deceitful but alluding to the planned CVWT asylum.

This project proved to be a difficult task for the CVWT. In 1860, they had a capital of mere 400 Mk, and requested support from the Prince Regent Wilhelm, later Emperor Wilhelm I. Fürstenberg argued that an asylum for deaf elders would benefit the deaf and the hearing equally, since the burden and nuisance of taking care of and communicating with older deaf would be lifted from the hearing. Similar difficulties also faced deaf patients and hearing caregivers in ordinary hospitals, he argued, and therefore, the CWVT also planned to open a hospital.[97] The request for support was unspecific but still prompted an investigation of the matter, resulting in a negative response the following year. According to the report's suggestion of declination, there was a genuine need for help to elderly and physically disabled 'deaf-mutes', but an asylum as intended by CVWT was not the answer. The reason for this was that deaf people generally shunned asylums, preferring a struggling existence to giving up their freedom. Moreover, as a 'deaf-mute' man, Fürstenberg was deemed incapable of founding and running an institution.[98]

The first part of the argument shows a misunderstanding of the project. Whereas it might be correct that deaf adults avoided institutions – we have seen examples of this in the previous chapters[99] – the CVWT asylum was not comparable to existing asylums. What the CVWT planned was a specifically deaf asylum, a space where the social problems affecting their kind of people could be tackled within the community. Therefore, the second argument was an inversion of facts: Fürstenberg was in fact qualified to lead the project precisely *because* he was deaf.

Practical feasability, however, was another matter. Fürstenberg did not live to realize his plans.[100] When the asylum was finally inaugurated in 1909, it was

---

97   Fürstenberg to the Prince Regent, 20 September 1860, pp. 24-25, GStA PrK HA I., Rep. 89 Nr. 22575.

98   Reports to the King [signature unintelligble] 17 January 1861, 8 July 1861, pp. 20-23, GStA PrK HA I., Rep. 89 Nr. 22575.

99   V. above pp. 85, 136.

100 In the mid-1870s, it seemed as if the project was at last progressing, when the CVWT was endowed with a patch of land close to Königs-Wusterhausen. August Schenck, "Das Hospital der Taubstummen," TsF 18 (1875), pp. 102-103; A ceremonial laying of the cornerstone was held in 1876. The report on this event published in the TsF suggests why the building was never completed: Although the

situated in Hohen-Schönhausen on the outskirts of Berlin. The long history of the project was recalled in a report from the opening ceremony, published in the TsF: The first deaf club had conceived of the idea, which was then slowly realized step by step. Fürstenberg and the Berlin deaf clubs were honoured for having originated the idea, but to realize it a cooperation of several instances had been needed: Teachers lobbying for the project, authorities approving it, and individual donors paying for it. In the end, the result was an asylum led by Carl Rumpf, president of the CVWT, and Anna Schenck.[101] The unity of the CVWT with teachers, religious leaders and the state manifested at the opening ceremony connected the project to the strategies used by its originator. It was not an asylum built and run by deaf people only, but it did combine in its management

---

CVWT had obviously been successful in collecting funds for the asylum, and in 1876 had a capital amounting to 27 000 Mk, this was, according to the club itself, far from enough to complete the asylum. "Die Grundsteinlegung," TsF 17 (1876), pp. 67-68; "Die Feier der Grundsteinlegung," TsF 18 (1876), pp. 66-67. In the following years, it was never again referred to the progress of the project. Collection of funds was continued, but the cornerstone ceremony appeared to have been a climax instead of a starting point. "Bekanntmachung," TsF 18 (1877), p. 69; "Lotterie," TsF 12 (1879), p. 45; When publication of the TsF was disturbed in the years before Fürstenberg's death, the project disappeared into obscurity. The lot apparently remained in the hands of the CVWT, but an asylum was never built on it. "Kassenbericht," TsF 12 (1899), p. 63; Instead, August Schenck submitted a revision of the history of the asylum project in 1887. Although he had inspected the lot in Königs-Wusterhausen in 1875, he now claimed that Eduard Fürstenberg's parental home in Berlin was the intended locality, which had evaded the CVWT due to disagreement over the inheritance. According to Schenck, the Berlin deaf would surely have had a functioning asylum by 1887, had it not been for the unjust deprivation of the Fürstenberg house. August Schenck, "Berliner Taubstummen-Tageschronik," TsF 10 (1887), p. 39; In 1892, the CVWT bought a house in Berlin which served as a substitute for the asylum. Needy deaf people could obtain free housing in the building, and a permanent deaf space was created. Julius Heinrich, "Das neuerbaute Berliner Taubstummenheim in Hohen-Schönhausen," TsF 19 (1909), p. 106; "Vereinswesen," TsF 9 (1899), p. 43; Eulenberg, von Schelling, and Bohse to the Emperor, 13 February 1894, pp. 86-87, GStA PrK HA I., Rep. 89 Nr. 22575.

101 Julius Heinrich, "Das neuerbaute Berliner Taubstummenheim in Hohen-Schönhausen," TsF 19 (1909), p. 106.

representatives of the two most dominant groups in the early deaf movement: deaf men and the Fürstenberg family.

Deaf associations in Bavaria and Württemberg also picked up the idea of building asylums for deaf people. In 1913, the *Württembergischer Taubstummen-Verein* applied for royal protection of its asylum project. With reference to the Paulinenpflege in Winnenden, the request was declined. As has been described above concerning Berlin, the authorities referred to the declining demand for institutional care of deaf people, and regarded the planned asylum as unnecessary.[102] Lack of government support, however, did not discourage the WTV, which was able to open a club-owned asylum in 1930.[103]

Bavarian authorities did not question the need for deaf asylums, but rather facilitated the attempts made by the deaf movement.[104] It was not, however, the more or less volatile social clubs that engaged in this issue, but another type of association. The *Zentral-Verband für das Wohl hilfsbedürftiger Taubstummen* (ZVWhT) was a mutual-aid society with the purpose of assisting deaf people in need, and collecting funds to erect an asylum.[105] It was essentially an association for regulating reciprocal support between deaf people. Although a teacher of the deaf presided over the club, the statutes caused distress at the Royal Institute in Munich and the government. In 1912, the superintendent of the institute, Anton Hofbauer, expressed his concern in a letter to the Ministry of the Interior: The present board was said to consist of reliable people, but given the decisive power of the deaf members, this could quickly change. Therefore he recommended that any decisions associated with costs exceeding 300 Mk should be made by a

---

102 Junghans to the Kabinet des Königs, 12 August 1913; Statement by the Zentralleitung für Wohltätigkeit in Württemberg, 29 August 1913, HStA Stuttgart E 14 Bü1388; Paulinenpflege Winnenden to the Zentralleitung des Wohltätigkeitsvereins, 27 August 1913, StA Ludwigsburg E 191 Bü 3938.

103 Festschrift des Württemberg. Taubstummen-Fürsorge-Vereins Stuttgart e. V., pp. 8-9, StA Ludwigsburg E 191 Bü 3938.

104 They were allowed to arrange lotteries, which was an effective way of collecting funds. According to Anton Hofbauer at the Royal Deaf-Mute Institute in Munich, the government also gave monetary contributions to the cause. Correspondence between the ZVWhT and the Staatsministerium des Innern 1909-1910, Staatsministerium des Innern to the Reg. von Oberbayern, Kammer des Innern, 15 November 1911, Hofbauer to the Staatsministerium des Innern, 14 April 1912, BayHStA, MInn 73077.

105 Satzung des Zentral-Verbandes für das Wohl der Taubstummen Bayerns (e.V.), §2.1-2.2.c, BayHStA, MInn 73077.

board of trustees. This board should have a hearing majority and be headed by a "higher civil servant".[106] Part of Hofbauer's argument was that the *Verein zur Gründung eines Taubstummen-Heims in Oberfranken zu Bamberg* (VGTHOB) had previously been compelled to change its statutes to this effect. The statutes of the latter association stipulated a board of trustees in which a deaf majority could never be achieved, making deaf people the objects of the VGTHOB rather than its subjects.[107] By withholding the permission to hold lotteries, an important source of funds, the ministry of internal affairs pressured the ZVWhT to change its statutes accordingly, changing it from a club where deaf subjects administrated their support of each other, to a charity organization with deaf objects.[108] The funds that had been gathered to create autonomous deaf spaces were thus effectively lost, as the projects metamorphosed into building institutions for the deaf controlled by the hearing. In a sense, the government had stopped the two associations from realizing their intentions, even while allowing them to carry on the projects.

The character of the sources does not allow us to determine in detail what the motives of the asylum projects were. Several analyses are possible, and it is likely that the projects served more than one purpose. Within Deaf History scholarship, club-owned asylums have been seen as answering to two main needs: maintaining the deaf community, or network, and manifesting its independence and success.[109] The participation in deaf networks was often conditional on a certain social status. Loss of livelihood due to old age or physical infirmity could lead to dependence on others and therefore loss of the space of action where one could choose to take part in the deaf networks. As Fürstenberg pointed out in his letter to the prince regent, institutionalization often meant

---

106 "höherer Beamter", Hofbauer to the Staatsministerium des Innern, 14 April 1912, BayHStA, MInn 73077; *cf.* Kgl. Reg. von Oberfranken to the Staatsministerium des Innern, 18 January 1911, BayHStA MInn 73131.

107 Statuten des Vereins zur Gründung eines Taubstummen-Heims in Oberfranken zu Bamberg (E. V.) §6-9, §14-15, BayHStA, MInn 73077.

108 Staatsministerium für Kirchen- und Schulangelegenheiten to the Staatsministerium des Innern, 18 July 1912, Staatsministerium des Innern to the Reg. von Oberbayern, Kammer des Innern 4 July 1913; *Satzung des Landesverbandes für das Wohl hilfsbedürftiger Taubstummer Bayerns, e. V.*, print, §17-19, BayHStA, MInn 73077.

109 Burch, *Signs of Resistance*, pp. 83-88; Reginald Boyd and John Vickrey Van Cleve: "Deaf Autonomy and Deaf Dependence: The Early Years of the Pennsylvania Society for the Advancement of the Deaf." in *The Deaf History Reader*, ed. Van Cleve, pp. 164-167.

communicative isolation. A club-owned asylum could be the solution to this, by offering a signing environment to elderly and infirm deaf. The asylum projects can also be interpreted as real manifestations of the imagined deaf community. Buildings were physical proof of the strength of organizations.

Another plausible motive was the possibility offered by such projects to position oneself as a competent and capable person. Eugen Traub argued in a 1905 article in the DTZ that homes for infirm and unemployed deaf people were not only a solution to 'the social question', but would also earn recognition among the authorities. When they had proven themselves able to shoulder this responsibility, the "intelligent deaf-mutes" would be in a better position to claim further rights for themselves.[110]

Homes founded and managed by and for the members of a certain organization were not unique to the deaf community. In a study on railroad workers' unions in late 19th century United States, John Williams-Searle argues that the distribution of aid, for instance in shape of club-owned asylums, was used as a tool to assert the masculinity of the (temporarily) able-bodied workers. According to Williams-Searle, independence was the core of late 19th-century masculinity. Industrial capitalism posed a threat to the independence of craftsmen and artisans, and implanted in them a deep fear of becoming 'wage-slaves'.[111] This must have been an urgent issue especially for deaf men: given that dependence was the main social effect of deafness in 19th century Germany according to the dominant image, their masculinity was severely threatened. Their exclusion from military service further enhanced the crisis in their masculinity. Only a fraction managed to obtain the independent status expected of a stereotypical man. Even those who did reach this position sometimes faced exclusion and reduction to being, after all, a 'deaf-mute', that is, a person expected to be dependent.[112] Integration to the point where one would be as respectable as a hearing man was thus beyond reach for most, due both to socio-economical and cultural factors. The deaf men needed to find other strategies to assert their independence and masculinity. Managing homes for elderly and otherwise needy deaf could be one way of doing this. Through distributing charity to others, deaf leaders drew up a border between givers and receivers.

---

110   Eugen Traub, "Die 'soziale Frage'," DTZ 51 (1905), [n.p.].
111   John Williams-Searle, "Cold Charity. Manhood, Brotherhood and the Transformation of Disability, 1870-1900," in *The New Disability History*, eds. Longmore and Umansky, pp. 157-186.
112   *Cf.* the reply to Fürstenberg above p. 246.

'Deaf-mute colonies', as were suggested by some,[113] would not have achieved this, since they implied that all 'deaf-mutes' were unable to cope in mainstream society. Asylums run by hearing people implied a homogenous group of 'deaf-mutes', who were inferior to the hearing, and thus needed their help. Deaf-club-owned asylums, on the other hand, marked a division where those deaf people who could cope in fact managed so well that they supported those unfortunates who could not.

REACTIONS

Many of the demands made within the deaf community debate lay outside the space of action available to deaf people themselves. In order to change methods in education or the situation on the labour market, they needed to win the sympathy of hearing people for their causes. In this section, I will ask how those in power responded to appeals from deaf individuals and deaf movement organizations.

We have already seen examples of interaction between authorities and deaf organizations in the cases of the church feasts and the asylum projects.[114] The most noteworthy example, however, of such communication was the 1891 petition to the Emperor. John Pacher, the esteemed deaf leader and factory owner, was the initiator of this move in the midst of the most intensive methods debate. The petition circulated in German deaf clubs and gained 800 signatures.[115] It consisted of a description of the current situation in deaf education, whereby the educators were collectively accused of standing in the way of success. The petitioners now saw themselves having to turn to the very highest instance with their plea: that the Emperor would release an order to the effect "that the question of deaf-mute education be reconsidered, and that, in addition to spoken

---

113 As a solution to the communicative and social isolation as well as poor material conditions of deaf people, calls for creating a 'deaf-mute colony' emerged across the Western world throughout the 19th century. In Germany, it was the hearing teacher of the deaf at the Berlin Royal Asylum, Ludwig Grasshoff, who made this proposition in 1820. Schumann, *Geschichte,* pp. 191, 657; Buchanan, *Illusions of Equality,* pp. 10-11; Rée, *I See a Voice,* p. 200; Van Cleve and Crouch, *A Place of their Own,* pp. 60-70; Quartararo, *Deaf Identity and Social Images,* p. 99.

114 V. above pp. 184, 247.

115 "Massenpetition," TC 10 (1891), p. 119; Fischer, Wempe, Lamprecht, and Seeberger, "John E. Pacher," pp. 261-263.

language, the long yearned for introduction of the sign language in the teaching of deaf-mutes be realized."[116] Methods in deaf education were essentially not a concern of the Imperial government, and the oral method was not official German policy.[117] For that reason, the petition could seem to have had slim chances of success *per se*, but this was not the reason for dismissal. The Minister of Education, Robert Bosse, replied with an official statement in which he emphasised the gravity of the issue and referred to thorough investigations he had performed in order to reach a decision. In the reply, he categorically rejected all claims in the petition – the total exclusion of signing in the school, the use of the combined method in other countries, and the widespread abuse in the institutions – as unfounded.[118] Evidently, the information Bosse founded his reply on originated in the mainstream of European deaf education. In the words of Joseph Murray, "Bosse rejected the personal experience of deaf Germans in favor of reports generated by the regular monitoring functions of the state"[119] – and, it might be added, of dominant opinions among German teachers of the deaf. Turning to the highest instance of appeal thus led only to the educators having the last word, this time through the Minister.

As is demonstrated in this example as well as in the cases of the asylum projects and church feasts, attitudes among the educators were the main influence on the way authorities interacted with deaf adults. The hearing teachers of deaf children were considered experts on the entire group of 'deaf-mutes'. Their response to the positions and requests brought forth by deaf organizations and individuals therefore played a pivotal role in the success or failure of deaf movement cases.

During the period of time studied, Germany had two major periodicals for teachers of the deaf, the *Organ der Taubstummen-Anstalten in Deutschland und den deutschredenden Nachbarländer* and the *Blätter für Taubstummenbildung*.[120]

---

116 "dass die Frage der Taubstummenbildung aufs neue erwogen und neben der Lautsprache die lange ersehnte Einführung der Geberdensprache in den Unterricht der Taubstummen zur Thatsache werde." The petition, quoted in: "Eine Massenpetition," TC 3 (1892), p. 27.
117 Eduard Walther, "Die Taubstummen als Unterrichtsmethodiker," *Blätter* Vol. 4. No. 22 (1891), p. 339.
118 "Ein abschlägiger Bescheid," TC 12 (1892), pp. 147-148.
119 Murray, *Touch of Nature*, p. 143.
120 *Organ* was first published under the title *Organ der Taubstummen- und Blinden-Anstalten in Deutschland und den deutschredenden Nachbarländer* in 1855. The title was changed in 1880 to make it a journal only about deaf education, and it

A survey of these journals shows that teachers of the deaf paid very little attention to what went on in the deaf movement before 1891. Mirroring the tendency in the deaf elite, the teachers seem to have let the adult deaf mind their own business. Altogether, only a handful of articles, all in a respectful and moderately paternalistic tone, reported on deaf clubs, the Silent press and deaf leaders during the first 35 years of the teachers' press.[121] As we shall see, it was when the Heidsiek debate flared up that the interest increased and the tone hardened.

Thereby, there was a clear difference between the *Organ* and the *Blätter*. The older periodical kept its sober character and did not resort to ridicule or attacks on the anti-oralist deaf debaters. In two articles reflecting on the methods debate, influential teacher Johannes Vatter seemed offended by the lack of loyalty from some of the adult deaf.[122] He said that he acknowledged their right to have an opinion, but that they had gone too far in their criticism. At the core of this argument, as benign as it may appear, was however a graver matter. What Vatter reacted against was that the deaf criticized a system that had brought them "everything that they are able to think, speak and do".[123] He saw the deaf as the products of the deaf education system, and was shocked to see them turned against the institutions that had made them into what they were. It was to him, in a sense, like a machine that turned against its creator. Vatter was able to comfort himself with a few letters from loyal former pupils, which he quoted in his first article, and decided that the anti-oralist advocates represented a generation out of touch with the present deaf education.

In the *Blätter*, reactions were decidedly harsher. We have already seen some of the attacks on deaf leaders by Eduard Walther. During 1891 and 1892, several

---

continued to be published until 1915. *Blätter* was issued from 1887 by the teacher's association "Bund deutscher Taubstummenlehrer." It is the predecessor of the contemporary professional journal *Hörgeschädigtenpädagogik*.

121 M., "Der Centralverein für das Wohl der Taubstummen in Berlin," *Organ* Vol. 18. No. 112 (1872), pp. 192-195; O. Danger, "Die Taubstummenvereine," *Organ* Vol. 20. No. 7 (1874), pp. 116-117; On *Hephata*, a new periodical, *Organ*, Vol. 21. No. 3 (1875), p. 44; Obituary on Eduard Fürstenberg, *Organ* Vol. 31. No. 1 (1885), p. 15.

122 Johannes Vatter, "Eigene Gedanken, sowie beachtenswerte Stimmen Taubstummer gegenüber dem 'Notschrei der Taubstummen'," *Organ* Vol. 37. No. 3 (1891), pp. 65-72; idem, "Der gegenwärtige Kampf gegen die Lautsprachmethode," *Organ* Vol. 37. No. 11 (1891), pp. 313-321.

123 "alles, was sie zu denken, zu reden und zu thun imstande sind", Vatter, "Kampf gegen die Lautsprachmethode," pp. 313-321.

articles of this type appeared in the *Blätter*. Although it might be argued that this, too, was motivated by hurt feelings in a profession that took pride in being the benefactors of the deaf, the main expression it took was ridicule. Walther and other authors conveyed an image of themselves as adults who in indulgence and amusement shook their heads at precocious children – the deaf leaders. Their pretension to have a say in the methods debate was made into a joke.[124] Also, Heidsiek and the deaf elites were accused of instrumentalizing other deaf for their purposes.[125] Sometimes, the two approaches were combined, as in this quote by Walther from an article about the Heidsiek debate:

"Unfortunately, the deaf-mutes, also the more cultivated, are easily exploited, especially if one somewhat gratifies their vanity, and a certain overestimate of themselves that is found in many of these unfortunates, as well as a limited worldview caused by the deaf-mutism, mislead them to take steps that a hearing person with equally limited education would hardly decide to take."[126]

Similar to Vatter's articles, *Blätter* authors also made frequent references to deaf individuals and groups who were loyal to the teachers and who favored oralism.[127]

---

124 Eduard Walther, "Die Taubstummen als Unterrichtsmethodiker," pp. 337-346; idem,"Agitation erwachsener Taubstummer," pp. 268-269; "Die Leipziger Taubstummen," *Blätter*, Vol. 5. No. 4 (1892), p. 59; G. Hp. i. E., "Auch ein Traum," *Blätter*, Vol. 5. No. 14-15 (1892), pp. 220-223.

125 Franke, "Aus den Erlebnissen eines Hephata-Abonnenten," *Blätter* Vol. 5. No. 16 (1892), pp. 254-255; Eduard Walther, "Die Taubstummen als Unterrichtsmethodiker," pp. 337-339.

126 "Leider lassen sich die Taubstummen, auch die gebildeteren, leicht missbrauchen, zumal wenn man ihrem Ehrgeize etwas entgegenkommt, und eine gewisse Selbstüberschätzung, die sich bei vielen dieser Unglücklichen findet, sowie eine beschränkte Weltanschauung, die ihren Grund in der Taubstummheit hat, verleiten sie zu Schritten, die zu gehen ein Vollsinniger von gleich begrenzter Bildung sich schwerlich entschliessen würde." Eduard Walther, "Die Taubstummen als Unterrichtsmethodiker," pp. 337-338.

127 G. Schlott, "Urteile erwachsener Taubstummer über den Lautsprachunterricht in der Taubstummenanstalt," *Blätter*, Vol. 4. No. 23 (1891), pp. 367-368; "Erklärung Taubstummer," *Blätter*, Vol. 5. No. 1 (1892), p. 14; P., "Der deutsche Taubstummen-Kongress," *Blätter*, Vol. 5. No. 12 (1892), p. 188; "Kirchenfest in Marien-

After the dismissive response to the petition in 1892, sentiments cooled down in the teachers' press. Articles about deaf clubs or relating to deaf movement debates were again featured more infrequently. However, the break between the teachers and the deaf leaders was evident also in the teaching community. The mild benevolence that dominated before 1891 had given way to a contemptuous attitude, which surfaced also in the *Organ*.[128]

The background of the paternalistic attitude, which fuelled the mocking reactions, and cast deaf people as incompetent to enter the discussion on teaching methods, was their lack of double status as *bourgeois* and *hommes*.[129] This was true regardless of the actual situation of the deaf individual. Deafness had the character of a 'master status' paramount to all other attributes such as educational, professional, and financial status.[130] Eduard Fürstenberg, notwithstanding his solid background, his education, and his respectable professional position, remained to the establishment a 'deaf-mute secretary', who was not estimated competent enough to found an asylum.[131] Fürstenberg and many other deaf people had private lives, their own home and families, as well as making an independent living. They did, too, participate in a 'deaf public sphere' where the participants acknowledged each other and were able to express and develop ideas. It is probably correct to assume that the prominent figures in the movement perceived of themselves as 'co-equal' to the hearing. However, the rest of society did not share this view. To the authorities the deaf elite turned to, they were still no private people, but pathological objects of administration, and not different in kind from the communicatively isolated, uneducated, rural deaf. Thus, their demands were declined, and their events and organizations interfered with.

---

burg," *Blätter*, Vol. 5. No. 13 (1892), p. 204; K. Franke, "Vom Kirchenfeste in Schleswig," *Blätter*, Vol. 5. No. 14-15 (1892), pp. 218-220.

128 *Cf.* R. K., Notice on planned deaf congress in Geneva, *Organ*, Vol. 42. No. 8 (1896), pp. 255-256; "Nachteile der Taubstummen-Vereine," *Organ*, Vol. 45. No. 9. (1899), p. 279; *cf.* also Eduard Walther, "Stimmungsbilder vom V. Taubstummenkongress zu Berlin," *Blätter*, Vol. 15. No. 17 (1902), pp. 269-271.

129 *V.* above, pp. 99, 105ff.

130 Higgins, Outsiders in a Hearing World, pp. 131-135.

131 *V.* above, p. 246f.

STRATEGIES

In terms of power and influence, the sense of co-equality lacked actuality. Being deaf was not a matter of being different-but-equal, but was, in most settings, a severe stigma. In the deaf club, in deaf networks, and in deaf families, alternative sets of values and hierarchies may have existed, but to live one's entire life in these communities was impossible. The very foundation of the modern deaf community, the school, was built on the assumption that being deaf is less desirable than being hearing. This is of course especially true of oral education, but the socialization of pupils to become as similar to the hearing as possible was central to all varieties of deaf education in the 19th century. At the same time, the practices and experiences in the emerging deaf networks were sources of much pleasure and pride for the participants.

In the early years of the deaf movement, these two tendencies were symbiotic. Deaf people could be loyal to their *alma mater* and to the teachers' profession without ending up in a conflict between deaf community- and mainstream values. There was a reciprocal politeness between deaf elites and educators. However, the unequal distribution of power between the two groups was an underlying threat to their calm co-existence. Teachers had always interfered with the affairs of deaf people, but as soon as the latter group started to make demands towards the former, the polite surface crumbled. It had relied on the non-resistance of the deaf. Due to the stigma, the attempts by the deaf elite to position themselves and the educators as equal sides in a conflict failed. They had to invent other strategies to be able to make claims and demands within a framework where hearing was always cast as superior to deaf.

The first strategy was perhaps the simplest. To evade their own master status as 'deaf-mutes', deaf leaders and organizations could use hearing agents to raise attention to their causes. Erwing Goffmann has described this as a typical strategy of stigmatized people. The hearing agents had the role of what Goffman calls 'the wise': they were people familiar with the particular stigma of deafness and had an accepting attitude towards it.[132] Since they did not share it themselves, however, they could enter areas where 'deaf-mutes' were unable to go. In the case of deafness, the symbolical significance of hearing agents was enhanced by the language barrier, which made relationships with 'wise' hearing people almost indispensable for managing both personal and public affairs. Anna Schenck, whom we encountered in previous chapters, was such a 'wise' hearing

---

132 Erving Goffman, *Stigma. Notes on the Management of Spoiled Identity* (Englewood Cliffs, N.J.: Prentice-Hall, 1963), pp. 19-31.

person, who played a vital part in the lives of many deaf people.[133] Her space of action was, however, the every-day concerns of individual deaf, whereas other hearing agents acted in the public sphere.

At the end of the 19th century, there were no longer any deaf teachers at German schools, which meant that the meetings and publications of the educators were virtually closed to deaf people.[134] Since hearing people owned the issue also in the wider public and administrative spheres, hoping for 'wise' hearing people to agree at least in part with the deaf movement was potentially more effective than repeating the own agenda at internal events.[135] Of the hearing people who appeared as agents in the public sphere, Johann Heidsiek was the most notable. His engagement for the use of Sign was not limited to the pedagogic realm, but was coupled with personal association with deaf adults. Contact between teachers and deaf adults was by no means unusual, but Heidsiek's deaf acquaintances were of a rare type. He visited August Schenck as one might visit any colleague, enjoying Schenck's and his wife's hospitality on an apparently equal footing. He corresponded with deaf leaders, and in his writings initially took an open and interested attitude towards the deaf as a group, instead of patronizing.[136] It seems that he sought allies in his cause with little regard to their sensory disposition, befriending both manualist teachers and deaf activists, and presenting at teachers' – as well as deaf congresses.[137] Why he had such a different approach to deaf people than most teachers may have been simply a matter of personality, but the claim that he was prompted to seek support for his views among the deaf after being rejected by his hearing colleagues probably also has some validity.[138]

---

133   *V.* above p. 123.

134   Except for the lay preacher and poet Eugen Sutermeister, who regularly published pro-oralist articles in the teacher's press. *Cf.* above, p. 237.

135   This was recognized by an anonymous hearing man, probably a teacher, in his report from the 1902 deaf congress. "Der 5. Taubstummen-Kongreß zu Berlin," TsF 22 (1902), p. 113; *cf.* "Der 5. Taubstummen-Kongreß zu Berlin," TsF 19 (1902) p. 92; J. Heinrich, letter to the editor, TsF 23 (1902), p. 121.

136   "Das 50jährige Jubiläum des Localvereins in Berlin," TC 6 (1898), pp. 53-54; Albin Maria Watzulik, "Der Empfang Heidsieks in Amerika," TC 7 (1898), pp. 66-68; Heidsiek, *Der Taubstumme und seine Sprache,* pp. 5-6, 10-33, 84, 111-112, 132-133; above, p. 235.

137   Muhs, *Johann Heidsiek,* pp. 12-17.

138   He was kept from presenting at the II. German educators' congress in Cologne in 1889. *V.* Schumann, *Geschichte,* p. 425.

Around the same time that Heidsiek was at his most active, Franz Bossong in Wiesbaden emerged as another hearing ally to the deaf movement.[139] He made his first public appearance with a pamphlet against Heidsiek, which was accompanied by declarations from three deaf clubs. Bossong claimed to be speaking for the deaf when he argued for the value of speech in every-day life and rejected Heidsiek's bleak prognosis for the chances of success in articulation.[140] Unlike Heidsiek, Bossong did not come from any of the usual factions of the methods debate. How he, a hearing publisher, became involved in the deaf movement is unknown. In his local community, he had obviously gained the trust of the organized deaf and been cast in the agent role. He was president of the deaf club in Wiesbaden and of the regional deaf association of the Rhineland. Nevertheless, reactions were everything but trustful when he entered the pan-German public debate in 1892. The TC called him an intruder who had nothing to do with the issue of deaf education. The methods debate was described as a conflict between two sides – the teachers and the deaf – in which outsiders had neither the appropriate knowledge, nor plausible motives to get involved. Bossong's views on deaf education were, in fact, not very different from either Heidsiek's or those usually found in the TC, although he presented them as if this were the case. The reason for the fierce reaction against him was not the contents of his writings, but his conduct. His alleged habit of presenting himself as a benefactor of the deaf, boasting for instance how he helped them to write letters, suggested dependence on the part of the deaf adults. This was, as the TC pointed out, embarrassing for the deaf who aspired to display themselves as competent and independent.[141] Some, however, considered an alliance with Bossong to be tactically wise: after the Wiesbaden congress in 1894, Ludwig Neubauer of Stuttgart praised his less confrontational tone, hoping that the moderation he brought the debate might render the decision makers more sympathetic to the deaf movement's demands.[142]

Relying on 'wise people' is precarious. The stigmatized always risk losing the good will of the wise person, who possesses a strong weapon, should he or

---

139 *Cf.* above p. 180.

140 Franz Bossong, Die Kampf der Taubstummen um die Laut- und Gebärdensprache (Wiesbaden: J. Bossong, 1892).

141 Review of *Die Kampf der Taubstummen*, TC 4 (1892), p. 47; "Der Hecht im Karpfenteich," TC 10 (1892), pp. 117-118.

142 Ludwig Neubauer, "Hannover-Wiesbaden-Augsburg. Einige Betrachtungen," TC 8 (1894), p. 86.

she turn against the former protégés: the stigma.[143] In Bossong's case, he appears to simply have lost interest in the issue after the 1894 congress, leaving the deaf movement behind.[144] Heidsiek, who was entwined with the matter by profession, took a different turn. A visit to the United States in 1898 left him impressed by American schools, and changed his mind about idiomatic Sign Language. In his travelogue published in 1899, he claimed that the superior method in deaf education was based on fingerspelling. In sharp contrast with his earlier work, he now ridiculed deaf adults for their poor language skills and called Sign a language for the uneducated and uncultivated. As such, it may be suited for the deaf to use among themselves, but for the forthcoming generations he envisioned fingerspelling as the saviour bringing them to think in spoken language.[145] This argument was not as complete a break with his earlier ideas as it might seem, although the rhetoric was certainly transformed. Heidsiek's main issue with the oral method had been its failure to acknowledge deaf people's disposition towards the visual. Fingerspelling kept the visual mode, which to him was more important than any loyalty with the deaf. When his interest in Sign no longer motivated him to align with the deaf community, the deaf adults no longer fit his purpose.

What is remarkable is the lack of reaction to this within the deaf community. Although Heidsiek in 1899 used the same type of language as had Walther in 1891, there was never a break in his relations to the deaf. Heidsiek continued to appear at deaf congresses and in the deaf press.[146] In a review of his new work, Albin Maria Watzulik asserted that Heidsiek only marginally had changed his mind. Furthermore, he declared his continued support.[147] When Heidsiek was mentioned in the TC thereafter, it was always in positive terms, although there were noticeably fewer articles on him than before.[148] This illustrates just how

---

143 Goffmann, *Stigma,* p. 31.

144 *Cf.* above, p. 180.

145 Johann Heidsiek, Das Taubstummenbildungswesen in den Vereinigten Staaten Nordamerikas. Ein Reisebericht und weiterer Beitrag zur Systemfrage (Breslau, self-published by the author, 1899), esp. pp. 46-51.

146 Protokoll über die Verhandlungen des IX. Allgemeinen Deutschen Taubstummen-Kongresses zu Breslau, am 31. Mai und 1. Juni 1914 (n.pl.: AATD, 1915), p. 3; Muhs, Johann Heidsiek, p. 17.

147 Albin Maria Watzulik, "Herr Heidsiek und sein neuestes Buch," TC 4 (1899), pp. 38-39.

148 "Der internationale Taubstummen-Congress in Paris," TC 6 (1900), p. 62; "Die Wahrheit – eine Gasse!" TC 5 (1901), pp. 49-53.

vital hearing agents were to the deaf movement: Heidsiek was almost the only influental hearing person on their side in the 1890s methods debate. They had invested a great amount of hope in him. To denounce him would be too great a loss to a collective which relied on the good will of the 'wise'. This also adds to the understanding of the reactions to Bossong. When he positioned himself in opposition to Heidsiek, loyalty towards the latter prompted a negative response. The result was that a conflict between two hearing agents threatened to cause divisions within the deaf community. Although none of the 'wise men' were present at the 1892 congress, delegates saw themselves having to take great care not to upset either agent. Greetings were sent to both to avoid conflict.[149]

Much in the same way that oralists, such as Johannes Vatter, quoted letters from loyal former students to support their case, the use of agents to advocate Sign foremost gave a few hearing individuals access to deaf people as supporters. There is no evidence that either Heidsiek, Bossong, or any other hearing person taking on the agent role were, on their part, significantly influenced by the deaf movement. Due to the assymmetry of power, the deaf could only hope that their hearing agents would be inclined to make demands reasonably compatible with their own. If they were, deaf individuals and organizations could take sides and declare support or otherwise further the spread of their ideas.[150] In doing so, they saw the deaf movement's issues gain some attention, but without being able to actively influence the debate.

An alternative to turning to hearing agents was trying to rearrange the dichotomy of deaf and hearing. In order to be acknowledged by people subscribing to negative stereotypes, deaf individuals and groups often used demarcations between themselves and other deaf people. As we shall see, instead of challenging the stigma of deafness, they accepted it, but projected it on deaf people who were different from themselves in some way.

The social significance of deaf education has been stressed throughout this study. Given the decisiveness of access to education in determining the outcome of a deaf person's life, the use of education as a discursive demarcation lies at

---

149 Carl Bente, "Der Taubstummen-Kongreß zu Hannover am 5., 6. und 7. Juni 1892," TsF 30 (1892), p. 124.

150 For instance, Albin Maria Watzulik encouraged the readers of the TC to buy copies of Heidsieks brochure *Hörende Taubstumme* and send them to policy makers. Albin Maria Watzulik, "Aufruf," TC 1 (1898), pp. 7-8. As part of a debate in the *Frankfurter Zeitung*, sparked by this same publication, three deaf clubs sent a declaration in support of the manualist teachers. "Allerlei aus der Taubstummenwelt," TC 4 (1898), pp. 39-40.

hand. Central to this distinction was the German concept of *Bildung*, meaning both education and cultivation, and thus a both elastic and powerful denominator. It was also a very convenient way of defining those deaf people who took part in the deaf movement debate; as we have seen, they were almost without exception educated. The 'uneducated' or 'uncultivated' deaf were evoked as pitiful or frightening images to which negative stereotypes could be attached. No opposition was to be expected, as the uneducated themselves were not present to counter this image. Thus appeared three instead of two categories: hearing, educated deaf, and uneducated deaf – or, in another context, blind, educated deaf, and uneducated deaf. Educated deaf people were cast as co-equal with the hearing, whereas the uneducated deaf allegedly lived in wilderness, isolation, or deepest unhappiness, were unfortunates in need of philanthropic care, or animal-like savages.[151]

As time progressed, the figure of the 'uneducated deaf-mute' lost some of its gravity. The number of 'educated deaf-mutes' grew so that the category became less exclusive. Among them, there were people from whom the deaf elite wished to distance itself. Thus, there was a gradual change in vocabulary, from 'educated' to 'intelligent' or 'talented', and a change in the use of *Bildung* from referring to 'education' to meaning 'cultivation.' Then, a person could have received education, but still not qualify as having *Bildung*.[152]

Once established, the demarcation between educated, intelligent, or cultivated deaf on the one hand, and their opposites on the other, could be used in two ways by deaf authors and advocates. To make demands for aid or other special accommodations for the own group was problematic. A group in the need of, for instance, institutional care or court interpreters, risked not being taken seriously when discussing policy, educational, or linguistic matters. By distinguishing between themselves and 'uncultivated' or otherwise less intelligent

---

151 Presentation by Eduard Fürstenberg at the II. Deaf congress in Vienna, in "Protokoll," TsF 7-8-9 (1874), p. 55; "Die von der Natur stiefmütterlich bedachten Viersinnigen," TC 1 (1885), pp. 2-3, TC 2 (1885), pp. 15-16; Josef Gläsner, "Der Taubstumme ohne Bildung und Erziehung," TC 10 (1887), p. 111-112; "Unrichtige Urtheile über die psychischen Eigenheiten der Taubstummen," TC 9 (1888), pp. 97-98; Wilhelm Gans, "Der Bildungslose Taubstumme," TC 1 (1889), pp. 5-6.

152 Julius Neuschloss, "Der Taubstumme in öffentlichen Localen," TC 8 (1888), pp. 86-87; W. Schill, "Eine Stimme für die reinorale Methode," TC 6 (1896), pp. 66-67; Josef Tomalla, "Die Aufgaben gebildeteren Tabstummen," TC 1 (1897), pp. 1-3.

deaf, the elite could suggest such measures without threatening its own status.[153] To argue for the need for Sign was associated with the risk of exposing oneself as an 'oral failure', who had not been talented enough to benefit from oral education. Advocating Sign on behalf of other deaf people, who were not as intelligent as themselves, allowed deaf leaders to demand the use of Sign Language in the schools, while still maintaining the hierarchy where being as similar to the hearing as possible constituted high status. They did not go so far as to say that only the less intelligent deaf needed Sign Language, but they sometimes evoked the image of the less talented to strengthen their argument. August Schenck added as a final point in his 1891 polemics with Eduard Walther:

"If we look at our parroting, faintly talented companions-in-suffering, we are soon convinced that eternal spiritual night would surround these unfortunates, if they would not enter the deaf-mute club and there learn the indispensable sign-language, and there acquire the necessary knowledge, for with his [sic] small vocabulary he cannot extract spiritual nourishment from books and papers. And then the modern speech-fanatics want to deny any value of sign-language and, what's more, give it the blow of death!!"[154]

It was clearly not August Schenck himself who could not benefit from reading – he not only read, but contributed to the media that were inaccessible for the less talented deaf he described. He was not in need of Sign in order to avoid the 'eternal spiritual night', but that some other deaf people were, added gravity to

---

153 "Der IV. deutsche Taubstummen-Congreß in Leipzig," TsF 12 (1878), p. 44; M. Hötzold, "Anlage zu dem Protocoll," TsF 12 (1878), pp. 79-80; *Protokoll der Verhandlungen des Dritten Deutschen Taubstummen-Kongresses in Nürnberg am 24. und 25. Mai 1896* [appendix to the TsF 1896], p. 6.

154 "Werfen wir nun einen Blick auf unsere papageimässig abgerichteten schwachbegabten Leidensgefährten, so gewinnen wir bald die Ueberzeugung, dass diesen Bedauernswerthen ewige geistige Nacht umgeben würde, wenn sie nicht in den Taubstummenverein giengen, und die unentbehrliche Zeichensprache dort erlernten, und die nothwendige Kenntnisse sich dort aneigneten, denn vermöge seines geringen Wortvorrathes kann er doch nicht aus den Büchern und Zeitungen geistige Nahrung schöpfen. Und da wollen die modernen Lautsprach-Fanatiker der Geberdensprache jeden Werth absprechen und noch obendrein den Todesstoss geben!!" August Schenck, "Nachwehen des Berliner Kirchenfestes – Kritik der 'Blätter für Taubstummenbildung' über dasselbe – Abwehr und Berichtigung," TC 10 (1891), p. 112; *cf.* a similar remark by Josef Obhlidal in a letter to the editor, TC 12 (1891), p. 138.

his demand for its use. In the series of letters against oralism collected and edited by Watzulik, it was a common argument that only the few benefit from oral education, whereas all deaf can be taught in Sign. Watzulik added that Sign made communication possible even with deaf 'idiots'. At the same time, he and the other contributors repeatedly emphasised their own oral skills and those of their acquaintances.[155]

Another potential in the division between cultivated and uncultivated deaf was to open up the public sphere for deaf participants. Claiming that deaf people in general were entitled to discuss educational and policy matters, and be listened to, was too far-fetched given the stigma associated with deafness. By adding the word 'cultivated' or 'intelligent', however, those deaf people who aimed at entering the public sphere cast themselves as exceptions to the rule. For instance, the editor of the TK occasionally suggested readings not to all, but to 'the cultivated deaf-mutes'.[156] In an article about the deaf clubs and Silent press, Albin Maria Watzulik described both as results of the institutional education of deaf people. The institutions had produced a class of 'cultivated deaf-mutes', for whom he demanded the right to enter the public sphere, meaning not only the internal deaf community debate, but also the general discussion about issues concerning deaf people. Hence, he did not demand this right for deaf people in general, but took great care outlining a certain category of deaf people before making his claim.[157] Heinrich Enge, a glasswork master from Eilenburg, used the same rhetorical tool in a suggestion anticipating the 1914 Breslau congress: He envisioned committees at each deaf school monitoring the disciplinary measures and the use of donations, as well as offering different kinds of assistance to the graduates. The members of these committees should be "about six older cultivated deaf-mutes, one older cultivated deaf-mute lady, and three hearing, adult

---

155 "Der Methodenstreit," TC 6 (1895), pp. 63, 65-67, TC 7 (1895), pp. 75-77, TC 8 (1895), p. 89; v. also Albin Maria Watzulik's footnotes to the letter from Richard von Tieschowitz-Tieschowa, where he points out that he and his acquaintances effortlessly integrate and function in hearing (and speaking) society. Albin Maria Watzulik, "Der Methodenstreit," TC 7 (1897), p. 74.

156 Editorial footnote to "Wer ist der Schöpfer der natürlichen Gebärdensprache?" TK 6 (1909), p. 45; "Plan einer Neuausgabe von Samuel Heinicke-Schriften," TK 7 (1910), p. 55.

157 Albin Maria Watzulik, "Die Vereine und die Presse der gebildeten Taubstummen," TC 3 (1891), p. 26-27.

gentlemen (children of deaf-mute parents)".[158] Only the deaf members needed to be distinguished by their cultivation or *Bildung* to qualify for such a body – also, it set them apart from those Enge envisioned the committee helping, "orphaned or uncultivated deaf-mutes".[159]

Negative stereotypes, such as the allegedly "simian" appearance of Sign Language, could be relativized according to the level of cultivation and intelligence. An article in the DTZ expressed concern about disagreeable signs and advocated the improvement of the language. However, the aesthetically unpleasant signs were associated with the "personality of the less gifted deaf-mutes". On the other hand: "It is above all the outer appearance and the level of cultivation of the speaker that creates such a beautiful sign."[160] Thus, the writer, Max Lummert, was able to defend Sign Language while at the same time not challenging stereotypes connected to it. The 'less gifted' deaf played the part of the scapegoat, to which the stigma of deafness could be attached.

CONCLUSION OF CHAPTER 4

The media where deaf people expressed their views in written German were closely associated with the deaf movement. It was when clubs and associations started to hold conferences and issue periodicals that deaf people entered the public sphere with their views on a significant scale. Thus, the sphere they had access to was to a great extent separate from that of the hearing professionals they wished to influence.

The separate spheres of teachers and deaf adults were, at first, also maintained in the expressions appearing in the Silent press. Until the 1890s, deaf writers took great care not to 'meddle in the teachers' business'. Below the surface, however, there was widespread discontent with the treatment of the deaf in the education system, but these views did not appear until the hearing Johann

---

158 "etwa sechs älteren gebildeten Taubstummen, einer älteren gebildeten taubstumme Dame und drei hörenden, erwachsenen Herren (Kinder von taubstummen Eltern)", Heinrich Enge, letter to the editor, TK 2 (1914), p. 18. From the context it is clear that Enge here uses the concept of *Bildung* in the sense of cultivation.

159 "elternlosen oder ungebildeten Taubstummen", ibid.

160 "affenhafte", "Person des minderbegabten Taubstummen", "Es ist zunächst die äußere Erscheinung und der Bildungsgrad des Redenden, die eine solche schöne Gebärde erzeugt." Max Lummert, "Gebärdensprache und Schönheissinn," DTZ 5 (1903), [n.p.].

Heidsiek put the topic on the agenda. When deaf writers joined him in his cause and revealed their critical standpoint towards the oral method, the dominant voices from the education system insisted on the division previously upheld by the deaf. The teachers considered the deaf adults incompetent to make judgements about educational matters, thus not acknowledging them as participants in the methods debate. Since also the government accepted the teachers, and not deaf people, as experts on the matter, the deaf movement was unable to influence policy.

In the face of this problem, the deaf elite used two strategies to assert their status as *Bürger,* and thus be recognized as participants in the decision making concerning deaf people. The first strategy was the use of hearing 'agents', or, as Erving Goffman refers to such individuals, 'wise' people outside of the stigmatized group. Although discontent had probably existed among the deaf before, Heidsiek and other 'wise' hearing people were able to bring these issues into another sphere: that of printed, public, German discourse. This had several effects: one, that the adult deaf were made targets of attacks from oralist teachers who opposed Heidsiek, further, that some deaf writers openly expressed criticism of the professionals and institutions, and that they at the same time came to rely on the good will of their 'agents'.

The second strategy was to construct and emphasise demarcations within the group. Several different 'other deaf' were evoked to fit the dominant image of the deaf and to contrast this image with the deaf elite: Uneducated deaf, unintelligent deaf, feeble-minded deaf, vagrants, peddlers, beggars and the workshy. At times, the divisions appeared in statements denouncing these groups and calling for discipline. On other occasions, they were used as targets onto which negative stereotypes encountered in the mainstream or among professionals could be projected, in an attempt to divert these attitudes from the deaf elite. Finally, taking on and preserving hierarchies mirroring mainstream society was a way to gain respectability. Educated, able-bodied, well situated deaf men could manifest the status they believed belonged to them by interacting with deaf people with additional disabilities, elderly, working class, or poor deaf. Through distributing charity to others, deaf leaders drew up a border between givers and receivers. Charity from hearing people implied that deaf people were unable to cope in society. Club-owned asylums and other types of charity practiced in deaf clubs instead positioned some deaf as highly capable, which set them clearly apart from the indigent deaf they were helping.

5. Epilogue: The Deaf Movement during and after World War I

Shortly after the ninth German deaf congress was held in Breaslau in 1914, the First World War broke out. For the deaf movement, this meant that many activities were suspended. During the war, the debate was restrained, and the planned 1917 congress had to be cancelled. Instead, the Executive Committee for the Wellbeing of the German Deaf-Mutes (*Arbeitsausschuss für das Wohl der deutschen Taubstummen,* AWdT) in 1916 decided to hold a 'war conference' (*Kriegstagung*) for representatives of the individual deaf clubs. The agenda was shorter and the debate less vivid than at the earlier congresses.[1]

In spite of a request from the, deaf people were not used as soldiers.[2] Hopes of being able to do their part in the war as relief workers, or to benefit from the increased demand for labour, were only partly fulfilled. In some cases, deaf people were employed in civil service, which had been a demand from the AWdT's predecessor already before the war. In other cases, employers refused to accept deaf workers in spite of the labour deficit, preferring to exploit prisoners of war.[3]

The political polarization of Weimar Germany was evident also in the deaf movement. Division between different political factions had appeared in the debate already before the war, as had politically denominated deaf clubs. This

---

1 Ludwig Neubauer, "Zur Jahreswende," ATZ 1 (1915), pp. 1-2; Wilhelm Gottweiß, "Zur gefl. Beachtung!" ATZ 13 (1916), p. 75; Max Lummert, "Kriegstagung in Berlin," ATZ 17 (1916), pp. 95-96, ATZ 18 (1916), pp. 99-100.
2 "Die Taubstummen und der Krieg," ATZ 9 (1915), p. 45; Ludwig Neubauer, "Die Taubstummen und der Krieg," ATZ 10 (1915), p. 49.
3 Ludwig Neubauer, "Zur Jahreswende," ATZ 1 (1915), pp. 1-2; Wilhelm Gottweiß, "Zur gefl. Beachtung!" ATZ 18 (1915), p. 87; "Bericht des Arbeits-Ausschusses für das Wohl der deutschen Taubstummen E. V.," ATZ 3 (1917), pp. 13-14.

tendency gained in significance following the 1918/19 revolution and continued throughout the 1920s. The Imperial Union of the German Deaf-Mutes, *Reichsverband der Taubstummen Deutschlands* (RTD), was formed in 1919. It was an umbrella organization of deaf clubs, functioning mainly as a lobby organization, but also aimed at offering legal and other aid.[4] Due to its lack of political agenda, representatives of the social-democratic deaf clubs were dissatisfied with the organization, and chose instead to form a special section of the SPD, called the *Taubstummen-Parteibund* (TPB), Deaf-Mute Party Union.[5] The two organizations had a strained relationship.[6] The leading deaf movement periodical, the *Allgemeine Taubstummen-Zeitschrift*, remained loyal to the AWdT and RTD, although it was to some extent open for debate about socialist and communist ideas.[7]

Simultaneously, the AWdT resumed their activities. Johann Heidsiek joined them again in the campaign against the 'pure oral method'.[8] Shortly after the war, the AWdT directed a petition to the government, in which they called for access to higher education, employment of deaf teachers, introduction of supervisory committees of deaf people at the schools, and, of course, the use of Sign

---

4   "Tagung der deutschen Reichs-Konferenz am 20. und 21. April 1919 im ehemal. Herrenhause zu Berlin zwecks Gründung eines Reichsverbandes," ATZ (1919), pp. 49-51; "Satzung des Reichsverbandes der deutschen Taubstummen," ATZ 15 (1919), pp. 82-83.

5   Also formed in 1919. Paul Stolzenberg, "Gründung, Zweck und Ziel des Taubstummen-Partei-Bundes Deutschlands," *Wochenschrift des Taubstummen-Partei-Bundes Deutschlands*, 2 (1919), pp. 10-13.

6   "Tagung des Reichsverbandes deutscher Taubstummen am 22./23. August 1920 in Berlin," ATZ 18 (1920), p. 81; W. Ehlert, "Die Reichsverbandstagung in Berlin," *Wochenschrift des Taubstummen-Partei-Bundes Deutschlands* 31 (1920), p. 149; Carl Brachmann, "Fazit," *Wochenschrift des Taubstummen-Partei-Bundes Deutschlands* 36 (1920), pp. 153-154.

7   V. for instance Eugen Traub, "Politische Taubstummenvereine!" ATZ 8 (1920), pp. 41-42, and H. Stollfuß, "Sozialismus," ATZ 9 (1920), p. 45; idem, "Kommunismus," ATZ 11 (1920), p. 52.

8   Johan Heidsiek, "Revolution und Reform," ATZ 13 (1919), p. 70, ATZ 14 (1919), p. 73; idem, "Ein Gutachten zu der Eingabe des Arbeits-Ausschusses für das Wohl der deutschen Taubstummen an den Herrn Minister für Wissenschaft, Kunst und Volksbildung vom 18. August 1919," ATZ 2 (1920), p. 12, ATZ 3 (1920) pp. 15-16.

in the education.⁹ However, the petition did not even generate a reply. In a renewed effort, the TPB and RTD summoned a meeting in Berlin in 1921 to start negotiations between the deaf, the teachers, and parents of deaf children on the methods issue. The result was a compromise with very little success for the deaf movement. After a series of meetings, the teachers and deaf movement representatives took a resolution declaring that 'natural' signs were to be used with small deaf children, and that interpreters and those wishing to socialize within deaf clubs must learn Sign Language. However, the resolution also stated that this was, strictly speaking, not a language at all, but a translation of spoken language.¹⁰

Notwithstanding, these activities brought the demands of the deaf movement to the teacher's attention. At a teachers' congress in Hildesheim in 1922, the topic "[t]he demands, deriving from the circles of adult deaf-mutes, concerning the organization and methods of deaf-mute education, and our position towards them"¹¹ headed the agenda. It turned out that the teachers agreed with the deaf movement in most issues, concerning for instance the right to education, higher standards, and secondary education. More controversial were Sign Language use, deaf teachers, and supervisory committees; these suggestions were declined. Wilhelm Gottweiss, president of the RTD, had attended the meeting. Afterwards, he took a resigned position, calling for peace among the members. The approval of some of the issues should be enough, he argued. Now, the deaf and the teachers should join efforts instead of opposing each other.¹²

Given the political tension, it was instead the opposition between different deaf movement subgroups that grew. Not only the social democrats, but also communists and Nazis, gained deaf followers during the 1920s.¹³ In 1927, the

---

9   Letter from Wilhelm Gottweiss to Minister Haenisch, printed in ATZ 17 (1919), pp. 91-92.
10 Schumann, *Geschichte*, pp. 419-420.
11 "Die aus Kreisen erwachsener T[aubstummen] in bezug auf Organization und Methode der T[aubstummen]-Bildung erhobenen Forderungen und unsere Stellung dazu." Schumann, *Geschichte*, p. 420.
12 Schumann, *Geschichte*, pp. 420-421.
13 In Hamburg, the movement was split between the SPD-section and the more teacher-friendly organization Allgemeine Taubstummen-Unterstützungsverein. Hannen, *Von der Fürsorge zur Barrierefreiheit*, pp. 18-31; Jochen Muhs counts around twenty-five deaf clubs in Berlin in 1932, many of which were political. Jochen Muhs, "Deaf People as Eyewitnesses of National Socialism," in *Deaf People in Hitler's Europe*, eds. Donna F. Ryan and John S. Schuchmann (Washington, D.

Reichsverband der Gehörlosen Deutschlands, Imperial Union for the Deaf in Germany, (REGEDE) was formed, and from the beginning had connections to the national socialists. When the Nazis seized power in 1933, all deaf organizations were disbanded and reorganized as parts of the REGEDE, by then a suborganization to the NSDAP. Oppositional deaf activists and Jewish members were shut out of the movement, depriving them of their base for public influence, leisure, and social support. Others, who embraced the new regime, were rewarded with marks of distinction: uniforms, titles, and the status of helpers of and spokespersons for the deaf.[14]

This is not the place to elaborate any further on the gruesome history of the deaf under National Socialism. A few works on the topic exist; surely, more will follow.15 It shall suffice to point out that division and hierarchies among the deaf was nothing new, or imposed by the Nazis. An all-encompassing solidarity between the 'companions-in-suffering' had never existed. As we have seen, German deaf leaders had already in the 19th century been prepared to differentiate between themselves and others, in that case less educated, cultivated, or intelligent deaf, in order to add gravity to their arguments, or recognition to themselves.

C.: Gallaudet University Press/ United States Holocaust Memorial Museum, 2002), pp. 80-81.

14   Muhs, "Deaf People as Eyewitnesses of National Socialism," pp. 81-84, 90-94; Groschek, *Unterwegs in eine Welt des Verstehens,* pp. 315-321.

15   On the forced sterilizations of deaf people and the collaboration of teachers, clerics, institutions, and deaf leaders, v. Horst Biesold, *Klagende Hände. Betroffenheit und Spätfolgen in bezug auf das Gesetz zur Verhütung erbkranken Nachwuchses, dargestellt am Beispiel der "Taubstummen".* (Solms-Oberbiel: Jarick Oberbiel, 1988). In Ryan and Schuchman (Eds.), *Deaf People in Hitler's Europe*, there are also several essays on the situation of deaf people in Nazi Germany, from the eugenics and euthanasia programs, to the deaf movement and deaf education, and the persecution of deaf Jews. On the deaf *Hitlerjugend*, v. Lothar Scharf: *Gehörlose in der Hitlerjugend und Taubstummenanstalt Bayreuth. Zeitgeschichtliche Dokumentation der Jahre 1933-1945.* (Berlin: Pro Business, 2004) and Malin Büttner, *Nicht minderwertig, sondern mindersinnig...: Der Bann G für Gehörgeschädigte in der Hitlerjugend,* (Frankfurt a. M.: Lang, 2005).

6. Conclusion

The deaf in 19th and early 20th century Germany appeared not as one, but as several groups of people. They were very different kinds of groups: demographic subcategories used for statistical averages; informal circles of friends; formal organizations; target groups of public or private welfare, of special institutions, or criminal investigation; patients with a certain diagnosis; advocates of certain causes. Thus, they appeared on levels from the concrete, personal relationship, to the conceptual bond between people imagining the existence of each other. Some groupings were made on paper, such as the demarcation of 'the deaf mutes' in the population, others, like the friendship between certain deaf men, emerged in dormitories and taverns. Yet other groups were summoned by calls from employers wanting deaf workers, or charities offering them contributions. Finally, there were people who did not belong to any group at all, but appear as such through my categorization of them as having something in common as 'unknown deaf-mutes'.

The people, real, calculated, and imagined, who made up the groups were no less diversified. Even without considering cultural and linguistic aspects, deafness is not absolute, but exists in varying degrees and is furthermore contingent upon several other factors than the hearing organs themselves. The variations in degree and type of hearing loss, the time at which it occurred, if and how it is treated[1] co-determine if a person is deaf or not. Nevertheless, there have always been deaf people, regardless if anyone counted them or built institutions for them. In that sense, deaf people were certainly not invented or "made up" by any

---

1   Today, hearing aids make many people who would in the 19th century have been 'deaf-mute' merely hard of hearing.

administrative, scientific, or organizational efforts.[2] However, the deaf who constituted the deaf movement were something more than just a kind of people who could not hear very well.

Statisticians identified the 'deaf-mutes' as people mostly in the lower ranks of society. According to the statistics, they tended to work in manual trades at subordinate positions, and to be confined to living in other people's households rather than starting a family of their own. At the same time, governments, institutions, and professionals were concerned with managing people who had much in common with the 'average deaf-mutes' of the statistics. The measures they took were designed to direct these people towards a position not at the very bottom, nor in the higher ranks of society. This – both the description and the practice – had remarkably little to do with (not) hearing. The hearing loss and associated properties, such as linguistic skills, were not the main issues. Instead, it was demographic and social characteristics that drew the attention of governments and experts. The 'deaf-mutes' became a subcategory in the population. As such, they were made up, for they did not exist as a group before classification made them into one. The 48 750 'deaf-mutes' counted in the German Empire in 1900 had no relationship to each other except being listed in the same statistical charts.

From the difficulties involved in producing such statistics, one can infer a change in content of the concept 'deaf-mute'. Various people, such as police, clergy, and laypeople, were involved in counting 'deaf-mutes'. Looking through their records, or visiting local households, they came across individuals they categorized as 'deaf-mute', apparently a familiar category to them. Sometimes they asked the household head, relying on him or her to make the judgement. A medical diagnosis or pedagogic evaluation of the individual case was usually not involved. The result must be regarded as a social categorization more than anything else. However, this was not what the statisticians desired. The development of different methods of counting 'deaf-mutes' was a constant struggle to sort people into a medical and pedagogic slot for those with early-enough, severe-enough, and disabling-enough loss of hearing. This did not apply to everyone who was considered 'deaf-mute' at first glance, by people who knew them well, or possibly even by themselves. The ultimate thruth of 'deaf-mutism' was pedagogic and medical. As we saw in the cases of a couple of 'unknown deaf-mutes', this was recognized in the individual treatment of apparently 'deaf-

---

2   Cf. Ian Hacking, "Making Up People," in *Reconstructing Individualism. Autonomy, Individuality, and the Self in Western Thought*, eds. Thomas C. Heller et al. (Stanford: Stanford University Press, 1986), pp. 222-236.

mute' persons. Belonging to the category 'deaf-mute' was not a matter of labelling oneself, or appearing deaf and mute to the surroundings, but of fulfilling a set of criteria developed above all in the educational realm.

Once there were people in this way classified as 'deaf-mutes', and treated as such, there started to emerge new kinds of people as results of that treatment. Above all, this applies to the institutional education of the deaf. Education provided the earliest and one of the most important motives for counting 'deaf-mutes': First came the revelation that deaf people were educable, then the methodological and institutional consolidation of this practice towards the end of the 18th century. This made deafness an educational matter, and therefore a concern for the state. The authorities wanted to know the extent of the need for deaf schools in their area, thus, they needed to count 'deaf-mutes'.

This classification and counting, that is, the creation of a group of people on paper, lead to some of the classified being brought together to form a very real and distinct group in the classroom. There, they were equipped with skills and knowledge that opened up the possibility for them to independently earn their living. Moreover, the pupils were socialized in the same way as, and together with, other deaf. Not only skills, but also cultural and moral values were taught at the schools. Children who would otherwise have been brought up in diverse social, regional, and cultural settings were instead growing up together, or at least under similar circumstances. The way in which they were socialized was similar, even if they attended different schools. Thus, the group that had begun as a mere number on paper now became flesh on the basis of a shared experience and personal relationships. They were now a kind of people: Educated, urban people with *bürgerliche* values, who earned their living in crafts or as skilled workers, or sometimes as artisans or artists. They were used to sharing many aspects of their lives with others who were deaf and sought each other's company through informal networks. This kind of person had not been "lurking about in nature",[3] but was the result of very specific theoretical, institutional and administrative efforts.

Compared to 'the deaf-mutes' of statistics and professional literature, this kind of people appeared significantly different. The 'deaf-mutes' were thought of as dependent on traditional social structures, typically in a rural-agricultural setting. Helping on the homestead, or surviving by complementing their low incomes with support from relatives, were typical life circumstances. The appropriate way to manage this kind of people appeared to be measures that somewhat increased their income and protected them from the very bottom ranks

---

3   *Cf.* Davidson, quoted in Hacking, "Making Up People," p. 222.

of society. That is why schools were built, apprenticeships were solicited, and bonuses were paid. However, this lead to a looping effect where those people that were classified as 'deaf-mutes' and treated accordingly changed as a result of that very classification and treatment. They moved, geographically and socially, from rural singularity to urban groupness, from dependence and need to working- or middle-class relative comfort. Thus, hand in hand with the development of the 'deaf-mute' as a demographic concept, and the measures designed to manage that group, the people in the category changed. Many of them no longer fit the slot that had been created for them, and they set about claiming yet another way of being deaf.

The educated, urban deaf men joined to elect boards and adopt statutes of clubs, which not only gave them the chance to socialize and support each other, but also had the ambition of bringing together and representing the deaf. Although they also spoke of 'the deaf-mutes', what they imagined were not the same kind of people as the statisticians, educators, and bureaucrats thought of, but people like themselves – educated petty bourgeoisie, deaf *Bürger*. Yet another way to be deaf had emerged, and this time it was in the hands of the deaf themselves. Instead of behaving in the prescribed manner – that is, by means of education becoming as similar to the hearing as they possibly could – they enjoyed life as deaf persons. They sought each other's company, went to deaf-friendly bars, read deaf newspapers, attended deaf congresses, married and employed each other.[4]

Through their education and material position, the new kind of deaf people felt entitled to enter the public sphere and influence the discussion about and, ultimately, treatment of, deaf people, foremost the suppression of Sign Language. Admittedly, most of them were no *Bürger* in the strict sense. Regarding class, they can more accurately be described as lower middle- or upper working class. They were skilled workers or craftspeople working for wages or, sometimes, owners of small businesses. Bourgeois deaf were a rare phenomenon, as were deaf professionals. Nevertheless, Habermas's model of the bourgeois public sphere is valuable to understanding their situation. As has been noted by Tim Blanning, even the public sphere of the 18th century was "a neutral vessel, carrying a diversity of social groups and ideologies."[5]

---

4 In a way very similar to what Ian Hacking describes in the case of multiple personalities in the late 20th century. V. *Rewriting the Soul. Multiple Personality and the Sciences of Memory* (Princeton, N.J.: Princeton University Press, 1995), pp. 37-38.

5 Tim Blanning, *The Culture of Power and the Power of Culture. Old Regime Europe 1660-1789* (Oxford: Oxford University Press, 2002), p. 15.

Deaf people who sought access to the public sphere of late 19th and early 20th century Germany did so based on a certain level of independence, and because they recognized that public reasoning was a potential way to collectively influence their situation. They wanted to influence authorities, professionals, and the public opinion, and possessed the material and intellectual means to do so. However, since they emerged not from the private realms of the family, but from public institutions, the deaf were unable to establish themselves as private people, a precondition for entering the public sphere. Through education, they had been able to free themselves from reliance on their families, poor relief or charity. As artisans, craftsmen or skilled workers, they had reached a certain level of respectability. Nevertheless, the social standing they had achieved relied on their access to special education in institutions, which meant a constant surveillance through teachers, doctors and administrators. Their upbringing was a public affair, taking place in state-owned, or similar, institutions, and their further conduct and situation continued to be a public concern.

Thus, deaf people were almost inevitably objects of interference by others, which explains why even deaf elites were unable to position themselves as rational subjects in the public sphere: They found themselves in a self-contradictory situation. To reach a certain standard of education and living, to be (quasi-) *Bürger* in the socio-economic sense, they had to go through institutions, which made them objects of constant intervention. As such, they were no private people, and therefore could not take part in what Habermas describes as the "sphere of private people come together as a public"[6]: the bourgeois public sphere. In other words, the exclusion of deaf people was different from the exclusion of, for instance, women. Women were restricted to the private sphere, whereas the deaf were assigned to the public sphere. The subject in the bourgeois public sphere did, however, have to be situated in both. Neither were they excluded in the same way as men without independence. Even though dependence on others was considered a common trait among 'the deaf-mutes', there were deaf people who fulfilled this condition, but still could not enter the public sphere.[7] From Habermas, we are familiar with public persons as the

---

6   "die Sphäre der zum Publikum versammelten Privatleute", Jürgen Habermas, *Strukturwandel der Öffentlichkeit*, p. 42.

7   *Cf.* Jürgen Habermas, "Further Reflections on the Public Sphere," in *Habermas and the Public Sphere*, ed. Calhoun, pp. 427-429. Habermas points at how the exclusion of women had a function in structuring the public sphere, whereas the exclusion of some other groups did not. Considering the function of deviance in constituting norms, as emphasized within Disability Studies, it would be an intriguing task to

opposite of the private people who constituted the public sphere, but he meant sovereign kings. The deaf of the 19th century were also public people, but in a completely different sense, as public charges.

This was, however, in the mainstream. For themselves, the educated, urban deaf were able to create a 'subaltern counterpublic', conditioned on their particular background. This, in turn, left many – probably most – deaf people out. The most extreme examples of this were uneducated and impoverished deaf vagrants, who through their communicative isolation were excluded from what Habermas calls culture, society, and personality.[8] With them, the only possible interaction was by the means of power and money. Furthermore, the counterpublic was not independently created by the deaf. Whether or not a deaf person was placed in the situation where he could enter it depended on decisions made in the mainstream public sphere, where deaf people had little or no influence. Thus, even when they developed in ways that were unforeseen by the experts, the deaf ultimately remained dependent on their judgements. Without being labelled 'deaf-mute' and treated as such at an early stage, one was highly unlikely to enter a deaf club.[9] Once there, the manner in which the deaf organized, the values they expressed, and the tools they used in their emancipatory struggle were modelled on the mainstream public sphere.[10]

In the media belonging to the subaltern counterpublic, the deaf movement, the writers initially seemed content with a separate-but-equal approach to their own and the educational realm. They did not want to 'meddle in the teachers business', but at the same time reserved the right for deaf adults to form a signing community. Refraining from questioning the educational policy did, however, not suffice to ensure an uncontroversial existence for the deaf movement. Its sociable function was in itself a challenge to an educational system aiming at assimilation. An underlying conflict was there from the beginning and surfaced in the repeated alliances between teachers and authorities to restrict deaf movement activity. The deaf counterpublic was not simply an alternative public sphere, but clearly a subaltern one caught up in an innate conflict with teachers and authorities. The status quo could therefore only be an illusion, caused by their limited power to set the agenda.

---

    determine if and how the exclusion of deaf people and other public charges had a functional dimension in the bourgeois public sphere.

8   Jürgen Habermas, *Theorie des kommunikativen Handelns* Vol. II., pp. 219-220.

9   *Cf.* Hacking, Rewriting the Soul, p. 38.

10   *Cf.* the description of the proletarian public sphere in Negt and Kluge, *Öffentlichkeit und Erfahrung*, pp. 108-111.

When one hearing teacher brought up the issue of Sign Language in the schools, the deaf movement was compelled to take a stand. In this debate, they encountered as their opponents hearing teachers who considered deaf people unqualified to have an opinion. The teachers and other hearing professionals thought of 'deaf-mutes' as objects of welfare and control, with the characteristics found in the statistic surveys. Thus, one kind of people – the educated, urban, petty bourgeois deaf men – were confronted with another – the dependent and indigent 'average deaf-mutes'. The medico-social classification worked as a stigma for all deaf people, even those who were urban, independent, and cultivated. In other words, both the classification and the treatment had similar consequences for the deaf movement. The classification erected discursive barriers, whereas the treatment provided the exclusion with a firm basis.

The strategy chosen by the deaf elite to counter this was also twofold. In order not to suffer from the stigma, they tried to distance themselves from underprivileged deaf people. Those who deviated from the way to be deaf preferred within the elite could be openly denounced or ignored in the debate as a way of emphasising what kind of people the deaf movement consisted of. Countering the practices that deprived them of an independent status was more complicated, since these very institutions were also preconditions to their cultural and financial position. Constructing an infrastructure of their own, with publications, events and spaces for their public sphere to unfold was an attempt to gain independence. Part of this was, however, setting up a hierarchy that modified but did not challenge the mainstream. The deaf elite consisted of men who, apart from being deaf, perfectly matched the norm. Their attitude towards less privileged deaf people was modelled on those that hearing people held towards all deaf, and their interaction with subaltern groups was also similar: they disciplined and called for education, paid contributions, built institutions and appealed for assistance on their behalf.

By disciplining deaf people who did not fit the picture of the respectable, independent deaf, or making themselves their benefactors, the members of the deaf movement tried to reserve for themselves a position where they could be deaf and be listened to. However, both the composition and values of their counterpublic were derived from dominant structures and ideas. At the same time accepting and challenging concepts and treatment of deaf people was of course futile. The deaf were unable to enter the public sphere as full participants, and failed to influence policy.

The radical content of the deaf movement instead proved to be its convivial nature. It did change the lives of deaf people, not by influencing policy or institutional practice, but by creating a space for deaf people to unfold their personalities, to enjoy each other's company and share each other's thoughts, beyond pathologization and administration.

Appendix: List of Deaf Press Biographies

OBITUARIES

Name	Lifetime	Occupation	Author	Source
Langner	1814-1872	Joiner	Ernst Meißner	TsF 3 (1872) pp. 20-21
Gustav Matthewes	?-1872	Locksmith's journeyman		TsF 3 (1872) p. 21
Alexander Dräge	1809-1873	Pianomaker	Ch. Rieckenberg	TsF 3 (1873) p. 25
H. Lübbers	1846-1872	Basket maker, cigar maker, worked on the family farm	Ch. Riekenberg	TsF 3 (1873) p. 24
Friederike Bosse	1846-1873	Took care of her father	Marie Strauß	TsF 12 (1873) p. 128
August Winckler	1810-1874	Porcelain turner		TsF 1 (1874) p. 2
Widow Harstrick, née Sprenger	?-1874	Teacher	Theodor Jacobs	TsF 5 (1874) p. 34
Ernst Battermann	1798-1874		J. Hirschberg	TsF 5 (1874) p. 37
Carl Heinrich Wilke	1800-1876	Teacher	Saegert – Heitefuß	TsF 3 (1876) p. 9
Ferdinand Stücken	1821-1877	Painter and photographer		TsF 19 (1877) p. 74
Otto Friedrich Kruse	1801-1880	Teacher		TsF 8-9 (1880) p. 30
Eduard Fürstenberg	1827-1885	Civil servant		TsF 1 (1885) p. 2; TC 2 (1885) pp. 13-15

Name	Dates	Occupation	Doctor	Reference
Gustav Schubert	1829-1885	Silver artisan	August Schenck	TsF 9 (1885) p. 36
Ferdinand Rasch	1831-1885	Teacher		TC 7 (1885) p. 74-75
Michael Schmaler	1818-1885	Engraver		TC 7 (1885) p. 80
Wilhelm Naglo	1842-1885	Engineer, factory owner; Telegraph constructor	August Schenck; anonymous	TsF 1 (1886) p. 3; TC 1 (1886) pp. 2-3
Joseph Ludwig Karl Beck	1822-1886	Joiner	August Schenck	TsF 5 (1886) pp. 19-20
Friedrich Hermann Gehrich	1844-1886	Lithographer and painter		TC 3 (1886) pp. 27-28
Paul Müller	1842-1887	Woodcutter, photographer	August Schenck; anonymous	TsF 11 (1887) p. 43; TC 11 (1887) pp. 125-126
Max Frühholz	?-1890		A.R.	TsF 34 (1890) p. 158
Klara Hötzold	1840-1891	Reading and female luxury articles		TC 4 (1891) p. 39
Wilhelm Vogt	?-1892		Friedrich Wilhelm Rung	TsF 6 (1892) p. 22
Michaelis Lichtenstein	1837-1892	Bookbinder	B.	TsF 21 (1892) p. 81; TsF 22 (1892) p. 86
August Schenck	1841-1892	Sculptor, secretary, photographer, teacher	Albin Maria Watzulik; anonymous	TsF 46 (1892) p. 195; TC 12 (1892) pp. 144-145
Carl Max Löwe	1834-1893	Teacher	Albin Maria Watzulik; anonymous	TsF 51 (1893) p. 207; TC 1 (1894) pp. 4-5
Oskar Faust	1841-1893	Portrait painter		TC 12 (1893) pp. 137-138
Wilhelm Rudolph	?-1894			TsF 30-31 (1894) p. 103
Carl Bente	1840-1895	Bookbinder		TC 3 (1895) pp. 26-27
Ludwig Wolff	1871-1895	Printer		TC 6 (1895) pp. 78-79
Carl Haar	1852-1896	Cigar maker	"Columbia"	TsF 17 (1896) p. 85
Karl Fuchs	1839-1896	Engraver		TC 2 (1896) pp. 16-17

Samuel Collin	1824-1897	Leather worker	Adam Brehler; anonymous	TsF 11 (1897) p. 51; TC 6 (1897) p. 66
Conrad Gehrmann	1832-1897	Schoemaker		TsF 10 (1897) p. 45
M. Horbart	?-1897	Wagoner		TsF 18 (1897) p. 89
John Pacher	1842-1898	Lithographer		TC 3 (1898) p. 25
Albert Lorenz	1854-1899	Ciseleur		TC 12 (1899) p. 138
Alfred Steinthal	1833-1901		A[nna] S[Schenck]; anonymous	TsF 12 (1901) pp. 53-54; TC 7 (1901) pp. 73-74
Max Löwenthal	?-1901	Sculptor	M.L.	TsF 1 (1902) p. 2
Carl Pesch	1860-1901	Baker (journeyman)	R.K.	TsF 2 (1902) p. 7
Heinrich Kolde	1859-1901	Shoemaker	R.K.	TsF 2 (1902) p. 7
Karl Krieger	1853-1901	Bookbinder		TC 1 (1902) pp. 2-5
Moritz Schubert	1834-1906	Goldsmith/ Engraver	Günther	TsF 21 (1906) pp. 107-108
Joseph Schäfer	1877-1906	Shoemaker	F.W.R.	TsF 15 (1906) p. 72
Moritz Lederer	1844-1908			TsF 7:1908 p. 37
Gustav Büchting	1834-1910		Heinrich	TsF 1 (1911) p. 3
Herr Marsch	1835-1911			TsF 4 (1911) p. 17

OTHER CELEBRATIONS

Name	Occupation	Occasion	Source
Joseph and Friederike Wurster	Modeler; none	25th wedding anniversary	TsF 1 (1873) p. 6
R. Borschitz	Domestic servant	Long service	TsF 4 (1875) p. 23
Beck	Carpenter	25th wedding anniversary	TsF 12 (1877) p. 45
L. Löwenberg	Lithographer	25th occupational anniversary	TsF 18 (1877) p. 70
Otto Friedrich Kruse	Teacher	77th Birthday	TsF 6 (1878) pp. 24-25

Name	Occupation	Type	Source
John Pacher	Factory owner/ printer	Business anniversary	TC 3 (1890) pp. 25-29
Johann Hörl	Shoemaker	Display of an invention:.	TsF 2 (1891) p. 6
John Pacher	Factory owner/ printer	Wedding	TsF 39 (1893) p. 158
Peter von Woedtke	Artist	Scholarship	TsF 26-27 (1894) p. 90
Paul Ritter	Artist	Birthday	TsF 4 (1899) pp. 16-17; TsF 6 (1899) pp. 29-30; TC 3 (1899) pp. 25-26
Carl Heinrich Wilke	Teacher	100th birthday, posthumous	TsF 22 (1899) p. 112
Ernestine Collier	Tailor	Occupational anniversary	TsF 1 (1902) p. 3
Moritz Hötzold	Teacher	Birthday	TC 3 (1903) pp. 25-26
Rudolph Reach		Wedding	TsF 12 (1905) p. 62
Albert Edel		Membership anniversary	TsF 3 (1908) p. 13
William Lipgens	Goldsmith	Received American citizenship	TsF 20 (1906) pp. 103-104
Richard Grützmacher	Engraver	Emigration to America	TsF 11 (1910) pp. 56-57

Warrants, Criminals, and Warnings

Name	Type	Occupation	Author	Source
Andreas Bitz	Criminal; news report	Cabinet maker		TsF 5 (1875) pp. 27-28; TsF 5 (1877) pp. 18-19
Heinrich Friedrich Rohde	Criminal; news report			TsF 15-16 (1877) p. 60
Carl Friedrich Gottlieb Schenck	Criminal; news report	Turner (journeyman)		TsF 6 (1887) p. 23-24
Xaver	Missing person; found	Aid worker		TsF 18 (1890) p. 95
Friedrich Bude	Criminal; warning	Tailor (journeyman)	Friedrich Keil	TsF 22-23 (1894) p. 78
Kanzick	Criminal; news report	Bookbinder (apprentice)		TsF 16-17 (1894) p. 56
August Rautenberg	Criminal; warning	Tailor (journeyman)	A. Obst	TsF 38-39 (1894)

Rahr	Criminal; news report			TsF 26-27 (1894) p. 91
Ernst Kettler	Criminal; news report	Fettler		TsF 11 (1897) pp. 51-52
Kastner	Criminal; warning	Shoemaker (assistant)	Jos. Röhrl	TsF 8 (1899) pp. 39-40
Unknown	Unknown person; found			TsF 22 (1902) p. 118
Fritz Bauschinger	Criminal; warning	Lithographer	Adam Brehler	TsF 2 (1904) p. 10
Isidor Haupt	Criminal; news report		M.	TsF 12 (1905) p. 60
August Boyry	Criminal; news report	Marble worker		TsF 11 (1906) p. 52
Margarete Duckert	Missing person			TsF 4 (1908) p. 19
Wilh. Becker	Criminal; warrant	Shoemaker	A. Rausch	TsF 3 (1908) p. 17
Joseph Willitschko	Beggar; news report			TsF 5 (1909) p. 29
Friedrich Eberle	Criminal; news report	Tailor		TsF 9 (1910) p. 42

Bibliography

ARCHIVES

Bayerisches Hauptstaatsarchiv Munich (BayHstA)

Ministerium des Innern
 Rep. MInn Nr. 46119
 Rep. MInn Nr. 46180
 Rep. MInn Nr. 73077
 Rep. MInn Nr. 79999
Ministerium für Unterricht und Kultus
 Rep. MK Nr. 17542
 Rep. MK Nr. 62324
 Rep. MK Nr. 62358
Ministerium für Wirtschaft
 Rep. MWi 1055

Brandenburgisches Landeshauptarchiv (BLHA)

Provinzialschulkollegium, Pr. Br. Rep. 34
 Nr. 1304
 Nr. 1305
 Nr. 1307
 Nr. 1312
 Nr. 1306
 Nr. 1314

Evangelisches Landeskirchliches Archiv, Berlin (ELAB)

Jerusalem-Gemeinde, Berlin
  Taufbuch 1800
Sankt-Marien-Gemeinde, Berlin
  Taufbuch 1802,1805, 1807, 1810, 1812, 1814, 1816, 1817

Gallaudet University Archives, Washington, D.C.

Presidential Papers of Edward Miner Gallaudet

Geheimes Staatsarchiv Preussischer Kulturbesitz, Berlin (GStA PrK)

Innenministerium
  I. HA Rep. 77, Tit. 3973, Nr. 1, Bd. 1
Finanzministerium
  I. HA, Rep. 151 I C 8121
Geheimes Zivilkabinett, jüngere Periode
  I. HA Rep. 89 Nr. 22575
  I. HA Rep.89 Nr. 22577

Landesarchiv Berlin (LA Berlin)

Polizeipräsidium Berlin
  A Pr. Br. Rep. 030 Nr. 1886
  A Pr. Br. Rep. 030-04 Nr. 3008

Staatsarchiv Amberg (StA Amberg)

Bezirksamt Amberg
  Nr. 779
Bezirksamt Eschenbach
  Nr. 4022
Bezirksamt Neustadt
  Nr. 3354
Bezirksamt Stadtamhof
  Nr. 4023

Bezirksamt Tirschenreuth
  Nr. 1766
Regiereung des Oberpfalz Kammer des Innern
  Nr. 12823
  Nr. 14597
  Nr. 15779
  Nr. 16231
  Nr. 17289
  Nr. 17619

Staatsarchiv Landshut (StA Landshut)

Bezirksamt/Landratsamt Passau
  Rep. 164/13 8457
  Rep. 164/13 8458

Bezirksamt/Landratsamt Pfarrkirchen
  Rep. 164/14 512
  Rep. 164/14 1711
Bezirksamt/Landratsamt Wolfstein
  Rep. 164/22 1203
  Rep. 164/22 1204

Staatsarchiv Ludwigsburg (StA Ludwigsburg)

Zentralleitung des Wohltätigkeitsvereins
  E 191 Bü 3533
  E 191 Bü 3938
  E 191 Bü 5053-5058
  E 191 Bü 5299
  E 191 Bü 5300a
Oberamt Welzheim
  F214 II Bü 112

Staatsarchiv Munich (StA Munich)

Jahres-Bericht über die Erziehungs- & Versorgungsanstalt taubstummer Mädchen in Hohenwart für das Jahr... 1900-1913

Landratsamt Garmisch-Partenkichen
  Nr. 105814
Landratsamt Laufen
  Nr. 141728
Landratsamt Weilheim
  Nr. 3181
Polizei-Direktion München
  Pol. Dir. 1445
  Pol. Dir. 2688
  Pol. Dir. 3674
  Pol. Dir. 3675

Württembergisches Hauptstaatsarchiv, Stuttgart (HstA Stuttgart)

Königliches Kabinett II
  E 14 Bü 1388
Königin Olga
  G 314 Bü 4

PRINTED SOURCES AND LITERATURE

Silent Press

Der Taubstummenfreund 1872-1911
Taubstummen-Courier 1885-1903
Deutsche Taubstummen-Zeitung 1902-1912
Allgemeine Deutsche Taubstummen-Zeitung 1913-1920
Neue Zeitung für Taubstumme 1912
Deutsche Taubstummen-Korrespondenz 1903-1914
Deutsche Gehörlosen-Zeitschrift Die Stimme 1930
Wochenschrift des Taubstummen-Partei-Bundes Deutschlands 1919-1920

Other Print Sources and Literature

Abrams, Lynn. *Worker's Culture in Imperial Germany. Leisure and Recreation in the Rheinland and Westphalia.* London: Routhledge, 1992.
Anderson, Benedict. *Imagined Communities. Reflections of the Origin and Spread of Nationalism.* Rev. ed. London: Verso, 1991.
Bab, Julius. *Die Devrients. Geschichte einer deutschen Theaterfamilie.* Berlin: Georg Stilke, 1932.
Bahan, Benjamin. "Upon the Formation of a Visual Variety of the Human Race." In *Open Your Eyes.* Ed. Bauman. pp. 83-99.
Barnes, Colin, Geof Mercer, and Tom Shakespeare. *Exploring Disability: A Sociological Introduction.* Cambridge: Polity Press, 1999.
Bauman, H-Dirksen L. (Ed.) *Open Your Eyes. Deaf Studies Talking.* Minneapolis: University of Minnesota Press, 2008.
Bayerisches Zentral-Polizei-Blatt 154 (1905); 35 (1890); 99 (1909); 108 (1905).
Baynton, Douglas. *Forbidden Signs: American Culture and the Campaign Against Sign Language.* Chicago: University of Chicago Press, 1996.
– "Disability and the Justification of Inequality in American History." In *The New Disability History.* Eds. Longmore and Umansky. pp. 33-57.
– "Beyond Culture: Deaf Studies and the Deaf Body." In *Open Your Eyes.* Ed. Bauman. pp. 293-313.
Behla, Robert. "Die Taubstummen in Preussen." *Zeitschrift des Königlich preussischen statistischen Landesamtes.* Vol. 52 (1912). pp. 279-303.
Bell, Alexander Graham. *Memoir upon the Formation of a Deaf Variety of the Human Race.* National Academy of Sciences lecture. Memoirs of the National Academy of Sciences [1883].

- "Die Ehe." Transl. Renz. *Organ der Taubstummen-Anstalten...* Vol. 38. No. 7. (1892) pp. 194-207.
Berger, Jane. "Uncommon Schools. Institutionalizing Deafness in Early-Nineteenth-Century America." In *Foucault and the Government of Disability*. Ed. Shelley Tremain. Ann Arbor, MI: University of Michigan Press, 2005. pp. 153-171.
Berghahn, Volker. *Das Kaiserreich 1871-1914. Industriegesellschaft, bürgerliche Kultur und starker Staat. Gebhardt Handbuch der deutschen Geschichte.* 10th Ed. Vol. 16. Stuttgart: Klett-Cotta, 2001.
Bernard, Yves. "Silent Artists". In *Looking Back. A Reader on the History of Deaf Communities and their Sign Languages.* Eds. Renate Fischer and Harlan Lane. Hamburg: SignumVerlag, 1993. pp. 75-85.
Bernd, Vera and Nicola Gallinger (Eds.) *"Öffne deine Hand für die Stummen." Die Geschichte der israelitischen Taubstummen-Anstalt Berlin-Weissensee 1873 bis 1942.* Berlin: Transit, 1993.
Bieritz, Karl-Heinrich. *Das Kirchenjahr. Feste, Gedenk- und Feiertage in Geschichte und Gegenwart.* Munich: Beck, 2001.
Biesold, Horst. *Klagende Hände. Betroffenheit und Spätfolgen in bezug auf das Gesetz zur Verhütung erbkranken Nachwuchses, dargestellt am Beispiel der "Taubstummen".* Solms-Oberbiel: Jarick Oberbiel, 1988.
Blanning, Tim. *The Culture of Power and the Power of Culture. Old Regime Europe 1660-1789.* Oxford: Oxford University Press, 2002.
Bogner, Ralf Georg. *Der Autor im Nachruf. Formen und Funktionen der literarischen Memorialkultur von der Reformation bis zum Vormärz.* Tübingen: Max Niemeyer Verlag, 2006.
Bohler, Karl-Friedrich. *Regionale Gesellschaftsentwicklung und Schichtungsmuster in Deutschland.* Frankfurt a. M.: Peter Lang, 1995.
Böhmert, Victor. "Die Statistik der Gebrechlichen im Königreich Sachsen in den Jahren 1834-1875." *Zeitschrift des Sächsischen Statistischen Bureaus.* 23 (1877) pp. 20-27.
Boicke, J. W. (Ed.) *Allgemeiner Wohnungsanzeiger für Berlin auf das Jahr... : enthaltend: die Wohnungsnachweisungen aller öffentlichen Institute und Privat-Unternehmungen, aller Hausbesitzer, Beamteten, Kaufleute, Künstler, Gewerbetreibenden und einen eigenen Hausstand Führenden, in Alphabetischer Ordnung.* Berlin, 1831, 1840, 1851.
Boissevain, Jeremy. *Friends of Friends: Networks, Manipulators and Coalitions.* Oxford: Basil Blackwell, 1974.

Bösl, Elsbeth, Anne Klein, and Anne Waldschmidt (Eds.) *Disability History. Konstruktionen von Behinderung in der Geschichte. Eine Einführung.* Bielefeld: transcript, 2010.
- "Was ist Disability History? Zur Geschichte und Historiografie von Behinderung." In *Disability History.* Eds. Bösl et al. pp. 29-43.
Bossong, Franz. *Die Kampf der Taubstummen um die Laut- und Gebärdensprache.* Wiesbaden: J. Bossong, 1892.
Boyd, Reginald and John Vickrey Van Cleve. "Deaf Autonomy and Deaf Dependence: The Early Years of the Pennsylvania Society for the Advancement of the Deaf." In *The Deaf History Reader.* Ed. Van Cleve. pp. 153-173.
Breivik, Jan Kåre, Hilde Haualand, and Per Solvang. *Rome – a Temporary Deaf City! Deaflympics 2001.* Stein Rokkan Centre for Social Studies, Bergen University Research Foundation, 2002. Working paper from the project *"Transnational Connections in Deaf Worlds".*
Brueggemann, Brenda Jo. *Lend Me Your Ear. Rhetorical Constructions of Deafness.* Washington D. C.: Gallaudet University Press, 1999.
- *Deaf Subjects. Between Identities and Places.* New York; London: New York University Press, 2009.
- "Introduction: Reframing Deaf People's Literacy." In *Literacy and Deaf People. Cultural and contextual Perspectives.* Ed. Brenda Jo Brueggeman. Washington, D. C.: Gallaudet University Press, 2004. pp. 1-26.
Buchanan, Robert M. *Illusions of Equality. Deaf Americans in School and Factory 1850-1950.* Washington, D.C. :Gallaudet University Press, 1999.
- "The Silent Worker Newspaper and the Building of a Deaf Community 1890-1929" in *Deaf History Unveiled.* Ed. Van Cleve., pp. 172-197.
Burch, Susan. *Signs of Resistance: American Deaf Culture History, 1900-1942.* New York: New York University Press, 2002.
Büttner, Malin. *Nicht minderwertig, sondern mindersinnig...: Der Bann G für Gehörgeschädigte in der Hitlerjugend.* Frankfurt a. M.: Lang, 2005.
Calhoun, Craig (Ed.) *Habermas and the Public Sphere.* Cambridge, MA: MIT Press, 1992.
Corker, Mairian. *Deaf and Disabled or Deafness Disabled? Toward a Human Rights Perspective.* Buckingham: Open University Press, 1998.
Danger, O. "Die Taubstummenvereine." *Organ der Taubstummen-Anstalten...* Vol. 20. No. 7 (1874) pp. 116-117.
Dann, Otto. "Conclusion. Sociabilité und Vereinsbildung." In *Sociabilité et société bourgeoise et France, en Allemagne et en Suisse, 1750-1850. Geselligkeit, Vereinswesen und bürgerliche Gesellschaft in Frankreich,*

Deutschland und der Schweiz, 1750-1850. Ed. Étienne François. Paris: Editions Recherche sur les Civilisations, 1986. pp. 313-319.

Dann, Otto (Ed.) *Vereinswesen und bürgerliche Gesellschaft in Deutschland.* Historische Zeitschrift, Beiheft 9. Munich: R. Oldenburg Verlag. 1984.

Davis, Lennard J. *Enforcing Normalcy: Disability, Deafness, and the Body.* New York: Verso, 1995.

– "Postdeafness." In *Open Your Eyes.* Ed. Bauman. pp. 314-325.

Davis, Lennard J (Ed.) *The Disability Studies Reader.* 3rd. Ed. New York: Routledge, 2010.

Dederich, Markus. *Körper, Kultur und Behinderung. Eine Einführung in die Disability Studies.* Bielefeld: transcript, 2007.

Degenne, Alain and Michel Forsé. *Introducing Social Networks.* Trans. Arthur Borges. London: Sage Publications, 1999.

Desai, Ashok V. *Real Wages in Germany 1871-1913.* Oxford: Clarendon Press, 1968.

Dreger, Alice Domurat. "Jarring Bodies: Thoughts on the Display of Unusual Anatomies." *Perspectives in Biology and Medicine.* Vol. 43, No. 2 (Winter 2000) pp. 161-172.

Ebbinghaus, Horst and Jens Heßmann. "Wie gefällt dir meine Stimme? Zur sozialen Wirklichkeit des Sprechens Gehörloser." *Das Zeichen* 2 (1987) pp. 24-29.

Eley, Geoff. "Nations, Publics, and Political Cultures: Placing Habermas in the Nineteenth Century." In *Habermas and the Public Sphere.* Ed. Calhoun. Cambridge, MA: MIT Press, 1992. pp. 289-339.

Elsner, Paul. "Ueber Taubstumme und ihre Erziehung" Lecture held on the 16th of March 1861 in the 'Ohrenclub', Berlin. *Archiv für Ohrenheilkunde* 5 (1870). pp. 170-187.

Engelmann. "Die Taubstummen im Deutschen Reiche nach den Ergebnissen der Volkszählung von 1900." *Medizinal-statistische Mitteilungen aus dem Kaiserlichen Gesundheitsamte. Beihefte zu den Veröffentlichungen des Kaiserlichen Gesundheitsamtes.* Vol. 9. Part 1. Berlin: Julius Springer, 1905. pp. 8-35, 71*-244* (*appendix)

– "Die Ergebnisse der fortlaufenden Statistik der Taubstummen während der Jahre 1902 bis 1905." *Medizinal-statistische Mitteilungen aus dem Kaiserlichen Gesudheitsamte. Beihefte zu den Veröffentlichungen des Kaiserlichen Gesundheitsamtes.* Vol. 12. Part 1. Berlin: Julius Springer, 1908. pp. 1-241.

"Erklärung Taubstummer." *Blätter für Taubstummenbildung.* Vol. 5. No. 1 (1892) p. 14.

Ersch, Johann Samuel and J. G. Gruber. *Allgemeine Encyclopädie der Wissenschaften und Künste in alphabetischer Folge von genannten Schrifts bearbeitet.* Vol. 38. Leipzig: Greiditsch, 1843.

Erting, Carol J. "Introduction." In *The Deaf Way. Perspectives from the International Conference on Deaf Culture.* Eds. Carol J. Erting, Robert C. Johnson, Dorothy L. Smith and Bruce D. Snider. Washington, D.C.: Gallaudet University Press, 1994.

Fandrey, Walter. *Krüppel, Idioten, Irre: zur Sozialgeschichte behinderter Menschen in Deutschland.* Stuttgart: Silberburg-Verlag, 1990.

Feige, Hans Uwe. *"Denn taube Personen folgen ihren thierischen Trieben..." (Samuel Heinicke). Gehörlosen-Biografien aus dem 18. und 19. Jahrhundert.* Leipzig: Gutenberg Verlag, 1999.

– "Samuel Heinickes Eppendorfer ‚Muellersohn.'" *Das Zeichen.* 48 (1999). pp. 188–193.

– "Die Geburt der ‚Taubstummenprämie' im Königreich Sachsen." *Das Zeichen.* 54 (2000). pp. 548-557

– "Lebenswirklichkeit gehörloser Kinder gegen Ende der frühen Neuzeit". *Das Zeichen.* 55 (2001). pp. 18-33.

– "Gehörlose Handwerker vor 200 Jahren." *Das Zeichen.* 58 (2001). pp. 526-535.

– "Carl Friedrich Wilhelm Teuscher und Carl Gottlob Reich. Der gehörlose Schüler und sein hörender Mentor." *Das Zeichen.* 59 (2002). pp. 8-22.

Fischbach, Rainer. *Von der Sonntags- und Fortbildungsschule zur Berufsschule. Ein Beitrag zur Wirtschafts und Sozialgeschichte des preußischen Siegerlandes 1815-1918.* St. Katharinen: Scripta Mercaturae Verlag, 2004.

Fischer, Renate, Saskia Abel, Brigitte Broth, Gesine Drewes, and Ulrike Lüdeke. "'mir mußten dann die Flügel abgeschnitten werden' Hörgeschädigte in einer Hamburger 'Heil- und Pflegeanstalt' in der ersten Hälfte des 20. Jahrhunderts." *Das Zeichen.* 39 (1997). pp. 20-33.

Fischer, Renate, Karin Wempe, Silke Lamprecht, and Ilka Seeberger. "John E. Pacher (1842-1898) – ein ‚Taubstummer' aus Hamburg. Zusammenstellung von Quellen als Versuch einer biographischen Skizze." *Das Zeichen.* 32 (1995). pp. 122-133[Part 1]; *Das Zeichen.* 33 (1995). pp. 254-266 [Part 2].

Fischer, Renate. "'Schläge auf die Hand rauben den Verstand'. Ein historisches Beispiel für den Zusammenhang von Strafe und Gebärdensprachverbot an Gehörlosenschulen." *Das Zeichen.* 61 (2002). pp. 336-342.

Foucault, Michel. *The Archaeology of Knowledge.* Trans. A.M. Sheridan Smith. New York: Pantheon Books, 1982.

Foucault, Michel. *The Discourse on Language*. Trans. Rupert Swyer (1971). In Foucault, *Archaeology*, pp. 215-237.
Franke, K. "Vom Kirchenfeste in Schleswig" *Blätter für Taubstummenbildung*. Vol. 5. No. 14-15 (1892). pp. 218-220.
Franke. "Aus den Erlebnissen eines Hephata-Abonnenten." *Blätter für Taubstummenbildung*. Vol. 4. No. 16 (1891). pp. 254-255.
Fraser, Nancy. "Rethinking the Public Sphere: A Contribution to the Critique of Actually Existing Democracy." In *Habermas and the Public Sphere*. Ed. Calhoun. pp. 109-142.
Freudenthal, Herbert. *Vereine in Hamburg. Ein Beitrag zur Geschichte und Volkskunde der Geselligkeit*. Hamburg: Museum für Hamburgische Geschichte, 1968.
Frishberg, Nancy. "Home sign." In *Gallaudet Encyclopedia of deaf people and deafness*. Vol. 3. Ed. John Vickrey Van Cleve. New York: Mc Graw Hill, 1987. pp. 128-131.
Fuchs, Petra. "Von der 'Selbsthilfe' zur Selbstaufgabe. Zur Emanzipationsgeschichte behinderter Menschen (1919-1945)." In *Der [im-]perfekte Mensch. Metamorphosen von Normalität und Abweichung*. Eds. Petra Lutz, Thomas Macho, Gisela Staupe and Heike Zirden. Cologne: Böhlau Verlag, 2003, pp. 435-447.
Eduard Fürstenberg, Obituary of. *Organ der Taubstummen-Anstalten...* Vol. 31. No. 1 (1885). p. 15.
G. Hp. i. E. "Auch ein Traum." *Blätter für Taubstummenbildung*. Vol. 5. No. 14-15 (1892). pp. 220-223.
G. Sch. Review of Johann Heidsiek's Der *Taubstumme und seine Sprache*. *Blätter für Taubstummenbildung*. Vol. 2. No. 17 (1889). pp. 268-272.
Gannon, Jack R. *Deaf Heritage. A Narrative history of Deaf America*. n.p.:National Association of the Deaf, 1981.
Garland-Thomson, Rosemarie. *Extraordinary Bodies. Figuring Physical Disability in American Culture and Literature*. New York: Columbia University Press, 1997.
Gay, Peter. "The Social History of Ideas: Ernst Cassirer and After." In *The Critical Spirit. Essays in Honor of Herbert Marcuse*. Eds. Kurt H. Wolff and Barrington Moore. Boston: Beacon Press, 1967. pp. 106-120.
Gessinger, Joachim. *Auge und Ohr. Studien zur Erforschung der Sprache am Menschen 1700-1850*. Berlin: de Gruyter, 1994.
Gläser, Käte. *Berliner Porträtisten 1820-1850. Versuch einer Katalogisierung*. Berlin: Verlag für Kunstwissenschaft, 1929.

Goetz, Thomas. *Poetik des Nachrufs. Zur Kultur der Nekrologie und zur Nachrufszene auf dem Theater.* Wien: Böhlau Verlag, 2008.

Goffman, Erving. *Stigma. Notes on the Management of Spoiled Identity.* Englewood Cliffs, N.J.: Prentice-Hall, 1963.

Gömmel, Rainer. "Gewerbe, Handel und Verkehr." In *Handbuch der Bayerischen Geschichte.* Vol. 4. *Das neue Bayern. Von 1800 bis Gegenwart.* Part 2. *Die innere und kulturelle Entwicklung.* 2nd. Ed. Ed. Alois Schmid. Munich: C.H. Beck, 2007. pp. 216-299.

Groce, Nora Ellen. *Everyone Here Spoke Sign Language. Hereditary Deafness on Martha's Vineyard.* Cambridge, MA: Harvard University Press, 1985.

Groschek, Iris. "John Pacher und die Hamburger Taubstummenvereine." *Das Zeichen.* 34 (1995). pp. 409-411.

- *Unterwegs in einer Welt des Verstehens. Gehörlosenbildung in Hamburg vom 18. Jahrhundert bis in die Gegenwart.* Hamburger historische Forschungen 1. Hamburg: Hamburg University Press, 2008.

Grötz, Heidi. "Der ,Taubstummen-Courier' – Eine Zeitschrift von Gehörlosen für Gehörlose." *Das Zeichen.* No. 30 (1994). pp. 412-421 [Part 1]. *Das Zeichen.* No. 31 (1995). pp. 8-13 [Part 2].

Guttstadt, Albert. "Die Taubstummen und Blinden in Preussen". *Zeitschrift des Königlich preussischen statistischen Landesamts.* Vol. 48 (1908). pp. 135-188.

Guttstadt, Albert. *Krankenhaus-Lexikon für das Königreich Preussen: die Anstalten für Kranke und Gebrechliche und das Krankenhaus-, Irren-, Blinden- und Taubstummenwesen.* Vol. 2. Berlin: Verlag des Königlichen Statistischen Bureaus, 1886.

Gutzmann, Albert. *Kleine Streiflichter auf die kirchliche, soziale und gesetzliche Stellung der Taubstummen.* Berlin: Elwin Staude, 1899.

- *Vor- und Fortbildung der Taubstummen.* Vol. 2. Berlin: Elwin Staude, 1899.

Habermas, Jürgen. *Strukturwandel der Öffentlichkeit. Untersuchungen zu einer Kategorie der bürgerlichen Gesellschaft.* 5th Ed. Neuwied: Luchterhand, 1971.

- *Theorie des kommunikativen Handelns.* Vol. 1. *Handlungsrationalität und gesellschaftliche Rationalisierung.* Vol. 2. *Zur Kritik der funktionalistischen Vernunft.* Frankfurt am Main: Suhrkamp, 1981.

- "Further Reflections on the Public Sphere." In *Habermas and the Public Sphere.* Ed. Calhoun. pp. 421-461

Hachtmann, Rüdiger. *Berlin 1848. Eine Politik- und Gesellschaftsgeschichte der Revolution.* Bonn: Dietz, 1997.

Hacking, Ian. *The Taming of Chance*. Cambridge: Cambridge University Press, 1990.
– *Rewriting the Soul. Multiple Personality and the Sciences of Memory.* Princeton, N.J.: Princeton University Press, 1995.
"Making Up People." In *Reconstructing Individualism. Autonomy, Individuality, and the Self in Western Thought.* Eds. Thomas C. Heller et al. Stanford: Stanford University Press, 1986. pp. 222-236.
"Kinds of People: Moving Targets." British Academy Lecture, 2006. *Proceedings of the British Academy.* Vol. 151 (2007). pp. 285-318.
Handbuch über den Königlich Preussischen Hof und Staat für das Jahr 1805. Berlin: Johann Friedrich Unger, n.d.
Hannen, Christian. *Von der Fürsorge zur Barrierefreiheit. Die Hamburger Gehörlosenbewegung 1875-2005.* Seedorf: Signum Verlag, 2006.
Härdtner Max. (Ed.) *Deutscher Taubstummenkalender auf das Jahr...* Leipzig: Hugo Dude, 1908-1922.
Hartewig, Karin. *Das unberechenbare Jahrzehnt. Bergarbeiter und ihre Familien im Ruhrgebiet 1914-1924.* Munich: C. H. Beck, 1993.
Hartmann, Arthur. *Taubstummheit und Taubstummenbildung nach den vorhandenen Quellen, sowie nach eigenen Beobachtungen bearbeitet.* Stuttgart: Ferdinand Enke, 1880.
"Hauptergebnisse der Ermittelung der Blinden, Taubstummen, Blödsinnigen und Irrsinnigen nach Regierungsbezirken, auf Grund der Volkszählung vom 1. Dezember 1871." *Zeitschrift des kgl. bayerischen statistischen Bureaus.* Vol. 8. No. 2 (1876). pp. 100-130.
Hauser, Susanne. *Die Geschichte der Fürsorgegesetzgebung in Bayern.* Inaugural dissertation, Ludwig-Maximilian University, Munich 1986.
Hedinger, A. *Die Taubstummen und die Taubstummen-Anstalten nach seinen Untersuchungen in den Instituten des Königreichs Württembergs und des Grossherzogtums Baden.* Stuttgart: Ferdinand Enke, 1882.
Heidsiek, Johann. *Der Taubstumme und seine Sprache. Erneute Untersuchungen über das methodologische Fundamentalprinzip der Taubstummenbildung.* Breslau: Max Woywood, 1889.
– *Das Taubstummenbildungswesen in den Vereinigten Staaten Nordamerikas. Ein Reisebericht und weiterer Beitrag zur Systemfrage.* Breslau: published by the author, 1899.
"Heinicke, Samuel." In *Neue Deutsche Biographie.* Vol. 8. Berlin: Dunker & Humblot, 1968. p. 303.

Henninger, Margarete. *Friedrich Jakob Philipp Heim. 1789-1850. Gründer der Paulinenpflege Winnenden. Ein Beitrag zur Frühgeschichte der Diakonie in Württemberg.* Winnenden: Paulinenpflege, 1990.

Hephata, a new periodical, about. *Organ der Taubstummen-Anstalten...* Vol. 21. No. 3 (1875). p. 44.

von Hermann, F.B.W. (Ed.) *Beiträge zur Statistik des Königreichs Bayern.* Vol. 1. Munich: J. G. Cotta'schen Buchhandlung, 1850.

– (Ed.) *Beiträge zur Statistik des Königreichs Bayern.* Vol. 8. Munich: J. G. Cotta'schen Buchhandlung, 1859.

Hesse, Gertrud. *Beiträge zur Geschichte und Methodik der deutschen Taubstummenstatistik.* Inaugural-Dissertation, Johann Wolfgang Goethe-Universität, Frankfurt a. M.; Saarlouis: Haufen Verlagsgesellschaft, 1935.

Higgins, Paul C. *Outsiders in a Hearing World. A Sociology of Deafness.* Beverly Hills, CA: Sage Publications, 1980.

Hill, Friedrich Moritz. *Der gegenwärtige Zustand des Taubstummen-Bildungs-Wesens in Deutschland : eine Mahnung an die Taubstummen-Lehrer und ihre Vorgesetzten, die Communal- u. Kreis-Schulbehörden, die Geistlichen und Aerzte, die Staatsregierungen und Landesvertreter.* Weimar: Böhlau, 1866.

von Hippel, Wolfgang. "Wirtschafts- und Sozialgeschichte 1800 bis 1918." In *Handbuch der baden-württembergischen Geschichte.* Vol. 3. Ed. Hansmartin Schwarzmaier. Stuttgart: Klett-Cotta, 1992. pp. 477-784.

Hoerder, Dirk, Jan Lucassen, and Leo Lucassen. "Terminologien und Konzepte in der Migrationsforschung." In *Enzyklopädie Migration in Europa. Vom 17. Jahrhundert bis zur Gegenwart.* Eds. Klaus J. Bade, Pieter C. Emmer, Leo Lucassen, and Jochen Oltmer. Munich: Wilhelm Fink, 2007. pp. 28-53.

Hoerner, Ludwig. *Agenten, Bader und Copisten. Hannoversches Gewerbe-ABC 1800-1900.* Hanover: Reichold Verlag, 1995.

Hof- und Staatshandbuch des Königreichs Württemberg. Vol. 1. n.pl., 1907.

Högg. (Ed.) *Polizeiliches Verzeichnis der im Lande umherziehenden stummen, tauben, blödsinnigen und geisteskranken Personen.* Knittlingen: Beesenmayer, 1856.

Hueber, Alfons. "Das Vereinsrecht in Deutschland des 19. Jahrhunderts." In *Vereinswesen und bürgerliche Gesellschaft in Deutschland.* Ed. Dann. pp. 115-132.

Huschens, Jakob. *Die soziale Bedeutung der Taubstummenbildung. Ein Beitrag zur richtigen Bewertung des der menschlichen Gesellschaft wiedergegebenen sprechenden Tauben.* Trier: Paulinus-Druckerei, 1911.

Im Hof, Ulrich. *Das gesellige Jahrhundert. Gesellschaft und Gesellschaften im Zeitalter der Aufklärung*. Munich: C. H. Beck, 1982.

K. E. Sch. Review of Heidsiek's *Der Taubstumme und seine Sprache. Organ der Taubstummen-Anstalten...* Vol. 35. No. 9 (1889). pp. 280-286.

Kätzke, Bertha. "Der Unterricht in weiblichen Handarbeiten." In *Handbuch der Taubstummenbildung*. Ed. Walther. pp. 702-707.

Kellenbenz, Hermann. "Zahlungsmittel, Maße und Gewichte seit 1800." In *Handbuch der deutschen Wirtschafts- und Sozialgeschichte*. Vol. 2. Eds. Hermann Aubin and Wolfgang Zorn. Stuttgart: Ernst Klett Verlag, 1976.

Kellinghaus, Christoph. *Wohnungslos und psychisch Krank. Eine Problemgruppe zwischen den Systemen. Konzepte – empirische Daten – Hilfsansätze*. Münster: Lit Verlag, 2000.

Kerer, Franz X. *Dominikus Ringeisen von Ursberg. Ein Lebens- und Charakterbild*. Regensburg: G. J. Manz, 1927.

"Kirchenfest in Marienburg." *Blätter für Taubstummenbildung*. Vol. 5. No. 13 (1892). pp. 203-204.

Klessmann, Christoph. *Polnische Bergarbeiter im Ruhrgebiet 1870-1945. Soziale Integration und nationale Subkultur einer Minderheit in der deutschen Industriegesellschaft*. Göttingen: Vanderhoeck & Ruprecht, 1978.

– "Long-Distance Migration, Integration and Segregation of an Ethnic Minority in Industrial Germany: The Case of the 'Ruhr-Poles.'" In *Population, Labour and Migration in 19th- and 20th- Century Germany*. Ed. Klaus J. Bade. Lemington Spa: Berg, 1987. pp. 101-114.

Klose, Olaf and Christian Degn. *Die Herzogtümer im Gesamtstaat. 1721-1830. Geschichte Schleswig-Holsteins*. Vol. 6. Neumünster: Karl Wahholtz, 1960.

Kocka, Jürgen. *Das lange 19. Jahrhundert. Arbeit, Nation und bürgerliche Gesellschaft. Gebhardt Handbuch der deutschen Geschichte*. 10th Ed. Vol. 13. Stuttgart: Klett-Cotta, 2001.

– "Bürgertum und Bürgerlichkeit als Probleme der deutschen Geschichte vom späten 18. zum frühen 20. Jahrhundert." In *Bürger und Bürgerlichkeit*. Ed. Kocka. pp. 21-63.

Kocka, Jürgen. (Ed.) *Bürger und Bürgerlichkeit im 19. Jahrhundert*. Munich: dtv, 1988.

Kockelmann, Paul. *Taubstummenbildung und Taubstummenfürsorge. Ein Wort der Aufklärung für alle gebildeten, besonders für Seelsorger, Lehrer und Lehrerinnen und für die Eltern Taubstummer Kinder*. 2nd Ed. Düsseldorf: L. Schwann, 1914. pp. 54-57.

Krentz, Christopher. *Writing Deafness: The Hearing Line in Nineteenth-Century American Literature.* Chapel Hill, NC: University of North Carolina Press, 2007.

Kruse, Otto Friedrich. *Der Taubstumme im uncultivierten Zustande nebst Blicken in das Leben merkwürdiger Taubstummen.* Bremen: Kaiser, 1832.

- *Über Taubstumme, Taubstummenbildung und Taubstummenanstalten; nebst Notizen aus meinem Reisetagebuche.* Schleswig: Published by the author under commission of the Prussian administration, 1853.

- *Zur Vermittlung der Extreme in der sogenannten deutschen und französischen Taubstummen-Bildungs-Methode. Ein Versuch zur Vereinigung beider.* Schleswig: Verlag der Schulbuchhandlung Hermann Heiberg, 1869.

- *Bilder aus dem Leben eines Taubstummen. Eine Autobiographie des Taubstummen.* Altona: Published by the author, 1877.

Kubach-Reutter, Ursula. (Ed.) *Spätromantik im Industriezeitalter. Die Nürnberger Künstlerfamilie Ritter.* Nuremberg: Museum Industriekultur, 2007.

Kudlick, Catherine. "Disability History: Why We Need Another 'Other'." *American Historical Review.* Vol. 108. No. 3. June 2003. pp. 763-793.

Lane, Harlan, Richard C. Pillard, and Mary French. "Origins of the American Deaf-World: Assimilating and Differentiating Societies and Their Relation to Genetic Pattering." In *The Deaf History Reader.* Ed. Van Cleve. pp. 47-73.

Lane, Harlan, Robert Hoffmeister, and Ben Bahan. *A Journey into the Deaf-World.* San Diego, CA: DawnSignPress, 1996.

Lane, Harlan. *When the Mind Hears. A History of the Deaf.* New York: Vintage Books, 1989. [Reprint; first ed. by Random House, 1984].

- *The Mask of Benevolence: Disabling the Deaf Community.* New York: Alfred A. Knopf, 1992.

Lane, Harlan. (Ed.) *The Deaf Experience. Classics in Language and Education.* Cambridge, Mass.: Harvard University Press, 1984.

Lang, Harry G. "Genesis of a Community: The American Deaf Experience in the Seventeenth and Eighteenth Centuries." In *The Deaf History Reader.* Ed. Van Cleve. Washington D. C.: Gallaudet University Press, 2007. pp. 1-23.

Langewiesche, Dieter. "Republik, konstitutionelle Monarchie und 'soziale Frage.' Grundprobleme der deutschen Revolution von 1848/49." In *Die deutsche Revolution von 1848/49.* Ed. Dieter Langewiesche. Darmstadt: Wissenschaftliche Buchgesellschaft, 1983.

"Leipziger Taubstummen, Die." *Blätter für Taubstummenbildung.* Vol. 4. No. 4 (1891). p. 59.

Lemm, Werner, et al. *Schulgeschichte in Berlin.* Berlin: Volk und Wissen, 1987.

Lenger, Friedrich. *Industrielle Revolution und Nationalstaatsgründung. (1849-1870er Jahre.) Gebhardt Handbuch der deutschen Geschichte.* 10th Ed. Vol. 15. Stuttgart: Klett-Cotta, 2001.

Lepsius, M. Rainer. "Zur Soziologie des Bürgertums und der Bürgerlichkeit." In *Bürger und Bürgerlichkeit.* Ed. Kocka. pp. 79-100.

Lingelmann, Heinrich. *Aus der Taubstummen-Welt. Biographien, Charakterzüge und Erzählungen aus dem Leben der Gehörlosen für Leser jeden Standes.* Berlin, 1876.

– *Aus der Taubstummen-Welt. Biographien, Charakterzüge und Erzählungen aus dem Leben der Gehörlosen für Leser jeden Standes.* 2nd Ed. Berlin, 1878.

List, Günther. "Assimilation durch Zweisprachigkeit. Die preußisch-deutschen Projekte Taubstummen-Bildung und Polenpolitik im 19. Jahrhundert." *Das Zeichen.* Vol. 68 (2004). pp. 338-347.

– "Deaf History: A Suppressed Part of General History." In *Deaf History Unveiled.* Ed. Van Cleve. pp. 113-126

– "Zeit-Schriften. Periodica als Quellengattung für die Geschichte der Gehörlosen bis zum Beginn des 20. Jahrhunderts". *Das Zeichen.* Vol. 29. (1994). pp. 278-287.

– "Pädagogische Inklusion und die 'Bildbarkeit' der Taubstummen". *Das Zeichen.* Vol. 51 (2000). pp. 8-18.

– "Nationale Inklusion und die Gebärdensprache der Taubstummen". *Das Zeichen.* Vol. 52 (2000). pp. 186-196.

Longmore, Paul and Lauri Umansky. (Eds.) *The New Disability History.* New York: New York University Press, 2001.

Löwe, Armin. "Gehörlosenpädagogik." In *Geschichte der Sonderpädagogik.* Ed. Světluše Solarová. Stuttgart: Verlag W. Kohlhammer, 1983.

Lucassen, Leo. "Eternal Vagrants? State Formation, Migration, and Travelling Groups in Western-Europe, 1350-1914." In *Migration, Migration History, History. Old Paradigms and New Perspectives.* Eds. Jan Lucassen and Leo Lucassen. Bern: Peter Lang, 1997.

M. "Der Centralverein für das Wohl der Taubstummen in Berlin." *Organ der Taubstummen-Anstalten...* Vol. 18. No. 112 (1872). pp. 192-195.

Marx, Karl. *Das Kapital. Kritik der politischen Ökonomie.* Vol. 1. [1890] Berlin: Dietz Verlag, 1982.

Marx-Jaskulski, Katrin. *Armut und Fürsorge auf dem Land. Vom Ende des 19. Jahrhunderts bis 1933.* Göttingen: Wallstein Verlag, 2008.

Mayr, Georg. *Die Verbreitung der Blindheit, der Taubstummheit, des Blödsinns und des Irrsinns in Bayern nebst einer allgemeinen internationalen Statistik dieser vier Gebrechen.* Beiträge zur Statistik des Königreichs Bayern. Vol. 35. Munich: Adolf Ackermann, 1877.

Mieck, Ilja. "Von der Reformzeit zur Revolution." In *Geschichte Berlins.* Vol. I.: *Von der Frühgeschichte zur Industrializierung.* 3rd Ed. Ed. Wolfgang Ribbe. Berlin: Berliner Wissenschafts-Verlag, 2002. pp. 405-602.

Mirzoeff, Nicholas. *Silent Poetry. Deafness, Sign, and Visual Culture in Modern France.* Princeton, NJ: Princeton University Press, 1995.

Möckel, Andreas. *Geschichte der Heilpädagogik.* Stuttgart: Klett-Cotta, 1988.

Muhs, Jochen. *Johann Heidsiek. Einer der letzten großen Vorkäpfer für gebärdensprachliche Erziehung Gehörloser an Taubstummenanstalten (1855-1942).* Deaf History 1. Berlin: Deaf-History Deutschland, 1998.

- "Eduard Fürstenberg." *Das Zeichen.* Vol. 30 (1994). pp. 422-423.
- "Margaretha Hüttmann." *Das Zeichen.* Vol. 28 (1994). pp. 156-157.
- "Johann Heidsiek (1855-1942) – Wegbereiter des Bilingualismus." *Das Zeichen.* Vol. 47 (1999). pp 11-17.
- "Deaf People as Eyewitnesses of National Socialism." In *Deaf People in Hitler's Europe.* Eds. Donna F. Ryan and John S. Schuchmann. Washington, D. C.: Gallaudet University Press and United States Holocaust Memorial Museum, 2002. pp. 78-97.

Müller, Hans-Heinrich. (Ed.) *Produktivkräfte in Deutschland 1870 bis 1917/18.* Berlin: Akademie-Verlag 1985.

Murray, Joseph. *"One Touch Of Nature Makes The Whole World Kin:" The Transnational Lives Of Deaf Americans, 1870-1924.* Ph.D. Dissertation, University of Iowa, 2007.

"Nachteile der Taubstummen-Vereine." *Organ der Taubstummen-Anstalten ...* Vol. 45. No. 9 (1899). p. 279.

Nathaus, Klaus. *Organizierte Geselligkeit. Deutsche und britische Vereine im 19. und 20. Jahrhundert.* Göttingen: Vandenhoech & Ruprecht, 2009.

Negt, Oskar, and Alexander Kluge. *Öffentlichkeit und Erfahrung. Zur Organizationsanalyse von bürgerlicher und proletarischer Öffentlichkeit.* Frankfurt a.M.: Suhrkamp, 1972.

Nipperdey, Thomas. *Deutsche Geschichte 1800-1866. Bürgerwelt und starker Staat.* Munich: C. H. Beck, 1987.

- ""Verein als soziale Struktur in Deutschland im späten 18. und frühen 19. Jahrhundert. Eine Fallstudie zur Modernisierung I." In *Gesellschaft, Kultur, Theorie. Gesammelte Aufsätze zur neueren Geschichte.* Göttingen: Vanderhoeck & Ruprecht, 1976. pp. 174-205.

Oblinger, Hermann. "Johann Evangelist Wagner und Dominikus Ringeisen als Wegbereiter der Behinderten- und Sonderschulpädagogik im 19. Jahrhundert." In *Handbuch der Geschichte des Bayerischen Bildungswesens.* Vol. 2: *Geschichte der Schule in Bayern. Von 1800 bis 1918.* Ed. Max Liedtke. Bad Heilbronn: Verlag Julius Klinkhardt, 1993.

P. "Der deutsche Taubstummen-Kongress." *Blätter für Taubstummenbildung.* Vol. 5. No. 12 (1892). pp. 187-188.

Padden, Carol and Tom Humphries. *Deaf in America. Voices from a Culture.* Cambridge, Massachusetts: Harvard University Press, 1988.

– "Deaf People. A Different Center." In *The Disability Studies Reader.* Ed. Davis. pp. 393-402.

Padden, Carol. "The Deaf Community and the Culture of Deaf People." In *Sign Language and the Deaf Community. Essays in Honor of William C. Stokoe.* Eds. Charlotte Baker and Robbin Battison. National Association of the Deaf, 1980.

Pongratz, Georg. *Allgemeine Statistik über die Taubstummen Bayerns. Zugleich eine Studie über das Auftreten der Taubstummheit in Bayern im 19. Jahrhundert.* Munich: Max Kellerer's Hof-Buchhandlung, 1906.

Preussische Statistik. (Amtliches Quellenwerk.) Herausgegeben in zwanglosen Heften vom Königlichen statistischen Bureau in Berlin. Vol. 69: *Die Gebrechlichen in der Bevölkerung des preussischen Staates nach den Ergebnissen der Volkszählung vom 1. December 1880.* Berlin: Verlag des Königlichen Statistischen Bureaus, 1883.

*Preussische Statistik...*Vol. 148: *Die endgültigen Ergebnisse der Volkszählung vom 2. December 1895 im preussischen Staate.* Part 2. Berlin: Verlag des Königlichen statistischen Bureaus, 1898.

Prillwitz, Siegmund. "Der Lange Weg zur Zweisprachigkeit im deutschen Sprachraum." *Das Zeichen.* 12 (1990). pp. 133-140.

Prinzing, Friedrich. "Die Methoden der medizinischen Statistik." In *Handbuch der biologischen Arbeitsmethoden.* Ed. Emil Aberhelden. Vol 5. Part 2. Berlin: Urband & Schwarzenberg, [1928].

Protokoll der Verhandlungen des dritten Deutschen Taubstummen-Kongresses zu Nürnberg. Appendix to the TsF 1896.

Protokoll der Verhandlungen des Vierten Deutschen Taubstummen-Kongresses zu Stuttgart. Appendix to the TC 1899.

Protokoll des VI. Allgemeinen Deutschen Taubstummen-Kongresses zu Leipzig im Saale des Krystallpalastes. Leipzig: n.pub.,1905.

Protokoll über die Verhandlungen des IX. Allgemeinen Deutschen Taubstummen-Kongresses zu Breslau. n.pl.: Arbeitsausschuss für die Allgemeinheit der deutschen Taubstummen, 1915.

Quartararo, Anne T. *Deaf Identity and Social Images in Nineteenth-Century France.* Washington D.C.: Gallaudet University Press, 2008.
- "Republicanism, Deaf Identity and the Career of Henri Gaillard in Late-Nineteenth-Century France." In *Deaf History Unveiled.* Ed. Van Cleve. pp. 40-52.
Radomski, Josef. *Statistische Nachrichten über die Taubstummen-Anstalten Deutschlands und deren Lehrkräfte pro 1901.* Vol. V. Kommissionsverlag Friedrich Ebbeke: Posen, 1901.
- *Statistische Nachrichten über die Taubstummenanstalten Deutschlands und der russischen Ostseeprovinzen, sowie über deren Lehrkräfte für das Jahr 1906.* Posen: Friedrich Ebbecke, 1908.
R. K. Notice on planned deaf congress in Geneva. *Organ der Taubstummen-Anstalten...* Vol. 42. No. 8 (1896). pp. 255-256.
Rée, Jonathan. *I See a Voice. Deafness, Language and the Senses – A Philosophical History.* New York Metropolitan Books, 1999.
Reith, Reinhold. "Zur beruflichen Sozialisation im Handwerk vom 18. bis ins frühe 20. Jahrhundert. Umrisse einer Sozialgeschichte der deutschen Lehrlinge." *Vierteljahrschrift für Sozial- und Wirtschaftsgeschichte.* Vol. 76 (1989). pp. 1-27.
Richter, August. "Die Eingliederung des Taubstummen in die deutsche Kulturgemeinschaft." In *Handbuch des Taubstummenwesens.* Ed. Schumann.
Richter, Wilhelm. *Berliner Schulgeschichte. Von den mittelalterlichen Anfängen bis zum Ende der Weimarer Republik.* Berlin: Colloquium Verlag, 1981.
Rinneberg, Karl-Jürgen. *Das betriebliche Ausbildungswesen in der Zeit der industriellen Umgestaltung Deutschlands. Deutsches Institut für Internationale Pädagogische Forschung: Studien und Dokumentationen zur deutschen Bildungsgeschichte.* Vol. 29. Cologne: Böhlau Verlag, 1985.
Ryan, Donna F. and John S. Schuchmann. (Eds.) *Deaf People in Hitler's Europe.* Washington, D. C.: Gallaudet University Press and United States Holocaust Memorial Museum, 2002.
Sachße, Christoph and Florian Tennstedt. *Geschichte der Armenfürsorge in Deutschland. Vom Spätmittelalter bis zum Ersten Weltkrieg.* Stuttgart: Kohlhammer, 1980.
Sacks, Oliver. *Seeing Voices. A Journey into the World of the Deaf.* [Berkeley, CA: University of California Press, 1989] London: Picador, 2000.
Saegert, C.W. *Das Taubstummen-Bildungswesen in Preußen.* Berlin: Verlag der Expedition des Taubstummenfreundes, 1874.
Sarasin, Philipp. *Reizbare Maschinen. Eine Geschichte des Körpers 1765-1914.* Frankfurt a. M., Suhrkamp, 2001.

Scharf, Lothar. *Gehörlose in der Hitlerjugend und Taubstummenanstalt Bayreuth. Zeitgeschichtliche Dokumentation der Jahre 1933-1945.* Berlin: Pro Business, 2004.

Schlott, G. "Urteile erwachsener Taubstummer über den Lautsprachunterricht in der Taubstummenanstalt." *Blätter für Taubstummenbildung.* Vol. 4. No. 23 (1891). pp. 367-368.

Schlotter, P. *Die Rechtsstellung und der Rechtsschutz der Taubstummen. Eine juristische Plauderei.* Leipzig: Hugo Dude, 1907.

Schlüter, Anne. *Neue Hüte – alte Hüte? Gewerbliche Berufsbildung für Mädchen zu Beginn des 20. Jahrhunderts – Zur Geschichte ihrer Institutionalisierung.* Düsseldorf: Pädagogischer Verlag Schwann-Bagel, 1987.

Schmaltz, Heinrich. *Die Taubstummen im Königreich Sachsen. Ein Beitrag zur Kenntniss der Ätiologie und Verbreitung der Taubstummheit.* Leipzig: Breitkopf & Härtel, 1884.

Schmidt, Friedrich August, and Bernhardt Friedrich Voigt. *Neuer Nekrolog des Deutschen.* Vol. 4. [1826] Part 2. Ilmenau: Bernhard Friedrich Voigt, 1828.

Schmidt, Walter et al. *Illustrierte Geschichte der deutschen Revolution 1848/49.* Berlin: Dietz, 1988.

Schorsch, Ernst. *Das Taubstummenwesen der Stadt Berlin. Anläßlich des fünfzigjährigen Bestehens der Städtischen Taubstummenschule.* Berlin: Verlag der Städtischen Taubstummenschule, 1925.

– "IV. Deutsche Taubstummenlehrer-Versammlung in Dresden vom 29. September bis 2. Oktober 1897." *Blätter für Taubstummenbildung.* No. 20 (1897) pp. 309-317.

Schott, Walter. *Das k. k. Taubstummen-Institut in Wien 1779-1918.* Vienna: Böhlau Verlag, 1995.

– *Das Allgemeine österreichische israelitische Taubstummen-Institut in Wien 1844-1926.* Vienna: Published by the author, 1999.

Schröder, Wilhelm Heinz. *Arbeitergeschichte und Arbeiterbewegung. Industriearbeit und Organizationsverhalten im 19. und frühen 20. Jahrhundert.* Frankfurt a. M.: Campus Verlag, 1978.

Schumann, Paul. *Geschichte des Taubstummenwesens vom deutschen Standpunkt aus dargestellt.* Frankfurt a. M.: Moritz Diesterweg, 1940.

Schumann, Paul. (Ed.) *Handbuch des Taubstummenwesens.* Osterwieck am Harz: Erwin Staude Verlagsbuchhandlung, 1929.

Shakespeare Tom. "The Social Model of Disability." In *The Disability Studies Reader.* Ed. Davis. pp. 266-273.

Söderfeldt, Ylva. "Lebenswelt eines ‚taubstummen Vaganten' – Die Befragung eines gehörlosen Bettlers als Ego-Dokument zur Geschichte der Gehörlosen." *Das Zeichen* 83 (2009). pp. 375-379.

– "Taubstumme Genossen. Vor 100 Jahren wurde eine spezielle Sektion der SPD gegründet." *junge Welt,* supplement *Behindertenpolitik.* 24. August 2011. p. 6.

Spivak, Gayatri Chakravorty. "Can the Subaltern Speak?" In *Colonial Discourse and Post-Colonial Theory. A Reader.* Eds. Patrick Williams and Laura Chrisman. New York: Harvester/Wheatsheaf, 1994. pp. 66-111.

Statistik des Deutschen Reichs herausgegeben vom Kaiserlichen Statistischen Amt. Vol. 111. Berlin: Puttkammer & Mühlbrecht, 1899.

Statistik des Deutschen Reichs herausgegeben vom Kaiserlichen Statistischen Amt. Vol. 150. Berlin: Puttkammer & Mühlbrecht, 1903.

Statistisches Jahrbuch für das Deutsche Reich 1897. Berlin: Puttkammer & Mühlbrecht, 1897.

Steinmetz, Georg. *Regulating the Social. The Welfare State and Local Politics in Wilhelmine Germany.* Princeton: Princeton University Press, 1993.

Stichnoth, Tomas. *Taubstummheit. Die medizinische Behandlung der Gehörlosigkeit vom 17. Jahrhundert bis zur Gegenwart.* Kölner medizinhistorische Beiträge: Arbeiten der Forschungsstelle des Instituts für Geschichte der Medizin der Universität zu Köln. Vol. 37 (1985)

Stoe, Norman and Geoffrey Barraclough. (Eds.) *The Times Atlas of World History.* 3rd Ed. London: Times Books, 1990

Stolte, H. *Über die Erziehung des Taubstummen zur Religiosität und Sittlichkeit. Ein Beitrag zur Methodik des Religionsunterricht in der Taubstummenschule.* Soest: P. G. Capell, 1891.

Sutermeister, Eugen. "Hie Lautsprache – hie Gebärden!" *Blätter für Taubstummenbildung.* Vol. 10. No. 22 (1897). pp. 349-351.

– "Wider die Gebärdensprache." *Blätter für Taubstummenbildung.* Vol. 10. No. 12. (1897) pp. 183-187.

Tenfelde, Klaus. "Bergmännisches Vereinswesen im Ruhrgebiet während der Industrialisierung." In *Fabrik, Familie, Feierabend. Beiträge zur Sozialgeschichte des Alltags im Industriezeitalter.* Eds. Jürgen Reulecke and Wolfgang Weber. Wuppertal: Peter Hammer Verlag, 1978. pp. 315-344.

– "Die Entfaltung des Vereinswesens während der industriellen Revolution in Deutschland (1850-1873)." In *Vereinswesen und bürgerliche Gesellschaft in Deutschland.* Ed. Dann. pp. 55-114.

Teuscher, Carl-Wilhelm. "Bemerkungen über meines Denkens Form." In Carl Gottlob Reich. *Blicke auf die Taubstummenbildung und Nachricht über die*

Taubstummenanstalt zu Leipzig seit ihren 50jährigen Bestehen, nebst einem Anhange über die Articulation. 2nd. Ed. (Leipzig: Leopold Voß, 1828) pp. 93-99.

Thieme, Ulrich and Felix Becker. *Allgemeines Lexikon der bildenden Künstler von der Antike bis zur Gegenwart*. Vol. 25. Ed. Hans Vollmer. Leipzig: E.A. Seemann, 1931.

– *Allgemeines Lexikon der bildenden Künstler von der Antike bis zur Gegenwart*. Vol. 31. Ed. Hans Vollmer. Leipzig: E.A. Seemann, 1937.

Tornow, Ingo. *Das Münchner Vereinswesen in der ersten Hälfte des 19. Jahrhunderts, mit einem Ausblick auf die zweite Jahrhunderthälfte*. Neue Schriftenreihe des Stadtarchivs München. Munich: Kommissionsbuchhandlung R. Wölfle, 1977.

Tramer, Moritz. "Vaganten (Arbeitswanderer, Wanderarbeiter, Arbeitsmeider) einer 'Herberge zur Heimat' in der Schweiz." *Zeitschrift für die gesamte Neurologie und Psychiatrie*. 35/1 (1916). pp. 9-34.

Unser neues Recht in gemeinfasslichen Einzeldarstellungen. Vol. 12: Die Vormundschaft Berlin: Pass & Garleb, 1900.

Van Cleve, John Vickrey and Barry A. Crouch. *A Place of Their Own. Creating the Deaf Community in America*. Washington D.C.; Gallaudet University Press, 1989.

Van Cleve, John Vickrey. (Ed.) *The Deaf History Reader*. Washington D. C.: Gallaudet University Press, 2007.

– *Deaf History Unveiled. Interpretations from the new Scholarship*. Washington, D. C.: Gallaudet University Press, 1993.

Vatter, Johannes. "Der gegenwärtige Kampf gegen die Lautsprachmethode." *Organ der Taubstummen-Anstalten...* Vol. 37. No. 11 (1891). pp. 313-321.

– "Eigene Gedanken, sowie beachtenswerte Stimmen Taubstummer gegenüber dem 'Notschrei der Taubstummen'." *Organ der Taubstummen-Anstalten...* Vol. 37. No. 3 (1891). pp. 65-72.

Vogel, Helmut. "Otto Friedrich Kruse (1801-1880). Gehörloser Lehrer und Publizist." [Part 1.] *Das Zeichen*. No. 56 (2001). 198-207.

– "Otto Friedrich Kruse (1801-1880). Mahner gegen die Unterdrückung der Gebärdensprache." [Part 2.] *Das Zeichen*. No. 57 (2001). pp. 370-376.

Waldschmidt, Anne. "Warum und wozu brauchen die Disability Studies die Disability History?" In *Disability History*. Eds. Bösl et al. pp. 13-27.

– "Brauchen die Disability Studies ein ‚kulturelles Modell' von Behinderung?" In *‚Nichts über uns – ohne uns!' Disability Studies als neuer Ansatz emanzipatorischer und interdisziplinärer Forschung über Behinderung*. Eds. Gisela Hermes and Eckhard Rohrmann. Neu-Ulm, AG SPAK, 2006. pp. 83-96.

Walther, Eduard. *Handbuch der Taubstummenbildung.* Berlin: Elwin Staude, 1895.
- *Die Königliche Taubstummenanstalt zu Berlin in ihrer geschichtichen Entwickelung und gegenwärtigen Verfassung. Ein Beitrag zur Geschichte des Taubstummen-Bildungswesens in Preussen. Festschrift zur Feier des hundertjährigen Bestehen der Anstalt.* Berlin: Elwin Staude, 1888.
- "Agitation erwachsener Taubstummer gegen die deutsche Methode." *Blätter für Taubstummenbildung.* Vol. 4. No. 17. (1891). pp. 268-269.
- "Rückblick." In *Blätter für Taubstummenbildung.* Vol. 4. No. 1 (1891). pp. 1-8.
- "Stimmungsbilder vom V. Taubstummenkongress zu Berlin." *Blätter für Taubstummenbildung.* Vol. 15. No. 17 (1902). pp. 269-271.
- "Die Taubstummen als Unterrichtsmethodiker." *Blätter für Taubstummenbildung.* Vol. 4. No. 22 (1891). pp. 337-346.
Wehler, Hans-Ulrich. "Wie 'bürgerlich' war das Deutsche Kaiserreich?" In *Bürger und Bürgerlichkeit.* Ed. Kocka. pp. 243-280.
Weigl, Franz. *Johann Evangelist Wagner. Gründer der J.E. Wagnerschen Wohltätigkeitsanstalten in Bayern. Regens am Priesterseminar Dillingen a. D. Eine Lebensgeschichte.* Munich: Seyfried & Comp., Schnell & Söhne, 1931.
Weise, Wilhelm. "Der Knaben-Handarbeitsunterricht." In Walther. *Handbuch der Taubstummenbildung.* pp. 604-701
Weißback, Kurt. "Die Gebrechlichen und ihre Versorgung." *Zeitschrift des Sächsischen Statistischen Landesamtes.* 64/65 (1918/19). pp. 116-141.
Weithaas, Heinz. "Die Leipziger Taubstummenanstalt und die Gebärde – Ein geschichtlicher Rückblick." *Das Zeichen.* No. 24 (1993). pp. 163-165.
Wellman, Barry, Peter J. Carrington, and Alan Hall. "Networks as personal communities." In *Social Structures: A Network Approach.* Ed. Barry Wellman and S. D. Berkowitz. Cambridge: Cambridge University Press, 1988. pp. 130-184.
Werner, F. Review of Bell, *Marriage. An Address to the Deaf. Blätter für Taubstummenbildung.* Vol. 5. No. 4 (1892). pp. 62-64.
"Wiener Bilder. Das Kaffeehaus der Taubstummen." *Illustrirte Zeitung.* No. 2122. 1 March (1884). pp. 173, 176, 179.
Wilhelmy, Petra. *Der Berliner Salon im 19. Jahrhundert.* Berlin: Walter de Gruyter, 1989.
Williams-Searle, John. "Cold Charity. Manhood, Brotherhood and the Transformation of Disability, 1870-1900." in *The New Disability History.* Eds. Longmore and Umansky. pp. 157-186.

Wilmanns, Karl. "Das Lanstreichertum, seine Abhilfe und Bekämpfung." *Monatsschrift für Kriminalpsychologie und Strafrechtsreform.* Vol. 1 (1904/5). pp. 605-620.

Winkler, Joachim. (Ed.) *Erwin Spindler. 1860-1926. Werkverzeichnis.* Hamburg: Signum Verlag, 1998.

Winkler, Joachim. "Der gehörlose Leipziger Maler Erwin Spindler." *Das Zeichen.* No. 41 (1997). pp. 334-344.

Wolff, Sylvia. "Von der 'Taubstummen-Unterrichtskunst' zur Didaktik des Gehörlosenunterrichts". *Das Zeichen* 42 (1997). pp. 502-7 [Part 1]. *Das Zeichen* No. 43 (1998). pp. 10-18 [Part 2].

- "'Taubstumme zu glücklichen Erdnern bilden' – Lehren, Lernen und Gebärdensprache am Berliner Taubstummen-Institut. Teil I: Selbstverständlich Gebärdensprache! Ernst Adolf Eschke in der Zeit von 1788 bis 1811." *Das Zeichen.* No. 51 (2000). pp. 20-29.

- "Lehren, lernen und Gebärdensprache am Berliner Taubstummen-Institut. Teil II: Die Willkür der Zeichen.". *Das Zeichen.* No. 52 (2000). pp. 198-207.

- "Gehörlose im Land Brandenburg zwischen 1750 und 1900. Teil I: Von Zöglingen, Künstlern und Handwerksgesellen – Schulleben und berufliche Bildung". *Das Zeichen.* No. 68 (2004). pp. 348-357.

Wrigley, Owen. *The Politics of Deafness.* Washington D.C.: Gallaudet University Press, 1996.

Württembergische Jahrbücher für Geschichte, Geographie, Statistik und Topographie. Vol. 1833, No. 1. Stuttgart: J. G. Cotta'sche Buchhandlung, 1834.

Zeise, Roland and Bernd Rüdiger. "Bundesstaat im Deutschen Reich (1871-1917/18)." In *Geschichte Sachsens.* Ed. Karl Czok. Weimar: Hemann Böhlaus Nachfolger, 1989.

Ziolowski, Theodore. *Berlin. Aufstieg einer Kulturmetropole um 1810.* Stuttgart: Klett-Cotta, 2002.

From Pathology to Public Sphere
The German Deaf Movement 1848-1914

YLVA SÖDERFELDT

Abstract
Ph. D. Dissertation in History
Stuttgart University 2011

The topic of this dissertation is the history of the German deaf movement considering the social history of deaf people and the cultural image of deafness in the 19th and early 20th centuries. It aims to determine the social and ideological foundations of the deaf organizations, and to explore their activity and impact.

Periodicals from the deaf movement, protocols from deaf congresses, as well as files from the clubs themselves, are sources for a comprehensive and thorough analysis of the emergence and development of the movement. In order to place it in the context of German society and culture, medical and population statistics, pedagogic and medical literature, files from institutions, welfare- and police authorities amend the body of source material.

Instead of the traditional view on disabled people as mere objects of welfare, medicine, special education, etc., recent scholarship within Disability Studies and Disability History suggest the use of disability as a central analytical category on *a par* with, for instance, gender and class. Accordingly, this study attempts to regard deaf people as subjects and to place them at the centre of analysis. Furthermore, an intersectional perspective connects the history of the deaf as disabled to other social and cultural structures of power.

The first deaf club in the German-speaking world was founded in Berlin in 1848. In the following decades, the movement gradually expanded, until, at the end of the 19th century, the growth gained momentum. In 1913, nearly 300 individual clubs existed. The club activity consisted of everything from sociable events and sports to mutual aid, public events such as congresses, and the publishing of periodicals. A central organization was planned and attempted several times, but without sustainable success during the period of time studied.

The press associated with the deaf movement played a central role. Before the first German deaf periodical, the Taubstummenfreund ("Deaf-Mute's friend") appeared in 1872, published texts by deaf Germans were extremely rare. With the emergence of periodicals by and for deaf people, they achieved a space for debate and self-manifestation, whereas deaf people in earlier print media only appeared as objects. Further periodicals were founded, so that the German deaf press of the early 20th Century constituted a pluralistic landscape of different local, national and international papers of various genres and political leanings.

A further project pursued by some deaf clubs was the founding of asylums for elderly and disabled members. Through such establishments, the protagonists hoped to offer an alternative to the isolation in mainstream institutions and hearing families, and to let the inhabitants grow old within their community. These projects were also public manifestations of the capability of the movement, and, similar to the mutual aid societies and charity initiatives, a possibility to position oneself as giver, not as receiver, of aid.

The emergence of the deaf movement is located in the context of the bourgeois public sphere (Habermas) as a constitutive principle of the German society. Based on the self-image expressed in the deaf press, an elite of urban, educated deaf men can be distinguished. This elite strived to establish themselves as a respectable, independent petty bourgeoisie, which was a prerequisite to be acknowledged as rational participants in the public sphere.

Regardless of their individual backgrounds, deaf school alumni shared a common socialization and level of education and often performed the same type of skilled or semi-skilled manual labour. Thus, the schools were not only the birthplaces of local deaf networks, but also fostered an "imagined community" (Anderson), based not on personal acquaintance but on the idea of cultural connectedness. This idea was expressed through the foundation of numerous clubs, associations, periodicals and meetings, where the elite established themselves as representatives of the deaf. Towards the end of the 19th century, they began to use these platforms for defending their interests, foremost demanding the use of Sign Language in deaf education.

In this study, the self-image of the deaf quasi-bourgeoisie is compared with the 'average deaf-mutes' that appeared in statistics and professional literature. These were described as unfortunate beings, mostly rural, highly dependent on their families and on interventions by the educational and welfare authorities, or on charity. This image affected all people who were deaf, regardless of their individual circumstances.

Instead of challenging the prejudices in their entirety, the deaf elite by and large agreed, but tried to project them on other groups. Thus, they distanced themselves from certain kinds of deaf people, such as beggars and vagrants, or the uneducated. Whereas these groups were criticized or even denounced, rural deaf and deaf women were given scarce attention in the public sphere of the deaf movement. One further strategy was to position oneself as advocate or benefactor of less fortunate deaf people. Through these measures, the deaf elite hoped to achieve a position where they could escape the stigma (Goffman) of deafness.

It was only in the 1890s that the deaf movement started to turn to the schools and authorities with demands. At the time, deaf education was dominated by the oral method, by which the children are supposed to learn spoken language. Articulation and lip reading were used as means to diminish Sign Language use and to assimilate the deaf in hearing society. Even though an underlying discontent can at times be detected, the first explicitly critical statements appeared after a hearing teacher of the deaf published works discrediting the oral method and demanding the use of Sign.

In the debate that followed, the deaf were rebuked by leading teachers for criticizing the methods of education. According to the teachers, the deaf did not possess the necessary competence to express opinions about pedagogic matters. A petition to the Emperor demanding the use of Sign was turned down with reference to the teaching community as the experts on the topic.

This and other similar examples show that the attempt of the deaf movement to reach political aim was a failure. Prerequisites of the position of the deaf elite were public support and intervention, meaning emergence not from the private, but from the public sphere. Even if they were propertied and cultivated, the deaf, in the eyes of the mainstream, remained objects of welfare and special education. Thus, they were unable to claim the status as private people and participants in the public sphere of the German Empire. Their public reasoning was not acknowledged and their demands refused. The impact of the German deaf movement was of another kind: it gained no political influence, but formed a community engaging in sociable activities, forging personal relationships, and preserving a cultural heritage, at odds with the assimilatory efforts of the authorities.

Aus der Pathologie in die Öffentlichkeit

Die deutsche Gehörlosenbewegung 1848–1914

VORGELEGT VON YLVA SÖDERFELDT

Zusammenfassung
Von der Fakultät 9 der Universität Stuttgart
zur Erlangung der Würde eines Doktors der Philosophie
(Dr. phil.) genehmigte Abhandlung

Diese Arbeit untersucht die Geschichte der deutschen Gehörlosenbewegung im Kontext der sozialen Lage der Gehörlosen und des Bildes von Gehörlosigkeit im 19. und frühen 20. Jahrhundert. Dabei wird der leitenden Frage nachgegangen, auf welcher sozialen und ideologischen Grundlage sich Gehörlose organisierten.

Hierfür herangezogene Quellen sind Zeitschriften der Gehörlosenvereine, Protokolle von Gehörlosenkongressen, Fachliteratur wie z. B. Bevölkerungs- und Medizinalstatistiken, pädagogische und medizinische Werke der Zeit, Archivalien der Gehörlosenvereine und anderer Institutionen für Gehörlose sowie Einzelfallakten der Polizei- und des Fürsorgewesens.

Bis heute werden Menschen mit Behinderung häufig nur als Objekte von Fürsorge, Medizin, Sonderpädagogik etc. studiert. In den letzten Jahren sind jedoch die „Disability Studies" bzw. die „Disability History" als Ansätze hinzugekommen, die Behinderung als eine analytische Kategorie neben „Gender" und „Klasse" zu betrachten und die jeweiligen Betroffenen in den Vordergrund treten zu lassen. Die vorliegende Arbeit stellt einen Beitrag zu einer Geschichte von gehörlosen Menschen *als Subjekte* dar und bringt zugleich die historische Analyse einer Behindertengruppe mit anderen Strukturen der Macht in Verbindung.

Der erste Gehörlosenverein im deutschsprachigen Raum wurde im Jahre 1848 in Berlin gegründet. In den folgenden Jahrzehnten wuchs die Bewegung langsam, die Entwicklung beschleunigte sich jedoch am Ende des Jahrhunderts.

Für das Jahr 1913 konnten knapp 300 Gehörlosenvereine ermittelt werden. Die Vereine veranstalteten Treffen geselliger Natur, unterstützten bedürftige Mitglieder und traten durch die Presse und Kongresse öffentlich in Erscheinung. Von Beginn an gab es Bestrebungen, die Vereine in einem Zentralverband zu vereinigen, was aber im untersuchten Zeitraum nicht nachhaltig gelang.

Besondere Bedeutung hatte die mit der Bewegung verbundene Presse. Vor dem Erscheinen der Zeitschrift *Der Taubstummenfreund* im Jahre 1872 gab es nur vereinzelt deutschsprachige Veröffentlichungen von Gehörlosen. Ab diesem Zeitpunkt war ein Medium für die Debatte und Eigendarstellung gehörloser Menschen gegeben, die zuvor fast ausschließlich als Objekte in der Literatur zu finden waren. Es kamen weitere Zeitschriften hinzu, so dass die Gehörlosenpresse am Anfang des 20. Jahrhunderts ein pluralistisches Bild abgab.

Ein weiteres Projekt einiger Gehörlosenvereine war die Gründung von Heimen für alte und arbeitsunfähige Mitglieder. Sie wollten damit die Möglichkeit anbieten, die Isolation in gewöhnlichen Institutionen und hörenden Familien zu vermeiden und stattdessen innerhalb der Gemeinschaft alt zu werden. Die Bauprojekte waren auch äußerliche Erfolgsmanifestationen der Bewegung. Weiter waren sie, wie auch die Unterstützungskassen und Sammlungen für bedürftige Gehörlose, eine Möglichkeit, selbst als Wohltäter, nicht bloß als Empfänger von Wohltätigkeit aufzutreten.

Das Entstehen der Gehörlosenbewegung wird im Kontext der bürgerlichen Öffentlichkeit (Habermas) – als konstitutives Prinzip der deutschen Gesellschaft – erklärt. Basierend auf der Selbstdarstellung in der Gehörlosenpresse wird gezeigt, dass eine Elite von städtischen und gebildeten gehörlosen Männern versuchte, sich als respektables, selbstständiges Kleinbürgertum zu etablieren. Dabei ging es ihnen darum, einen Platz als gleichberechtigte Teilnehmer der bürgerlichen Öffentlichkeit zu erlangen.

Die in den Gehörlosenschulen ausgebildeten Gehörlosen hatten unabhängig von ihrem Wohnort und Hintergrund ähnliche Lebenserfahrungen gemacht, standen auf dem gleichen Bildungsniveau und waren auch in beruflicher Hinsicht relativ homogen. Die Schule wurde somit nicht nur Entstehungsort von lokalen Gehörlosennetzwerken, sondern auch von einer „imagined community" (Anderson), die statt auf persönlicher Bekanntschaft auf der Idee der Gemeinschaft beruhte. Diese Idee fand ihren Ausdruck in den Vereinsgründungen, Zeitschriften und Versammlungen, wo die gebildete Elite sich mit Gleichgesinnten in Verbindung setzte und sich als Vertreter der Gehörlosen inszenierte.

Ab den 1890er Jahren fingen die Vertreter der Gehörlosenbewegung aktiv an, sich an Schulen und Behörden mit Forderungen zu wenden. Der Unterricht von gehörlosen Kindern war zu dieser Zeit von der Erlernung der Lautsprache beherrscht. Durch Artikulation und Lippenlesen sollte die Gebärdensprache verdrängt und die Gehörlosen damit assimiliert werden. Obwohl Anzeichen einer Unzufriedenheit mit diesem System früh zu erkennen sind, kamen kritische Stimmen erst auf, nachdem ein hörender Taubstummenlehrer die Lautsprachmethode angriff.

In der folgenden Debatte wurden die Gehörlosen von den einflussreichen Taubstummenlehrern zurechtgewiesen: sie hatten aus der Sicht der Lehrer nicht die nötigen Kenntnisse um zur Methodenfrage eine Meinung zu vertreten. Als die Gehörlosenbewegung sich mit einer Petition an den Kaiser wandte, wurden sie mit Hinweis auf den Expertenstatus der Lehrer abgewiesen.

Das Selbstbild der gehörlosen (Quasi-)Bürger wird in der Arbeit dem Bild der „Durchschnittsgehörlosen" in der Fachliteratur gegenübergestellt. In Statistiken, medizinischen Arbeiten und pädagogischen Handbüchern werden die Gehörlosen als abhängige, ländliche Objekte und Empfänger für private und staatliche Unterstützung dargestellt. Die Vorstellung von einem solchen Menschentyp wurde allen Gehörlosen zugeschrieben; ungeachtet ihrer individuellen Lebensumstände.

Statt die Vorurteile konsequent in Frage zu stellen, wurden sie von der gehörlosen Elite weitgehend akzeptiert, dabei jedoch auf andere Betroffene projiziert. So distanzierte sich die Elite von bestimmten Gruppen von Gehörlosen, wie z. B. Bettlern und Ungebildeten und griff diese sogar in Debatten an. Andere, vor allem Frauen und die Gehörlosen auf dem Land, erhielten wenig oder gar keinen Platz in den öffentlichen Äußerungen der Bewegung. Eine andere Strategie bestand gleichwohl darin, sich zu Wohltätern und Fürsprechern von weniger erfolgreichen Gehörlosen zu machen. Dadurch versuchte die gehörlose Elite sich in eine Position zu erheben, von wo aus sie dem Stigma (Goffman) der Gehörlosigkeit entfliehen konnte.

Dieser Versuch ist, so wird festgestellt, fehlgeschlagen. Die Voraussetzung für die bürgerlichen Verhältnisse der gehörlosen Elite war die Unterstützung durch öffentliche Instanzen. Als Objekte des Sonderschul- und Fürsorgesystems waren Gehörlose, auch wenn sie über Besitz und Bildung verfügten, keine Privatleute. In der bürgerlichen Öffentlichkeit des Kaiserreichs konnten sie sich deswegen trotz ihrer Bemühungen nicht als Teilnehmer behaupten. So blieben im gesamten untersuchten Zeitraum ihre Forderungen unentsprochen.

Die Bedeutung der Bewegung war eine andere: sie erreichte keinen politischen Einfluss, aber sie wurde im Widerstand gegen Assimilationsforderungen der Politik und des Bildungswesens zu einer identitätsstiftenden kulturellen Gemeinschaft.